RELATIONS OF NDA AND UPA WITH NEIGHBOURS

RELATIONS OF NDA AND UPA WITH NEIGHBOURS

Dr. Rajkumar Singh

GYAN

Relations of NDA and UPA with Neighbours
Rs. 850

ISBN: 978-81-212-1060-7

Published in 2010 in India by
Gyan Publishing House
23, Main Ansari Road, Darya Ganj
New Delhi-110002
Phones : 23282060, 23261060
Fax : 011-23285914
E-mail: books@gyanbooks.com
Website: www.gyanbooks.com

Laser Type Setting by: Rudra Computer Graphics, Delhi
Printed at : Chawla Offset Printers, Delhi

Dedicated to

Late Ram Lakhan Singh

Uncle

Contents

List of Abbreviations

ACDA - Arms Control and Disarmament Agency
ADB - Asian Development Bank
AL - Awami League
ANC - African National Congress
ANNFSU - All Nepal National Free Student's Union
BDR - Bangladesh Rifles
BJP - Bharatiya Janata Party
BIPPA - Bilateral Investment Protection and Promotion Agreement
BNP - Bangladesh Nationalist Party
BOPs - Border Out Posts
BPKISH - B P Koirala Institute of Health Sciences
BSF - Border Security Force
CBMs - Confidence Building Measures
CBT - Cross-Border Terrorism
CCCI - Ceylon Chamber of Commerce and Industry
CCT - Comprehensive Convention on Terrorism
CDM - Clean Development Mechanism
CEPA - Comprehensive Economic Partnership Agreement
CHT - Chittagong Hill Tracks
CPNML - Communist Party of Nepal Marxist Leninist
CRP - Central Reserve Police
CTBT - Comprehensive Test Ban Treaty
CWC - Ceylon Workers Congress
DMK - Dravida Munnetra Kazhagam
DPR - Detailed Project Report

DRDO - Defence Research and Development Organisation
DTAA - Double Taxation Avoidance Agreement
EPB - Export Promotion Bureau
EPR - Exempt from Police Reporting
ESAF - Enhanced Structural Adjustment Facility
FATA - Federally - Administered Tribal Area
FBI - Federal Bureau of Investigation
FICC - Federation of Indian Chambers of Commerce
FICCI - Federation of Indian Chamber's of Commerce and Industry
FOCs - Foreign Office Consultations
FPCCI - Federation of Pakistan Chamber of Commerce and Industry
FTA - Free Trade Agreement
GDP - Gross Domestic Product
GoI - Government of India
HMT - Hindustan Machine Tools
HUJI - Harkat-ul-Jehad al Islami
HUM - Harkat-ul-Mujahideen
IBCCI - India-Bangladesh Chamber of Commerce and Industry
ICT - Information and Communication Technology
ICU - Intensive Care Unit
ICRC - International Red Cross Committee
IGMDP - Integrated Guided Missile Development Programme
IIGs - Indian Insurgent Groups
IOJ - Islamiya Okiya Jote
IMF - International Monetary Fund
IPCCI - Indo-Pak Chamber of Commerce and Industry
IPKF - Indian Peace-keeping Force
IRCON - Indian Railway Construction
ISI - Inter-Services Intelligence
JBWG - Joint Boundary Working Group
JI - Jamaat-e-Islami
JKLF - Jammu and Kashmir Liberation Front
JMB - Jamaatul Mujahideen Bangladesh
JMJB - Jagrata Muslim Janata Bangladesh
JP - Jatiya Party
JRC - Joint Rivers Commission

JUI - Jamiat-ul-Ulema-e-Islam
JWG - Joint Working Group
LBA - Land Boundary Agreement
LeT - Lashkar-e-Taiba
LoC - Line of Control
LTTE - Liberation Tigers of Tamil Eelam
MBTs - Main Battle Tanks
MFN - Most Favoured Nation
MJF - Madhesi Janadhikar Forum
MoU - Memorandum of Understanding
NAM - Non-Aligned Movement
NDA - National Democratic Alliance
NF - National Front
NPT - Non-Proliferation Treaty
NWFP - North-West Frontier Province
NWFZ - Nuclear Weapon Free Zone
OIC - Organisation of Islamic Conference
PA - People's Alliance
PCJSS - Parbatya Chattagram Jana Samhati Samity
PLO - Palestinian Liberation Organisation
PoK - Pak-occupied Kashmir
PRC - Peoples Republic of China
PRGF - Poverty Reduction and Growth Facility
RAW - Research and Analysis Wing
SAARC - South Asian Association for Regional Cooperation
SAFTA - South Asia Free Trade Area
SAGQ - South Asian Growth Quadrangle
SAPTA - South Asia Preferential Trading Arrangement
SOFA - Status of Forces Agreement
SLMP - Sri Lankan Muslim Party
SPA - Seven Party Alliance
TULF - Tamil United Liberation Front
ULFA - United Liberation Front of Assam
UF - United Front
UMLCP - United Marxist Leninist Communist Party
UN - United Nations

UNDP - United Nations Development Programme
UNEP - United Nations Environment Programme
UNHRC - United Nations Human Rights Commission
UNP - United National Party
UPA - United Progressive Alliance
UPFN - United People's Front of Nepal
USD - United State's Dollar
VAT - Value Added Tax
WTO - World Trade Organisation

Preface

The book '*Relations of NDA & UPA with Neighbours*' gives us an issue-wise account of India's relations with South Asian countries-Pakistan, Nepal, Bangladesh and Sri Lanka in particular, right from the first non-Congress Government of Morarji Desai formed in March 1977 to the third BJP-led Government formed in October 1999, and succeeded by the Government of United Progressive Alliance (UPA) led by Indian National Congress and headed by Dr. Manmohan Singh till May 2009. The coming of Janata Party to power raised a measure of doubt and uncertainty in the country and outside about several aspects of India's foreign policy. Unlike its predecessors, the new dispensation disavowed its hegemonistic ambition that created a favourable climate in the subcontinent for the improvement of India's relations with its neighbours had come to harbour about it since the beginning of the 1970s.

Further the successive non-Congress Governments headed by the leaders of National Front in 1989, United Front in 1996, quickly followed by mid-term poll and assumption of powers by the Bharatiya Janata Party in March 1998 with the help of pre and post election alliance of political parties witnessed a relaxation of tension in South Asia. Without making any basic change in India's foreign policy, as it was based on factors of permanent nature, the regimes tried their level best to remove the prevailing atmosphere of suspicion and distrust. Even in post-Gujral Doctrine phase the multi-party coalition under the banner of National Democratic Alliance (NDA) and Congress-led coalition government of the UPA attempted to remove big-brotherly image of India and adopted an accommodative policy towards neighbours. It establishes the bipartisan character of India's foreign policy. In utmost possibility the Congress-led government which took over on May 22, 2009 again under the premiership of Manmohan Singh is likely to continue the policy in India's interest keeping in view the national, regional and global considerations.

Encouragement, co-operation and goodwishes of the institutions and individuals that I received are acknowledged with gratitude. Several central libraries as well as the book stocks of different Departments have been consulted in the completion of the book. Librarians and staff of the institutions deserve cordial thanks.

Among teachers Dr. D. N. Mallik, Dr. Kirtyanand Singh, Dr. R. N. Kumar and Dr. M. R. Kazmi, retired Professors of the University Department of Political Science, B.R.A. Bihar University, Muzaffarpur, have been a constant source of guide and encouragement at every stage. Colleagues Dr. Chandra Prakash Singh, University Department of History, B. N. Mandal University, West Campus, Saharsa, Dr. Ram Naresh Kumar, Professor and Head, University Department of Chemistry, B.N. Mandal University, Madhepura, Dr. Dhirendra Narayan Singh, Department of Political Science, MLT College, Saharsa, are thankful for their cooperation and goodwishes. Eldest brother the late Suryanath Singh, elder brother Shri Bhuvneshwar Prasad Singh and father-in-law Shri Ramanand Singh, retired Professor and Head, University Department of Physics, BRA Bihar University, Muzaffarpur, deserve deep sense of gratitude for their sincere goodwishes. I am thankful to Dr. Ranjeet Kumar for his pains in composing the book in a scheduled time. The author is also grateful to colleagues and staff of the BN Mandal University, West Campus, P. G. Centre, Saharsa.

I must extend my honest goodwishes and gratitude to the family members including my wife Dr. Hemlata Singh, son Aditya Priyadarshi and Apurv Adarsh in the completion of the book.

All responsibility for the defects and misjudgements, however, rests with me alone.

Rajkumar Singh
Chanakyapuri,
Ward No. 19
Saharsa-852201
(Bihar)

Introduction

1977 was an important year for India: even more important than 1947 when India became formally free. For the first time in the 30-years of its career as the ruling Party, the 90-year old Indian National Congress was voted out of office at the centre. With the defeat of a political party at the polls emerged a milieu congenial to the flowering of democratic institutions in a healthy atmosphere. Over the years, the primary objective of India's foreign policy had been the erection of a stable inner balance on the subcontinent, in which India, as the principal power would play an integrative role. Jawaharlal Nehru, the chief architect of country's external policy fashioned the ambiguous tool of non-alignment with a view to maintaining the autonomy of Indian diplomacy in a world polarized between two mutually hostile blocs. Since then, the rapid sophistication of international politics—the result of new inputs like weapon system, technology, strategic resources like petroleum, and fiscal and monetary issues—had robbed foreign policy in the latter half of the century and made the translation of foreign policy motivations into diplomatic operations a highly complex and difficult task.

In early seventies the world in general and South Asia in particular became India–conscious. The military victory of India over Pakistan in 1971 made it the "dominant power" on the subcontinent. It had earlier concluded a treaty of friendship with the Soviet Union which buttressed its position as a regional power. The Pokhran nuclear blast of May 1974 and integration of Sikkim into the Indian Union had conclusively established it as the dominant power of the region. India's diplomacy took a dramatic turn and appeared to be based on the assumption that a subtle structure of peace in South Asia could not be built without the acceptance, however, implicit, of New Delhi's dominant position in the region by its neighbours as well as others. Such a policy made India's neighbours apprehensive of its motives and designs and an image of a hegemonistic India sunk deep into the psyche of its neighbours which was reinforced by the assumption of authoritarian powers by Mrs. Gandhi's Government. It was in this background that Mrs. Gandhi's Government of the Congress Party was replaced by Desai's Government of the Janata Party at New Delhi in 1977.

However, over the years, India's foreign policy and relations had formed a pattern of linkages and alignments which had served the interests of the nation reasonably well and which, in any case, had stemmed not so much from what the Government had considered desirable as from what became inevitable in the light of India's varied engagements with regional and world realities and forces. The country's national interests had become more or less stably defined; the ups and downs in the fortunes of external engagements had trained the foreign policy bureaucracy to distinguish the practicable from desirable, the friends from the enemies. Thus, it was in the light of the changed world realities that the Janata Government began to respond to events, trends and processes. Indian foreign policy objectives have not changed. What have changed are India's perceptions of world and regional realities, its self-perception and, to some extent, India's diplomatic style.

When Desai-Vajpayee team took charge of India 's foreign policy and set out to define its policy towards neighbours, the Janata Government first undertook a critical scrutiny of its predecessor's policy on the subject. In this scrutiny it was found that the previous government's policy suffered from a duality of using "good neighbourliness" as a clique on the one hand and adoption of a superior and imperious tone on the other. Then there was a certain lack of credibility and that the task, the Janata Government set to itself, was to eliminate the duality and restore credibility. This could be done by buildings bridges of trust and co-operation with our neighbours-with dialogue and trust".

The Janata Party Government from the first day of its existence, as emphasised by Vajpayee, set out deliberately to clear the cobwebs of suspicion, remove misunderstanding and banish the fear of interference. We have not only professed strict non-interference in the internal affairs of its neighbours, but also practised it. The regime had gently tried to explain to them the mutuality of advantage in bilateralism and allowed the irresistible logic of geography to assert itself. The Janata regime took a number of measures to lower India's dominant power profile and to reassure the smaller neighbours that India was willing to accept them as they were rather than measure their credibility and friendship-worthiness in the scale of its own ideological preferences and power calculus.

As a follow up of the new diplomatic style, India supported Pakistan's participation in the Belgrade meeting of the Foreign Ministers of non-aligned states as a "guest observer" and concluded in April 1978 an agreement for the construction of the Salal Hydroelectric Project without waiting for a settlement of the dispute over a section of the Chenab River. Relations with Bangladesh improved rapidly. The Janata regime recognised the legitimacy of the post-Mujib regime in Dacca, signed with it a five–year agreement on the waters of the Ganges, and assured it that pro-Mujib elements would not be allowed to carry on their activities against the Bangladesh regime from Indian bases. With Nepal the Janata Government concluded separate trade and transit accords and offered to provide the necessary facilities for Nepal's trade with Bangladesh and other countries across Indian territory. During the period its relations with Sri Lanka and other South Asian countries also improved considerably.

Apart from this, with a view to diffuse the polarisation in world politics, Indira Gandhi took determined steps and cemented India's long-tested friendship with the USSR. During the Indian election campaign, Janata Party leaders spoke of ending the "special relationship" with the Soviet Union. The new government lowered its profile of dominant power and the profile of Soviet-Alliance. The lowering of profiles did not mean that India would cut back on its military power to diffuse its friendship with the USSR. Profile is a matter of projection and style. Hence the Janata government proceeded to end India's special relationship with the Soviet Union and at the same time to keep, even to strengthen, friendly co-operation between the two nations. The second move was aimed at normalising relations with the United States and the People's Republic of

China. To facilitate normalisation, the new dispensation coined a rather spurious concept viz. "genuine non-alignment". But the Jarata Party Government in India could project its policy towards India's immediate neighbours or South Asia in general as a major show-piece of success in the realm of foreign policy. India's relations with the neighbours were more relaxed than eversince Independence.

Like 1977, the year 1989 witnessed the formation of second non-Congress government at the centre under the premiership of Vishwanath Pratap Singh as leader of the National Front and supported by the BJP from outside. It was not merely the change of government. It was, in fact, a culmination of the struggle waged by a section of India's political elite against what it perceived to be the force of authoritarianism which, under their dispensation had allegedly destroyed democratic institutions and severely undermined democratic rights of the people. This struggle achieved some success in 1977 when 'total revolutionaries' putting on the garb of democracy and individual liberty defeated the forces of 'authoritarianism'. In other words, the opponents of the so-called authoritarianism found themselves, either inadvertently or by design, standing side by side with world imperialism as their cry for the 'restoration of democratic norms' in India found a favourable echo in the United States and other parts of the "Free World".

In the international context, this struggle between 'authoritarianism' and democratic values has generally been co-terminus with the conflict between socialist world and the democratic world, the latter being another name for the 'free world', the modern democracies or the capitalist world. India, however, remained on the side of the victims of imperialism and friendly with the socialist world and adhered more firmly to the objectives of India's foreign policy even during the reign of Rajiv Gandhi. In 1989, the triumph of the forces which had continued their campaign against what they perceived as anti-democratic, corrupt and oppressive regime of the Congress I, coincided with the euphoric upsurge of democratic forces in the socialist world. There was Glasnost and Perestroika through which ideological distortions and socio-political and economic bureaucratisation of society and polity are sought to be put to an end to. The happenings in the socialist world had projected the United States and the system which it sustains as superior and worthy of emulation.

Amid these national and international developments, a minority government of National Front, supported by the BJP from outside took the reigns of administration in India. The new regime felt that the government under Rajiv Gandhi had severely damaged India's relations with immediate neighbours and here there was need to do everything possible for restoring the confidence and trust, which had been lost owing to the previous government's allegedly high-handed policies and arrogant behaviour. However, unintentional it might have been the diplomatic style of Rajiv Gandhi's government gave an impression to the neighbours that India was acting like a "regional bully". This was particularly true in the wake of the dispatch of IPKF to Sri Lanka, even though many in the island and most people in India believed that the IPKF played a very useful role in the preservation of the territorial integrity of the island republic. Rajiv Gandhi's foreign policy was said to be a "muscular policy". Tension had followed between New Delhi and Kathmandu on account of the expiry of the trade and transit treaty of 1978. In that perspective New Delhi's attitude towards the neighbours was perceived of a big brother rather than that of a cooperative friend.

Consequently review of relations with both Nepal and Sri Lanka and restoration of traditional friendly relations with them was felt to be the need of the hour. In the National Front manifesto it was stated that they will "weave a new pattern of co-operative relationship with the neighbours". Committing the Front to "the safety and security of the Tamils in Sri Lanka, "the manifesto clearly announced that the IPKF will be withdrawn from Sri Lanka and with Nepal, it stated that negotiations will be started on all issues of contention to find an amicable solution". and also help "strengthen the economy of Nepal and honour her self-respect.

Obviously, the National Front's Government consciously played India's diplomacy in such a way that such an image of India may be dispelled. To this end, therefore, the new policy makers were following a low diplomatic stance vis-à-vis the neighbours. To quote V. P. Singh :

> Our approach to the neighbouring countries will be one of friendliness, no any arm-twisting or any bullying tactics. I want to make this clear. Strength lies in mutual understanding.

It was probably with this in mind that the new government took steps to shed off India's "big brother" image by publicly announcing that India's defence expenditure will be cut; and second that India will enter into dialogue with all the neighbouring countries to find a way out of some of their outstanding issues with them. Final withdrawal of the Indian Peace-keeping Force took place peacefully a few days before 31 March 1990 and in the same year in June, during the visit of Nepalese Prime Minister K. P. Bhattarai the National Front Government signed an understanding that brought an end to almost a year long stalemate. Government of India's agreement to open all the traditional points of transit for trade purpose and a few more to allow foreign tourists to visit Nepal had indeed been widely acclaimed in Nepal.

Considering South Asia as the critical core of the foreign policy, initiatives have also been taken in regard to the other neighbouring countries, like Bangladesh and Pakistan. With Dacca, the most outstanding of all the disputes was the Sharing of Ganga waters and it found a welcome development in the resolution of her pending disputes with New Delhi. Even with Pakistan–the most complicated and yet the most important of all of India's South Asian neighbours, the National Front Government's record had been creditable. Despite the developments in Kashmir Valley and a certain amount of militancy in Islamabad's attitude, V. P. Singh's Government considered it appropriate to keep the dialogue open. He laid special emphasis to the need to revitalising and strengthening of ties with the neighbours in South Asia and declared that his Government will spare no effort to resolve outstanding bilateral issues with neighbouring countries, consistent with national interest, usher in an era of stability, confidence and co-operation endeavour in our region.

The 1996 experiment was no different. The United Front was a post-poll alliance of largely regional formations and it banked on Congress support from outside. Under H.D. Deve Gowda's dispensation Inder Kumar Gujral became the new Minister for External Affairs. Coming of the new team marked a new beginning in India's relations with South Asian countries. Major positive developments took place in India's foreign relations that showed a different direction. India during the regime launched an initiative of peace through the "Gujral Doctrine". The atmosphere in South Asia was more hopeful, and promised to herald a new era of durable peace in a region, frequently marked by hostility and misperceptions. The traditional fear of "India's big bullying tactics" had declined in some ways in the present atmosphere.

The "Gujral Doctrine" was a much–needed initiative. The new trend after the cold war that witnessed conflict resolution and conflict management some people in Indian Foreign Policy establishment believed that if peace could reign in Combodia and between the formerly dead enemies such as Egypt and Israel and Jordan, and Israel and PLO, why not in South Asia. The second most important rationale behind the doctrine was the disintegration of the former Soviet Union that had a far-reaching effects on world politics in general and India's area of "special relationship outside the South Asian powers in particular. In the changed world perhaps the most significant achievement of the Gujral Doctrine was a conscious decision by our Foreign Office to make the nation's foreign office less Pakistan-centric. The Policy has enhanced India's image abroad and has also been successful, to a considerable extent, to check the outside interference in the regional problems in South Asia. It promised to bring about changes in the security environment of the region and is in conformity with the ongoing world-wide changes.

India's relations with other neighbours had also promised a marked reduction of tensions with the increasingly intrusive diplomacy being pursued by Gujral. With the signing of the historic treaty with Bangladesh on the sharing of the Ganga waters, a long standing irritant had been replaced with a cordial relationship. Other areas of disagreements have also been accommodated or agreed to solve between New Delhi and Dhaka. With Nepal, the conclusion of the Mahakali water treaty was another landmark. Similarly with Colombo, New Delhi had been extending maximum co-operation to restore peace and stability in its Northern and Eastern Provinces. Even Kofi Annan, the U. N. Secretary General, had welcomed the initiatives taken by Prime Minister I.K.Gujral in pursuing the policy of good-neighbourliness.

With the help of pre and post election alliance of political parties, a BJP Government under the premiership of Atal Bihari Vajpayee had taken over on 19 March 1998. The new Prime Minister, in his first foreign policy pronouncement had rightly emphasised importance of bilateral diplomacy. Despite the profound strategic and technological changes in the world since 1980s, the bilateral approach remains the best for tackling bilateral problems. The new regime will "strain every nerve" to accelerate the process of building better ties with neighbours. He asserted that his regime is determined to be friendly with all and precisely because we happen to be the larger country, we shall be all the more sensitive to the aspirations and needs of our neighbours. Under the new dispensation, New Delhi's relations with South Asian countries is likely to strengthen further. Even with Pakistan, despite a chain of nuclear explosions from both sides Vajpayee had offered for bilateral talks and suggested Islamabad to resolve all the bilateral issues in accordance with the Simla Pact, signed much earlier between the two countries.

By the end of July 1998 the negative effects of nuclear explosions began to recede as the two Prime Ministers met in Colombo in the 10th Heads of Government Meeting of South Asian Association for Regional Co-operation. Further their positive thinking took a visible shape in the third week of September that year in Newyork, where they assembled to address the session of UN General Assembly. Among the other decisions, they agreed was to start a bus service from New Delhi to Lahore. After having a formal agreement in this regard Atal Bihari Vajpayee took a historic visit of Pakistan with the inaugural bus service in February 1999. The occasion reflected an attitudinal change in India and Pakistan as well. Through this handshake and Lohore Declaration the two Prime Ministers had tried to carve out some political space for themselves both domestically and internationally. Despite the fact that Islamabad did not miss any opportunity to remind the solution of Kashmir issue as a pre-condition for normalisation of Indo-Pak relations, their interests can be further safeguarded by creating a stable infrastructure of confidence building measures as military, non-military, and conventional as well as nuclear related levels.

Vajpayee's Government, on the one hand decided to go for nuclear explosions and, on the other assured the small neighbours that New Delhi has no ill-will, but it is for its security sake only. It should be credited for the invitation of a healthy relationship with Bangladesh, Nepal and Sri Lanka. In June 1998 Sheikh Hasina, the Prime Minister of Bangladesh came to New Delhi on a goodwill visit and held discussions on matters of mutual interest. The nuclear explosion by India was followed by K. R. Narayanan's visit to Kathmandu to allay its fears and anxieties, while Sri Lanka's President Chandrika Kumaratunga during her visit to New Delhi in December 1998 signed a trade pact which paved the way for further economic gains between the two countries.

In a surprising moment on 17 April 1999, Atal Bihari Vajpayee's Government lost the confidence of the Lok Sabha by the razor-thin margin of one vote (269 in favour and 270 in against). Minutes after his fall Vajpayee drove to Rashtrapati Bhawan and submitted resignation. The President asked Vajpayee to continue in office in a caretaker capacity till alternative arrangements were made. Commenting on the developments *The Newyork Times* (Newyork) wrote, "India's divisive ethnic and regional politics have produced one political crisis after another in recent years. Now these tensions have caused the collapse of the Hindu nationalist government led by the Prime Minister Atal Bihari Vajpayee, which lost a vote of confidence by a single vote. India's challenge is to prevent the present political turbulence from undermining the drive to make peace with its neighbours and among the warring groups within its borders." In view of *The Independent* (London) the BJP's government was mean, but not all, bad. It did little to prevent a wave of violence against Christians and continued with nuclear testing. It brought a measure of stability to India and showed Congress that it had a fight on its hands. Even Nawaz Sharif, the Prime Minister of Pakistan, after the fall of Vajpayee's Government lauded his sincere efforts to solve issues and hoped that the event would have no impact on Lohore Declaration as it was not signed by two people but by two governments.

On 26 April 1999, President K. R. Narayanan dissolved the 12th Lok Sabha on the Union Cabinet's recommendation and assessing the political situation of the country the Rashtrapati Bhawan, in a communiqué, observed, "the ruling coalition had lost its majority because of a lack of cohesion within its ranks and those who voted out the alliance showed the same lack of cohesion when trying to form an alternative government". Having consulted nation's political parties, M. S. Gill, the Chief Election Commissioner of India, announced that the poll dates for the 13th Lok Sabha would be in September-October and the new House (Lok Sabha) would be constituted before 21st October, 1999.

By the time Atal Bihari Vajpayee made a hattrick of being the Prime Minister of India on October 13, 1999, both the country and the outside world witnessed a sea of changes in respects more than one. Domestically the political leadership is increasingly becoming aware of the politics of growth to ensure better economic development. Things improved fast and India entered in a new period with major shifts in the development models and public policies. The revolution of information technology, telecom upsurge, fast movement in the financial sector, and flexibility shown by the private entrepreneurs in adjusting to the new globally competitive situation announce the arrival of India on the world map.

The behaviour on foreign and security policies is singularly Indian and is not peculiar to the BJP or Congress, the dominant political parties in contemporary India. Since the 1998 nuclear tests, substantive dialogue on nuclear matters between India and Pakistan has been minimal and in general for two years after Kargil misadventure, India rejected official dialogue with Pakistan. A policy of diplomatic isolation or nuclear non-engagement prevailed at cross-purposes to the pursuit of risk reduction. Ultimately ground for peaceful diplomacy between India and Pakistan was first prepared by Prime Minister Atal Bihari Vajpayee in April 2003. On the other the policies of President Musharraf also showed flexibility and innovative thinking in offering different proposals that could fulfil the aspirations of Kashmiris while keeping in mind the sensitivities of Indo-Pak relations. Favourable atmosphere led to the successful meeting between Vajpayee and Musharraf during the January 2004 SAARC meeting in Islamabad. It was the good beginning which spread at official as well as unofficial levels.

At the time Atal Bihari Vajpayee took over the premiership the political situation in the Himalayan Kingdom remained unstable and witnessed a series of change in the premiership. The later crucial developments in which King Birendra was gunned down in 2001 and King Gyanendra was made his successor along with the spread of Maoism in different parts of the country had made New Delhi confused on its policy towards Nepal. The regime of Vajpayee chanted the ideal of constitutional monarchy and lent almost total support to the King's authoritarian moves. Behind the policy was India's somewhat imprudent and unrealistic dislike for corrupt and power-hungry politician as well as its near hatred for the Maoists who were seen as a supporters of the Naxalite and insurgent groups in India. In case of Nepal during the period India failed to work as a quiet and honest facilitator.

The initial attitude of Vajpayee government towards Bangladesh was accommodative and adjusting, it however, received a setback with the coming of Bangladesh Nationalist Party's rule in 2001. The new Dhaka dispensation was known for its support of radical Islam, anti-Indian sentiments and actions, anti-secularism, anti-democracy and pro-China policies. In addition the development in the society and politics of Bangladesh had overshadowed the relations, political in particular, between the two friendly neighbours. It led to several misunderstandings in their relations in which India accused Bangladesh of harbouring both agents of Pakistan's intelligence services and separatist militants fighting in India's north-eastern states. As a result at the end of Vajpayee's regime there were several political issues which were yet to be resolved satisfactorily. Likewise India during the tenure of Vajpayee kept a vigil eye on Sri Lankan Tamils and made its policy clear that New Delhi would welcome a resolution of the current impass in the peace process and an early resumption of negotiations.

As a result of the 14th Lok Sabha a Congress-led UPA government was formed and Dr. Manmohan Singh replaced Atal Bihari Vajpayee as the new Prime Minister of India on May 22, 2004. The change of guard at New Delhi did not bring any change in its policy towards Pakistan and the earlier efforts initiated by the previous government continued further. Now without doubt, the economic struggle had taken primary over the political struggle and it was felt by both India and Pakistan. It is also to note here that with the rise of China and fall of Soviet system India is definite to have strategic role in international politics, security, diplomacy and anti-terrorism strategy. It is going to be the third pole, a balancing state between America and China, which can not be ignored by either. In the period of Manmohan Singh India's foreign policy adapted to the rapidly changing global environment. It concentrated on improving relations with all major powers and all its neighbours. India's diplomatic understandings with Pakistan improved further that led to exchange of visits at several levels. The political instability which was brought in Pakistan in 2007 ultimately led to the formation of a civilian elected government under the premiership of Yousuf Raza Gillani in 2008, but at the end of the year a terror attack was made in Mumbai at different places made India-Pakistan relations strained and created a war-like situation between the two countries.

India's dilemma over its relations with Nepal continued during the premiership of Manmohan Singh. As earlier the political uncertainty prevailed in Nepalese politics and society which was heightened by Gyanendra's taking over of direct rule in the country in February 2005. The emergency rule of King Gyanendra did not last long and it ended in April 2006 which led further the election to the members of Constituent Assembly and formation of a Maoist-led coalition government under the premiership of Pushpa Kamal Dahal 'Prachanda'. Although Prachanda visited New Delhi after taking a tour to Beijing his ideological proximity with China and support of anti-India activities in Nepal continued to remain a cause of concern for New Delhi.

A number of developments also took place in Indo-Bangladesh and Indo-Sri Lanka relations since the installation of Manmohan Singh's government in May 2004. In case of Bangladesh India, as earlier, continued to constructively engage with the governments in Dhaka. Having remained for two years under a caretaker government, in a general election held in December 2008, Sheikh Hasina and her Party Awami League along with its allies registered a victory and formed the government in Bangladesh. On her assumption of office the people and Government of India have hoped a recalling of close and friendly relations with Bangladesh. Like Dhaka the change of government at New Delhi did not witness any policy shift in regard to Sri Lanka and as earlier regular contacts at different levels continued. Throughout the period New Delhi remained careful in regard to the interests of Sri Lankan Tamils and extended every possible help whenever it was sought by Colombo.

1

India-Pakistan Relations

REGIME OF JANATA PARTY

Premiership of Morarji Desai (24 March 1977-28 July 1979)

The New Setting

On the eve of Janata Government assumption of office in New Delhi the general climate in the sub-continent appeared to be quite favourable for the improvement of relations between India and Pakistan. The signing of Simla Agreement in 1972 had set in motion of the relaxation of tensions and normalization of relation between the two countries.[1] When the Janata Party assumed office in New Delhi in March 1977 many hopes and fears were expressed in India and abroad in respect of India's relations with Pakistan, as a former Jana Sangh leader, Atal Bihari Vajpayee, had taken over as the Minister for External Affairs in India. However, it was the proclaimed policy of the Government of India to concentrate on improving relations with immediate neighbours.[2] Pakistan stood at the top of Government of India's priority list. Fears about Vajpayee proved unfounded. He faithfully and sincerely carried out the task assigned to him by his Government and proved equal to the task. As a result the trend of normalization of relations set in motion in 1972 continued unabated during the Janata regime in India.

However, it was not a one-sided affair. Had Pakistan not been interested in normalization of relations and co-operated with India hardly anything could have been achieved. The Government of Pakistan was quite responsive to India's initiatives. It moved cautiously and abstained from doing anything that could obstruct the growing understanding between the two countries. Thus on the occasion of its defence day on 6 September 1978 the censorship authorities of Pakistan ordered the press not to highlight the 1965 war.[3] Government of Pakistan found support from the press and public opinion on its new course. Early in 1978, *The Pakistan Economist* (Karachi), a right-of-centre weekly waged a campaign for amity with India. It suggested in its editorial on 2 February 1978 that an effort be launched both in Pakistan and India to create more enlightened understanding among their people about the sub-continent and its history. It added, "The quest for cheap popularity and going along with popular emotions at all times has to be replaced with rationalism and courage to do what is right."[4] M. B. Naqvi, commenting on Agha Shahi's visit to India, wrote in an editorial page article in *The Pakistan Times* (Lahore) on 19 April 1978 that the visit, as he thought, had brought the Kashmir issue to the top of Indo-Pakistan agenda, but that realistically, ramification of Kashmir should be treated a long-term goal. He further added that Pakistan need not suffer from the cold war mentality which forbade détente with the adversary.[5] The Political correspondent of *The Dawn* (Karachi), wrote on 2 November 1978 that the Afghan revolution had created an entirely new situation in which Pakistan could not afford to ignore the Soviet Union and India. He argued that Pakistan needed a political decision based on national consensus to resolve the dilemma whether it was worthwhile to move towards complete normalization with India while the Kashmir question remained unresolved.[6] By 31 March 1979 this magazine was bold enough to write editorially, "we have always succumbed to the temptation of trying to isolate India and to be one up on it. It is a pointless quest to find possible allies against India. Nor is the policy of perpetual confrontation with it in any way beneficial to Pakistan. It is no longer possible to sustain it."[7]

Growth in Understanding

As a result of their new policies New Delhi and Islamabad soon reached a level of understanding that some observers started describing as better than that during the Bhutto regime. On 15 April 1977 the two countries concluded a three-day trade talks and both sides agreed to set up an institutional mechanism in the form of a joint committee at secretaries level to review periodically the flow of trade and sort out the problems found impending it.[8] India agreed to buy more goods from Pakistan and Pakistan offered to sale items like industrial alcohol, gypsum, rock salts, besides dried and fresh fruits to India. In 1977 two agreements were signed between the two countries. The first agreement signed on 31 August 1977, provided for air services between India and Pakistan.[9] The second agreement, signed on 1 October 1977 at Islamabad, concerned the regulation and improvement of the communication services between the two countries which had been put into operation under an agreement signed in September 1974. Indian ambassador K. S. Bajpayee and Pakistan's Post and Telegraph Director General S. A. Siddique, signed the agreement.[10] By themselves these two agreements did not achieve much and were not very significant. But their signing created an extremely favourable climate in the two countries for further pursuit of friendly and co-operative relationship between the two countries.

The Government of Pakistan took the initiative and invited Vajpayee to visit Islamabad. Responding to that invitation Vajpayee paid a goodwill visit to Islamabad 6-8 February 1978. The new Janata Government in New Delhi was genuinely interested in improving relations with its neighbours, particularly Pakistan. With this aim in view Vajpayee went to Islamabad with the new government's goodwill for Pakistan.[11] In Pakistan itself it appeared that a realization was growing that co-operation with India was preferable to confrontation.[12] Vajpayee's visit to Islamabad resulted in several concrete advances in Indo-Pak relations. A decision was taken for mutual stationing of journalists in the two countries and an agreement was reached to exchange teams of officials for trade negotiations and for the study of each other's agricultural system. However, far more important than these agreements was the way in which each side handled the conversations. The conclusion of the visit was marked by mutual appreciation and understanding.[13]

In course of the visit a fresh emphasis was given on the expansion of trade and cultural exchange between the two countries. Vajpayee proposed the idea of an Asian Common Market. But Pakistan was not in its favour and expressed the fear that, if established, it would be dominated by India.[14] Thus, though some improvements resulted from Vajpayee's visit to Islamabad, the main problem of Kashmir which had plagued Indo-Pak relations since 1947, remained unresolved. On 6 February 1978 at a banquet given in the honour of Vajpayee, Agha Shahi said that Pakistan fervently believed that a just solution of the Kashmir problem would usher in a new era of fruitful and harmonious relations between the two countries.[15] However, the two sides agreed that the matter deserved deeper study.[16]

Relations between the two countries continued to improve. Welcoming Vajpayee at a banquet at Islamabad Agha Shahi said that he was encouraged by the constructive and statesman-like approach of Vajpayee to Indo-Pakistan problems. Shahi paid the return visit to New Delhi 10-14 April 1978. His visit to New Delhi resulted in the signing of an agreement on 14 April on Salal Hydroelectric Project. Under the terms of the agreement the height of the dam, to be constructed by India at the project, was fixed at a little less than 10 metres, so that it did obstruct the free flow of water to Pakistan. Originally, the height of the dam was fixed at 12 metres.[17] Thus, the new Janata Government by agreeing to reduce the height of the dam gave ample evidence of its friendly attitude towards Pakistan.[18] Vajpayee informed the Lok Sabha that the discussion were held in atmosphere of understanding and cordiality which reflected a desire to foster friendly and good neighbourly relations in order to usher in an era of co-operation and confidence between the two countries. At this time New Delhi appeared to be thinking that it was not only laying the foundation of a friendly and good neighbourly policy towards Pakistan but that it had considerably succeeded in it. Commenting on the Salal Agreement Vajpayee said in the Lok Sabha that the agreement demonstrated that the Janata Government respected the inherited obligations and sought to build with greater vigour co-operative relations with immediate neighbours.[19] It was expected that the signing of the agreement would strengthen the base for solving other outstanding problems between the two countries.

In September 1978, Khwaja Ahmed Safdar, Federal Minister for Agriculture, Government of Pakistan , visited India. During the visit an agreement was signed providing for supply of 5270 tonnes of wheat seeds to Pakistan. The Government of India seemed to be ready to co-operate in the growth of such relations to the extent Pakistan was willing to go.[20] A number of problems existed between the two countries and it was an illusion to entertain the hope that the relations between them could improve without their solution. It was not surprising, therefore, that a downward slide in their relations started soon.

The Opening of the Karakoram Highway

In June 1978 an incident occured which set off the downward slide in Indo-Pak relations. On 18 June General Zia formally opened the 500-mile all weather Karakoram Highway in the presence of Geng Biao, a Chinese Deputy Premier. The highway ran from Havelibad 60 miles north of Islamabad to Gilgit in Azad Kashmir and crossed the Karakoram range through the 16,000 feet Khunjerab pass into the Chinese province of Sinkiang.[21] The initiative for the project had come from the Chinese and Pakistan had accepted the offer after the Indo-Pak war of 1965.[22] The highway was built by a working force of Pakistan and China.

The highway improved the strategic position of Pakistan vis-à-vis India by opening up the hither to inaccessible northern regions through a communications network.[23] What was more disturbing for India was that the highway gave the Chinese direct access to Gilgit and from there to the heart of Pakistan. Even more important, it opened up for the Chinese a backdoor entry to the Arabian Sea, and hence, an indefinitely shorter route to West Asia and Africa.[24]

Pakistan tried to play down the strategic significance of the highway and emphasised its importance as a nation-building effort necessitated by the obvious need of national integration and concrete socio-economic unity.[25] However, in view of India's strained relations with China it could hardly look at these developments without concern. But there was little it could do in the matter except lodging formal protests to the parties concerned. Ever since 1969, when the Government of India received confirmed reports of the construction of this highway, it had taken up the issue and lodged protests from time to time. Once again, when it came to know of its opening, it did the same. India's Foreign Secretary, Jagat Mehta, drew the attention of the Chinese ambassador and the Pakistani Charged' Affairs to the protest lodged by India in 1969 against the construction of the Karakoram Highway that stated that neither Pakistan nor China had any locus standi in Kashmir.[26] Later Government of India took up the matter with China also.[27]

Soviet Intervention in Afghanistan

The Soviet intervention in Afghanistan in the last week of December 1979 was an event of great significance and involved all the potentialities of straining Indo-Pak relations. Though the event affected the entire sub-continent, Pakistan was affected more directly. The incident had dramatically transformed its geo-strategic situation. The mountains, deserts, and ravines of Afghanistan, which for long had separated Russia from the sub-continent, disappeared overnight. Pakistan now faced the spectre of Soviet troops virtually every where along the thirteen hundred mile frontier. India was not affected that much directly. It made little difference to India whether Russian troops were stationed on the Amu Darya or the Khyber.[28] It was not surprising, therefore, that Pakistan and Indian troop dispositions changed very little following the incident. On 11 January 1980, participating in the debate in the General Assembly. India's permanent representative at the UN put the primary responsibility for developments in Afghanistan on "the attempt by some outside Powers to interfere in the internal affairs of Afghanistan by training, arming, and encouraging subversive elements to create disturbances inside Afghanistan."[29] It was interpreted to mean that India justified the Soviet move as a defensive response to the activities of "certain foreign powers", implying US and Pakistani responsibility for the Soviet venture.

As the intervention erupted the United States became excessively sympathetic to Pakistan. The day after the invasion, President Carter telephoned President Zia offering his help. In Washington's eye, Pakistan became a "frontline" state sharing a thirteen hundred mile frontier with a country the Soviet Union now sought to control. Carter saw Soviet success in Afghanistan as a great danger to "the region as a whole". Responding to the event the USA offered military aid worth Rs. 85 crores to Pakistan immediately.[30] Carter ordered speeding up in delivery of military equipment to Pakistan which had earlier been suspended to "discourage" arms race in the sub-continent.[31] It made India anxious, and Charan Singh's Government conveyed to the United States that the arming of Pakistan would provide no solution to the problem.[32]

Fear of Indo-Soviet collusion had long prevailed in Islamabad. India's 1971 venture in Bangladesh, launched within months after the conclusion of the Indo-Soviet Treaty of Friendship, lent substance to that fear. Under the circumstances, India's reluctance to condemn the Soviet intervention in Afghanistan and its opposition to US military aid to Pakistan were bound to cause serious misgivings and anxieties in Islamabad. In the first few months of the Soviet intervention, it appeared that the situation had all the potentialities of reversing the process of normalisation of relations between India and Pakistan which had begun with the signing of the Simla Agreement between the two countries in 1972. To some the initial Indian reaction suggested "a return to the 1950s.

However, it was not easy for India to make a choice. Afghanistan was a non-aligned state and, as such, it presented a test case for India. Moreover, there was no gainsaying that it vitally affected India's strategic environment and impinged on its relations with the super powers as well as with the immediate neighbours. The situation demanded a deft handling. Soon India fashioned quite a mature and sophisticated approach to the problem and the worse fears entertained in certain quarters in the first few months of the crisis did not come out true.

The Problem of Kashmir

Both India and Pakistan held different views on Kashmir. Ever since 1947 it had been (and continues to be) a bone of contention between the two countries. Government and people in India viewed Kashmir as an integral part of India, whereas Pakistan took the stand from the very beginning that normalisation of relations was possible only after the solution of the problem of Kashmir. For both the countries, it was not simply a territorial dispute but at the sametime involved historical, psychological, and sentimental aspects.[33] After the creation of Bangladesh in 1971 Pakistan was no longer in a position to alter the status quo in the sub-continent by force. Its emancipation weakened pro-Pakistan elements in India-held Kashmir.[34] However, following the assumption of office by Janata Government in New Delhi in March 1977, Kashmir once again became a hot issue between the two countries.

The Government of Pakistan repeatedly reiterated that full normalisation of relations between the two countries was possible only after the settlement of Kashmir problem.[35] Agha Shahi said that Pakistan fervently believed that a just solution of the Kashmir problem would usher in a new era of fruitful and harmonious relations between the two countries.[36] It had also been seen that the issue came up for a brief discussion in course of Vajpayee's visit to Islamabad in February 1978 and that the parties agreed that the matter deserved deeper study.[37] When Shahi visited New Delhi 10-14 April 1978 the problem once again figured in his talks with Prime Minister Desai. In course of the talks with Desai on 12 April he took the stand of normalisation of relations between the two countries depended on the settlement of the problem of Kashmir.[38] Shahi's visit to India resulted in some concrete achievements. But the problem of Kashmir remained unresolved, and when Zia met Desai in Nairobi in the first week of September 1979 in course of Kenya's President Kenyatta's funeral, he told him that Pakistan's main problem with India was Kashmir.[39] Early in September General Zia made a reference to the Kashmir problem at the Havana Conference of Non-Aligned Nations.[40] The Janata regime in India ended before any definite progress for the solution of the problem of Kashmir.

The Nuclear Issue

Successful explosion of a nuclear device at Pokhran in May 1974 by India introduced a new irritant in Indo-Pak relations. The decision to explode a nuclear device was earlier made in the first half of the 1971 when events in East Pakistan posed a serious threat to India's security and not to deflect public attention from the current political and economic difficulties of the country as is widely believed[41] Pakistan's reaction to the test were strident. It was understandable as the test, coming in the wake of the emancipation of Pakistan by the loss of East Bengal, had sharply tilted the strategic balance in India's favour. In September that year Pakistani delegation to the General Assembly of the United Nations, sidetracking the issue of Peace Zone in the Indian Ocean, sponsored a resolution declaring South Asia a Nuclear Weapon Free Zone (NWFZ). Thereafter, Pakistan attempted to introduce the same resolution on NWFZ on South Asia year after year.[42] India treated this as a deviationist strategy of Islamabad. It also secretly embarked on acquiring nuclear capability under the leadership of Dr. A. Q. Khan, a nuclear scientist. As a counterbalance to India's power superiority Zia made the acquisition of nuclear capability a main plank of his foreign policy.[43]

So long as Pakistan's nuclear ambition and design remained secret it could not become a concern for India. It was during the Janata regime that information about Pakistan's efforts to acquire nuclear capability started coming trickling down. On 28 June 1977, in course of the discussion in the Lok Sabha on the demand for grants of the Ministry of External Affairs. Dr. Henry Austin drew Government's attention towards Pakistan's nuclear intentions.[44] He quoted Pakistan's Foreign Minister, Aziz Ahmed, as saying that, inspite of American opposition France had agreed to supply the uranium processing plant to Pakistan. Quoting *The Jung* (Karachi), he said that there had been a ten-fold increase in budgetary allocation for Pakistan's nuclear programme. A large part of the allocation would go to the nuclear reprocessing plant to be supplied by France. As he said, the current year's (1977-78) allocation was Rs. 55 crores as compared Rs. 5.5 crores in 1966-67 and Rs. 4.79 crores in the previous year.[45]

India's concern over the issue was growing. In the middle of February 1979 Desai wrote a letter to President Zia expressing concern at reports of Pakistan's efforts to acquire nuclear explosion capability. In his reply to Desai, early in March, Zia allayed India's apprehensions and wrote that those were based on misleading reports about Pakistan's nuclear programme which was entirely geared for peaceful purposes. He urged that India and Pakistan should make a joint declaration renouncing the manufacturing of nuclear weapons and stated that if India accepted full scope safeguards for nuclear facility or acceded to the Nuclear Non-Proliferation Treaty of 1968, Pakistan would do the same.[46] Vajpayee informed the Rajya Sabha on 2 March 1979 that Government had reports that Pakistan had embarked on a nuclear programme which might not be entirely for peaceful purposes. He added that Government had collected information from its own sources and it was not based on press reports. India's growing concern over the issue once again found expression in Prime Minister Charan Singh's address to the nation on the Independence Day. He warned that if Pakistan persisted with its plans and exploded an atomic bomb India would have reconsider its nuclear options. He added that Pakistan had no major dispute with any other country in the region and, as such, the bomb was aimed at none else, but India. He asserted that such a bomb in the hands of Pakistan would be a serious threat to India's peace and security.[47] Making an oblique reference to Charan Singh's Independence Day speech General Zia said to the Indian correspondents attending the Havana Conference of Non-Aligned Nations in September 1979 that any suspicion that Pakistan wanted to make nuclear bombs was utterly baseless. He asserted that Pakistan had neither money for it nor the desire to make it. This was his message to his "brothers and friends in India." He requested the media men to carry this message with them and convey them to the people of India.[48] Pakistan's delegate to a conference of the International Atomic Energy Agency at New Delhi Munir Ahmed Khan stated on 5 December that it was not Pakistan's policy to acquire or develop nuclear weapons. He proposed that Pakistan and India should jointly declare South Asia a nuclear free zone and bar development, manufacture and entry of nuclear weapons in the region. Two days later the Indian delegate to the conference rejected his proposal.

The divergence of positions of the two countries on the nuclear issue was obvious. Government of India wanted to be satisfied that Pakistan was not engaged in the making of a nuclear bomb. Pakistan on the one hand, assured India repeatedly to that effect, wanted it to believe its version, adopted other diversionary tactics and, on the other, secretly engaged itself in the making of the bomb.[49] Subsequent developments confirmed it. By, November 1986 Pakistan became "a nuclear weapon power in all but the name".[50]

REGIME OF NATIONAL FRONT

Premiership of V.P. Singh (1 December 1989 -7 November 1990)

The second non-Congress Government took over the reigns of administration in New Delhi with Vishwanath Pratap Singh the new Prime Minister of India. As was known to all the foreign Policy was not an issue in the Parliamentary elections of November 1989. The National Front, in its election manifesto stated that they will weave a new pattern of co-operative relationship with the neighbours. Elaborating the new pattern V. P. Singh said :

Our approach to the neighbouring countries will be one of friendliness, no any armtwisting or any bullying tactics. I want to make this clear. Strength lies in mutual understanding.[51]

Probably the most complicated and yet the most important of all of India's South Asian neighbours is the case of Pakistan and keeping this fact in view the new government took steps to shed off India's "big power" image by publicly announcing that India's defence expenditure will be cut : and, second, that India will enter into dialogue with all the neighbouring countries to find a way out of some of their outstanding issues with them.

The assumption of new government in New Delhi was followed by taking Kashmir issue at an alarming stage. Both countries have been obsessed with an inexorable state of "new cold war" on the subcontinent. Particularly in the light of Pakistan's covert or overt support to secessionists in Punjab and Jammu and Kashmir New Delhi felt the need for a slightly more aggressive posture and in a mild threatening, a foreign office spokesman said, "It is our hope that Pakistan will exercise similar restraint and desist from giving encouragement to terrorism directed against India. Such action violates bilateral, regional and international obligations including the terms of the Simla Agreement and is not conducive to peace in the region.[52] Most of the Indian People viewed Islamabad's recent disturbances in Kashmir to test whether the leadership of the minority government led by the Janata Dal is weak or indecisive and whether Pakistan could use this opportunity to realise its long cherished dream of seizing Kashmir. Actually Pakistanis are encouraged by the Azerbaijani uprising in USSR and feel that they will have the support of Islamic countries all over the world and also of China and the US.[53] Sensing the deterioration in Kashmir the Indian Prime Minister V. P. Singh referred to the provocative statements being made by Pakistani leaders. Despite India's best efforts to improve relations with neighbours, it was unfortunate that the developments in Pakistan were not conducive to it, he added.[54] Needless to say, the political atmosphere of India and Pakistan was charged with emotions and resentment against each other. Interestingly, despite a threatening posture adopted by the respective regimes and hawkish elements of the two countries, the normalisation process has not been entirely abandoned and talks on nuclear non-proliferation, Siachen, Wuler Barrage, Sir Creek and improve economic ties continued. In three respects, the National Front Government's record has been credible. First, inspite of developments in the Kashmir Valley and a certain amount of militancy[55] in Islamabad's attitude, V. P. Singh's Government considered it appropriate to keep the dialogue open. Secondly, when Benazir's Government was dismissed, New Delhi avoided making any comments except for wishing well for a strong and stable Pakistan.[56] Third, India's active diplomacy in the Arab countries and western world it was instrumental, to a large extent, in containing Pakistani efforts to internationalise the Kashmir issue.[57]

The Problem of Kashmir

Once again the long-pending issue of Kashmir became hot between the two countries. The new government of India suggested Islamabad not to continue intervention in Jammu and Kashmir and its support and encouragement to terrorism. It was not conducive to maintenance of peace in the region on the one hand and such an approach would be detrimental to Indo-Pak relations on the other.[58] But in utter disregard of the advice for restraint Pakistan had stepped up interventionist actions in Punjab and Kashmir through training and supply of arms to subversives and incitement to violence. Inder Kumar Gujral, the Minister for External Affairs under new dispensation discussed the issue with Abdul Sattar, Pakistan's Foreign Secretary, during latter's visit to India in January 1990. Although his visit was termed as of exploratory nature, it was a welcome sign that Ms. Bhutto was interested in sustaining the momentum of the efforts to improve Indo-Pakistan relations.[59] Gujral also took the opportunity to impress upon the Sahabzada Yakub Khan, the Foreign Minister of Pakistan when he visited New Delhi in quick succession of Sattar's tour to India. The Indian side utilised the opportunity to convey to him its concern over Pakistan's role in training and arming saboteurs for destabilisation and violent activities in the Kashmir Valley.[60] Pakistan's Foreign Minister denied that Pakistan was encouraging subversion and terrorism in India and reiterated Pakistan's well-known position regarding Kashmir and self-determination.[61] In the meantime Benazir's statement that no compromise would be done with India on the question of "the right of self-determination for the people of J & K added fuel to the fire that compelled India's ruling as well as opposition circles to react sharply. Ms. Bhutto in a state-run television broadcast announced that a joint session of parliament would be convened in the first week of February to discuss the "deteriorating situation in Kashmir."[62]

Protesting strongly against Pakistan's attempt "to interfere and intervene" in the internal affairs of India the Congress-I President and ex-Prime Minister of India Rajiv Gandhi condemned the Pakistan PM's statement on J & K. He also called upon the Government of India to refute the statement and take all steps required to repulse attempts by Pakistan to interfere and intervene in our internal affairs.[63] Gandhi also asked the Prime Minister to cancel the scheduled visit of Gujral to Pakistan and even warned, "The National Front Government cannot sell the country like this, we will not allow it", the AICC (I) President declared.[64] India had very convincing evidence of Pakistan's interference in its internal affairs and V. P. Singh had categorically told Islamabad that Pakistani Policy makers would be well-advised to keep in mind that people and the Government of India have the capacity and the requisite political will to safeguard India's territorial integrity and other interests as stated by Inder Kumar Gujral earlier. He also disclosed that the views have been made clear to both Pakistani dignitaries who visited India recently.[65]

At the moment, peace between India and Pakistan hangs by a slender thread. Kashmir is in turmoil. The turn of events in that troubled state will determine the future of peace and stability in these two countries, both in terms of domestic politics as well as their bilateral relations.[66] In a meeting the Consultative Committee of Parliament of the Defence Ministry which declared unanimously that Jammu and Kashmir is an integral part of India and interference in India's internal affairs would not be tolerated from any quarter whatsoever.[67] During the discussions, members from all political parties declared that the whole nation was behind the Government and the Armed Forces are engaged in defending the territorial integrity of the nation.[68] In this tense situation a balanced statement of Pakistani President Ghulam Ishaq Khan appeared that Pakistan can not afford war and added that there was no immediate threat from India. Pakistan, he said, would continue to make consistent efforts to improve relations with all its neighbours. But at the sametime we will continue to provide whatever resources are necessary to safeguard our independence, freedom and honour.[69] I. K. Gujral, in an interview to the Chief Editor of *The Pakistan Times* stressed that it was very important for both India and Pakistan to resolve their differences through dialogue and confidence building measures to promote peace and co-operation in South Asia.[70]

As per the need of the hour, the issue of Kashmir had been used for purposes more than one. The immediate cause of the present Kashmir problem as felt by Inder Kumar Gujral, is the internal political conflicts in Pakistan that have forced that country to build up a hysteria and whip up the Kashmir issue. It was largely the Nawaz Sharif-led Punjab and some ex-Kashmiri fundamentalists who for their internal hegemony were ranking up the issue and building up a war mood.[71] Benazir's uncompromising attitude continued and she, in her address to the joint session of Parliament declared that Islamabad's elected government will take all necessary steps in accordance with the "aspirations and wishes of the People of Pakistan on the issue".[72] Reacting to Ms. Bhutto's statement External Affairs spokesman said that the Indian government strongly objected to her address to the joint session of Parliament in which she claimed that the Kashmiris had never accepted Indian occupation and struggled against it with determination.[73]

The actual situation, as felt by the observers, was that India being the larger and stronger nation must do everything possible to prevent another war. Absence of help from the United States and China is likely to restrain Pakistan more than anything else. The United States is already putting a pressure on the Pakistani military to hold back from irresponsible brinkmanship. The Soviet Union has also contributed to regional peace and stability by reiterating its traditional support for India.[74] At this critical juncture, most of the Indians put forward the conclusion that Indian Policy must be a mixture of toughness and tenderness. Only iron toughness will subdue the liberationists in the Valley and their supporters in Pakistan. A simultaneous soft policy aimed at the minds of sober Pakistani political and intellectual elements is also an absolute necessity. But in any case, unlike Pakistanis, Indians must not get trapped in war rhetoric.[75] On the other hand, international change had deprived Pakistan of much of the clout it used to enjoy for many years with two of the principal global actors, the United States and China, as well as the countries of the Persian Gulf, the Middle East and South Asia. In practice,

Pakistan had got no support in the world community for its bid to internationalise the Kashmir issue, to trash the Simla Agreement and sent the Kashmir ball back to the court of the UN Security Council.[76] Perhaps, in the circumstances Ms. Bhutto apparently softened her touch stance and expressed Pakistani willingness to initiate a dialogue with the Kashmir issue in the spirit of Simla Agreement while addressing Joint Press Conference with the visiting French President Mitterrand.[77]

Exchange of allegations and counter-allegations on both the sides continued. Despite the efforts, Pakistan failed to project Kashmir on the world stage. The major powers of the world had other pre-occupations and were not willing, in anyway, to add a hoary contentious issue to their agenda.[78] *The Times* (London) wrote more appropriately. "Talk of war continues to escalate in both countries, fanned by Ms. Benazir Bhutto's attempt to out flank her opponents in Pakistan and by the burgeoning confidence of Hindu Hardliners in India.[79] It was also said that behind the rhetoric, there is a desperate and determined desire by Islamabad and Delhi to avoid conflict. Each side is taking tough because of domestic compulsions, with neither believing it will come to war.[80] In addition both are ruled by weak governments. In India we have a minority government, supported by the Bharatiya Janata Party from outside, while in Pakistan, although the government is more stable than it was, it is beholden to the army and to the President to remain in office. In contrast to India, Pakistan lacks the tradition of having and constitutionally changing democratic governments.[81]

The Foreign Ministers of India and Pakistan met in Newyork, where they were to attend the Special UN General Assembly, called to discuss economic issues. Even before their meeting, the two sides expressed the hope to be a meaningful discussion. The Indian spokesman, when Gujral left for Newyork, said, "It is our hope that the up coming dialogue between the two foreign ministers will yield positive results, so as to help relax the current tension resulting from the dispute over Kashmir in the interests of peace and stability in South Asia.[82] Gujral too, expressed optimism about his talks and said that he remained hopeful inspite of aberrations.[83] In the talks the two foreign ministers agreed on steps to ease tension and avoid a military confrontation. They decided that the directors general of military operations in India and Pakistan would remain in touch with each other. Both sides also agreed that they should exercise restraint and channels of communications should be opened at all levels.[84] For India, the Newyork meeting was an occasion to impress on Pakistan (i) that the unthinking manner in which it violated the Simla Agreement was fraught with grave implications (ii) that it will lead to a free for all, not healthy for the delicate bilateral ties (iii) that there will be no compromise on territorial integrity of India and that this had been demonstrated through the firmest of steps, and (iv) that the improvement of relations with Pakistan was the long-term objective which would continue to be pursued.[85] In the changed circumstances, Benazir Bhutto said, her country does not want a war with India as "it was only proved a useless instrument" to solve the Kashmir issue. Speaking at a banquet, hosted by her for visiting Japanese PM To Shiki Kaifu she also added that the previous two wars over the Kashmir issue had not yielded a solution and Pakistan wants "Peace and stability in its region."[86] However, the two countries adopted a divergent approach on United Nation's peace-keeping operations which include an observer group in Kashmir.[87]

There can be no doubt that India is the victim of sustained low-level aggression by secessionist forces encouraged and abetted by Pakistan. Depending entirely on the hope that resumption of negotiations would end the problem would be as self-delusory as the original mistake of agreeing to a ceasefire when Indian troops were rolling the Pakistani invaders back in 1948.[88] In the present day circumstances, adequate defence preparedness will not only provide credible deterrence against direct war, but also go a long way in imposing constraints on Pakistan in the conduct of its proxy war. Winning the proxy war itself requires a cool assessment of the evolving situation and the elements of the Pakistani strategy so as to evolve appropriate responses, political as well as military.[89] It is certainly important that the present government has taken the initiative in withdrawing some of the forces from advance posts apart from suggesting a whole package of confidence building measures. While all this is commendable, much more needs to be done. For it is not only a question of repairing the damage, but seeking to build an edifice of friendly relations.[90]

Foreign Involvement in Kashmir

For the last 50 years the problem of Kashmir between India and Pakistan has been an international issue. The major world powers have been taking active interest in the matter for their own reasons. Apart from facing a war-like situation on several occasions the two had fought in 1965 and 1971, that proved, to a large extent, futility of war in solving the problem. Although with the coming of V. P. Singh's Government nothing happened new with regard to the Kashmir problem except the fact that he headed a minority government supported by Bharatiya Janata Party from the outside. Islamabad viewed the new dispensation as weak and once again tried to hot up the issue by calling for a "thousand year war" and for "Jehad".[91]

Pakistan, in a well-thought strategy began to generate fresh extremism and violence in Jammu and Kashmir. Special Kashmir funds for supporting insurgency had been created. Government sponsored media campaign had increased manifold. Advertisements were appearing in the press asking for 'Jehad'. Fatehas were being read in the Mosques and in the Parliament for the terrorists. A Pakistani citizen sitting in USA was owing up responsibilities for kidnappings and killings, and also openly asking his so called followers to assassinate the Prime Minister and the leader of the opposition in India.[92] In the circumstances Stephen solarz, United States Congressman and Chairman of the House of Representatives Foreign Affairs Sub-committee on Asia and Pacific, has initiated inquiries into India's allegations that Pakistan is heavily involved with violence in the State of Jammu and Kashmir. According to a spokesman from Solarz's office he was "quite disturbed and concerned at continued differences between India and Pakistan on the Kashmir issue."[93]

New Delhi, as a part of its diplomatic efforts to appraise major world powers sent S. K. Singh, country's Foreign Secretary to USA and in response, the Bush Administration had reaffirmed US support for the resolution of the Kashmir question in the "Simla Agreement", which called for peaceful resolution of all bilateral matters between India and Pakistan.[94] At the same time the United States had rejected a bid by Pakistan seeking American support for bringing a resolution on Kashmir to the United Nations Security Council. The present dispensation in US had also appreciated new Indian Government's willingness to discuss and sort things out through a dialogue.[95] The new Prime Minister of India V. P. Singh, in a letter to the US President George Bush had welcomed

Washington's understanding of India's position on the criteria for resolving its problems with Pakistan. He noted with satisfaction the US endorsement of the principle that all issues involving New Delhi and Islamabad should be sorted out peacefully and bilaterally.[96] However, despite all this Pakistan was slowly but surely sought to internationalise the Kashmir issue through the UN ignoring the advice of the United States that the Simla Agreement of 1972 offers the best option for resolving the dispute between the two countries.[97]

At the end of three-day visit of India's Foreign Secretary S. K. Singh to USSR and his consultation with top Moscow officials the Foreign Minister of the country said, "The Soviet Union condemns foreign interference in any form in the affairs of India and assured all round co-operation.[98] The Soviet Union is also of the view that Pakistan must recognize the reality that Kashmir is an integral part of India.[99] Abdul Wakil, the Foreign Minister of Afghanistan in a meeting with his Indian counterpart extended full support to India on the Kashmir issue and had unequivocally condemned Islamabad's interference in the affairs of that state as well as its efforts to internationalise the issue. In the meantime, French President Mitterrand, in a banquet speech reply in Islamabad favoured peaceful solution of the problem and said. "It would not be good if the efficacy of the Simla Agreement was brought into question."[100]

The Peoples Republic of China being a major Power seemed sandwiched between its two objectives. Far from wanting to promote any conflict in South Asia, they are keen to avoid it. They do not want on the one hand, the slow progress of the normalization and improvement of relations with India to be reversed or impeded and wish to retain their special strategic equation with Pakistan on the other which had served their interests well.[101] Even earlier Peking had offered mediation over the Kashmir crisis[102] but the possibility of China or any other country mediating between India and Pakistan was ruled out. A foreign office spokesman said that New Delhi's stance on this matter is "absolutely clear". The Simla Agreement provided the framework for sorting out bilateral differences.[103] Peking's comment on the issue came only after Ms. Bhutto had sent her foreign policy adviser Iqbal Akhund to Beijing to persuade them to speak in support of the Pakistani position. Perhaps, for the sake of satisfaction to Pakistan, the Chinese leaders described

Kashmir as a "dispute" and a problem left over by history with a reference to the "UN decisions" relating to Kashmir. But they also mentioned the Simla Agreement, which the Chinese had seldom taken note of before Li wanted the two countries to settle the Kashmir issue "in conformity" with "Panchsheel". Most significantly the Chinese leaders have asked India and Pakistan to "set peace and stability in South Asia above everything else.[104] India has never been in favour of third party involvement or mediation as all issues between the two countries were to be settled bilaterally and through peaceful methods as per the provisions of the Simla Agreement.

Confidence Building Measures

The Confidence Building Measures have been proposed by New Delhi and Islamabad over the years to avoid war and normalize ties. Major disputes between India and Pakistan are an obstruction to the course of normalisation, but the progress in other areas could ultimately help settle these disputes. In fact, both sides undermine the necessity to simultaneously adopt military and non-military CBMs. India has its own reasons to emphasise the adoption of non-military CBMs before settling the Kashmir dispute whereas Pakistan feels it meaningless to go far these CBMs without settling its disputes with India. Although some circles quote the Simla Agreement as a model for the Indo-Pakistan normalization process, especially references concerning the peaceful settlement of disputes. Institutional measures for co-operation taken by India and Pakistan in the post-Simla accord period, however, account for only partial success. There have been frequent ups and downs owing to political tension.[105]

During the premiership of V. P. Singh in the summer of 1990, the Kashmir dispute threatened a new outbreak of hostilities in the sub-continent. India and Pakistan decided to launch bilateral talks at the foreign secretary level for de-escalation of tension and normalization of relations. A spokesman of India's External Affairs Ministry said that India was committed to exploring all avenues to establish a constructive and co-operative relationship with Pakistan for peace and stability in the region.[106] As a gesture of confidence building measure India unilaterally withdrew an armed division from a key area along the tension-ridden Indo-Pakistan border.[107] India also offered a package of Confidence Building Measures that laid particular emphasis on non-military steps to be taken :

The seven-point proposals are

- Exchange of information on military exercises;
- Communication (of troops movements) between local commanders;
- Joint border patrolling to prevent infiltration smuggling of weapons and explosive for purposes of carrying out terriorist activities;
- Memorandum of Understanding on prevention of air space violation by military aircraft;
- Exchange of visits by armed forces delegation;
- Prevention of acts detrimental to maintenance peace and harmonious relations and non-interference in each other's internal affairs; and
- Reiteration of commitment to abide by the Simla Agreement including non-use of force, resolution of bilateral differences through peaceful means and cessation of hostile propaganda and rhetoric.[108]

However, the recent trends in Indo-Pak relations would agree that notwithstanding the concrete package of measures suggested by India for confidence building between the two countries, Pakistan had yet to overcome certain psychological barriers.[109] The new wave of reconciliation that is sweeping over all parts of the world must touch our shores.[110] India had accepted Pakistan's suggestion that the Foreign Secretaries of the two counties meet to try and defuse the prevailing tension. According to a decision Muchkund Dubey, India's Foreign Secretary and Tanvir Ahmed Khan, his Pakistani counterpart met in Islamabad 18-20 July 1990 for talks to defuse the year long tension between the two countries over Kashmir. Benazir Bhutto, the Pakistani Prime Minister was happy with the forthcoming meeting and described Indian response as "positive".[111] Soon after his arrival in Islamabad Muchkund Dubey, speaking to reporters said that India had absolute sincerity and a constructive flexibility approach on the talks for which no agenda has been fixed.[112] In the talks India and Pakistan failed to make much headway to defuse tensions between them with the two sides sticking to their different perceptions on the situation in Kashmir.[113] The meeting ended without agreeing on any confidence building measure but it was decided to continue the dialogue in Delhi, tentatively in the second week of August 1990.[114]

Amid the dismissal of Benazir Bhutto's Government and Organisation of Islamic Conference (OIC) not endorsing Pakistan's call on Kashmir, India in August 1990 proposed five non-military and seven military CBMs to improve relations with Pakistan :

- Statements (should be) made by political and military leaders in Pakistan disassociating themselves from (acts of) terriorism and subversion in the (Indian states of) Punjab, Jammu and Kashmir.
- The handing over of (ten) fugitives who have been operating from Pakistan. India also asked Pakistan to hand over Jammu and Kashmir Liberation Front leader Amanullah Khan. Such a request was promptly turned down by Pakistan.
- Seizure (by Pakistan) of arms and ammunition (that are) being smuggled into India and the arresting of infiltrators (who have been) crossing into India.
- Cessation of official statements and pronouncements from Pakistan inciting violence and striking communal passion in India.
- Closure of officially sponsored funds that have been put in Pakistan in connection with recent developments in Jammu and Kashmir.[115]
- Military CBMs presented by India were :
- Prior notice of military exercises including troop movements;
- Regular contacts between military establishments;
- Prevention of air violations;
- Exchange of military delegations;
- Joint patrolling;
- Closure of camps stoppage of supply of arms and supports to political intruders;
- Reaffirmation of certain elements of the Simla accord that envisaged step by step resolution of all bilateral disputes and issues.[116]

The secretary-level talks between the two countries had some success as disclosed by Muchkund Dubey, India's Foreign Secretary. India asked Pakistan in the meeting five minimum measures including the cessation of its interference in Kashmir and Punjab to create conditions for withdrawing of troops to peace time positions. Pakistan side too had given an assurance that these proposals would be considered seriously.[117] Describing the talks as satisfactory Dubey said that the two sides had narrowed down their differences considerably on two subjects. One, advance notice of military exercises and manoeuvres and two, non-violation of each others air space by military air craft. The two agreements, he said were likely to be signed soon.[118] However, the future of the coming talk appeared bleak as Gujral, while addressing the Council on Foreign Relations in Newyork said, "Despite India's sincere efforts, the relations with Pakistan have deteriorated and tension increased as Islamabad is openly training, arming, funding and motivating the subversives in Punjab and Jammu and Kashmir.[119] New Delhi deeply regretted Pakistan's decision to raise the J & K issue at Havana Conference[120] and in the circumstances, the third round of foreign secretary level talks to normalize Indo-Pak relations was postponed.[121]

Chandra Shekhar
(10 November 1990-21 June 1991)

Chandra Shekhar succeeded V. P. Singh as the next Prime Minister of India on 10 November 1990. His regime was no less important for Indo-Pak relations as, it witnessed many good signs. The postponed secretary-level talks between the two countries was held 18-20 December 1990. Although the three Foreign Secretary-level talks failed to break the deadlock caused by their contradictory stands on Kashmir situation. While India refused to talk to Pakistan on Kashmir as it was its internal matter, Pakistan insisted that the main cause of tension was Kashmir.[122] Perhaps, one major factor that reversed this onward trend in Indo-Pakistan relations during the outgoing year was the political instability which followed indecisive results of the general elections in 1988 in Pakistan and 1989 in India. Whether he succeeds in his efforts or not Prime Minister Chandra Shekhar certainly merits commendation for the preservance and courage with which he tried to reach out to Pakistan. On 10 January 1991, in course of the late night session of the Lok Sabha, he declared, "I will take five steps for everyone that Pakistan takes".[123] Added credit is due to him for making the effort at a time when Pakistan is more unpopular in this country than it has been of most times in recent decades. Fortunately, at the regional level there have been two improvements, first, other South Asian countries are no longer taking sides between India and Pakistan. Second, for the first time ever, all South Asian countries with the small exception of Bhutan are now more or less democratic.[124]

In a significant development the India's High Commissioner in Pakistan J. N. Dixit on 25 January 1991, deposited instruments of ratification of the agreement on prohibition of attack on nuclear installations and facilities with Pakistan's acting Foreign Secretary Afsal Quadir. Special mention should be made of Article 2 of the agreement which provided that the two countries would inform each other the latitudes and longitudes of the nuclear installations and facilities in their respective countries at the beginning of each year and would inform each other of any changes in locations.[125] Pakistan's President and Prime Minister expressed happiness over the understandings reached between the two countries and hoped that Pakistan and India can enhance mutual trust and achieve the shared objectives of establishing tension free and good neighbourly relations.[126] In response, Chandra Shekhar said that the government was committed for improving relations with Pakistan and all possible efforts would be made to remove tension from the subcontinent.[127]

Fruitful conversations between the two Prime Ministers on the mournful day of the funeral of Rajiv Gandhi had somewhat cleared the climate of India-Pakistan relations of the clouds of conflict. A welcome result of the visit was the agreement, in principle that they agreed to meet later this year after adequate preparations. During the visit, Nawaz Sharif met with the President of India and other leaders of the Congress, the Janata Da! and BJP. In the talks L.K. Advani said that his party wants restoration of cordial relations between India and Pakistan.[128]

Despite New Delhi's good gestures Islamabad continued to encourage the insurgents in Kashmir and attempted to raise the issue at international forums. Reacting to a statement of Pakistani foreign office about human rights violation in Kashmir, the Indian side criticized the press release and maintained that the statement is not based on facts, but on distortions and misrepresentation.[129] "We sincerely hope that the Government of Pakistan will realize the necessity of building a co-operative and mutually beneficial relationship between India and Pakistan in accordance with the Simla Agreement.[130] In April 1991 a Pak-occupied-Kashmiri leader reported in a statement that the Kashmir issue will be raised in the UN by Pakistan.[131] In Labour Conference, in Geneva, in June 1991, when Islamabad tried to take up the Kashmir issue and alleged that its efforts to improve people's living standards were being hampered by the situation in Kashmir, Ambassador Chadha, outrightly rejected the Pakistani allegation and appealed to refrain from indulging in "empty rhetoric, but let its deeds speak for themselves and to abandon its confrontationist approach and join India in a spirit of co-operation to herald peace in the region.[132]

REGIME OF UNITED FRONT

Premiership of H. D. Deve Gowda (1 June 1996-21 April 1997)

H. D. Deve Gowda, as a leader of the United Front, formed the government on 1 June 1996. The Pakistani Prime Minister and Foreign Minister sent the message of felicitations on 4 June 1996 which was responded favourably by Indian Prime Minister and Inder Kumar Gujral, India's new Minister for External Affairs. Deve Gowda, in reply said "My Government stands ready to work together, with your Government, to address all issues of mutual concern. The bilateral approaches and agreements which have been devised earlier can guide us in our future exchanges on all matters, including those on which we might have differing perceptions.[133] Gujral too, in a message to his Pakistani counterpart hoped that it is our constant endeavour to implement the desire of the people and Government of India to establish a relationship based on friendship and co-operation between our two countries.[134] With the coming of Deve Gowda the policy underwent a process of refinement and was being extended to the diplomatic and political spheres by the present government. The political turn of events, especially the successful completion of elections in Jammu and Kashmir gave the United Front government the advantage, which the previous Congress government headed by P. V. Narasimha Rao did not enjoy. Many commentators attribute this new policy to Inder Kumar Gujral, the Foreign Minister in Deve Gowda cabinet." It is part of Gujral's earthy Punjabi approach to diplomacy which does not stop at embracing the other person.[135] Ms. Bhutto, in her congratulatory message to Godwa, had offered to resume talks with India unconditionally and as a gesture, took a major initiative on bilateral trade by "approving" the most favoured nation status for India.[136] New Delhi expressed its readiness for resumption of secretary-level talks but the response was low-key because Gujral tried his level best to break the long-time impression, going around in the international community that India's foreign policy is tied down to Pakistan and Pakistan alone. Though in reality this is not correct, it was getting projected that way. India adopted the policy of unilateralism and wanted to build bridges with the people of Pakistan, bypassing those in power in Islamabad.[137]

The unilateral proposals, made by New Delhi were aimed at creating "an atmosphere of friendship and positive environment where it is possible to talk".[138] Pakistanis were encouraged to visit India at any time of the year. According to a spokesman of India's Ministry of External Affairs, any bonafide Pakistani citizen wishing to visit India will not be denied a visa. As against 150 visas being issued prior to June 1996, the number went up to 225 to 250 per day. In fact, the Ministry spokesman said that they are not able to meet the rush due to inadequacy of the staff at our mission in Islamabad.[139] As against this Indian policy, Pakistan not only denied visas to a number of Indians, but also imposed severe restrictions on the number of Muslims who can make it to Pakistan in a calender year.[140] Islamabad was not happy with the way India acquired a high profile in the Afghan imbroglio by October 1996 and it unnerved the Pakistani armed forces/ISI. What Pakistan's Afghan policy makers have been assiduously trying to block for the last 17 years, that is keeping India away from the Afghan problem, seemed to have been reversed suddenly. This reversal was accompanied by accusations of Pakistan's active involvement in the Afghan civil war. In other words, Pakistan was put in the dock by the major players in Afghanistan, while India got projected as a country trying to use its good offices to find a way out.[141]

In fact, Pakistan was envious to the image India received against Islamabad in international arena. All these developments forced Pakistani armed forces/ISI to do something drastic to vitiate the atmosphere and they got the opportunity. The special branch of Delhi Police arrested the Pakistani embassy officials from a posh South Delhi residential area, while he was reportedly collecting secret documents concerning the south naval command from a local contact and was handed over to the Pakistani High Commission. Retaliatory action was expected but Pakistan went a step further and levelling similar charges against Ashok Kumar Wahi, an Indian authority in Islamabad, picked him up from his residence by the Pakistani intelligence official on 26 October 1996, taken to an unknown place in a vehicle and was brutally beaten. When his wife Renu Wahi tried to save her husband she was also assaulted.[142]

Strong protest was lodged over this shocking and unfortunate diplomatic event. Riaz Khokkar, the Pakistani High Commissioner was summoned by the Secretary, Ministry of External Affairs twice in twenty four hours and was told that the type of treatment meted out to Ms. Wahi constituted a gross violation of international convention on diplomatic behaviour, the bilateral code of conduct and was an affront to human dignity.[143] This particular incident vitiated, to a certain extent, and the United Front government's unilateralism received a setback. Gujral too had warned Pakistan on "unacceptable and uncivilized" incident and said "the best policy for India to follow was to keep a silent and watchful eye" on its neighbour.[144] The statement came in the wake of dismissal of the elected government of Ms. Benazir Bhutto and emergence of a whole set of 'nominated people' in positions of power. However, the development in Pakistan is an internal affair but it causes concern, he asserted.[145] A "change of tone" appeared in Pakistan's greetings extended by Farooq Leghari and the caretaker Prime Minister Malik Meraj Khalid, on 26 January, 1997, in a language of bilateral dialogue. Even as the official Pakistani media sustained its propaganda against India in relation to Kashmir both the leaders conveyed their greetings to the people of India on "the auspicious occasion of the Republic Day of India.[146]

New Delhi welcomed and responded favourably to the desire expressed by the newly elected Prime Minister of Pakistan Nawaz Sharif for talks at the ministerial level. Soon after becoming the Prime Minister, in a brief reference to Pakistan's troubled relationship with India he said in Lahore that the two countries "have to learn how to live as good neighbours".[147] The public opinion in Islamabad also favoured amicable relations with India as Benazir herself admitted in a television interview on 5 February 1997 and said, "we had more hawkish policy on India but he (Nawaz Sharif) is the one who had come with a three-fourth majority. So obviously people have endorsed his stand to open negotiations with India and they have rejected our stand that unless India moves on the Kashmir dispute there should be no talks".[148] Indian response at the moment was hopeful and H. D. Deve Gowda expressed India's readiness in an interview to editor S. Nihal Singh, to discuss minor adjustments in relation to Kashmir within the scope of the Simla Agreement.[149] However, Inder Kumar Gujral, India's Minister for External Affairs made it clear on 6 March 1997, that India would not have any pre-condition on Kashmir for resumption of the bilateral dialogue stalled since January, 1994.[150]

As decided earlier, the official level talks between the two countries were held 28-31 March for which both sides were hopeful and showed ample gestures. Pakistan's Foreign Minister Gohar Ayub Khan was of the view that the present government would be able to take "bold steps" to resolve its problems with India. New Delhi too on 20 March 1997, announced unilateral concessions to Pakistan in visa-related matters. Giving details in Parliament, Gujral said that the measures were designed to add to the goodwill between the people of the two countries. "They are an emblem of our earnest desire to establish and maintain relations of friendship and co-operation with our neighbour, Pakistan".[151] Earlier, Islamabad decided to repatriate 38 Indian children detained in Pakistan as a gesture of goodwill aimed at improving the atmosphere for the bilateral talks. The announcement said, "The Government has decided to make the "unilateral gesture, on humanitarian considerations" to create a propitious climate" for the forthcoming talks between Pakistan and Indian Foreign Secretary.[152] However, the much publicized and awaited talk between the two countries, despite its pleasant beginning, did not make any headway. The Pakistan side stressed the primacy, given by it, to the Kashmir issue, while India expressed its willingness to consider all outstanding problems. On the otherhand, while Islamabad was unrelenting on the urgent need to "meaningfully address the core issue of Kashmir, New Delhi asked its counterpart to stop meddling in its internal affairs.[153]

Problem of Kashmir

The Problem of Kashmir remained as in yester years, a burning issue between India and Pakistan. Each and every progress in their relations revolved round the Kashmir. After the United Front government had come to power Pakistani Prime Minister Benazir Bhutto, in her congratulatory letter to Deve Gowda, had expressed willingness to resume bilateral talks with New Delhi. India responded favourably with the offer but the Pakistani mood suddenly changed and it expressed "difficulty" in resuming negotiations with India because of the continued "deadlock" over Kashmir.[154] Perhaps Islamabad was also disturbed over the successful completion of Assembly and Parliamentary elections in Jammu and Kashmir which was appreciated by many world powers including the Great Britain. Asif Ali, the Pakistani Foreign Minister criticized the holding of elections in J & K and asserted, "Firstly, elections can not be a solution to the Kashmir issue. Had this been so then all the elections in the past would have solved the Kashmir problem. Secondly it is an international dispute and the people want plebiscite there.[155] In the same vein further, Ms. Bhutto, in an address to the nation on 28 June 1996, criticized India on Kashmir. In the circumstances, it was natural for New Delhi to raise serious doubts over Pakistan's intention to resume bilateral talks. A spokesman of the Indian Foreign Office said. "The tone of Ms. Bhutto's address was at variance with the letter sent to the Prime Minister. We wonder which to take seriously."[156] Pakistan also requested Bangladesh to politically support Islamabad's stand on Kashmir but had cold shouldered the proposal as disclosed by Nijamuddin Shaikh, Pakistan's Foreign Secretary, and was told that Bangladesh has difficulties on the question of Kashmir.[157] Even the dismissal of Ms. Bhutto's government and the coming of nominated government made no difference on the issue who in a statement on 5 February, before a gathering, assembled to observe the "Solidarity Day" declared that the people of Pakistan would continue to stand staunchly behind their Kashmiri brethren in their struggle to achieve their inalienable right to self-determination.[158]

In the general elections, held in Pakistan Nawaz Sharif got the landslide victory and became the next Prime Minister of the country. In his first remark after assuming office he chosen to articulate a "serious dialogue" between India and Pakistan and "not confrontation" is the foreign policy mantra. New Delhi too, was keen to have mutual dialogue and discussions with Pakistan to sort out our pending problems.[159] However, Deve Gowda, perhaps viewing attitude not encouraging said on 13 February 1997 "so far the Kashmir issue is concerned, it is a closed chapter". He added that J & K is a part and parcel of India and there is no question of its compromise.[160]

Foreign Involvement in Kashmir

From the beginning the major powers of the world have been taking alive interest in the affairs of Kashmir for their own reason, suited to their objectives. During the regime of H. D. Deve Gowda the United States has for the first time acknowledged that Pakistan is responsible for the terrorist activities in Kashmir. A State Department spokesman Nicholas Bums on 8 June 1996 said, "we have made this a big issue in our relationship with both the countries (India and Pakistan), and we are willing to do whatever we can to get these people out".[161] However, the US had some reservations concerning the conduct of Assembly and Parliamentary elections in J & K. In reply to a question on the western press reports, a State Department spokesman said earlier that US is always concerned about the reports of voting irregularities in the countries around the world and we have seen the reports of coercion having occured in districts in Kashmir. While the British Minister of State for Foreign and Commonwealth Affairs Jeremy Hanley said that there was a fair participation in recent Jammu and Kashmir elections.[162] When a separate question was asked on Kashmir the minister made it clear that Britain favoured a solution to the Kashmir issue amicably between India and Pakistan through bilateral negotiations.[163]

In a fresh move to settle the problem of Kashmir between India and Pakistan the UN Secretary General Boutros Boutros Ghali on 17 September 1996, in a report on the working of the organisation to the General Assembly laid emphasis on the urgency of the issue and said' "I am ready to render whatever assistance may be needed in this regard, should both countries find it useful."[164] Sometimes the US too, appeared sincere in solving the issue and perhaps in a bid, foiled Islamabad's attempt again to internationalise the issue. Benazir Bhutto on 4 October 1996, proposed a multilateral dialogue for peace and security in South Asia with the participation of India, Pakistan, the five permanent members of the Security Council and other major powers like Japan and Germany. But the US, apart from suggesting to resolve the issue through bilateral talks, charged Pakistan that "in the opinion of the United States, it is Pakistan that is reluctant to hold a dialogue with India on Kashmir.[165] In the background of India's readiness to resume the dialogue and Nawaz Sharif becoming the new elected Prime Minister of Pakistan, Robin Raphel said that the US finds the present stage congenial for Indo-Pakistan dialogue. The US Administration had favoured such a course in the past and would encourage the two sides to have meaningful contacts, she asserted. The country went a step further and sent its envoy Wisner on a three-day visit to review the post-poll situation in the state. During the visit when he was asked a question, denied the allegation that the US Government was having a tilt towards Islamabad in its policy on Kashmir.[166] But the US neutrality regarding Indo-Pak relations was questioned by Farooq Abdullah, the Chief Minister of J & K who refuted the claim of Wisner that America was neutral on the Kashmir issue. He added further that Pakistan had inflicted war on us and if US stops arms supply to Pakistan, the impass would have been sorted out once and for all.[167] The US was requested to give up its emphasis on maintaining a strategic balance between India and Pakistan. Indian Ambassador, Naresh Chandra, in an interview with *Washington Times,* on 14 February1977 said that the US attitude implied the assumption of continued confrontation between India and Pakistan rather than looking to the potential for bilateral and regional co-operation.[168]

Perhaps, as a result of the above statements indicating US attitude towards Kashmir as well as Indo-Pak relations, the United States tried to impress India when its Assistant Secretary of State Robin Raphel described that the tension between India and Pakistan over Kashmir is a key issue for South Asia and it is up to the two countries to decide about how they fit Kashmir into that equation.[169] Fortunately, the present dispensation of Nawaz Sharif got a landslide victory in recently held general elections on a pro-India plank. He has so far identified "some progress on the core issue of Jammu and Kashmir as a pre-requisite, not necessarily a pre-condition, for normalisation of ties with India, although Sharif was blamed for seeking talks under India's missile shadow."[170] New Delhi responded favourably to the Pakistani proposal for talks and the two countries conducted talks, after a gap of three years in March 1997. UN Secretary General Kofi Annan welcomed the development of understanding between New Delhi and Islamabad.

Defence

Soon after the taking over of the reigns of Administration by H. D. Deve Gowda on 1 June 1996, Pakistan had deployed M-11 missiles acquired from China. Apart from the deployment, Islamabad went ahead in its efforts to produce a missile capable of delivering 1,000 kg. of payload at a distance of 600 km. aimed at targeting New Delhi. Pakistan is almost on the verge of completing a high-tech domestic missile production on facility with the

Chinese help in the mountains of Fatehganj area, south of Islamabad. The acquirement of M-11 missiles from China could well represented the tip of an iceberg of Sino-Pakistan co-operation in the development of long-range missiles and it appears that Pakistan would co-produce or license-produce M-11s.[171] Pakistan is indigenously developing the Hat f-3 with a range of about 800 km. The Hat f-3 would be capable of striking Delhi from positions deep inside Pakistan. Given the range of Sino-Pak co-operation, it is probable that the Chinese would have provided extensive technological assistance, reducing the time and cost of Hat f-3 development. There are reports that it is nearly ready.[172]

The news of deployment of M-11 sparked off reactions from the sections more than one. V. P. Singh, former Prime Minister of India demanded that India go ahead with the development of Prithvi and other long-range missiles as a possible counter to M-11. "We can not keep our flanks open in view of this grave development across the border.[173] He also warned both countries not to enter an arms race with each other. A spokesman of External Affairs Ministry Arif Khan said, "The Government has seen reports in the US press on deployment of M-11 missiles by Pakistan". The acquisition of the missiles was a well known fact and a matter of "great concern" to India. He also stated further that India will take all necessary steps to safeguard its security and national interests according to its own threat perceptions". New Delhi had also lodged strong protest when the reports of Pakistan acquiring the M-11 missiles from China first appeared in the media. The Pakistani sources said it a misleading report of American press, an attempt to impede the improving US-Pak relations after the passage of the Brown Amendment which provided $ 368 million worth of arms to Pakistan.

Although indirectly, on 13 June 1997, the United States had confirmed that Pakistan has deployed the Chinese built and supplied M-11 missiles as part of a 'conspiracy' between the two governments. At the sametime it strongly denounced the leak of a CIA report to that effect. But China had rejected US intelligence reports that Pakistan had deployed nuclear-capable Chinese missile and said the reports are entirely groundless. The dealing with the Peking is not an easy one. Correct assessment of the Chinese changing position was made by Assistant Secretary of State Winston Lord when he said, "we are dealing with a complex, difficult and princkly partner whose power is growing, whose leadership is in transition, and whose government is turning increasingly to a nationalism that is conditioned by thousands of years to experience as the dominant "Middle Kingdom" and more than a century of humiliation by foreigners.[174]

Because India was pursuing the policy of unilateralism and wanted to build bridges with Pakistan, it did not respond to the wild and baseless Pakistani charges about "atrocities" committed by the Indian armed forces in Jammu and Kashmir. The Indian Defence Ministry did not consider it worthwhile to refute a film telecast by Pakistani Television on "Operation Dwarka", which was a propaganda film with professional artists, made by the Pakistani Navy's publicity wing on the so-called bombing of Dwarka port in the Indo-Pak war of 1965.[175] India's response to PTV report on the destruction of a mosque in Lucknow at the time of the Uttar Pradesh Assembly elections in 1996 was similar.[176]

The representatives of India and Pakistan Arundhati Ghose and Munir Akram respectively, exchanged hot discussions at the UN that showed their divergent approach on the nuclear issue. At the tenth meeting of the first committee of the General Assembly which was discussing issues relating to disarmament and international security, Akram laid emphasis that the international community must realize that a solution to South Asia's problems was indispensable for the success of global endeavours at nuclear disarmament and non-proliferation. He quoted the Kashmir issue as the cause of tension in South Asia.[177] While India's representative expressed concern at the illicit traffic in small arms and the excessive production, development and transfer of conventional weapons beyond country's legitimate security needs.[178]

The two countries had also a divergent approach on the fencing of 180 km-long border in the Jammu region which could not take off in the past two years due to stiff resistence by Pakistan. R. S. Mehta IG (Jammu border) had charged that Pakistan had been resorting to unprovoked firing in the region to intimidate the workers on the border whenever the task of fencing is taken up. The delegations of India and Pakistan met on the issue led by BSF IGs of Rajasthan, Punjab and Jammu, officers of the Narcotics Control Board, while the Pakistani delegation comprising six officers led by Director General of the Pakistan Rangers Major General

Sayeed-ul-Hasan Zaidi.[179] The security understanding had a further deterioration in sequence when Pakistan received first batch of 15 tanks of the 320 T-80 UD main battle tanks (MBTs) from Ukraine worth over $ 15 million. Although Russia had said earlier that it will block the sale because it did not want to promote the growth of Pakistani's military potential in that region to the detriment of India.[180] On 16 April 1997, Pakistani Premier Nawaz Sharif slammed India's nuclear and missile programmes. He said, "Pakistan is seriously concerned about India's nuclear and ballistic missile programme". Pakistan could not ignore the 'threat' to its security and it must have the capability to deter aggression.[181] He was very hopeful about the newly opened dialogue with New Delhi. These developments had vitiated the defence atmosphere between India and Pakistan for the time to come.

Inder Kumar Gujral
(21 April 1997-19 March 1998)

The Indian National Congress, a supporting party of the minority Government of United Front succeeded in getting a change of leadership from H. D. Deve Gowda to I.K. Gujral. The development followed the assumption of premiership by Inder Kumar Gujral on 21 April 1997 who was Minister for External Affairs in Deve Gowda dispensation. The year 1997 had already witnessed an elected government in J & K and a clearly discernible turn way from support to militancy by the Kashmiri population. It also saw the political leadership in India and Pakistan taking control of negotiations on a commonly agreed agenda. The political initiatives taken by the two countries in recent past had got a world wide response. The Prime Minister of India, in reply to the felicitations sent by his Pakistani opposite number on 24 April 1997, reiterated that India was determined not to spare any effort for widening co-operation in "mutually beneficial areas".[182] However, the perception is gaining ground that Pakistan has got the better of the Indian approach of sweet reasonableness the hallmark of the current policy. There is little doubt that New Delhi's conscious approach of friendliness towards the Nawaz Sharif Government has been interpreted as that of a weakening who can be paid back in a different coin altogether.[183]

A new wave of normalization of relations between the two countries shared when the two Prime Ministers had their famous rendezvous at Male on 12 May, 1997. It followed the resumption of talks between New Delhi and Islamabad, may well discern a definite pattern in our neighbour's responses and actions. Right from the beginning, Pakistan insisted that unless the "core issue of Kashmir was solved, bilateral relations would never improve. It also implied that the Indian approach of normalizing relations in other spheres would only serve to provide a cosmetic touch and would not materially alter the relations. While India continued to insist that it was ready to discuss Kashmir, normalization of relations in other spheres, especially commercial, economic and people to people, would help accelerate the process of normalization. India, without waiting for Pakistani reciprocity, went ahead with easing the access channels like visa issuance and selling scarce essential items in order to kick-start the normalization process. Being pressed by the inexorable economic conditions Pakistan seemed to have been persuaded and so the dialogue began.

As a follow up the second round of Foreign Secretary level talks was held in Islamabad between the two countries in June 1997. Apart from the good gestures, New Delhi in the haste to achieve forward movement, agreed to an entirely flawed concept of working groups and for providing the working group on Jammu and Kashmir in special status. Having got New Delhi to accept the special focus on Jammu and Kashmir, Islamabad had been predictably gleeful in subsequently seeing India seek to reinterpret what it had agreed to in Islamabad. The talks have stalled notwithstanding the rather brave political fronting by political leadership on both sides.[184] The eight point charter of priorities chalked out by the Foreign Secretaries during the talks included confidence building measures, Siachen, Tulbul navigation project and an amicable settlement of the Sir Creek boundary issue.

Before the commencement of the third round of Indo-Pakistan talks on bilateral issues, New Delhi began to mobilise the nations to become a permanent member of all powerful Security Council at the forthcoming session of the United Nations General Assembly. It was in the light of a US proposal, during the meeting, for five more permanent Security Council seats, three of them for developing world to broaden representation of the developing world in the Western dominated council.[185] Islamabad opposed Indian claim for the membership as well as any increase in the number of permanent seats, in the 15-member council on grounds of lack of consensus. The Pakistan's spokesman said, "As yet there is no consensus on expansion in the category.[186] Further, Pakistani Minister for Information and Media Development, Mushahid Hussain opposed Indian bid to secure a permanent membership in the United Nations Security Council saying it is unacceptable on moral, legal and diplomatic grounds. However, despite Pakistani opposition Gujral was optimistic about success of Indo-Pak talks and had full confidence that the outgoing dialogue with Pakistan could succeed and the two countries would find a "wayout on the Kashmir issue" He emphatically expressed India's readiness to establish a relationship of trust, friendship and co-operation with Pakistan and affirmed that the New Delhi's approach will be "constructive".[187]

Amid the speculations from both the sides, third-round of bilateral talks between India and Pakistan started in New Delhi in the middle of September 1997. Even earlier, Nawaz Sharif charged India with deploying ballistic missiles near its border and expressed fears that the recent incidents of firing along the Line of Control in Kashmir may undermine the forthcoming round of talks between the two countries.[188] Side by side, perhaps as a gesture, Islamabad started liberal visa policy for Indians. Under the new policy old persons and women were no longer required to report to the police that visa applications were being processed within two or three days. But without any change in its earlier stand, Pakistani Foreign Secretary Shamshad Ahmed led his country's delegation and confirmed that Kashmir would remain the main issue in the talks.[189] The Foreign-Secretary-level talks ended with no forward movement on outstanding bilateral issues, particularly a mechanism for discussing Kashmir due to the apparent lack of desire on Pakistan's part to show any progress. Although K.Raghunath, India's Foreign Secretary described the atmosphere of the talks as one comprising friendship and cordiality and there had been a "serious" and constructive exchange of views".[190] However, the latest round of India-Pakistan talks ended in a virtual deadlock. Ever since the initial enthusiasm about the resumption of talks had subsided, it became clear that the gap between the two sides were far too wide to be easily bridged. Pakistan wanted the entire focus to be on what it regards as the "core" issue of Kashmir while India favoured the idea of taking up other matters of mutual interest, including trade, cultural exchange, Siachin, terrorism and drug trafficking, etc. along with Kashmir.[191]

In a major breakthrough Indian Premier I. K. Gujral and his Pakistani counterpart Nawaz Sharif were to meet in Newyork on 23 September, 1997, to address the UN General Assembly. The two premiers were scheduled to meet US President Bill Clinton on September 22 when he addressed the General Assembly. It was expected that their meeting would set the tone for maximum co-operation between the two countries based on mutuality of interests and goodwill. Nawaz Sharif, while addressing the UN General Assembly, offered India to open talks on non-aggression pact and justified Pak nuclear and missile programmes.[192] The two Prime Ministers in their 40-minute meeting expressed the ways to initiate steps to generate confidence and goodwill. In view of the recent cross border firing, it was decided to enhance military-to-military contacts to the level of sector commanders. The discussions also included the issue of economic co-operation in the region as a whole with SAARC as the focus.

Despite the efforts for amicable Indo-Pakistan relations and continuation of the bilateral talks at the Foreign Secretary level, there were enough posture that clouded their relations. Before the third round talks, Pakistan expelled two officials of the Indian High Commission in retaliation to a similar act by India. Not much later the two sides repeated the expulsion of one diplomat from each other's for spying activities on 6 October, 1997. In the meantime, Islamabad blamed New Delhi for training of terriorists outside the Indian capital of Delhi. The report also claimed to have documentary evidence of the charge. However, in a rare occasion, India and Pakistan have expressed strong reservations over a proposal to create a new Department of Disarmament and Arms Regulations at the United Nations. In their third time meeting in Edinburgh, at the Commonwealth Summit, the two Prime Ministers agreed to immediately resume talks at the Foreign Secretary level for working out a mechanism for making progress on substantive issue.[193]

In the last quarter of 1997 much was not hoped keeping in view the political instability in India and Pakistan. Islamabad, being encouraged by its diplomatic victory at Organisation of Islamic Conference (OIC), which expressed the concern over the situation in Jammu and Kashmir pleaded for mediation on Kashmir during the visit of Madeleine Albright, US Secretary of State. Rejecting the Pakistani plea, she urged India and Pakistan to continue the dialogue process to resolve the Kashmir issue and reiterated Washington's policy of not playing the mediator unless requested by both the parties. In a significant move Washington perhaps for the first time identified Pakistan's direct involvement with terrorism in Jammu and Kashmir. This followed an assurance by Pakistani High Commissioner Ashraf Jehangir Qazi to India that Sharif Government is committed to bring about a "stable and predictable" relationship between the two countries.[194] But earlier, a negative trend in relations witnessed during the trilateral business summit of the SAARC countries (India, Pakistan and Bangladesh). Pakistani business delegation dubbed Gujral as a caretaker Prime Minister and tried to minimize the importance of his announcements at the summit on concessions to the SAARC countries.

Problem of Kashmir

India and Pakistan stuck to their earlier stand on Kashmir. Since the issue is a bilateral one, New Delhi sought its solution bilaterally and in accordance with the Simla Pact, signed between the two countries in 1972. While Islamabad treats the issue as a dispute between India and Pakistan and always emphasised on the third party mediation/intervention and wanted its solution as per the UN resolution. In recent years, despite repeatedly referring to the Kashmir dispute as possibly the most dangerous the United States too said that it should be settled on the basis of the Simla Agreement. Under the new dispensation second round of secretary-level talks between the two countries were held in Islamabad in June 1997. It was for the first time since 1972 that New Delhi agreed in black and white to have talks with Pakistan on Kashmir. Earlier India pledged our support to the Simla Agreement but did not discuss the future of Kashmir. We made ourselves believe that there was no need to have talks on Kashmir with Pakistan.[195] The Indian side, in course of the talks agreed to an entirely flawed concept of working groups for Kashmir in special status. New Delhi's argument is that such an approach will create the right atmosphere of mutual trust and goodwill and thereby help in tackling the Kashmir issue. But the proposal regarding the setting up of working groups had evidently got bogged down. Pakistan, of course, has used the deadlock to accuse India of retreating from its previous assurance.

Being encouraged by the second round of talks on Kashmir, Islamabad rejected India's claim of sovereignty over Jammu and Kashmir and described it as "universally recognized disputed territory" whose future has to be decided through a UN-supervised plebiscite. The spokesman also referred to a recent statement of a senior official of US State Department, George Pickart that Washington believed "Jammu and Kashmir", as a disputed territory", and said it was an example of "the international consensus on the disputed status of Jammu and Kashmir".[196] As expected, Pakistan sought some clarifications particularly on the Kashmir issue before the proposed third round of foreign secretary level talks with India. It said, "If the Indians do not honour their commitment made in the last Indo-Pak foreign secretary level talks, it will be extremely difficult for Pakistan to continue the talks with India. Apart from blaming New Delhi Premier Nawaz Sharif had urged the world to stop debating his country's nuclear capability and do more to help resolve the conflict over Kashmir.[197] However, despite tensions, allegations and counter allegations including the heaviest firing along the LoC in recent times the bilateral dialogue between the two countries resumed in the middle of September 1997. The deadlock on Kashmir issue continued as a Pakistani foreign office spokesman quoted "Pakistan considers Kashmir as the core issue which must be addressed urgently and effectively and a resolution on this contentious issue found in accordance with the UN resolutions. In the circumstances, the talk was bound to be inconclusive. The situation also provided Washington an opportunity to intervene in the matter as the two Prime Ministers were meeting with US President in this month. Although in Newyork, the Premiers of India and Pakistan agreed to continue the dialogue, Islamabad made it clear later on that the talks with India would continue only after the core issue of Jammu and Kashmir was given "due place" and discussed and negotiated in a "substantive and specific" manner. It asked New Delhi to change policy on Kashmir failing which no bilateral activity could bear any purpose or fruit without the prior resolution of the Kashmir issue.[198]

In a significant development the United States of America branded Harkat-ul-Ansar as a terrorist organization along with the 29 others. Ever since the involvement of Harkat-ul-Ansar in July 1995, in the kidnapping of six western hostages in the Kashmir Valley the affected western Government (US, UK, Germany and Norway) began to smell the Pakistani connection. The world also took note of the fact that Jammu and Kashmir is being governed by a popularly elected Government for over a year. However, the US had made it clear that it would not brand anymore group as terrorist outfit and it had turned down the request by US-based Kashmir Pandit groups that Washington name the Jammu and Kashmir Liberation Front (JKLF) and the Hizbul Mujahideen as terrorist groups. Even several scholars in the US had the view that India and Pakistan's stand on Kashmir was unfeasible.

The situation in Kashmir more or less remained the same. From the recent past Islamabad began to blame India for terrorism in different parts of the country. On 18 March, 1998, one day before Atal Bihari Vajpayee assumed the Prime Ministership, Pakistan's Foreign Minister Gohar Ayub Khan is expected to harangue the United Nations Human Rights Commission (UNHRC) on the so called "India-aided terrorist" allegedly plaguing his country. According to the Pakistani allegation, the Research and Analysis Wing (RAW) of the Indian Government has been master-minding the series of bomb-explosions that have rocked the country lately. The Pakistani Foreign Minister, in an effort to tarnish India's image abroad, virtually launched a campaign against New Delhi and refused any compromise on Kashmir at the outgoing Organisation of Islamic Conference at Dubai.[199] But the Indian Ministry of External Affairs appeared to be preferring a continuation of its policy of ignoring the habitual Pakistani abuses irrespective of the level at which they occur. Nawaz Sharif, in an interview with *The Khalej Times*, when his new counterpart is to assume office in New Delhi, hoped that India should come up with some gesture to demostrate its bonafides.Islamabad seemed convinced that "gestures" are a one way street.[200] Needless to remind that last time I. K. Gujral became the Prime Minister and announced a number of unilateral concessions despite criticism from certain quarters at home was forced to admit that Pakistan's ISI had been behind a series of bomb blasts in south India aimed at disruption of the recent elections.

Foreign Involvement in Kashmir

The United States of America took a lion's share of interest in Kashmir because New Delhi and Islamabad were face to face on the issue. US policy makers are highly pragmatic, highly cynical. They believed that through an intelligent exploitation of the Pakistani card they can exercise pressure on India. India is democratic, and tolerant; a society that wished not to confront or attack US policies and also hopes to receive from it hitech technology transfers. Regarding the "core" issue of Kashmir there is a wide gulf between New Delhi and Islamabad on the one hand and New Delhi-Washington on the other. Pakistan's single minded and unchanging pursuit had been to oppose and damage India in whatever manner feasible. India insists that the access of Kashmir to India is final and irrevocable. While the US, similar to Islamabad has maintained that it is a disputed territory. India asserts that Maharaja Hari Singh acceded to India of his own free will and that in any case he had the sovereign right to decide which domination he wished to join. There is a widely held view in the US, shared by the State Department that the accession took place under duress and at the very least needs to be revalidated by some sort of reference to the people.[201] Pakistan had been famous, for the decades, as an ally of US, and eventually a frontline state in its crusade against communism. The fallout of this on the Kashmir dispute was to distort each and every interpretation of events in Kashmir in a way that weakened India's case at the UN and strengthened Pakistan's. There is thus a well founded backlog of distrust that has to be dispelled if the US is to be accepted as a mediator by the Indian public.

On several occasions the US has offered mediation and Pakistan sought Washington's mediation/intervention in solving the problem. But New Delhi has been of the opinion that bilateral issues should not be solved through mediation of the third party. Coinciding with the Male meeting between Gujral and Sharif, in May 1997 reports from London and Washington spoke of J & K being on the agenda of the Blair-Clinton talks. The Beijing regime made extra loud promises of augmented military supplies during the Pakistani President's visit to China. In an effort to patch-up the differences between India and Pakistan having accepted New Delhi's position Clinton proposed a meeting with I.K. Gujral to be held during the UN General Assembly session. Since Pakistan has long been insisting on US intervention in the Kashmir "dispute" the entire rescheduling appeared to be a ploy to hold some kind of a tripartite meeting of the heads of Government of three countries.[202] Pakistan's Foreign Minister Gohar Ayub Khan, as a part of its strategy paid his four-day visit to China where he discussed the Kashmir issue with China, who has been carefully watching the Indo-Pak talks had expressed optimism that New Delhi and Islamabad would make unremitting efforts to seek a peaceful resolution of the Kashmir issue, thereby normalising bilateral relations.[203]

President Clinton, before his scheduled meeting with I. K. Gujral on 22 September 1997 laid stress on good Indo-Pak ties. He was also urged in a letter by Dan Burton, a Republican Congressman and other that his administration should devote "greater attention" to South Asia and help "facilitate a resolution of the Kashmir problem on the basis of the relevant UN resolutions and the wishes of the Kashmiri people".[204] Clinton and Gujral had an extremely warm and cordial 30-minute-plus meeting that engendered a pleasantly amiable ambience for the discussions. The US President sought to remove India's apprehensions by declaring that his country had no intention to interfere in its problems with Pakistan, an apparent reference to the Kashmir issue. When asked to a specific query, a senior State Department official said the two leaders were aware of the sensitivities on the subject. He made it quite clear that the US was very careful not to interfere in any way in the outstanding issues India had with Pakistan, although the US strongly supported the Indo-Pak dialogue that was underway. Washington made a fresh offer when Pakistan Foreign Minister visited USA, to assist India and Pakistan to resolve their differences but reaffirmed that it has "no intention to interfere" in the on going bilateral dialogue.

The United States of America in an important decision branded the Harkat-ul-Ansar, the Pakistan based terrorist group promoting terrorism in Jammu and Kashmir. Hailing the decision as a "welcome recognition" of the ground realities in Jammu and Kashmir the External Affairs Ministry hoped that Washington would follow up the decision by recognising "the true nature" of other similar terrorist groups operating from Pakistan.[205] The Indian officials also felt that as a next logical step Pakistan should at least be returned to the US State Department's watch-list of states which are believed to sponsor terrorism if not declare it a 'rogue' nation. In a Indo-US dialogue held in October 1997 the US Government acknowledged the seriousness of the problem of cross-border terrorism in Jammu and Kashmir.

In a renewed effort, Washington had dispatched its Secretary of State Ms. Albright with a view to create a positive impact on the stalled Foreign-Secretary level talks between the two South Asian neighbours. In course of her visit to Pakistan and India, the Chairman of the All Parties Hurriyat Conference, said that he would submit a memorandum to the visiting guest and added. "We will seek good offices of the US Government in resolving the Kashmir crisis by bringing all the concerned parties - India, Pakistan and Kashmiris into a single negotiation table". Such a situation he argued, would be "in the interests of peace and prosperity of South Asia".[206] In a fresh move Nawaz Sharif during his visit to China in February 1998 reiterated in familiar Pakistani stand on Kashmir and said Jammu and Kashmir was the primary cause of conflict between India and Pakistan. "It remains the flash point threatening regional peace and security."[207] However, Pakistani premier failed to garner Beijing's support against New Delhi and Kashmir issue never figured in any of the statements made by top Chinese leadership during the visit. Perhaps, Beijing was careful not to annoy India too much in the wake of renewed political and trade ties between Beijing and New Delhi after painstaking efforts from both sides.

Defence

The defence atmosphere during the premiership of Inder Kumar Gujral did not witness any basic change. The spheres of difference between the two countries were remained the same. Islamabad was mainly assisted by Beijing in the manufacturing of armaments as well as development of nuclear technology. Washington too, had been second to none in providing Pakistan's defence system a strong footing. Even today despite its efforts for disarmament and nuclear non-proliferation, US continued to be an important ally of Islamabad. The United States, even evades to react when Beijing used to supply defence related equipments to Pakistan. At present it is an established fact that Islamabad is being helped by China and USA, for the reasons, suited to each country.

With active support of the Beijing, Pakistan is making serious efforts to tip its missiles with nuclear warheads and is building a missile factory. Chinese experts were working on guidance and control systems, solid fuel and M-11 missile variants. It had also trained Pakistani personnel on assembling and use of the M-11 missile. In the series Pakistan test fired two missile systems - a surface-to-air missile named Azna and another anti-tank guided missile, Baktar Shikan at a firing range. Even earlier, in June 1997, Pakistan test fired its medium range surface-to-surface Hatf-III missile which reportedly had a range of nearly 800 kms.[208] Although Pakistani spokesman in a statement said that they were a routine affair and it has no high military significance. Reacting to the development, I.K. Gujral had told the parliament that Pakistan was maintaining a military arsenal far in excess of its legitimate defence requirement. His statement on Pakistani armed forces was rejected by Islamabad.

In August 1997, Pakistan suddenly started unprovoked firing in the Uri sector and Keran in Kupwara, in Jammu and Kashmir from across the border in which over 50 Pakistani soldiers are said to have been killed as a result of retaliatory firing by Indian troops. The Indian side also suffered a number of casualties, including the death of an Army Major. Commenting on the consistently heavy unprovoked firing by Pakistan the Indian sources said it was the handwork of "hawks" in the Pakistani military establishment and the notorious ISI to frustrate the normalising process between New Delhi and Islamabad through bilateral talks.[209] The second reason for Pakistan to resort to unusually heavy unprovoked firing was to "keep the pot boiling" in Jammu and Kashmir to ensure that it continued to hog international headlines. However, the immediate cause of this unprovoked firing was the fact that the Independence Day celebration passed off without any hindrance in Srinagar. The Pakistani army and the ISI had felt the need, therefore, to push in more armed militants and also boost the moral of those mercenaries already in the Valley by raising the temperature in the border region by their hostile activity.[210] Within a month of the incident New Delhi and Islamabad held an inconclusive bilateral talks at the Foreign Secretary level and Nawaz

Sharif discussed border firing with his Indian counterpart I.K. Gujral, when met in Newyork during UN General Assembly session. In their meeting the two Prime Ministers explored ways to initiate steps to generate confidence and goodwill. Measures have already been undertaken for Army Commanders to be in regular contact through a hot line and to inform each other about military exercises and Air Force flights.[211]

The recent unprovoked firing by Pakistan along the Indo-Pak borders, preceded by the announcement of Nawaz Sharif that Pakistan was a nuclear weapons state was a point of attention for New Delhi. The Pakistani premier while addressing the UN General Assembly on 22 September 1997 launched a propaganda barrage at India and, in the speech, tried to justify Pakistan's nuclear and missile programmes. Probably, in response to the development in Pakistani attitude, I.K. Gujral inaugurating the 23rd two-day Defence Research and Development Organisation (DRDO) stressed the need for evolving a rationalised defence imports policy and called upon scientists to take up the challenge to make the country more self-reliant in defence systems.[212] It was for the government to ensure how the scientists could give their best. The country's past experience too had shown that depending on imports in defence equipment carried grave risk of the supplies drying up at critical moments.[213] A recess in tension between the two countries appeared when the two premiers talked twice in the first week of October 1997 through recently reactivated hot-line to help de-escalate the warm atmosphere. However, Pakistani army Chief General Jehangir Karamat denied any possibility of peace and insisted, "the real issue is not the LoC situation. The bigger issue is Kashmir and without its solution there can be no peace. Ultimately normalcy prevailed and guns fell silent on 15 October 1997 after India and Pakistan agreed to maintain peace along the international border as reported by K. S. Vohra, DIG, Border Security Force.[214] In the coming days New Delhi and Islamabad seemed busy either in developing arms of their own or purchasing it from the outside.

Development of nuclear technology has been an important area of dispute between New Delhi and Islamabad. World Powers most of whom having sophisticated nuclear capability are anxious enough and tried their level best to mobilise South Asian countries, particularly India and Pakistan. The said two have been constantly refusing to sign the international treaties, such as, Nuclear Non-Proliferation Treaty (NPT) and Comprehensive Test Ban Treaty (CTBT) for the reasons of their own apart from blaming its discriminatory nature. However, a balanced view was expressed by Dr. Lawrence Scheinmam, former assistant director, US Arms Control and Disarmament Agency (ACDA) that in order to gain access to advance nuclear technology to meet the growing energy needs that India and Pakistan should probe ways of assuring nuclear states on non-proliferation without compromising on their known stands of security.[215] He laid stress that the South Asian nations and nuclear states could proceed through a set of "mutual bargains" wherein expertise could be forwarded on agreed steps towards non-proliferation.

REGIME OF BHARATIYA JANATA PARTY

Premiership of Atal Bihari Vajpayee (19 March 1998-12 October 1999)

The day Atal Bihari Vajpayee took the oath of the office of India's Prime Minister hopes and fears were apprehended by many in respect of country's relations to Pakistan. On account of a variety of reasons Islamabad has proved to be the most complicated of India's neighbours. Although Vajpayee's first public engagement after being sworn in was to witness the first India-Pakistan hockey test match at the National Stadium, at New Delhi, on 19th of March 1998 which was claimed as a "special gesture" by a spokesman of the External Affairs Ministry who said, "It reinforced the message of friendship and goodwill towards Pakistan and the need to have normal and co-operative relations with that country." On the same day after the swearing-in-ceremony Vajpayee himself told a questioner that India would have "friendly" relations with Pakistan and other neighbouring countries. Nawaz Sharif the Pakistani Prime Minister expressed his country's readiness to go extra mile in building co-operative and good- neighbourly relations with India. In a message of 'sincere felicitations to Vajpayee, Sharif said resumption of the dialogue between Pakistan and India stalled over the Kashmir dispute will save the way for such an outcome. Inviting his Indian counterpart "to work closely with us for ushering in a new era of durable peace and stability in South Asia he hoped that the Bharatiya Janata Party Government under your leadership can bring forth a firm resolve to build a happier, more prosperous future for our people. He also used the occasion to remind Vajpayee that Pakistan and India stand at the crossroad at a time of massive global transformations. We are the inheritors of proved civilizations, but our rich potential for economic growth has remained subdued."

However, the other side of the coin was not the same. Even before the taking over of BJP Government in India, malacious and contradictory statements were issued by the leaders and officials of Pakistan. Islamabad was anxious, in particular, for BJP's election manifesto that believed that the time has come to re-evaluate country's nuclear policy and induct nuclear weapons. It was not much different from its 1996 election manifesto and so the coming of power had spurred commentators to take more serious note of it. Till now the successive Indian governments have been adopting the ambiguous stance that nuclear weapons are terrible tools of destruction which must be eliminated; but at the same time, no one has expressed the readiness to give up the nuclear option, which has always remained "open". Many in India, feel that it is high time that India should come out of the nuclear closet and done away with what has always been the country's greatest diplomatic weakness. Thus, to go by both the BJP manifesto and the alliance's national agenda of undertaking India's first ever strategic defence review and the re-evaluation of the nuclear policy and the option to induct nuclear weapons would prove contentious not only internationally but its relations with Pakistan too.

Islamabad, in a swift reaction, on 19 March 1998, threatened to review its nuclear policy which it has so far claimed to be totally peaceful in response to what it called the "dangerous development" of the new Indian Government's decision to keep its options open on nuclear weapons. Meanwhile, Gohar Ayub Khan, Pakistan's Foreign Minister, reacting to the new Indian Government's stand on the issue, said it would push South Asia into 'a dangerous arms race'. Addressing the Conference on Disarmament in Geneva said, "recent public utterances and pronouncements by the BJP leader Atal Bihari Vajpayee, and also now in their manifesto, that India will 'go nuclear' and acquire and develop nuclear weapons should evoke global concern. When the new Indian Government was to assume power in New Delhi, Pakistan's top nuclear scientist. Dr. Abdul Quadeer, disclosed that his country was capable of responding to any nuclear challenge by the Bharatiya Janata Party Government and that Islamabad's missiles could target every city in India in case of war. The new Indian policy, a spokesman said, "will multiply manifold the threat to Pakistan's security besides dealing a grievous blow to global and regional efforts at nuclear non-proliferation". "We urge the international community to take serious note, as it deserves of Indian intentions and to exert pressure on India to show restraint". Despite the exchange of good expressions on both sides New Delhi and Islamabad, once again, remained stick to their earlier position and Nawaz Sharif, a day after assuming the new Indian Government said that normalisation of relations with India was not possible without settlement of the Kashmir issue.

A charged atmospheric Pakistan decided to go ahead with a secret test firing of a new 1,500 km. range surface to surface missile "Ghauri" from a base on the Baluchistan coast. A spokesman of the Ministry of External Affairs, in response, maintained that New Delhi would do all necessary in accordance with its security perception in the wake of reports from Islamabad. He also pointed out to take resolute steps to meet any threat to India's security. George Fernandes, India's Minister for Defence took the serious view of the successful test firing of Ghauri "missile and said that steps would be taken at "appropriate time" to counter this threat. The test firing was criticized by several countries of the world but, Islamabad, not taking any care thereof make it clear to the US that it would go ahead with the experiment whatever the cost of relations with Washington. It even decided to undertake that if India goes ahead with a fresh nuclear test, it would also conduct a nuclear test without any delay for its defence needs, as quoted by the largest circulated Urdu daily, *The Jung.*

In the circumstances, New Delhi took a historic decision and exploded its nuclear devices on 11 and 13 May 1998 at Pokhran (Rajasthan). Apart from world-wide condemnation of the Indian action, Islamabad reacted sharply and Nawaz Sharif said that his Government's response to India's nuclear test would not be dictated by foreign powers. Pakistan had the right to take any steps which were essential for its security. "This is our job and we alone have to decide about it". In retaliation Islamabad evened its nuclear account with New Delhi by exploding five nuclear devices on 28 May and went ahead by one more on 30 May 1998. This nuclear tit-for-tat made the relations between the two countries tense and a series of allegations and counter allegations continued till the two Prime Ministers met at the 10th meeting of Heads of Government of SAARC Countries held in Colombo. In the post-summit phase, Vajpayee appeared to have initiating a damage control exercise to revive the Indo-Pak dialogue. In his statement in Parliament, he reiterated India's commitment to normalise relations with Pakistan and desire to revive bilateral political and official discussions. He had also a unilateral declaration of no-first use of India's nuclear weapons capacities, which should partially address Pakistan's security concerns. Everybody analysed the current state of Indo-Pak relations from the revival of the bilateral talks in 1996 and the year marked a positive breakthrough. Actually, the nuclear tests made Kashmir an international issue. Since Kashmir was where the conflict was occurring, the world demanded that India and Pakistan either denuclearise themselves or settle the Kashmir dispute. The world could no longer afford even-handedness. It had to choose between urging upon the two countries one of two courses of action to change the status quo or to accept it.

The next meeting of the two Prime Ministers took place in Newyork, on 23 September 1998, where they gathered to attend the session of United Nations General Assembly. The meeting had a different kind of outcome, at least in some degree. Major developments have taken place since the Colombo meeting. Optimism was encouraged by the India-Pakistan agreement to resume Secretary-level discussions broken off a year ago. A government spokesman in Islamabad had said that Pakistan is "hopeful of positive results". The Colombo meeting followed by a terrorist blasts at the US embassies in Nairobi and Dares-Salaam and the retaliatory American missile attack in Sudan and Afghanistan. The missile attacks in Afghanistan turned out to be uncomfortable for Sharif in Islamabad. Consequently their meeting proved to be a fruitful one and following was the outcome of the talks held between them :

(i) Direct bus service between Delhi and Lahore.
(ii) Road-rail link between Manaboo (Rajasthan) and Khokrapar (Pakistan).
(iii) Restarting hot line between the two Prime Ministers.
(iv) Visa rules to be relaxed.

(v) Cultural exchanges to be increased.
(vi) Firing on LoC to be stopped.
(vii) Propaganda against each other to be checked.
(viii) Modalities to be worked out for buying electricity from Pakistan.

As a follow up of the decision taken during Newyork meeting India and Pakistan held a stalled secretary-level talks in Islamabad in the middle of October 1998. Foreign Secretary K. Raghunath headed Indian delegation while his Pakistani counterpart Shamshad Ahmed led the Pakistani delegation to the talks. In course of the talks Indian side conveyed to Pakistan that nuclearisation of the two countries had added a new dimension to the security environment of South Asia and this new reality must be taken into account while talking about peace and security of the two countries. The two sides discussed the seemingly intractable issue to Jammu and Kashmir and agreed to continue further the dialogue on the subject in the next round of talks. In the joint statement issued after much wrangling said that on the peace and security issue "both sides underscored their commitment to reduce the risk of a conflict by building mutual CMBs in the nuclear and conventional fields." Unfortunately, they even failed to agree on minor confidence building measures because of their reiterated positions on Jammu and Kashmir. Pakistan's attitude was that it had a territorial right over Kashmir and that if the persistent use of force or sponsored terrorism does not help it realise its claim, then international brokering certainly would. But India believes that neither sponsored subversion nor external pressure can force it to move on the question of Kashmir. The Indian belief was that the sovereignty and the legality of Jammu and Kashmir is not going to change. It appeared that Pakistan, of course, might have helped in reading a more congenial atmosphere if its representative had not claimed the right to speak on behalf of the Kashmiri people.[216]

Notwithstanding such negative impressions, the fact that the two sides have decided to persist with the talks should be seen as a positive sign. It was necessary that both the sides lay their cards on the table so that there is a clearer understanding of each other's positions. Apart from this, it would be futile to deny that domestic and outside pressure had not played any part. The talks were held in the background of political uncertainty and internal pressure from which both Nawaz Sharif and Atal

Bihari Vajpayee suffer. Both Pakistan and India were in difficult economic circumstances. They were subject to international pressure resulting from their nuclear weaponisation. Vajpayee was handicapped by coalition politics, factionalism within his own party centrifugal agitations affecting different parts of India and the deeply felt suspicions about Pakistan's intentions in India. Nawaz Sharif was grappling with the aftermath of his army Chief General Jehangir Karamat's resignation on political grounds, a profound economic crisis, agitation in Sind and the North-West Frontier Province, as well as controversies generated by the measures which he was introducing for the further Islamisation of Pakistan.[217] At the end, perhaps, due to pre-negotiation attitudes Sartaj Aziz said that the results of the talks were less than expected while Vajpayee expressed satisfaction about the talks.

As part of the second leg of the revived dialogue between the two countries, a 'Pakistani defence delegation arrived New Delhi' for talks in the first week of November 1998. This 12-member team headed by Pakistan's Defence Secretary Lt. General (Retd.) Chaudhary Iftikhar Ali Khan, consisted of officials from the Defence and Foreign Affairs Ministries, the Pakistani Army and diplomats from Pakistani High Commission in New Delhi, stayed in India and held six separate rounds of negotiations, spread over nine days on a range of issues, including the Tulbul Navigation Project, Siachin, the Sir Creek boundary question, cross-border terrorism and drug trafficking. At the end of the dialogue a senior Pak official remarked, "The series on the whole has not been positive. We came with high hopes that have not been fulfilled" New Delhi, too, was not hopeful and Vajpayee himself admitted in the Rajya Sabha, on 3 December 1998 in response to an anguished question by Gulam Nabi Azad (Congress), that forward movement in India-Pakistan dialogue is difficult to achieve because the neighbouring country wants to retain international attention on the Kashmir issue. Describing India-Pakistan relations as being in a flux and commenting that there were inherent contradictions in these he said "This does not mean that we should stop the dialogue". He expressed the "hope" that Pakistan would one day leave the path of violence and terrorism.

At a time when India and Pakistan were neither at war nor at peace with each other, many in the two countries felt that increasing people-to-people contact could be the most important confidence building measure between the two neighbours. This could be achieved through the enhancement of cultural, educational and sporting contacts, relaxation of visa regimes and evolution of practical mechanism to deal with the humanitarian issue of civilian prisoners and fisherman held in either country. Even in recent past New Delhi had taken several unilateral steps to considerably relax the visa regime for Pakistani citizens. It granted group visas for tourists, multi-entry visas for Pakistani businessmen recommended by their SAARC Chamber of Commerce, facilitation of commercial performances by Pakistani artists, an increase in the number of places to visit from 8 to 12, extension of exempt from police reporting (EPR) to every young, elderly, prominent personalities in the field of media, literature and business etc. Although Islamabad's response in this regard had been disappointing, yet there is a tremendous desire among the people of India and Pakistan for freer contact, the political will to promote this has been lacking on the part of their governments. As a follow up of the Newyork meeting of Vajpayee and Sharif, India and Pakistan made a substantial progress on 3 December 1998 towards reaching an agreement for starting a bus service between New Delhi and Lahore. Both sides expressed happiness over the agreement and termed the talks as "highly fruitful".

Diplomacy by Bus

Prime Minister Nawaz Sharif's invitation to Prime Minister Vajpayee to travel to Lahore by the newly inaugurated bus service and Vajpayee's prompt response accepting the invitation had caught the imagination of people in both countries. The general atmospherics of Indo-Pakistan relations in recent weeks had been characterised by some positive trends. The latest observations by the two Prime Ministers suggested a distinct thawing of relations which witnessed excellent prospects for meaningful negotiations. It was possible that the renewal of the Test series after a decade long interval, and the remarkable sporting atmosphere free of any feeling of animosity in which the Chennai match was played, had been responsible for fastering the feeling that a beginning could be made. It has always been known that an enormous fund of goodwill and the desire to have close ties have marked the attitude of the common people of both countries inspite of the three wars and the proxy war in Kashmir and terrorist activity elsewhere. Prime Minister Atal Bihari Vajpayee's reference to the possibility of a no-war pact with Pakistan marked yet another initiative in the present efforts to improve India-Pakistan ties. Externally, the nuclear tests and the looming American presence in the background had forced the two neighbours to reassess their options. Both have realised that their mutual hostility could only invite increasing pressure from the US and the world community. But, above all, Vajpayee, on his part, appeared keen on removing the impression of the weakness and ineptitude of his government through a bold foreign policy measure which, apart from enhancing his liberal image, would be widely acclaimed and establish his place in history.

For Nawaz Sharif, compulsions were probably more economic than anything else, apart from pressure from the US to which Pakistan is more vulnerable than India. His change of focus from Kashmir to investment, trade, business, shorts and culture and regret over wasting resources or an arms race point to a refreshing reappraisal of his country's stand, which must be cagerly grasped by India. There was undoubtedly a US pressure on the Pakistani establishment to talk to India. The World Bank and IMF adamantly gave prescription after prescription for the sick economy, and had also exhorted Pakistan to improve trade with India. It is pertinent to note here that Pakistani premier had toured Washington in the first week of December 1998, to emphasise the special place Islamabad had consistently enjoyed in the US Presidential considerations. Given the kind of difficulties that the Pakistani Prime Minister was facing back home, he could have asked for nothing better than a few tokens that he could flaunt back home to silence his domestic critics. Instead, he came back from Washington almost empty-handed. He could not get sanctions on the conventional military assistance lifted, nor did Washington agreed to mediate on the Kashmir issue. Bill Clinton, as a consummate and pragmatic politician had proved that when it comes to weighing India and Pakistan on the scales of America's geostrategic and economic calculus, India came out way ahead. Despite America's traditional sympathy for Pakistan as a cold war ally and a willing Afghan Mujahideen conduct, Clinton did bend over backwards to avoid any impression of favouring

Pakistan over India. The fact that Sharif had to return empty-handed was of the first indications of things to come unless Islamabad embraces reality.

Thus, at present there are two Prime Ministers who are inclined to reason together. Public opinion in both countries desire normalcy and an end to confrontation. The power structures and their respective political compulsion in both countries, however, were not supportive of this positive attitude. The nuclearisation of the subcontinent had transformed the chemistry of Indo-Pak relations which should compel both countries to be anxious to achieve durable stability in their interaction. On the other hand, it could also encourage mutual assertiveness. The international community was keen that the subcontinent did not become a nuclear flashpoint. But important powers in the community cannot intervene in bilateral relations to remedy these concerns beyond a certain point.

In the circumstances, the announcement that Indian Prime Minister Atal Bihari Vajpayee would travel to Pakistan on the inaugural Delhi-Lahore bus service, had raised high hopes in New Delhi and Islamabad. A spokesman of the Indian External Affairs Ministry said that the path-breaking exercise will be one more manifestation of India's abiding desire to build peaceful, friendly and co-operative relations with Pakistan. Sartaj Aziz, Pakistan's Foreign Minister, when informed about the planned visit of Vajpayee welcomed it and said that it would go a long way in establishing good ties with India. Sources on the Indian side maintained that the bus service was geared to work as part of confidence-building measures towards normalisation of Indo-Pak relations. The service will facilitate movement of passengers from both the sides leading to greater interaction between the peoples of the two neighbouring countries. However, on two different occasions, Sartaj Aziz and Nawaz Sharif reminded the pitfalls ahead. In fact Aziz had made it clear that Pakistan would like India to move "beyond its present emphasis on the peripheral areas" and try to resolve our fundamental differences. Pakistan has repeatedly made it clear in recent years that there can be no normalisation of relations with India unless the Kashmir issue is first resolved, in accordance with the wishes of Pakistan. But what exactly would be achieved through this much publicised visit, was the implied message that this initiative could lead to the cutting of the Gordian Knot by resolving the present impasses in bilateral relations, and sweetness and light would soon prevail between the two countries.

On 20 February 1999, the much awaited moment came in the history of Indo-Pak relations when Atal Bihari Vajpayee entered the Wagah border after 37 kms. journey by bus from the Amritsar airport in Punjab. The Prime Minister went straight to receive the BSF guard of honour and he proceeded to address the press where he read out the prepared message. "I am visiting Pakistan today at the invitation of Prime Minister Nawaz Sharif. When I cross that gate, and throughout my visit, I will draw inspiration from the knowledge that the prayers and goodwill of the people of India are with me. My message to the people of Pakistan will be short and simple. Put aside the bitterness of the past, together, let us make a new beginning". In his arrival statement Vajpayee described the bus journey as a "defining moment and exhorted Sharif to join him, while speaking at a banquet at Lahore Fort in the evening, in developing "trust, confidence and amity" he noted that his current visit was only the beginning and that "we will together, give direction to our officials to accelerate what we have jointly set in motion. However, the anti-Indian demonstration by the Jamaat-e-Islami in Lahore, and the protests against Vajpayee's decision to go to Pakistan by Kashmiri Pandit's in Mumbai showed, the path to peace is strewn with boulders. The reference of Kashmir in a speech by Pakistan's President Rafiq and Nawaz Sharif's reminder of the issues at the official banquet were the hurdles that lie ahead. But it is undeniable that despite the bitterly acrimonious history of India-Pakistan relationship, with its roots going back to the pre-British period of the subcontinent's past, every new effort to make a fresh beginning is characterised by great optimism. What it probably denotes is a deep underlying desire among the common people of the two countries to bury the past, perhaps motivated by the memories of having lived together at one time. What Vajpayee had tried, apparently was to convey through the gesture of travelling in a bus was to re-establish the snapped links between the ordinary people of the two countries through a regular service. His trip marked a defining moment, as he said, because it was expected to be a turning point where the emphasis will change from suspicion and hostility to trust and co-operation.

On 21 February Vajpayee visited the Minar-e-Pakistan, a memorial to the 1940 resolution of the Pakistan Muslim League that constituted the basis of the two-nation theory. He became the first Indian premier to visit the place because neither Pandit Nehru nor Rajiv Gandhi who travelled Pakistan, while in office had never come to Lahore. From the historic Minar-e-Pakistan he assured the people of Pakistan of his country's deep desire for lasting peace and friendship. He noted in the visitors' book that a stable secure and prosperous Pakistan is in India's interest. Let no one in Pakistan be in doubt about it. India sincerely wishes the people of Pakistan well.

A joint declaration signed by the two Prime Ministers was issued on 21 February 1999, which resolved to intensify efforts to solve problems. The two leaders held discussion on the entire range of bilateral relations, regional co-operation within SAARC and issues of international concern. They will meet periodically to discuss all issues of mutual concern, including nuclear related issues. As per the declaration, they expressed satisfaction on the commencement of a bus service between Lahore and New Delhi, the release of fisherman and civilian detainees and the renewal of contacts in the field of sports. Apart from this, pursuant to the directive given by the two Prime Ministers, the Foreign Secretaries of Pakistan and India signed a Memorandum of Understanding on the same day, identifying measures aimed at promoting an environment of peace and security between the two countries.

Vajpayee's visit to Pakistan was hailed by the United States of America and its President Bill Clinton. In an unusual move he had welcomed the Lahore Summit between Indian Prime Minister and his Pakistani counterpart Nawaz Sharif and promised all help to the two countries in promoting progress in the region. In a statement in Washington he noted, "I commend the two Prime Ministers for demonstrating courage and leadership by coming together and addressing difficult issues that have long divided their countries." The US President seemed satisfied with the Lahore declaration and maintained "South Asia and indeed, the entire world will benefit if India and Pakistan promptly turns these commitments into concrete progress adding that we would continue our own efforts to work with India and Pakistan to promote progress in the region. Domestically, the declaration was hailed by BJP and its allies of the government, the efforts made by Vajpayee for taking the initiative and at the same time, praised Pakistan's Prime Minister Nawaz Sharif for responding to Vajpayee's call to improve Indo-Pak relations. However, to build upon their positive intent, as outlined in the Lahore Declaration, the two leaders would need to show forward movement on contentious issues, or else, their bus of hope might not proceed beyond Wagah. Despite these all, Benazir Bhutto termed the declaration as "disappointing" because Sharif had missed a golden opportunity to reach an agreement with his Indian counterpart A. B. Vajpayee on signing the Comprehensive Test Ban Treaty (CTBT). "Had Nawaz Sharif had any experience of international affairs, he could have convinced Vajpayee of the dramatic repercussions for security in South Asia for both sides to announce simultaneously a firm and early date for the signing of the Test Ban Treaty, Mrs. Bhutto added.

Jaswant Singh, India's Minister for External Affairs, who accompanied Vajpayee along with others to Pakistan was very hopeful and said, the declaration, is a "movement towards a no war situation but not a movement towards a no war pact and ruled out foreign intervention in sub-continent. India's Minister was replying the questions who were aimed to seek clarifications on Vajpayee's visit to Pakistan. Earlier, the statement mentioned that the tour was the most significant engagement between India and Pakistan in over a quarter of a century. In fact, the measures of declaration, if implemented honestly, would enable the people of the two countries to sleep in greater security. An agreement on the nuclear question, of course, was never expected to pose any great difficulty. What would be the problematical is the issue of Kashmir and the related question of the "Proxy War" waged by Pakistan there for nearly a decade. It would be on these issues that the ingenuity and sincerity of the two sides would be tested. However, both the countries now know that in view of the impossibility of a war, or even proxy war which could bring the two to the brink, a negotiated settlement is the only way out. It may take time. In any case, no one expects an overnight solution. But the mood of reconciliation created by Vajpayee's visit should help to smooth out the rough edges and pave the way for a settlement. The two countries have never had a chance better than this one in recent years to bury the past and build a future of friendship.

Economic Relations

Independent India, for many years, remained a major partner of Pakistan. In the mid 50s, over 40 per cent of Pakistan's exports was from India. But since the beginning of the 1960s, the share of India in Islamabad's total trade started declining and reached a low of less than one per cent in 1997. This is despite the fact that Pakistan has increased the list of freely importable items from India from 42 in 1975 to 601 in 1998. There are several factors responsible for the diversion of trade of Pakistan away from India and the much touted issues of political tension has been secondary.[218] In fact, Pakistan shifted its trade focus increasingly to countries offering machinery on a suppliers' credit basis. It was estimated in the 1960s that the prices of commodities supplied to Pakistan under a number of tied credit agreements had exceeded the lowest quoted price in the international market by up to 170 per cent. This deprived the Pakistani consumers from other competitively priced sources and made Pakistan an artificially high cost economy. Apart from this, the politically driven trade policy of Pakistan[219] has been one of the reasons behind the diversion of Pakistani trade away from India.

All these restrictions closely followed a large scale unauthorised trade taking place along the 625-mile long border with India. Studies commissioned by the Benazir Bhutto Government had shown the extent of that trade to be as high as Rs. 2 billion both ways. Besides many household items which made their way to Pakistan through border transaction the most vital are liquor, food items, textile machinery, spares and equipment, tanneries and machine parts. New Delhi, taking a liberal view of Indo-Pak trade, accorded the Most Favoured Nation status to Pakistan long ago and, of late, it has removed, unilaterally, all the quantitative restrictions on the imports of 2,000 products from the South Asian countries whereas Pakistan has not done anything in response. Islamabad feared that giving Most Favoured Nation status to New Delhi would lead to the opening of floodgates to Indian goods which may dislodge a large section of Pakistani industries. However, Pakistan had several gains from free trade with India :

(i) Benefits of specialisation in sectors where the economies are competitive;

(ii) Where the economies are complementary, the productive capacity can be accelerated through cheaper industrial inputs and possible sub-contracting;

(iii) Induction of new technology through extension of the market;

(iv) Import of machinery directly from India at lower prices will make products competitive;

(v) Transfer of technology will benefit the engineering industry;

(vi) India and Pakistan both will get additional leverage in negotiations with the developed countries and other trading blocks.

By the time Atal Bihari Vajpayee assumed power in New Delhi on 19 March 1998, Indo-Pak trade relations were in a good shape. The prevailing mutual suspicion and mistrust in each other's affairs continued and a fresh irritant and tension started on nuclear issue. On 11 and 13 May 1998 the new regime exploded five nuclear devices followed by six by Islamabad in quick succession. The major world powers imposed economic and defence related sanctions on India and Pakistan that necessitated the economic needs of the two and mounted a fresh pressure on their economy. A fast deteriorating economic condition in Pakistan had placed the Nawaz Sharif Government under increasing pressure. However, the government on its behalf assured that it was taking all measures for strengthening the national economy and hard days would end soon. Pakistan, in the three-day meeting on custom co-operation held at Jaipur (India) in August 1998, submitted an indepth study of the draft agreement that favoured the uniformity, simplification and harmonisation of custom laws and procedures besides preparing the commodity description code for the region.

Sharing of Electric Power

As a follow up of the meeting between Indian Prime Minister Atal Bihari Vajpayee and his Pakistani counterpart Nawaz Sharif in Newyork in September 1998,Indian proposal to import 2000 MW of power from Pakistan had been agreed to in principle by this country. The scope for co-operation in the energy sector between India and Pakistan is vast. India suffers from power shortage and Pakistan has surplus power. The World Bank and the Asian Development Bank, which assisted Pakistan in developing the hydel resources of the Indus river system, have been putting pressure on Islamabad to sell surplus power to New Delhi. Further, at the SAARC

Summit in the Maldives an agreement was signed by the member states to share the natural resources of the subcontinent. In fact co-operation between Pakistan and India in the field of power should eventually become the nucleus of such co-operation in the entire SAARC region. Nepal, Bhutan and Bangladesh have ample hydel resources waiting to be developed.

Gohar Ayub Khan, Pakistan's Power Minister, disclosed in Islamabad on 15 January 1999 that the final agreement with India on supply of power would be signed soon. Dispelling the notion that Pakistan was back tracking from its commitment to supply electricity to India, but said, "We have to consider certain factors such as local requirements and the rates of electricity before entering into contract with India". Another Minister of Commerce and Finance Ishaq Dar said in Dhaka that Political conflict between India and Pakistan were no bar to increasing trade between the two countries because the governments in New Delhi and Islamabad were firm on improving the situation. In India too a national seminar was organised by the Punjab Industries and Export Corporation Limited in collaboration with Jalandhar Chambers of Industries. A number of issues relating to office of Director of Foreign Trade, duty entitlement, pass book scheme, advance licence scheme were discussed and a vociferous demand for opening of Indo-Pakistan trade route to enhance exports from Punjab to Pakistan and other adjoining countries was made.

In a major breakthrough in Indo-Pak trade relations the Federation of Indian Chamber of Commerce and Industry (FICCI) and Federation of Pakistan Chamber of Commerce and Industry (FPCCI) have decided to form Indo-Pak Chamber of Commerce and Industry (IPCCI). With a view to identify the areas of mutual co-operation between neighbours they had also urged upon their respective Governments to remove the artificial barriers that would facilitate mutual trade and business between both the countries. Sudhir Jalan, President of FICCI said that currently export from India to Pakistan is just Rs. 550 crore while import from Pakistan Rs. 150 crore. By taking some of the steps the total trade between the two countries will increase to Rs. 3000 to Rs. 3500 crore in three years time. Trade would certainly bring businessmen from both sides together more often and dispel some of the distrust of working together. Both India and Pakistan have much to gain in jointly fighting the WTO agenda as many of the industries affected by it are common. Both have to face protectionist pressures from the Western countries and are suffering on account of various non-tariff barriers with social issues being linked to trade. With the relations between the two neighbours showing signs of improvement, greater economic co-operation would signal a faster integration of both into the world economy. Syed Babar Ali, former Finance Minister also felt that lack of direct contact and interaction between Indian and Pakistani businessmen has severely restricted the full realisation of trade potential between the two countries. As decided earlier the two countries signed a Memorandum of Understanding on 10 April 1999 for the setting up of India-Pakistan Chamber of Commerce and Industry. Sheikh Jamil Mehboob Magoon, leader of the delegation and Advisor, Ministry of Industry and Production, Government of Pakistan, had termed it a historic landmark that would give a kick start to the bilateral trade and investment. A new emphasis on improving India-Pakistan economic relations is to be welcomed because even though complete free trade between the two neighbours will take much longer to become a reality, a bold gesture has been made.

Defence

The major ups and downs took place in Indo-Pak defence relations and perceptions since the Government of Bharatiya Janata Party and its allies assumed power in India, on 19 March 1998. Tension between the two was charged in general but particularly on nuclear matters. Although Islamabad had been increasing its defence expenditures disproportionately for the last several years, in a fresh initiative, it decided to procure state-of-art fighter planes from Russia, Sweden and France to bridge a gap with India in the field of conventional arms. On 6 April 1998 Pakistan successfully test-fired its Intermediate Range Ballistic Missile (IRBM), Ghauri, capable of carrying nuclear warheads that, as claimed by the Pakistani scientists can target most major cities in India. New Delhi termed the development as a "setback" in Indo-Pak relations and a spokesman of the External Affairs Ministry said, "We will draw appropriate conclusions from the development and take resolute steps to meet any threat to India's security. After the test-firing there was a general feeling in India that New Delhi should now wake up to the fact that it cannot afford to back-pedal on its integrated guided missile development programme. Years of studied neglect and the lack of political will have resulted in the country maintaining deployable rather than deployed missile system capabilities. The absence of a missile deterrent force in India's defence armoury is too glaring and having foresworn in chemical and biological options, the only way for India is to correct this by building appropriate delivery systems. The development was also a setback for US efforts for reducing tension in the sub-continent and persuading India and Pakistan to take a softer view on NPT and CTBT. Major western countries had condemned it because it had made the situation more complicated, specially by the fact that the new government of New Delhi is largely untested in foreign affairs, particularly on Indo-Pak relations and nuclear non-proliferation.

Less in response and more for its defence sake, India, on 11 and 13 May 1998, exploded its five nuclear devices at Pokhran (Rajasthan).In retaliation Islamabad exploded its six nuclear devices at the end of that month. The development was an ominous signal for Indo-Pak relations and a chain of allegations and counterallegations started between the two countries. Nuclear blasts by India and Pakistan had surprised the world, particularly nuclear powers of the world. The United States along with others imposed economic and defence-related sanctions on New Delhi and Islamabad. Even earlier, in March 1998, Britain had threatened to cut off aid to Pakistan unless it reduces its defence expenditure. Considering the expenditure as "disproportionate" Claire Short, British Minister for International Development, assured House of Commons, during question hour that Britain would try to persuade to cut its defence expense. Peking, despite being an important supplier of defence equipments to Pakistan was also shocked over India and Pakistan's nuclear-charged tension. Japan too, in its annual report maintained that the explosions had threatened security balance in Asia and had affected not only the security of South Asia, but also efforts towards the non-proliferation of weapons of mass destruction.

Grounds for normalising the Indo-Pak relations were prepared during the 10th SAARC Conference of Heads of Government, held in Colombo at the end of July 1998. On the occasion Vajpayee and Sharif held bilateral discussions pertaining to mutual interest that paved the way for taking concrete decisions in September 1998 when they met in Newyork, in course of the session of the UN General Assembly. In their meeting both the Prime Ministers had agreed to stop firing on the Line of Control (LoC) and check the propaganda against each other. Although they agreed to continue at the Foreign-Secretary level on all aspects including Kashmir but it is no secret that the Kashmir issue has been psyched up to such intense levels in both countries that any government on either side of the border would find itself, accused of surrender if it displays even a hint of accommodation. As a follow up of the Newyork meeting the two sides held Foreign Secretary level talks but because of their mutual intransigence on how to approach the intractable Jammu and Kashmir issue they failed to agree even on minor confidence building measures. The two sides also held, in November 1998, a detailed discussion on defence related matters, particularly, on Siachen, Sir Creek, terrorism and drug trafficking but without success.

New Delhi, in its efforts to restore some normalcy in relation to Pakistan after the nuclear explosion it had offered a no-first-use agreement to Islamabad which had been rejected by the latter. Following the rejection, in a spirit of accommodation and rational compromise, India had discussed measures to bring about strategic restraint in terms of nuclear weapons and missiles with Pakistan. Particularly in nuclear field, New Delhi has expressed itself emphatically and Prime Minister Vajpayee has broadly defined India's nuclear doctrine since the day he assumed office. He did this in Parliament, at the non-aligned summit in Durban and at the UN General Assembly in Newyork. However, India is coming to grips with the dilemmas emanating from the country's nuclear weaponisation and is in the process of forging a cohesive policy responsive to the multi-dimensional requirement of India's nuclear weapon status. India still has to cope with obstacles and challenges.

Nawaz Sharif, in course of his visit to the United States of America met President Clinton on 2 December 1998. The President made it clear that Pakistan had to take additional concrete steps to address America's non-proliferation and security concerns before Washington could even consider being more helpful. The sanctions imposed after the nuclear explosion had not only hurt the Pakistani economy, but also impaired its conventional capabilities. In the circumstances, Islamabad wanted the

US to be kinder but Assistant Secretary for South Asia Karl Inderfurth had brutally briefed, "We cannot help him unless he helps himself. For us to have any opportunity to address the conventional military needs of Pakistan, it will have to take further steps to address our concerns on non-proliferation". Pakistan's Premier hoped during the visit to discover a satisfactory solution to the long standing dispute over the F-16 aircraft, paid for by Islamabad, but not delivered because of Pressler Amendment restrictions. The US Administration also disappointed Nawaz Sharif on the issue of American mediation in the Kashmir dispute and he had received his most serious rebuff. Despite disappointments on defence count, as a new years' gift, in January 1999 Pakistan received from the US administration 464 million, most of it in cash, as reimbursement for the 28 F-16 combat jets, purchased a decade ago but never received.

The two Prime Ministers at their meeting at Newyork in September 1998 agreed to start a bus service from New Delhi to Lahore that followed an agreement between the two in December. Vajpayee made a visit to Pakistan by the first bus and entered in Pakistan's territory through Wagah border in Punjab. This much publicised bus diplomacy and Lahore declaration, issued at the end of the visit on 21 February 1999,marked a new era of understanding and amicable relations between the two countries. However, there was no compromise from both sides, on defence-related matters and they continued to prepare, as earlier, their nuclear armaments and test-firing of missiles. Despite very hopeful end of Vajpayee's visit to Pakistan, its President and Prime Minister hinted/ reminded Indian Prime Minister of the problem of Kashmir. Later in April 1999, Sartaj Aziz, the Foreign Minister of Pakistan, while addressing the United Nations Commission on Human Rights, at Geneva, was quoted as saying that complete and durable normalisation can become a political reality once a just and peaceful solution has been found to the core dispute over Kashmir.

In an important decision Pakistani cabinet decided to keep the country's missile testing option open as to counter to a possible launch of the long-range Agni missile by India. The nuclear scientist of Pakistan Abdul Qadeer had revealed that the Kahuta Research Laboratories can put a satellite of reasonable size into orbit and Islamabad is likely to go ahead of India in long range patrol submarines because it had signed a contract with France for three Agosta class submarines, one of which would have a Mesma stream-and-gas AIP system. It valued 950 million dollar and expected to reach Pakistan first in June 1999. New Delhi too, perhaps in response, had shown interest in air-independent propulsion technology produced by the Russian Federation for its Amur class submarine. The Russian Federation had offered the technology to India because joint development would reduce the costs incurred on it.

As expected by Islamabad and as a follow up of the Lahore declaration Pakistan was informed a bit earlier (on 9 April) and India successfully test-fired the extended range Agni-II intermediate range ballistic missile on 11 April 1999, in a bid to bridge a key gap in its nuclear deterrent profile. The salient features of this test-firing were demonstration of mobile launch capability, solid propulsion system; range in excess of 2,000 kilometres, features designed to carry special pay load; state-of-the-art navigation guidance and control systems and sophisticated on-board packages including advanced communication interface. India's Minister for Defence George Fernandes and Prime Minister Atal Bihari Vajpayee declared that the test-firing of Agni-II was "purely defensive" and strongly reiterated India's commitment to minimum nuclear deterrence, no first use of nuclear weapons and non-use against non-nuclear weapon states. They also congratulated the scientists, technicians, jawans and other defence personnel for it. The achievement had established India firmly in world missile club, but the shaky political coalition of Vajpayee had undermined the nuclear missile deterrent. The Political parties in opposition had charged that the test-firing of Agni-II meant for diverting attention from political crisis. Although Vajpayee failed to get the confidence motion passed from the Lok Sabha on 17 April 1999 by margin of one vote (269 in favour and 270 in against) yet he will go down in history as the man who freed India from decades of political poltroonery and began building a credible nuclear missile deterrent for India's security.

Islamabad, apart from criticizing the test-firing of Agni-II promised a tit-for-tat and Sartaj Aziz said, "Since India has gone ahead, we would probably have to respond fittingly. We will decide in a day or two". In retaliation Pakistan successfully test-fired its Ghauri-II missile on 14 April 1999 followed by the test-firing of Shaheen missile next day (15 April). It is a surface –to-surface missile having a range of 600 km with capacity of carrying nuclear warhead. The test-firing of Agni-II missile by India and Ghauri-II and Shaheen by Pakistan received world-wide condemnation. White House spokesman Joe Lockhart said that "Although these may not violate any existing arms control treaty; they certainly do nothing to enhance the environment in which co-operation between the countries is enhanced". Beijing too called on India and Pakistan to take steps to prevent an arms race and suggested that both sides should seek concrete avenues to avoid the acceleration of an arms race in South Asia so that peace and stability could prevail.

Second Term of Atal Bihari Vajpayee (13 October 1999-22 May 2004)

Having defeated by the margin of one vote in the Lok Sabha on April 17, 1999, Atal Bihari Vajpayee, the then Prime Minister of India, continued thereafter in the capacity of a caretaker till the next general election. The results of the scheduled election went in favour of the BJP–led coalition and for the third time in prime ministerial history he took the oath of this office on 13 October 1999. It was from his first term of office that India's relations with Pakistan had been charged and the two had detonated their nuclear devices in May 1998 successfully that followed a tensed relationship between them along with a world wide condemnation. The present dispensation of India had a lot of experience of its Pakistani counterpart who recently waged a war at Kargil and foiled the much debated Lahore Declaration which was signed when Indian Prime Minister took a journey by bus to Lahore. India's image in Pakistan is rather limited and bleak. Despite the shared culture, the dominant image of India is that of a hostile country. The limited people to people contact, in fact, has not allowed people on either side of the divide to develop a better understanding of each other or to appreciate the richness of their cultures.[220] In such a situation it is natural for the people in Pakistan not to appreciate the diversity in India's culture or politics.

Day before Vajpayee's assumption as the Prime Minister of India on October 12, 1999, in a bloodless coup the Pakistan Army once again ousted the civilian government. On that very day Nawaz Sharif, the Prime Minister of Pakistan, had sacked General Pervez Musharraf and appointed his crony General Ziauddin Butt as his successor which was refused by the senior generals who did not gave charge to Ziauddin. As Musharraf was out of the country and his way back from Sri Lanka he could not have done any thing to save himself. Once Musharraf landed, he dismissed the Government of Nawaz Sharif immediately, dissolved Parliament and suspended the constitution. A transitional government headed by the General, including a cabinet and a National Security Council was established. With this development another chapter of military rule was opened in Pakistan – a country that has been ruled by unelected governments for 25 of its 52 year history.

Countries of the world including India and the US have expressed their reactions over the military takeover in Pakistan. New Delhi expressed grave concern at the sudden turn of events in Pakistan and placed its armed forces in a state of full alert. The analysts in India viewed the latest political military turmoil as an extension of the consequences brought upon that country by the Kargil misadventure. J. N. Dixit, the former Foreign Secretary had described the situation as extraordinarily volatile.[221] Another analyst considered it a complex and unfortunate situation which is not conducive to normalisation of relations in South Asia. From Washington the senior officials of Clinton Administration had sent a message to the Pakistan Army through diplomatic channels that the US does not support any military takeover anywhere, that the constitution has to be respected and it would be not right to presume it would be business as usual after a democratically elected government is overthrown.[222] Among others the Commonwealth moved swiftly to suspend Pakistan and the European Union has been tougher than the US in demanding the restoration of democracy. The UN Secretary General had deplored it, and the International Monetary Fund director had declared that loans to Pakistan will be suspended until democracy is restored.[223] But genuinely speaking these measures meant only a moral sermon as it did not involve sanction or trade bars in regard to Pakistan. In general military coups are not fashionable in the post-cold war era as the world community's revulsion towards coups is now unequivocal.

Unlike the negative response of the coup world over the dismissal of Nawaz Sharif's government seemed to be welcomed by several quarters in the country. Under the cover of a crushing two-thirds majority Nawaz Sharif had tended to accumulate power for himself by molesting institutions, rules and conventions. The people had a feeling of relief at the end of his 31 months of chaotic rule. Almost all the political parties welcomed the military intervention. Benazir Bhutto, the exiled opposition leader, accused Sharif of antagonizing and provoking the military against his own government and in an interview with Sky TV she reported to have said that 'The people believe that that man is violating every rule of law and there is no one to stop him. The armed forces had to protect themselves as an institution.[224] However, as an exception to the general welcome the right wing fundamentalist Party Jammat-i-Islami in a statement issued on October 15, 1999, while urging the armed forces to give priority to making corrupt rulers accountable, criticized Musharraf's decision to declare a state of emergency and stated that it could not support the martial law and the suspension of fundamental rights.

Like other military rulers of the past General Musharraf promised to clean up Pakistan's corrupt elite, rebuild national confidence and morale, revive the economy, strengthening the crumbling bonds between the four provinces that make up the country, and cleanse institutions to install 'real democracy' before the army relinquishes power.[225] Similar to the first military regime of Ayub Khan, Musharraf kept army personnel in the background and ran the administration through civilian institutions and officials, described as the 'civil-military combine' by the military rulers. The military rulers establish monitoring cells at different levels to oversee and supervise the working of the civilian institutions. In a calculated way the new-ruler tried to introduce guided democracy as he needed to introduce civilian rule to get Western sanctions off his back. Accordingly he planned to make the district the country's basic 'governance and development unit. He was of the view that these local bodies would provide the country with a strong, grassroots level democratic foundation. Musharraf believed that Pakistan's face can be turned and the country can be made to walk in the right direction – and he is the man to do it.

In the circumstances India needed to know what destination the general had in mind for New Delhi. The spectre of the Kargil war of the summer of 1999 haunted Indian policy towards Pakistan and resulted in an uncertain policy of diplomatic non-engagement between nuclearised neighbours. The new ruler of Pakistan continued its anti-India policy and once again asserted that his country is committed to providing all diplomatic, moral and political support to the people of Kashmir in their 'just struggle for self-determination. Musharraf's India policy was underpinned by a military stance. There has been a qualitative and quantitative increase in Pakistani subversive violence against India and its military activities across the Line of Control. It gave birth to military camps and establishments, terrorist violence against civilian targets and infiltration of terrorists and weapons into India. The general's approach towards Kashmir is that it has to be settled on Pakistani terms and conditions, otherwise proxy war and terrorism will be continued by him. He considers confidence building measures as a farce. He wants discussions on Kashmir denovo.[226] The policy approach of Islamabad's new ruler was also confirmed by Jaswant Singh, the new Minister for External Affairs, in a written reply to Lok Sabha, 'The military coup in Pakistan has not altered its aggressive and hostile policies and propaganda towards India.[227] He quoted statements by Pakistani spokesmen after the military coup that indicate Pakistan's assertions of territorial claims in Jammu and Kashmir, he, however, assured the House that New Delhi was closely monitoring the situation and would take all necessary steps to safeguard India's security.

Pakistan's anti-India policy and other related terrorist activities continued unabated and in line the Indian Airlines IC-814 was hijacked by Pakistan-based elements and took it to Kandahar (Afghanistan) from where they put their initial demands through the Taliban. In January 2000 the large scale attacks against Indian posts in the Akhnoor-Chamb sector were executed that followed the Sikh massacre by militants in Chitthi-Singhpora in Anantnag on 20 March and the gunning down of 100 Amarnath pilgrims. But in contrast in the spring of 2000 India released leaders of the Hurriyat Conference from the prison and it showed an openness to the short-lived Hizbul Mujahideen ceasefire in summer that year. Further in the winter of 2000 the Indian Prime Minister declared the Ramzan truce which was broke down when New Delhi rejected the Hizbul Mujahideen's insistence on including Pakistan in the negotiations. As the last way out India invited Musharraf for talks in India in Agra in July 2001 which ended without any concrete gain on either side. Looking back it seemed strange that one summit between the leadership of the two countries, when one had Muslim hard liners and the other the Hindutva brigade to contend with, would end decades of mistrust was wholly unrealistic. There was some movement away from stated positions, Pakistan substituted the word 'issue' for the word 'dispute' as the adjective to Kashmir, in deference to Indian sensitivities, with the Agra summit ending in failure both sides retreated behind old antagonisms. Thus the liberalism and patience showed on the part of New Delhi was an indication that the then coalition government in India might just be capable of a little more pragmatism and goodwill than its predecessors in an attempt to grasp the Kashmir nettle.[228]

India remained sympathetic and soft in action towards Islamabad despite the Kargil, Kandahar and terrorism in Kashmir. Its policy had not only discredited the Lahore Declaration but also surprised the foreign policy experts and analysts. They felt in general that New Delhi is willing to be tough with Pakistan in view of the recent developments but not to the extent that it would upset Washington. In fact the seeds of the Lahore process were sown when Vajpayee and Nawaz Sharif visited Newyork in September 1998. It was also at the instance of Strobe Talbott that certain measures were incorporated in the Memorandum of Understanding (MoU) signed at Lahore, including advance notification of missile tests, bilateral consultations on security concepts, nuclear doctrines and nuclear-risk reduction.[229] The Vajpayee Government has invested so much in Indo-US ties that, despite the serious setbacks in relations with Islamabad, it is reluctant to deal with Pakistan independently of its relationship with the US. This situation in effect precludes measures to raise the costs for Pakistan of its strategy to slowly bleed India.[230] Therefore, it is no wonder that elementary steps to help break the back of ISI operations in India are a no-go. Although the Vajpayee Government has felt the gravity of the situation and continued to deliver tough statements on Pakistan that reflected the fury and frustration arising from government's willingness to strike-but-afraid-to-wound policy. Perhaps New Delhi had made a commitment to Washington not to escalate diplomatic or other tensions with Islamabad. The answer to Pakistan's strategy to haemorhage India is not tough words and barren action, but soft words and deterrent action.

On India-Pakistan relations every right-thinking people in both the countries feel that the conflict between the two is eminently resolvable. The benefits of peace between India and Pakistan are immense and the cost of conflict is far too apparent to ignore. This state of affairs has to do with several factors including the manner in which the two countries view each other, the differences in their national movements and how each one of them defined political freedom, the quest of Pakistan-being the smaller geographical part of the undivided whole for strategic parity with India. The aberrations in Indo-Pak relationship have been fed by Pakistan's quest for strategic parity with India. Such a quest necessarily leads to misplaced aggressiveness particularly when a smaller entity seeks parity with one many times its size.[231] In the changed circumstances and especially after its nuclear parity with India in May 1998 it is pointless to seek conventional military parity but Islamabad due to its obsession with India continues to behave as an insecure state. India can handle Pakistan only through a calibrated, carrot-and-stick approach that rewards good behaviour and imposes penalties for errant or belligerent behaviour.

Having a failed talk at Agra in July 2001 once again relations between India and Pakistan received a sudden jolt in view of the September 11, 2001, suicidal attacks in the United States and a terrorist attack on the Indian Parliament on 13 December. Earlier Islamabad had made no move to curb the terrorist groups based in Pakistan, which have been continuing violent attacks in Kashmir and other places. This reveals the fact that Pakistan has no interest in creating a conducive environment for the commencement of an India-Pakistan peace dialogue.[232] The terrorist attacks of September on the World Trade Centre and Pentagon in the US had resulted in a shift in all geo-political dynamics – international, regional and local. The extraordinary situation had forced the US to co-opt Pakistan – the foundation head of terrorist activities into its crusade against global terrorism. It had, in addition, put the military regime in Islamabad in the biggest dilemma Pakistan has ever faced. On the one side, the world's most powerful nation, wounded and angry, was bluntly telling the general that if he did not act as a friend now he would be considered as the enemy. On the other were the Taliban leaders of the most brutish police state in the world and their hordes who threatened jehad against the very country that had nurtured them. In the situation the military regime's options were limited to risking US punishment for supporting the Taliban, neutrality, or seeking strategic dividends by assisting the US. With a weak economy, a polarised polity, China backing Washington and the

Islamic bloc a virtual non-factor, Pakistan was left with no choice and General Musharraf decided to make a virtue of necessity and has proclaimed support for US moves. Musharraf's decision to support the American war on terror after the 11 September 2001 attacks strengthened his domestic position considerably.

By the event of September 11, 2001 India, for the first time found the opportunity to categorise all Islamist resistance to Indian armed forces in Kashmir as terrorism, and it wanted endorsement for its efforts to crush them and the US did declare multiple Islamist groups to be terrorist organisations.[233] India watched the further developments with concern and unfortunately found that Pakistan again emerged as a frontline state in the latest US assault on Afghanistan as Pakistan now had the chance to improve its economy and rehabilitate itself in the Western world. The United States' war against terror has changed the destiny of Pakistan and at the same time provided a lease of life to general's regime which was struggling hard for its legitimacy at home and abroad. All the sanctions related to the nuclear tests had been lifted and aid has started to flow, inconvenient facts about cross- border terrorism have been brushed under the carpet. Pakistan's profile in the eyes of the West, and particularly the US has changed completely. Islamabad's chance and US cooperation disappointed in India those who expected that Pakistan, source of cross-border terrorism, would be a prime target of the US war against terror.

The new situation emerged after the terrorist attacks on World Trade Centre completely favoured Pakistan and it made New Delhi more worried than ever before. It increased the terrorist attacks in the Jammu and Kashmir and a brutal suicide squad of JeM was made on the Kashmir Assembly complex on 1 October 2001. The relations between them deteriorated further as a result of the JeM terrorist attack on the Indian Parliament, located at the heart of the capital's high security zone on December 13, 2001. It was an attack on the pillar of Indian democracy-the Parliament which India said was orchestrated by Pakistani agents. The attack led to a dramatic build-up of troops along the Indo-Pakistan border, military exchanges and raised fears of a wider conflict.[234] It, however, carried two strident messages on behalf of Pakistan's Musharraf regime for New Delhi. The first was that despite the success of the United States-led coalition in the Afghan war, terrorism is alive and well. It had become imperative to send it to raise the morale of terrorists in India and Pakistan which had sunk to their boots following the collapse of the Taliban regime. The second message was that the attack was a proof of the fact that the Musharraf regime had not sold out to the US, and its alliance with the latter was meant to safeguard Pakistan's nuclear arsenal and prevent the US from including its cross-border terrorism against India in its anti-terrorist agenda.[235] But despite these once again Pakistan came under intense pressure to clamp down and reform the country into a moderate Islamic state.

After the terrorist attack on Indian Parliament Islamabad took some steps in right direction and arrested hundreds of terrorists including some top brass of the organisation. Jaswant Singh, India's Minister for External Affairs, considered the measures in right direct but hoped that such actions against terrorist groups targeting India including Jammu and Kashmir would be pursued vigorously and cross-border terrorism eliminated.[236] India also mounted pressure on Islamabad when Prime Minister Atal Bihari Vajpayee met Musharraf on the sideline of 11th SAARC summit held at Kathmandu in the first week of January 2002. In the summit India received the support of its South Asian neighbours for its principled stand that terrorism, no matter what form it took or cause it espoused, should be combated concertedly. Even the inauguration of the summit was marked by direct references to the December 13 attack on Parliament and member-countries strengthened their resolve to act on the convention on Terrorism. The Indian Prime Minister also gave a hard-hitting reply to Musharraf's address and recalled how Pakistan had repaid India's peace initiatives at Lahore and Agra with the Kargil aggression and later the attacks on the Jammu and Kashmir Assembly and Parliament House.[237] Earlier Pervez Musharraf, while supporting the 'SAARC Convention on Terrorism' maintained that it was equally important to distinguish between acts of legitimate resistance and freedom struggles on the one hand and acts of terrorism on the other.

In the meantime Pervez Musharraf in a televised address to the nation on January 12, 2002, as a skilful tactician and perception manager, had tried to carry conviction to India and the rest of the world that his determination to act against terrorism in all its manifestations was a definite change of policy and not just a change of posture. As an ally of the US in the war against terrorism the General had agreed publicly to wage the war domestically and make the choice which the US and the democratic world wants to make him. His speech and strategy to tackle the problem of terrorism was welcomed by the US, Britain and Russia and they expressed the hope that India would respond positively to Musharraf's remarks about resolving the Kashmir issue through peaceful means and to the ban on the extremist groups in Pakistan. Real intensions apart, it must be said to Musharraf's credit that no other Pakistani leader, political or military had ever condemned the activities of religious extremist and sectarian parties and highlighted their devastating effect on the Pakistani State and society in such strong terms as he did. Behind this tact was also the compelling facts of Islamabad's economy which was in total chaos when the military took over and was heavily dependent on foreign loans to meet deficit repayment obligations. Its Gross Domestic Product (GDP) slumped to mere 2.2 per cent and 3.4 per cent in fiscal years 2000-01 and 2001-02 respectively. These growth rates were the lowest in Pakistan's recorded history. Later from the fiscal year 2002-03 the overall economy of the country witnessed a sharp recovery due to American dollars in aid and in Paris Club creditors who restructured and rescheduled much of Pakistan's external debt.

For India the meaning of Musharraf's address was not positive, but not negative either.[238] Going by the reaction to Musharraf's speech the whole world seemed to be in a mood to give the General a standing ovation for his bold and visionary approach to tackle terrorism. Jaswant Singh, India's Minister for External Affairs in a measured response, welcomed the address as a major shift in Islamabad's policy but at the sametime reiterated India's stand that it would await ground level implementation of Musharraf's pious promises before taking the President's offer of dialogue in active consideration. As in the oft-repeated style Islamabad had exhibited no substantial change in its Kashmir policy and alleging India's policy in Jammu and Kashmir had called for an active role by the UN observers and international human rights organisations, New Delhi remained committed to bilateralism. In a clear message to Pakistan the Indian Minister hoped that Islamabad should operationalise its intention and move purposefully towards eradication of cross- border terrorism. In that case India will respond fully and be prepared to resume the composite dialogue process that includes Kashmir.[239] He was also of the view that Musharraf's goal to modernise Pakistan by reigning in the fundamentalists had a direct connection with external development of terrorist activities. The minister remarked that we are willing to take two steps for every one that Pakistan takes.

New Delhi was worried and concerned particularly on the problem of terrorism in Jammu and Kashmir. The much propagated speech of General Musharraf contained nothing on the vexed issue and it put India where it was. On the one hand Pakistan banned the Jaish-e-Mohammad and the Lashkar-e-Tayyeba, but attributed the ban to their activities inside Pakistan and not to their acts of terrorism in India. In this connection Islamabad spared the Harkat-ul-Mujahideen (HuM), whose jehadi organisations has the largest following in the Pakistani Army and had close links with the Taliban and Al Qaeda. Similarly it had also spared the Al Badr, another Pakistani organisation active in Jammu and Kashmir and was silent on the activities of Kashmiri organisations such as the Hizbul Mujahideen from Pakistani territory. In addition the leaders of the JeM, and LeT were arrested only after they had nominated their deputies, the bank accounts of both were frozen in a manner that had enabled them to withdraw a bulk of funds in advance. In other words Pakistan seems to be going through the motions of acting against them without hurting them. Even on the terrorists wanted by India Musharraf had taken the traditional Pakistani position that while Pakistan would try Pakistani nationals under its own laws provided credible evidence was forthcoming it would be willing to consider the extradition of non-Pakistanis if they are found in Pakistani territory.

Since the attack on Parliament the Indian government had played its card well and in cooperation with the US compelled Pakistan to reverse its jehad policy and ban the terror groups, it had nourished. However, this phase of change in Islamabad's policy was purely temporary and did not last long. The Pakistani State has been so hooked to bleeding India cheaply through surrogate terror groups only because it helps Pakistan to debilitate an enemy it can not confront militarily and to keep the spot light on the Kashmir dispute.[240] In his speech of 12 January, as an astute painter he painted on a wide convas with very broad strokes. He announced his intentions of drastically cleansing Pakistani society and polity of religious fundamentalism, violence and terrorism. It is humanly impossible for one man, working under heightened personal security and thus at considerable remove from the masses, to bring about social revolution and that too in a society that is deeply mired in illiteracy poverty, religious extremism and exclusiveness, and social conservatism. In the circumstances Musharraf is incapable of bringing about a qualitative change in Pakistani societal structures and making it democratic, plural, secular and terrorism free.[241]

In fact Pakistan is more India's problem than America's. Instead of waiting for the US to bring Islamabad to heel, Indian diplomacy should be vigorously seeking to influence Pakistan's behaviour and the American agenda on that country. India needs to maintain pressure through a durable strategy with clearly defined objective measures, but without the fickleness. Still Pakistan military and its ISI agency have not severed their links with terrorists operating against India, but rather asked them to lie low, as part of their strategy to buy time. At present New Delhi and Washington share the goal of deracinating the jehad culture from Pakistan. India should persuade Washington to also put reform of the Pakistan military on its agenda. In that kind of situation Musharraf expressed Pakistan's readiness for resolving all outstanding differences with India including Kashmir on March 23, 2002, which is observed as Pakistan Day as on this day in 1940 the Muslim League passed a resolution to form Pakistan.

Further direction of India-Pakistan relations did not witness any positive sign and General Musharraf had suddenly in April 2002 raised military tensions with a stark warning that he is prepared to use nuclear weapons in the event of war. He in an interview to Germany's magazine *Der Spiegel* warned that if the pressure on Pakistan becomes too great then as a last resort the atom bomb is also possible. Taking a new posture he also allowed Pakistani courts to free religious clerics jailed earlier during protests at the start of US military campaign in Afghanistan. The development compelled New Delhi to adopt a tough attitude and India asked Pakistan to recall its High Commissioner Ashraf Jehangir Qazi. A meeting of the Cabinet Committee on Security was also held in May 2002 which took stock of the ground situation after a briefing by the chiefs of the three services and three other officers.[242] India's hardened attitude continued and it ruled out a face-to-face dialogue between Prime Minister Atal Bihari Vajpayee and President Musharraf saying that this was not possible till Islamabad stopped cross-border terrorism. The two dignitaries met at the 16-Nation Conference on Interaction and Confidence Building Measures in Asia (CICA) held at Almaty in the first week of June 2002 but avoided each other studiously refusing to make eye contact. However, the gathering was a success despite differences between New Delhi and Islamabad and in the two-page Declaration on Eliminating Terrorism and Promoting Dialogue among Civilizations, it held the view that the fight against terrorism should be global, comprehensive and sustained, and not selective or discriminatory and should avoid applying double standards.

Ground for peaceful diplomacy between India and Pakistan was prepared first by Prime Minister Vajpayee's speech of 18 April 2003 in which he offered the hand of friendship and Zaffrullah Jamali, the then Prime Minister of Pakistan, responded favourably. The policies of President Musharraf also showed flexibility and innovative thinking in offering different proposals that could fulfil the aspirations of Kashmiris while keeping in mind the sensitivities of Indo-Pak relations. A helping hand was also extended by an intensive back-channel diplomacy in which secret talks were held in 2003 by Brajesh Mishra, India's National Security Advisor and Tariq Aziz, a senior civilian adviser to President Pervez Musharraf. Their talks led to the successful meeting between Musharraf and Vajpayee during the January 2004 SAARC meeting in Islamabad.[243] The joint statement signed on 6 January was a serous step towards the management of conflict pertaining to Kashmir. In the statement Vajpayee reiterated that in order to take forward and sustain the dialogue process, voilence, hostility and terrorism must be prevented. Likewise, President Musharraf reassured Prime Minister Vajpayee that he would not permit any territory under Pakistan's control to be used to support terrorism in any manner.[244] He further emphasised that a sustained and productive dialogue addressing all issues would lead to positive results.

For the India-Pakistan relations it was a good beginning which spread at official as well as unofficial levels. The joint statement also followed a joint press conference that the two leaders addressed on the occasion and Musharraf took the opportunity to declare, 'History has been made as Pakistan and India have reached an understanding to take the process of normalization of relations forward. We have never reached the point we have reached now.[245] The opportunity also held out the promise of expanded road, rail and air contacts, people to people exchanges, a new look at regional economic cooperation and even a discussion on Kashmir. Subsequently a number of unofficial dialogues sprang up, including a revival of the Neemrana group, a visit of high-level Indian businesspersons to Pakistan, and the prospect of cooperation between Bollywood and Lollywood-India's and Pakistan's film studios in Mumbai and Lahore respectively. This demonstrated that genuine diplomacy was possible between them. The change in style and method is just as important at this stage as any changes in substantive positions.

Further Strokes on Kashmir

Like earlier during the premiership of Atal Bihari Vajpayee India-Pakistan relations remained a hostage to the enmity generated by the partition. It is the liberation of Indo-Pak relation from the captivity of hostility that can create a soil of mutual confidence, strengthened by mutually beneficial cooperation across South Asia and beyond, that can help overcome historically rooted disputes in a process of reconciliation. The ideas of South Asian customs, economic and monetary union and collective security are so much inspiring and mutually useful that border disputes will disappear with the softening of borders while respecting the sovereign entities, and allowing the Kashmiris and so many other disposed peoples to realise their aspirations. The logic of hostility will have to be turned over into the logic of fraternity. There cannot be a new beginning for the Kashmiris without a good beginning between India and Pakistan and there can not be any beginning for South Asia without a friendly relationship between the twin brothers of subcontinent. We live in a ruthless world of unilateralist, globalization and militarization and cannot survive, nor find a respectable place in this world of great imbalances.

Basically the experience of independence and partition shaped the perceptions of the decision-makers on both sides. The mistrust with which the leaders view the actions of one another is rooted in their divergent conceptions and perceptions. From the Pakistani perspective, Kashmir is the 'core' issue and the root cause of bitterness in its relations with India. Pakistan maintains that Kashmir is a disputed territory and its accession to India in 1947 was invalid, so it has been unfinished agenda of partition. In Pakistan's eyes the accession to India without consulting the Muslim population of the state was null and void because this decision ignored the partition principles : both demographic considerations and geographical location demanded that Kashmir should join Pakistan.[246] What Pakistan wanted foremost was to press its claim to Kashmir.

In contrast from Indian points of view Kashmir is an *atool ang* (integral part) of India. In a speech to the Constituent Assembly on 25 November 1947, Prime Minister Jawaharlal Nehru justified it in these words, 'We were of course vitally interested in the decision that the state would take. Kashmir, because of her geographical position with her frontiers marching with three countries, namely the Soviet Union, China and Afghanistan, is intimately concerned with the security and international contacts of India. Economically also Kashmir is intimately related to India. Kashmir's 'accession' is described as absolute and final and the problem in Kashmir is interpreted as an issue of autonomy rather than an issue of plebiscite. Indian analysts do not believe that Kashmir is a 'core issue'.[247] Thus while Pakistan asserts it is the problem of Kashmir, India insists it is the problem in Kashmir as one analyst says that for Pakistan still it is the problem of Kashmir i.e. Kashmir is a disputed territory and an unfinished agenda of partition; for India it is the problem in Kashmir suggesting that the accession of Kashmir to India is final and complete and the challenge now remains of addressing cross-border terrorism, development and the grievances of the people of Kashmir.

However, over the decades there has been a shift in Pakistan's attitude regarding Indo-Pak relations and a number of reasons are responsible for it. Firstly, there are pressures from the people of Pakistan to have improved relations with India. The cable TV network and liberal visa to Pakistanis to visit India has shown to them the progress India has made and the prosperity that the average Indian is enjoying. Secondly, the post-partition generation is not so anti India as the older generation. They want to enjoy the life and know that it would be possible only if Pakistan has friendly relations with India. Thirdly, there are pressures from the American-European camp to have improved relations with India.

This group of nations sees in India a potential market that is huge. All economic surveys in the USA are showing that India would be a powerful economy in another forty years. The Pakistani business feels that if they do not have better trade relations with India, they would be left far behind. Fourthly, India has emerged as a powerful military nation.[248] Its capacity to buy armaments is huge and many countries producing tanks, submarines and fighter planes want to be on the right side of India. Pakistan has no such capacity and can purchase armaments only if military aid is provided to it.

The nationalist government which took over in New Delhi in March 1998 under Vajpayee's premiership conducted in May five nuclear tests and declared India to be a nuclear weapon state. In response Pakistan successfully exploded its six nuclear devices on 28 and 30 May 1998. Following the Indian suit Islamabad offered New Delhi to initiate a dialogue to ensure mutual restraint in the wake of nuclear tests by both sides but it should address all outstanding issues, including the thorny Kashmir problem. Tariq Altaf, a spokesman of Pakistani foreign office reiterated Nawaz Sharif's assertion saying that Pakistan was ready to have a non-aggression pact with India but after just settlement of Kashmir dispute 'Actually Kashmir is the core problem which is a cause of tension in the region he asserted and accused India of an illegal occupation and suppression of the people's rights in Jammu and Kashmir.[249] Nawaz Sharif also raised the matter on 6 June 1998 while addressing a joint session of the two Houses of Parliament to approve the imposition of emergency in the country, termed the Kashmir problem a 'challenge for the international conscience' and urged the world nations to take practical steps for solving the issue. Adhering to the earlier stand Vajpayee too while taking part in a debate on nuclear issue in the Rajya Sabha on 8 June reiterated New Delhi's desire for earliest resumption of official talks with Pakistan on all outstanding issues including Kashmir but ruled out any third party mediation in the dialogue process.[250]

Nuclear tests by India and Pakistan had further complicated the matter and not only changed the power equation in South Asia, but it also made deep impact on India and Pakistan by forcing political leaders to rethink and revisit their national security strategy differently. It drove South Asia to an uncertain and fragile situation and led the world leaders to raise myriad questions regarding possible nuclear confrontation in the region. In apprehension the United States ordered sanctions against both countries, freezing more than twenty billion dollar of aid, loans and trade. Japan ordered a block on about one billion dollar of aid loans. Several European countries followed suit, and the G-8 governments imposed a ban on non-humanitarian loans to India and Pakistan. The UN Security Council condemned India and Pakistan for carrying out nuclear tests and urged the two nations to stop all nuclear weapons programmes. In post-Pokhran phase while Kashmir does not receive the attention and press coverage of other political hotspots such as the Middle East, it is considered by many experts to be one of the most potentially explosives regions in the world. There have been innumerable direct bilateral negotiations between India and Pakistan on or including Kashmir, unfortunately all these discussions have not yielded any result. Robert G. Wirsing in his book '*Kashmir in the Shadow of War*' has rightly stated that India and Pakistan are far from free to settle the Kashmir dispute in their own terms. And Pakistan's nothing-except-Kashmir and India's everything-but-Kashmir stands even today.

After nuclear tests by both the two Prime Ministers – Atal Bihari Vajpayee and Nawaz Sharif met in July 1998 at the SAARC summit in Colombo where they instructed their Foreign Secretaries to discuss modalities for revival of Foreign Secretary level talks. Actually Islamabad knew that Colombo was only the first stage of a last, desperate, gamble to wrest Kashmir from India by literally blackmailing the world into imposing a solution to the Kashmir issue on India.[251] Under the strategy Pakistan proposed to get Kashmir discussed within the SAARC summit on the grounds that the nuclear tests had turned the Kashmir dispute into a regional threat to peace and security and a second one to establish a high council of foreign ministers who would discuss both bilateral and multilateral security and associated issues. Having failed at Colombo Pakistan unveiled its further strategy on August 2, 1998, in which Nawaz Sharif accused India of pushing the region to the brink of war with its barrage of artillery fire. He along with his Foreign Minister asked the world community to put pressure on India to desist from such actions. Pakistan's foreign minister warned that if New Delhi dared to attack in Kashmir Islamabad would use Chinese and North Korean missiles to hit

Indian cities with nuclear warheads. At the moment it is Pakistan's assessment that the more they prolong the crisis in Jammu and Kashmir through political, subversive and terrorist means, the greater the likelihood of direct international involvement in discussions on Kashmir and greater the pressure likely to be exerted on India on the issue.

In the middle of October 1998 the stalled Indo-Pak talks resumed with little hope for any breakthrough in view of the recent tough stand by both the countries on Kashmir. It was held in Islamabad in view of the agreement between Prime Ministers of the two countries during their meeting in Newyork where they reaffirmed their common belief that an environment of durable peace and security was in the supreme interest of both India and Pakistan and of the region as a whole.[252] Despite disagreements there was an agreement of discussing Jammu and Kashmir as part of a composite dialogue between the two countries and to move towards a solution which would be in the mutual interest. In the meeting the two side proposed each other the Confidence Building Measures (CBMs) relating to conventional and nuclear warfare, it however did not satisfy Shamshad Ahmed, the Foreign Secretary of Pakistan, who held the view that without any forward movement on the Kashmir issue, he said, 'working for settling other peripheral issues would amount to nothing more than papering over the cracks'.[253] The joint statement issued on the occasion also included the problem of Jammu and Kashmir and said that the two sides reiterated their respective positions. Pakistan's attitude was that it had a territorial right over Kashmir and that if the persistent use of force or sponsored terrorism does not help it realise its claim, then international brokering certainly would. But India believed that neither sponsored subversion nor external pressure can force it to move on the question of Kashmir. The Indian belief is that the sovereignty and the legality of Jammu and Kashmir is not going to change. However, Pakistan continued to urge India to abandon its negative approach on the Kashmir issue and enter into a substantive and result-oriented dialogue.

Relations between India and Pakistan improved in February 1999 when in the background of the meeting of two Prime Ministers in September 1998 in Newyork, Atal Bihari Vajpayee arrived Lahore on the inaugural Delhi-Lahore bus service. Vajpayee's visit created a nation-wide euphoria and expected to dawn a new era in South Asia. It was an atmosphere of friendship and reconciliation and the hope was natural that once both countries, now nuclear weapon states decide to live as equal sovereign states in a mutually beneficial economic and security framework there are endless possibilities of progress for both.[254] Even before the visit Nawaz Sharif had urged India to go beyond stated position on contentious issues facing the two countries. Pakistan had made it clear that there can be no normalization of relations with India unless the Kashmir issue is first resolved in accordance with Pakistan's wishes. In fact both the countries now know that in view of the possibility of a war, or even, proxy war which can bring the two to the brink, a negotiated settlement is the only way out.

On the last day of the visit (21st February) the Lahore Declaration was signed by the two Prime Ministers that brought a defining moment in South Asian history. They agreed on the resolution of all outstanding issues, including Jammu and Kashmir terming it as essential for the environment of peace and security and pledging to intensify their efforts to resolve all issues including Jammu and Kashmir. They also agreed to step up the composite and integrated dialogue process for an early and positive outcome of the agreed bilateral agenda. Besides the Lahore Declaration the two Prime Ministers issued a joint statement, and the two Foreign Secretaries signed a Memorandum of Understanding (MoU) and provided several steps to boost mutual cooperation and understanding. The Indian President K. R. Narayanan, after return of Vajpayee also expressed the hope that the visit would make a new chapter in bilateral ties. *The Hindu*, in a leading article appreciated their sincere efforts that demonstrated commendable determination to tread a new path of reconciliation and good neighbourliness, displaying rare courage to depart from scripts that had till now reduced the scope for positive action to improve bilateral relations.[255] The international community including USA, Russia, Britain and France have appreciated the Lahore process.

Good intentions of the Lahore Declaration took a 'U' turn soon after its signing as it failed to reflect any softening of the Pakistani position on Jammu and Kashmir. Expectations in Pakistan would be running high if the claim of Kashmir is sustained, making it difficult for any government in that to be accommodative to India in further negotiation. The developments at Lahore made aggressive to the opposition and fundamentalists and they apprehended a compromise on Kashmir. Under the circumstances Nawaz Sharif had threatened India to suspend talks if the Kashmir issue was not resolved within a specific time frame. He even used the occasion to declare that Islamabad would continue to give moral, diplomatic and political support to Kashmiris. The post-Lahore events that followed amply exihibited political immaturity on India's part as deadly serious issues are not resolved by emotional outbursts.

The intrusion and later war in Kargil sector had shattered the vision attached to the Lahore Declaration and it started in March 1999 when Pakistani troops fired on Kargil across the Line of Control (LoC). On March 18, 1999, George Fernandes, the Indian Defence Minister had admitted in the Lok Sabha that Pakistan's ISI agents in Kargil are suspected to be behind the accuracy of Pakistani firing in the Uri-Kargil sector. In the intrusion Pakistan's message was two-fold : one, we do not accept the LoC in any future map-making; two, the Jammu and Kashmir issue has to be discussed urgently under the changed terms or reference. But if Kashmir is the core issue for Pakistan, it is doubly so for India because it is the heart of its territorial disputes with Pakistan and China and the spring of externally sponsored terrorism. Islamabad failed in its entire game plan as Indian army demonstrated unprecedented determination and courage, and defeated the Pakistani intruders which included large number of regulars. In between the Kargil Pakistan also offered talks on prevailing situation and sent its Foreign Minister Sartaj Aziz to New Delhi on 12 June 1999. At the end of talks, it became clear that the stand-off would continue without any let-up. At the end of May Pakistan was on the verge of defeat diplomatically and militarily,[256] its firm stance that the aggression in Kashmir had occurred because of India's obdurate attitude on Kashmir issue. Islamabad also linked the crossing of the Line of Control in the Kargil and Drass sectors with the question of Kashmir and felt that such invasions and intrusions would continue to occur till the problem of Kashmir is resolved to Pakistan's satisfaction.

Ultimately as a follow up of Clinton-Sharif Communique in which Pakistan had committed to take concrete steps to restore the sanctity of the Line of Control (LoC) in Kashmir it decided to appeal to Mujahideen fighting the Indian Army while praising them for their courageous action leading to focussing of international attention to the Kashmir issue, to help resolve the Kargil situation. After Kargil India emerged from the war with enhanced capacity for negotiation and compromise while Pakistan stood with this capacity almost destroyed. But the end of Kargil war did not mean the end of continuing Pakistani hostility to India. In fact, Kashmir has always been a symbol, not the root cause of Indo-Pak conflict. As admitted recently by the army chief of Pakistan that even a settlement of the Kashmir issue would not usher peace in the region and the root of Pakistan's hostility are in history, religion, civilization and the politics of revenge. The gulf between the two is too wide to be bridged in the foreseeable future without major geostrategic or radical policy changes in the region. In post-Kargil periods, as feared was the calculated revival by Pakistan of cross-border terrorism, and resort to provocative anti Indian action along various points across the LoC. True to the faith there was an increase in subversive activities by Pakistan not only in Jammu and Kashmir, but also in other parts of the country. If Pakistan now decided to set-up its terrorist activities in Kashmir and elsewhere in India as a result of frustration, no one would have any doubt as to who was behind them.

Nawaz Sharif's doublespeak policy on Kashmir continued further in post-Kargil phase. In all his public pronouncements on the issue, had called for an immediate resumption of dialogue at the high political level but in another statement he made in the National Assembly said that though the volcanic eruption in Kargil had been brought under control, if India did not discuss Kashmir in a meaningful manner, other volcano would erupt. Even earlier his one statement was negated by the other. For instance, he urged Prime Minister Vajpayee to come and talk without wasting any further time while advancing the curious argument that the Mujahideen's occupation of Kargil was meant to attract world attention and that their withdrawal had paved the way for bilateral talks. But several analysts were of the view that such rhetoric was meant to deflect domestic criticism after a major military and diplomatic setback. In Pakistan there had been an increase in the number of attacks on security personnel, including planting of improvised explosive devices on convoy routes and throwing of hand grenades on security posts. The overall situation in the country also deteriorated fastly and in a dramatic way on October 12, 1999, the Government of Nawaz Sharif was overthrowned in a military coup by General Pervez Musharraf, Chief of Army Staff.

A day after the coup Pervez Musharraf, the new ruler of Pakistan, addressed the nation on television and counted the wrongs done by Nawaz Sharif. On the same day (13 October) a new government was took over in India under the premiership of Atal Bihari Vajpayee. Pervez Musharraf, as a gesture of goodwill towards India announced on 17 October 1999, unilateral military de-escalation along the border and pulling back of his troops that moved to the area in the recent past. The televised address also included an offer to resume result-oriented talks with India on all issues but said, 'Pakistan would continue its support to the Kashmiri people for their right to self- determination and added that India must honour all UN resolutions on Kashmir. India reacted Musharraf's offer in a guarded language and expressed its willingness to talk to any regime in Pakistan provided cross-border terrorism was stopped. India's Minister for External Affairs Jaswant Singh, when asked also ruled out any scope for India compromising on its demand that the dialogue could only be renewed after Pakistan had stopped cross-border terrorism in Jammu and Kashmir.[257] By the end of 1999 cross-border terrorism assumed new dimensions. It became very active in Jammu and Kashmir as even military posts inside India began to be attacked by armed terrorists. In December an Indian Airlines flight from Kathmandu to Delhi was hijacked by five armed men and in a high voltage drama New Delhi had to release three of the militants detained in Indian jails.

In the meantime after a long gap of 22 years Bill Clinton, the President of the United States of America paid a visit (March 19-25, 2000) to the South Asian region including India and Pakistan and talked with them on the issue of Kashmir. In course of the visit Clinton met Vajpayee on 21 March and discussed with him several aspects of Indo-US relations. The talks were held in the background of the killing of 36 Sikhs in Kashmir Valley by Pakistan sponsored terrorists. The United States, in a significant shift came out in clear support of India's stand that the dialogue with Pakistan could resume only if the Line of Control is respected and cross-border terrorism is ended. Bill Clinton made a nearly five-hour stopover in Pakistan on 25 March and in a televised address to the Pakistani People told emphatically to stop cross-border terrorism, create conditions for resumption of Indo-Pak dialogue and warned Islamabad of more isolation if it continued to support violence. Earlier Clinton in his talks with Pervez

Musharraf, firmely rejected his demand for American mediation on Kashmir issue. We (the US) can not and will not mediate or resolve the dispute in Kashmir. Only you and India can do that through dialogue. I hope you will be able to met the difficult challenges we have discussed today. The remarks made by the American President had frustrated Pakistani efforts to gain Kashmir through violence and General Pervez Musharraf's India policy had not convinced the US that Kashmir constituted the centrality of Indo-Pak feuds.[258] At the moment it became clear that the stark truth must also be faced-there is no military solution to Kashmir.

Contradictory position of India and Pakistan over the issue of Kashmir continued further and there was no policy change on Pakistan's part. For the nationalist establishment in Pakistan, Kashmir has always been a part of the unfinished agenda of partition. Pakistan has, in fact, remained incomplete without Kashmir. Annexing Kashmir is part of the nationalist agenda in Pakistan. The keepers of this agenda are the armed forces. A military government is therefore the very last one that can be expected to give it up. The nationalists' obsession with Kashmir has led Pakistan to the classic error of strategic overreach.[259] General Pervez Musharraf, the new ruler of Pakistan, in an interview to Doordarshan urged Vajpayee and the Indian government to enter into talks with him over Kashmir and to give it primacy over other issues. He pointed out, again very reasonably, that Kashmir was the only conflict between India and Pakistan. All other disputes were merely irritants. In a way Musharraf rejected India's equally reasonable demand that Pakistan cease to allow Islamic militants to cross the border to wage a proxy war in Kashmir before resuming talks. On the contrary he asserted that Pakistan would continue to help the freedom fighters in Kashmir. It, and indeed all Muslims, had a moral obligation to do so.[260] He also reiterated that if India responded to the proxy war by attacking Pakistan it would use nuclear weapons if it felt this was necessary to safeguard its national integrity.

On the other the new Indian government headed by Atal Bihari Vajpayee appeared to have changed the traditional policy over Kashmir and made the issue dialogue-centric. For the last six decades Kashmir has posed the single biggest challenge to India's security. Far from blocking or containing that challenge, New Delhi has been damaging its interests through its own inaptness. India's distinguishing trait is that it does not learn from mistakes. So, being unmindful of even the recent past India has embarked on a new experiment in Kashmir without undertaking any study or examining the consequences of another failure. The latest show in policy signals a fundamental shift in India's Kashmir posture. It tends support to the Pakistani contentions India has publicly disavowed : That Kashmir is the core problem; that its resolution holds the key to sub continental peace; and that a potential settlement demands a third party role.[261] Till date India's Kashmir policy has been guided by the Simla Agreement signed in 1972 between the two countries.

In July 2000, the Hizb-ul-Mujahideen (HUM), the leading Kashmiri group resisting India's armed forces, unilaterally offered a truce. Vajpayee, as part of new, accepted the offer and agreed to negotiate outside the framework of the Indian Constitution. The truce broke down when India rejected the HUM's insistence on including Pakistan in the negotiations. The same year in November India took the peace initiative to deal with the Kashmir problem, beginning with the declaration of unilateral ceasefire. Further in April 2001 New Delhi nominated the former defence minister and present deputy chairman of the Planning Commission K. C. Pant, as chief of negotiator. He was authorised to hold discussions on behalf of the government with all groups and segments of the people of Kashmir who were interested in a peaceful solution.[262] Vajpayee's had taken a definite initiative and his November move signifies three things – first, India genuinely believes that a solution has to be achieved through political negotiations with the people of Jammu and Kashmir; second, India accepts the need for a discussion with Pakistan to find a durable solution to the problem, and third, India wishes to continue the dialogue despite the terrorist violence perpetrated by secessionists.[263]

In the hope of major breakthrough on the issue of Kashmir in July 2001 Vajpayee invited Musharraf for talks in India in Agra which is also known as the Agra Summit. At the juncture the Government of India's Kashmir policy was severally criticized for its dilemmas. Earlier the government had announced a unilateral ceasefire to exploit the desire for peace among the people of Kashmir so that the ordinary citizens would recognise that India was sincere and hardliners would disown Pakistan and talk to us. Then later suddenly the government called off the cease-fire explaining that militants had continued to kill Indian soldiers but the simple fact was that the violence had not stopped, the people of Kashmir had not recognised India's sincerity and the Hurriyat were still taking orders from Islamabad. And then general Pervez Musharraf was invited to visit India. These all showed a mockery of our claim that we can settle the Kashmir issue internally and that Pakistan has no locus-standi. By linking the end of the ceasefire to the invitation to Musharraf, we have, in effect conceded that we can not solve the Kashmir problem without the involvement of Pakistan. Islamabad is still arming the militants but we are quite willing to talk to Musharraf.

On Kashmir we have one short-term policy goal and one long-term priority. The short-term goal is an end to Pakistan-sponsored terrorism. There is nothing in Musharraf's record to suggest that he will agreed to that. The Kashmir militancy is his own trump card, the only way of ensuring that Kashmir remains an international talking point and Pakistan becomes integral to any solution. There is no way that he will abandon this card. On the other the long-term policy goal is the speculation that Islamabad would accept the Line of Control as the international border. But, in fact no Pakistani government can concede that Kashmir is part of India and content itself with only Pak-Occupied Kashmir or Azad Kashmir. Not only will the government not allow this but public opinion in Pakistan had been whipped into such a frenzy about the atrocities being committed in Kashmir, that Pakistan will never accept a situation where Pakistan accepts that Kashmir is a part of India for all time to come. However, in between the apprehensions Prime Minister Atal Bihari Vajpayee assured an all party meeting, a gathering of 37 Parliamentary Parties, that the government would not make any concessions on Kashmir at the Agra summit. In a pre-visit all party meeting Vajpayee reiterated, 'Jammu and Kashmir is an issue linked to India's sovereignty and integrity. He rejected Pakistan's attempts to paint Kashmir as the 'core issue' of the talks. He stressed that India has never accepted religion as the basis of the partition of the country.[264] The Prime Minister also assured that all the discussions on Kashmir will be within the framework of the Indian Constitution, the Simla Agreement and the Lahore Declaration.

Pervez Musharraf's India visit that followed the Agra Summit was a total failure on the issue of Kashmir as revealed by Prime Minister Atal Bihari Vajpayee at the end of his reply in the Rajya Sabha on his July 24 statement on the Agra summit. He reiterated that dialogue with Pakistan would continue and we have been assured that Pakistan will raise the Kashmir issue at such forums. At the sametime he warned Islamabad that if it thought it could pressurise India by abetting terrorism in Jammu and Kashmir, the talks would not continue 'Talks and terrorist violence can not go together. In the Rajya Sabha Vajpayee held Pervez Musharraf responsible for his constant reference to the Kashmir issue, 'Musharraf was not prepared to discuss anything except Kashmir. He talks of the will of the people of Kashmir. But it was Pakistan which did not give the people of Kashmir freedom to decide which country they should join. Our position is strong and justified.The people of Kashmir have merged with India as per the Constitution. Musharraf was not prepared to discuss cross-border terrorism, and that was another for the deadlock at Agra.'[265] In nutshell, Musharraf reiterated broadly two thigns. One, till the Kashmir problem was resolved there could be no lasting peace in the subcontinent. Two, India must show a big-brotherly attitude in its dealings with smaller neighbours like Pakistan.

In post-Agra period it was widely believed that if Kargil was a failure of the Indian military leadership to assess the gathering hostile clouds over the area, the Agra fiasco was on account of the failure of our political leadership to gauge the mode of the team from across and prepare accordingly. Unfortunately, there was a complete failure on the part of the Indian side to understand him before and after Kargil. The Indian leadership and establishment as well did not visualise the three important developments that took place in Pakistani Prime Minister Nawaz Sharif to engage with India on a host of issues without undermining the centrality of the Kashmir dispute. Two, Pakistan's failure to do a Siachen on India in Kargil. Three, the coup by the Pakistani army which replaced Sharif with Musharraf. In addition Indian side was also blamed for not dealing with plainspeak required from our side.[266] For example there was no use harping on Kashmir not being a disputed area. The whole world knows that is a disputed-how else on earth is there an LoC and not a border. Our stand should be that what is disputed is not just Kashmir but the composite State of Jammu and Kashmir,which includes not just the Jammu and Ladakh region, but also Pakistan occupied Kashmir and Northern Areas and even some areas ceded to China. With India accepting that Jammu and Kashmir is disputed, it should reiterate its decision to solve the problem by peaceful means. This can be done only by putting an end to violence of all kinds. And it is at this stage that India could talk about cross-border terrorism. Then acceptance of Kashmir as the core issue and stoppage of cross-border or cross LoC-terrorism bring us to the third stage and at the point India could state that it has no problem in resolving the Kashmir dispute as per the wishes and aspirations of the people. But against the people of Jammu and Kashmir include not just of the Valley but also the people of other areas-including Jammu and Ladakh.

As there was no progress at Agra summit relating to the issue of Jammu and Kashmir between the two countries Islamabad, on its part, continued the terrorist activities. In October 2001 there was a devastating terrorist attack on the Kashmir Assembly in Srinagar in which 38 people were killed. The incident followed a request by Farooq Abdullah, the Chief Minister of India-administered Kashmir, to the Indian government to launch a war against militant training camps across the border in Pakistan. In succession another terrorist attack was made on December 13, 2001, on the pillar of Indian democracy, the Indian Parliament, which India said was orchestrated by Pakistani agents. These two incidents, and the last one in particular, had changed the political and strategic dimensions between India and Pakistan. It led to a dramatic build-up of troops along the Indo-Pakistan border, military exchanges and raised fears of a wider conflict. India deployed its armed forces along the border and moved missiles to where they could be launched against Pakistan. Islamabad responded in similar fashion.

In between the events on September 11, 2001, a terrorist attack was made on the World Trade Centre and Pentagon in the US that resulted in a shift in all geo-political dynamics-international, regional, and local. The suicidal attack brought a rapprochement between Pakistan and the West. The US response to the September 11 attacks confronted the political leaderships of both Pakistan and India with unique challenge and opportunities. Pakistan had to quickly choose whether it would become an adversary of the US and risk the expected consequences, or side with it, and confront its own Islamic fundamentalist allies in Pakistan and Afghanistan.[267] Musharraf's decision to support the American war on terror after the attacks strengthened his domestic position considerably.

Despite facing stiff opposition from the religious lobby, he boldly promised to curb Islamic militancy and restore Pakistan's image as a moderate member of the international comity of nations.[268] In the changed circumstances Pakistan is an ally of the US in the war against terrorism and Musharraf has agreed publicly in his January 12, 2002, address to the nation to wage the war domestically and make the choice which the US and the democratic world wants him to make. Thus, in the eyes of West and particularly the US once again Pakistan emerged as a frontline state in the latest US assault on Afghanistan as Pakistan had now the chance to improve its economy and rehabilitate itself. Sanctions imposed on Pakistan and India after the nuclear explosions of 1998, and Pakistan's military coup of 1999 were recinded.

India watched the developments relating to Pakistan with concern. For the first time, India found the opportunity to categorise all Islamist resistance to Indian armed forces in Kashmir as terrorism, and it wanted endorsement for its efforts to crush them and the US did declare multiple Islamist groups to be terrorist organisations. On the other despite its alliance with the US against the terrorism, Islamabad continued to highlight the issue of Jammu and Kashmir and get India pressurised to solve the problem in Pakistan's favour. Kashmir, Musharraf told his people and the world community, runs in Pakistan's blood and that the country would never give it up.[269] If Pakistan's understanding with the US on terror aspects strengthened, Musharraf may find many clever ways to ensure their transfer to Indian hands, and then the Pakistani leader would press for a dialogue on Kashmir preferably under international supervision. Since Kashmir is his current great interest, Musharraf will stretch out the negotiating process to extract the maximum diplomatic leverage he can with the US help.

Keeping the above strategy in view the Pakistani dictator appeared keen to resume talking Kashmir and also so confident of the strength of his post-September 11 equation with the US, that he is laying down markers, as though negotiations with India on Kashmir have already begun. His statement that converting the LoC in Jammu and Kashmir into an international boundary is not acceptable to Pakistan should be viewed in this background. It implied that Musharraf would like to settle for nothing less than all or at the very least, a substantial part of the Muslim-majority Kashmir Valley. In order to invigorate his diplomatic stance, the Musharraf's regime had also created a National Kashmir Committee charged with international lobbying and creating public opinion. General Musharraf's Kashmir related efforts were intended to create the impression that he seeks a genuine dialogue.[270] Perhaps intentionally Musharraf remained unmindful to the bilateral dialogue structure jointly put in place by the two countries at Simla and carried forward through Lahore. Both these agreements are peace-oriented documents that reject war as an option, and allow for bilateral dialogue on the premise that the other side has a point of view. The ruler of Pakistan had a strong belief that he is in a strong enough position with the US and also domestically to radically transform the rules of the game and convert Kashmir into an international football to be kicked once again by the world's major players so that they may help Pakistan score a goal.

However, from the analysis of ground realities and Indian points of view Pakistan's hope was totally misplaced. Even in post-cold war phase international life does not run to do the bidding of any single power, however influential. If this were not the case, many long pending issues would have already been settled to the sole satisfaction of the principal powers. What was true was that Musharraf was far less confident a leader than he was before September 11 and December 13. He is fighting for survival on the domestic front with his back to the wall. The unholy nexus which threw up the *Jehadi* monster was in some danger of being rupture. In order to save it Musharraf was desperately drumping up the so-called Kashmir cause. Operationally too Pakistan possessed a much weaker hand than before now that most of the *tanzeems'* have been curbed at for now at the US pressure. By suppressing the extremist elements in the government, he has sent a strong message about his stand on terrorism. But, he has no or very less control on some of the government organs in Pakistan which wholeheartedly supports and nurtures terrorist and extremist groups.

Continuing deep clouds in India-Pakistan relations were minimized as a result of the Ceasefire Agreement signed between the two countries on November 23, 2003. Bilateral dialogue reached a new height between them when President Pervez Musharraf met Indian Prime Minister Atal Bihari Vajpayee. It was a four year ceasefire agreement along the international border, the Line of Control and the Actual Ground Position Line in Jammu and Kashmir which took effect from November 27th. Leaving out minor skirmishes along the borders and intrusion of terrorists across the border, the usually volatile border between India and Pakistan, for the first time after the birth of these two nations tasted a lull of peace along the Kashmir borders. The diplomatic lull that ensured after Operation Parakram started to thaw. However, the Indian way at present, ahead was : restore relations to pre December 13 levels, end cross border terrorism (CBT), dismantle terrorist infrastructure, pick up the Lahore Memorandum of Understanding (MoU), adopt new Confidence Building Measures (CBMs) and reinvigorate old ones, and create conditions for the resumption of dialogue.[271]

The year 2004 started on a happy note in Indo-Pak relations. In January both the nations exchanged their annual lists of nuclear facilities. The 12th SAARC Summit which was held in the same month in Islamabad ushered in prospect and President Musharraf, while meeting the Indian leadership mentioned, 'We will have to deal with the extremists strongly. Pakistan has taken a number of measures and will take more steps to curb extremism. In May 2004 a foreign secretary level meeting of India and Pakistan was held in Islamabad in which a five point agenda was initiated and a path was drawn which would normalise relations between the two countries. It is difficult to expect an early solution of various India-Pakistan disputes, including differing perceptions on Jammu and Kashmir however, continuance of dialogue between them is right direction that would herald an era of civil society where prosperity, peace and happiness would receive utmost priority.

Terrorism and Reactions Abroad

Whenever, there is a terrorist attack, the fall guy is, rightly Pakistan, who has sheltered, trained and protected terrorists for the last over three decades. Whatever government may be in position in Pakistan, they have been following the policy of making 1000 cuts on India, repeatedly, so that it bleeds to extinction, by itself. Irrespective of the fact, whether it an army or a civilian ruler, they have been following a consistent anti-India policy. The question that is being debated all over, is that what are options to deal with the terrorism. Whenever there is a major terrorist attack, including the Kargil (1999) and the latest on Mumbai (November 26, 2008) one solution, which is always trouted is the war and to finish off the terrorist camps in Pakistan.[272] But once a war is started, then it is a no hold war, as each side would like to use is arsenal, including nuclear weapons to the maximum effect. There are no rules of game in the war, that one would fight only a conventional war and use only small weapons.

The monster of political violence in the form of terrorism has struck almost the whole of the world. The West and the rest – all reel under its impact. The fundamentalist militant groups and their activities have spread to several countries, including the world's mightiest power. Today it exists in many forms – bomb explosions, assassinations of selected people and indiscriminate killings, blackmailing and hijacking are only some of these.[273] India has lived under the shadow of cross-border terrorism and has seen and experienced it. The porous border, free flowing information and modern means of communication, all have made cross border terrorism an easy game. India shares 3310 km of land border with Pakistan. The border is most valuable along the whole length of the Punjab and Kashmir. In the case of Kashmir only 200 km of the border is demarcated with Line of Control (LoC) extending for another 790 km. These physical features make it easy for terrorists to infiltrate into Kashmir.[274] The unending proxy war in Kashmir is not only a threat to India's security but also a challenge to India's dignity as well as her credibility in the international circle.

The Islamist orientation of insurgency in Kashmir became more pronounced after the extremist and terrorist organisations like Hizbul Mujahideen, Jamiat-ul-Mujahideen, Harkat-ul-Ansar, Lashkar-e-Taiba, Markaz Dawa-ul-Irshad, which launched a religious crusade against the non-Muslim minorities, have been publicly taking pride for killing Hindus in the name of Jihad. The possibility of establishing a new Islamic Caliphate running from Kashmir to Pakistan through Afghanistan, Iran and Central Asia was being discussed by the Islamist extremist groups in Kashmir at a time when the Soviet troops had withdrawn from Afghanistan and the Muslim Central Asian Republics emerged as independent states following the disintegration of USSR. They were echoing the ideas of the Amir (Chief) of Jammat-i-Islami, Pakistan, Qazi Hussain Ahmed, who speaking on Kashmir Solidarity day in Rawalpindi in February 1992 declared that, 'a great Islamic state, spreading from Kashmir to Central Asia would emerge after the independence of Kashmir.[275] It is against this backdrop that there emerged close linkage between the Islamist insurgents from Kashmir and the Afghan Mujahideen with the pan-Islamic ideology binding them together. That thousand of such Kashmiri militants infiltrated to Pakistan and Afghanistan to undergo training in arms and guerilla warfare, with some of them later fighting alongside the Afghan Mujahideen lent new dimensions to the ongoing militancy in Kashmir.[276] Now the insurgency in Kashmir was not only losing its indigenous character, but was also being simultaneously taken over by the Islamist radicals and Afghan and Pak mercenaries as part of the new Pakistani strategy.

In the background of above considerations and strategy on Pakistan's part relations between the two had undergone a sea change when they exploded nuclear devices in May-June 1998. After the explosion Nawaz Sharif, the Prime Minister of Pakistan, reiterated that Pakistan was ready to have a non-aggression pact with India but after just settlement of Kashmir dispute. In post-nuclear phase violent and terrorist activities of Islamabad continued and the militants mostly from Afghanistan and Pakistan find it easier to shoot and kill the people in the mountainous parts of Jammu and Kashmir region. Pakistan's ISI wanted to involve the Jammu region in violence to show the international community that the entire Jammu and Kashmir was disturbed – to strengthen its points of plebiscite in the state.[277]

Almost at the sametime the *fidayeen* phase of insurgency commenced in terrorism as an additional feather and remain active in various regions for years. Three points may be made about this phase in Kashmir.[278] First, the use of suicidal tactics as a weapon of war is neither novel nor the monopoly of militant Muslims. Second, it is true that the main ideologues and practitioners of suicidal warfare in Kashmir war are radical Islamist groups of Pakistani provenance, it however, was not exclusively a cross-border phenomenon, but rather was the product of the incendiary infusion of the ideology and tactics of trans-national Islamist militancy into a brutalized, desperate local environment – that is, of a conjunction of internal and external factors. Third, that its most spectacular and most publicized attacks have been directed against such high profile targets as the Indian army's cantonment and operational headquarters at different places.

In the years following the *fidayeen* phase and even earlier thousands of Islamist terrorists have been pushed inside Kashmir, and to facilitate the infiltration of Islamist mercenaries, Pakistani forces resort to firing at Indian pickets along the LoC, to divert attention and to provide cover to the armed intruders. The pattern of Islamist mercenary activities in Jammu and Kashmir during the past few years suggest that their infiltration and terrorist operations have increased both in breadth and intensity, with the corresponding decline in the local support and popularity of militant groups in Kashmir. The Islamist mercenaries have extended their operations from Kashmir to Poonch in Himachal Pradesh, signals Pakistan's strategy of terrorising and forcing out the minorities.

As a result of Islamabad's strategy India had experienced more terrorist violence than any other country. There have been many attacks by these terrorists on the innocent people travelling in buses or on pilgrimage to Amarnath. There have also been suicidal attacks on the residential quarters of army personnel. No one considered to be hostile to the terrorists' interest is spared. By creating terror in the minds of local people these terrorists want to send the message that they consider Indian authorities feeble and incompetent. They mislead the youth often using Islam to spread hatred against other communities. They provide these misguided youths with arms and give them training in the use of these arms.[279] Many foreign mercenaries are also paid to carry on subversive activities in India. In order to gain popular support, the terrorists try to discredit the government by provoking it to adopt counter-measures, preferably repressive ones. This creates public disaffection and alienation. When such conditions are maintained for a long time they can be exploited by the terrorists. This gives them psychological and political advantage.

The terrorist attack on the World Trade Centre and Pentagon in the US on 11 September 2001 and launching of operation enduring freedom, it became obvious that the US is committed to stay in Pakistan and support the Pak President in his efforts to fight terrorism domestically and reform Pak Madrassas which have been churning out Mujahideen and Taliban. This development has far reaching implications for India, the sub-continent, and the region. Important geo-political developments have taken place on the sub-continent and on America's war on terrorism.

For the people of this region, such a situation would bear a disturbing resemblance to that which unfolded in 1980 after the Soviet invasion of Afghanistan. The US would be fighting a war in that benighted country and forced to depend heavily upon Pakistan for the success of its campaign. Throughout the Afghan civil war, the Taliban remained Pakistan's proteges. In his book on the Taliban, Ahmed Rashid estimated that, by 1998, no fewer than 80,000 Pakistanis had fought beside the Taliban in Afghanistan and returned to Pakistan.[280] In addition Pakistan contains a large number of battle hardened *jehadis* who have strong fraternal links with the Taliban. In fact the Taliban are products of extreme Deobandi Madrassas in Pakistan. Their spiritual mentor is the Jamiat-ul-Ulema-e-Islam (JUI), a quintessentially Pakistani religious organization.

General Musharraf, the ruler of Pakistan knew it all and first he did try for a bargain on Kashmir, but was politely ignored. If the campaign in Afghanistan becomes protracted, the US dependence on logistical support from Pakistan will increase. This could restore some of Pakistan's bargaining power. And if Musharraf fails, a significant American presence in Pakistan will rule out any possible use of the military option by India in the face of mounting *jehadi* assault in Kashmir. That will embolden the *jehadis* and their ISI backers. As US dependence increases and links get established between the Pentagon and the Pakistan army, a pro-Pakistan lobby will emerge once more in Washington and the tendency to turn a blind eye towards Kashmir will grow stronger.

Pervez Musharraf was to India what Osama bin Laden was to the United States – an architect of terrorism. In India those who expected that Pakistan, source of cross-border terrorism, would be a prime target of the US war against terror have been disappointed within a month of the Pentagon mishappening. On October 1, 2001, the brutal attack on the Jammu and Kashmir Assembly complex by a suicide squad of JeM was launched. This attack had a direct linkage with Pakistan's volatile situation emanating from *jehadi* violent demonstrations against Pakistan's decision to make common cause with US against the Taliban. Having joined the US in its fight against terrorism, General Musharraf needed as rarely before to pacify the *jehadis* and demonstrate his commitment to Kashmir.[281] It was also an indirect warning to India about joining any global war against terrorism. In response after many deaths in Jammu and Kashmir, Indian

Prime Minister Atal Bihari Vajpayee complained to Bush about Pakistan's role. In the context of Pakistan- supported cross-border terrorism in Jammu and Kashmir, the US did nothing more than listing the LeT and the JeM as foreign terrorist organizations. In a clear way Pakistan was playing a double game – helping the US offensive while trying to ensure that their old Taliban allies have a prominent role in post-war government. At the moment the biggest Indian foreign policy challenge was to ensure that the new US-Pak partnership does not work against India's interests in the way that the first US-Pak alliance did.

New Delhi's no clear and firm policy to tackle the issues related to terrorism was, in a way, encouraged the extremists to repeat the devastating history. On October 13, 2001, a terrorist attack on the Indian Parliament was made by the Islamic fundamentalist groups which was followed by the deployment of armed forces of both sides on the border had once again increased tension between India and Pakistan. Less than a year ago the militants belonging to Lashkar-e-Tayebba had stormed the Red Fort at New Delhi. Both Red Fort and Parliament House are a monument of the country's democratic transition and any aggression displayed in the precincts of these two complexes are hitting at the heart of the country's sovereign character.[282] The incident should serve as an eye opener for both the government as well as some opposition groups that terrorism in India is a reality which needs to strongly dealt with. For that a unified and a determined response is a pre-requisite and the entire nation should see this act as an assault on India's sovereignty. In fact India can learn a lot from the methodical, determined manner. America is waging its war on terrorism, especially the way it has created national heroes from the tragedy, the political unity it has shown, and the unanimous description of the suicide hijackers as terrorists and barbarians by US commentators. Contrast is the US and Indian policies on terrorism. America believes not in negotiations but in capturing terrorists, dead or alive. Our policy makers hope that the United States would fight our terrorism. But the reality is that the Americans are interested only in fighting their terrorism. As earlier on September 18, the White House had clarified that the US policy is to 'eliminate' terrorism around the world but only when it threatens the United States'.[283] Clearly now onwards Indian foreign policy appeared on a rough patch. Far from adopting an equidistance strategy, we should make it clear that combating terrorists is as much our first priority as it is of the US despite our opposition to an American aim of building a unipolar world.

As a result of the terrorist attack on the Indian Parliament New Delhi had hardened its attitude toward Islamabad and tension on both sides of the border increased. It followed the deployment of armed forces on borders as well as Line of Control and alarmed the world including Pakistan. The USA and the UK, in particular, exerted pressure on Islamabad to step up action on terrorists. American President George Bush asked General Pervez Musharraf to make a clear statement to the world that he intends to crackdown on terror and take further measures to help defuse the Indo-Pak situation. He expressed the belief that if he does that and continues to do what he is doing, it will provide relief on a situation that is still serious.[284] In line, Tony Blair, the British Prime Minister also reminded the commitment Pakistani dictator had made in front of him about rejecting terrorism in all its forms. But a mistake which not only the US and Britain but also some of India's neighbours have made is to think that a return to the table will automatically defuse the situation. That would have been possible if Pakistan was a normal country engaged in normal statecraft.[285] By the sametime India received a moral victory in the first week of January 2002 when in the 11th meeting of SAARC summit held in Kathmandu, Indian Prime Minister raised the issue of cross-border terrorism and the seven-member group declaration had endorsed India's position on the issue. The heads of state and government reiterated their support to the UN Security Council Resolution 1373, which makes difference to various forms of terrorism and affirmed their determination to redouble efforts collectively as well as individually to prevent and suppress terrorism in all its forms and manifestations. Almost simultaneously India's Home Minister L. K. Advani paid a visit to the US and during his meetings with Colin Powell, Secretary of State, told that India would not tolerate another betrayal on Pakistan's part.

In view of the growing pressure by major powers of the world and escalating tension on borders and Line of Control, Pakistan as an ally of the US war against the terrorism, Musharraf had agreed publicly in his speech of January 12, 2002, to wage the war domestically and make the choice which the US and democratic world wants him to make but at the sametime repeated his usual formula on the Kashmir issue and termed the problem as being part of every Pakistanis blood. Reacting to the speech India's Defence Minister George Fernandes ruled out the pull back of its troops from the border with Pakistan unless Islamabad ends cross-border terrorism. He said, 'We have had Musharraf's word. Now we wait for his deed and reminded that the ultimate purpose of Pakistani action must be to end cross-border terrorism for all time.[286] As understanding between them on border issue deteriorated further both the USA and the UK rather warned the Pakistani establishment not to play game about terrorism and asked Islamabad to hand over 20 terrorists and criminals wanted by India or try and convict them in Pakistan and added that this is very important to help reduce tension between the two countries. Harry Thomas, director-in-charge of South Asia in President George W. Bush's National Security Council pointed out that the terrorist attack on the Jammu and Kashmir Assembly and the Indian Parliament changed the whole Indo-Pak situation and was of the view that our highest priority right now is to keep India and Pakistan from going to war. A war is unthinkable and would be devastating for the global campaign against terrorism. The US had also rejected Islamabad's persistent demand for a plebiscite in Kashmir in accordance with the UN resolution.

In July 2002 when a war-like situation approached India committed itself to not attack on Pakistan in return for US assurance that Islamabad would cut loose the *jehadis* in Kashmir. Although New Delhi was not certain whether Washington will be ready to apply sufficient pressure on Pervez Musharraf, Colin Powell's message that Pakistan would be asked to act against those organizations which perpetrated the Jammu massacre, it had only partly abated New Delhi's concerns. Previously Pervez Musharraf was regarded as a tinpot dictator of a failed state whose chief exports were heroin and Jehad, was suddenly transformed into the respected leader of a frontline state in the global war against terror. At the heart of the problem is that India and the rest including the US and UK share different assessment of Musharraf's motives. New Delhi believes that Musharraf's promises to the US were largely tactical. The general would be expected to try and escape from them as soon as Washington looked the other way. The solution : Unremitting pressure on Pakistan. But the West takes the view Musharraf recognises that the *jehadis* must be brought to heel. However, he holds on to them because they are the only way he can bring India to hold a dialogue on Kashmir. The solution : Broker a deal exchanging an end to terror in return for dialogue.

Today terrorism all over the world and especially in Pakistan is blending with drug trafficking that feeds terrorists and is taking the shape of fully-fledged narco-aggression. It is in command of huge financial and material resources. It has become well organized and globally connected system that menaces the life of millions of people of the world. Continuing terrorist activities against India by way of cross border terrorism and several violent incidents of Pakistan itself is an indication that the latter is the main sanctuary of the dregs of the Taliban, Al-quaeda, the Chechens, the Uighurs, and the South East Asian terrorists who had escaped from Afghanistan after the US military offensive started on October 7, 2001,as well as of the *jehadis* operating in Jammu and Kashmir and other parts of India.

The *jehadi* training infrastructure previously located in Afghanistan is now located in Pakistani territory, mainly in the Federally-Administered Tribal Area (FATA), the North West Frontier Province (NWFP), Balochistan, Pak-occupied Kashmir (PoK) and the Northern Area-Gilgit and Baltistan.[287] The military regime of Pervez Musharraf continues to be reluctant to act effectively against the terrorist infrastructure in its territory. While the training to foreign *jehadis* in the Afghan camps used to be imparted by Arab and Chechan instructors, the training in the present Pakistani camps is being imparted largely by Pakistanis.[288] In the circumstances peace in relation to India and Pakistan can not be created by dramatic gestures or a few meetings between the top leaders, but through gradually increased confidence building measures. India and Pakistan have a long way to go before they can create a win-win situation on any of their problems. The best hope is that both countries can agree to create an atmosphere of trust and confidence : to live and let live.

Economic

In October 1999 when Atal Bihari Vajpayee in India and General Pervez Musharraf in Pakistan took over the reigns of administration relatively the economy of Pakistan was on the verse of total collapse.

Most economists agreed that there was no quick-fix solution to Pakistan's grave economic problems and they felt, the coup leaders would have to take some very painful measures to resuscitate a near dead economy. As part of its populistic programme for an economic revival General Musharraf promised to clean up Pakistan's corrupt elite, rebuild national confidence and morale, revive the economy, strengthen the crumbling bonds between the four provinces that make up the country and cleanse institutions to install 'real democracy' before the army relinquishes power. What the country needs is a crusade against wrong doing without the fear that it is going to be an unpopular move. Tax increases, raising electricity and gas tariffs, as well as petroleum prices will just be the beginning of any meaningful economic reforms.

One major step in the reform of the economy was the normalization of relations with India. Pervez Musharraf managed to bring in a major policy change in Pakistan's ties with India. As a result both India and Pakistan has been able to benefit from the growth of cross border trade. Under the new positive economic policy towards India, Musharraf gave the go ahead to talks on building a gas pipeline from Iran, through Pakistan to India. The project was estimated to generate dollar 700 million per year in transit fee for Pakistan. As a gesture of goodwill Musharraf pleaded in favour of the gas pipeline and on the request of Iranian authorities, ordered a re-examination of the case and lifted Pakistan's objection to its extension to India. In reply to criticism by the Islamic fundamentalist parties, he said that while Pakistan would continue to reject proposals for the normalization of the economic relations with India, it would treat the pipeline issue as a stand-alone issue without linking it to the Kashmir dispute. He justified his decision on the following grounds. First, Pakistan would need additional energy for diversifying its industrial capability and for stepping up production. Second, a gas pipeline required huge investment and no foreign company would be prepared to make that kind of investment for selling gas in Pakistan alone which would not bring adequate returns on the investment. Only its extension to India would make it profitable for the investors. Third, at a time when Pakistan's economy was in a state of collapse, it badly needed the US dollar 800 million per annum offered by Iran as transit fee for the gas.

Despite doing the best Musharraf could to revamp the economy of Pakistan in comparison to India and make Islamabad a economic power like the military one, he was not satisfied with the state of affair prevailing in the country. Three days before the announcement of the federal budget in June 2001, the ruler in a televised programme told the nation, 'Pakistan was a military power but its economic power was not commensurate with its military strength. Pakistan's survival depends on its economic revival.[289] In the situation, Shaukat Aziz, the Finance Minister of Pakistan, announced a freeze on the defence budget at last year's level. It was ostensibly first step towards this economic revival. The minister claimed that the step would not affect the operational side of the armed forces, but considering the 20% devaluation of the Pakistani currency and the 5% inflation rate, it actually amounts to a sizeable cut. He added that Pakistan's economy is a mess. The nation has been living beyond its means for more than three decades, and its dependence on foreign aid is a legendary.

In fact Pakistan has been in the trap of foreign debt for decades. Even recently between 1988 and 1998 Pakistan signed three bailouts with the IMF and the World Bank, a fourth has been hammered out by the present regime. Yet another one, a Poverty Reduction and Growth Facility (PRGF) is on the anvil. The perception that Pakistan is being kept afloat by the IMF and World Bank has gained ground. The continuation of the policy of 'borrowing from Peter to pay Paul' was practised by the regimes of Benazir Bhutto and Nawaz Sharif which Musharraf considered as the lost decade in Pakistan's history. However, he too was not out of the label as country's external debt currently stands significant. Up to 50% of its population lives below the poverty line and has no access to basic human needs like safe drinking water, sewerage education and primary health care. The rate of literacy is one of the lowest in South Asia.[290] At the moment, Dr. Pervez Hassan, former chief economist of the World Bank, suggested Pakistan to negotiate yet another debt relief package with donors, and seek dollar 6 billion in concessional aid from the IMF and the World Bank to repay dollar 20 billion due over the next four years.

The earlier normal economic relations between India and Pakistan which were in a good condition suddenly received a jolt by nuclear explosions by both and reached at the lowest during and after Kargil war. Indians, after Kargil, have started taking greater interest in national security matters and would not be prepared to compromise on its requirements. This led to a 28% increase in the defence budget soon after the war and about 10% increase in the year 2001. But in contrast, under the tremendous economic pressure in post-Kargil phase, Islamabad was forced to cap its defence budget. The defence budget of the country was reduced by Rs. 2 billion last year. In addition economic activities between the two were adversely affected by the terrorist attack on the state assembly of Jammu and Kashmir in October 2001, followed by an attack on Indian Parliament, the same year in December.

In response to unfriendly activities on Pakistan's part India closed its bilateral trade with Islamabad through land route with effect from January 1, 2002 and the matter was also discussed in the SAARC summit held at Kathmandu. The business community of Pakistan had termed the Indian step 'unfortunate' as now they have to cough up 20 times the amount as air freight. Even the sea route would take two months as against 10 hours on land. The closure would affect trade in 600 items allowed under the SAARC agreement between the two countries.[291] The SAARC summit which was held in a tense bilateral climate emphasised the need to reconvene the Independent Commission on Poverty Alleviation and felt the relations between India and Pakistan as key factor to the success of SAARC idea. Often, progress in economic and other areas has been held hostage to India-Pakistan relations. The failure in implementing such eminently sensible ideas as creating a South Asian Preferential or free trade area have remained a non-starter for the same reasons.[292]

In spite of strained India-Pakistan relations in respect of politics and defence, economy in general and trade through different routes, in particular remained on the top of the agenda. Even in this period India's export to Pakistan and its imports from Pakistan has been growing at an average rate of 62% and 65% since 2002-03. It was the year in which the government had taken a lot of initiatives for increased bilateral trade. Earlier the share of Pakistan's share to India in total exports rose from 0.5% in 2001-02 to 1.8% in 2005-06. However, the balance of trade had remained in favour of India. The main commodities of exports to Pakistan include sugar, dyes, plastic and petroleum products and cotton while the main import items from Pakistan are petroleum and crude products, fruits and nuts, cotton yam and fabrics and organic chemicals. Apart from this there are vast untapped trade and investment possibilities between the two countries which need to be exploited with significant welfare gains.

After the events of September 11, 2001, Pakistan became a frontline ally of the US. It is a popular belief that the terrorist attacks on the US have in certain ways benefited Pakistan's economy as the former has promised millions of dollars in assistance, waived sanctions and granted loans to the latter as a reward for its support to the war against terrorism. It was one of the reasons that Pakistan had not cooperated India and other developing countries in their fight against the discriminatory provisions of World Trade Organization (WTO). In post-9/11 phase Islamabad's real gains were in trade. Pascal Lamy, the EU Trade Commissioner, announced on October 17, 2001, dollar 1 billion worth of trade concessions for Pakistani textiles. Washington has also put together an aid package with a large trade component.[293] The Indian trade analysts felt that they have got more than they wanted. Pakistan's foreign exchange reserves have increased nearly seven-fold and consequently, the same dependence on third country imports from India is not there. But these all are not sufficient for Pakistan and still it is as keen as it was in the past for an early implementation of the project without linking it to the Kashmir issue because its expanding economy badly needs additional energy supplies. Even in respect of oil and gas from Turkmenistan, foreign investors are not prepared to invest heavily unless there is a possibility of the pipeline being extended to India.

As a result of the change in policy the Government of India decided not to discuss the issue directly with Pakistan and the latter too had begun to identify the other areas of cooperation which could be projected as stand-alone areas. The change of attitude on Pakistan's part was expressed by Shaukat Aziz, the Pakistani Prime Minister when he visited New Delhi in November 2004. He underlined Pakistan's continuing keenness to go ahead with this project despite the lack of progress in the talks on Kashmir. The Prime Minister of Pakistan had described the pipeline project as an important confidence building measure. Another area of cooperation between the two that Aziz had identified was agriculture. In a statement he referred to cooperation in the field of agriculture between Indian and Pakistani Punjabs as next possible stand alone-area which

Pakistan would be prepared to take up without linking it to the Kashmir issue. Pakistan's agriculture has not been doing as well as that of India, forcing it to import wheat periodically. This is an area which needs to be explored intensively. In the changed atmosphere India needs to keep up psychological pressure on Pakistan for the grant of the Most Favoured Nation (MFN) status, intensify the interactions with those sections of Pakistani business community who are in favour of early normalization of economic relations and other aspects of their relations, essential to boost the economic understanding between the two countries.

Defence

The makers of India's foreign policy faced with a daunting task of choosing priorities. Its dilemma is to balance the needs of security and the needs of development. Ideally, there need not be a conflict between national and human security, since real security complies protecting the people and safeguarding the borders. But a problem does arise in a poor and developing nation like India where there is glaring disparity between economic growth and human development. Though national security is still regarded as paramount, achieving it is linked with human security. India should recognise that national security can not be achieved in a situation where people starve and arms accumulate, where military expenditure, not social expenditure rises. The basic concerns of India's foreign policy may remain the same today as what they were at the dawn of independence.[294] But the seriousness and urgency for finding a balance between development and defence necessarily needs to be focussed.

Defence since partition of the subcontinent in 1947 never took a back seat either at New Delhi or at Islamabad. Both have gone to the extent of over looking the acute case of development and have demonstrated their ability to make nuclear devices and other defence-related equipments. In India there is a popular belief amongst the elites is that any increase in India's military capacity would eventually be used to dominate other smaller South Asian states, a situation that is totally unacceptable. There are also those who believe that internal political development in Pakistan such as correcting the imbalance in the civil-military relations depends on restoration of peace in the region, which, in turn, depends on India.[295] Such perceptions have remained constant since the country's independence. Moreover, the feeling of insecurity with regard to India has been the hallmark of all regimes irrespective of whether these have been military, military dominated, or civilian regimes.

Since the roots of security problems in South Asia are indigenous, the threat perceptions are sufficiently diverse to preclude a common approach. For India the major sources of threat continue to be China and Pakistan despite the march of normalisation processes and the advent of SAARC. Similarly, for Pakistan, and to a lesser degree, for Bangladesh, Sri Lanka and even Nepal, the main threats emanate from Indian policy pursuits. Undoubtedly, India is a dominant power in the region and in consequence its policies affect the security perceptions of other regional neighbours. South Asia is one such region where the nature of regional security issues are somewhat autonomous but the involvement of great powers directly affected the military balance within the region and introduced further complications. To cope with perceived threats, nations tend to seek power hoping that power alone may generate the desired level of security. Compared to Pakistan, Indian security perceptions visualise the major threats to the region stemming from the policy options exercised by Pakistan, the Chinese policy pursuits, and the periodic domestic upheavals in Bangladesh, Sri Lanka, Nepal and Pakistan. However, at the root of regional security problems are the differing security perceptions and the consequent divergent policy pursuit of both India and Pakistan along with the lack of regional pragmatism.

With the dawn of independence Pakistan's security perception remains India-centric. Perception and orientation, in turn, have led to an approach based on two opposing ends of spectrum : confrontation punctuated by short spells of rapprochement, and seeking extra-regional partnerships that could provide Islamabad with relative strength to counter its traditional adversary. It has produced either confrontational linkages or alignments that have been sought primarily to offset problems of military inferiority versus its main adversary India. Hence Islamabad's alignments have never been proactive and, in fact, have limited to seeking military or diplomatic assistance that could bolster Pakistan's position via-a-vis New Delhi. But in both the cases– conflict or peace with India, it is the military that tends to benefit. The best example of this pertains to the Musharraf regime that initially justified its ascendance to power on the basis of its ability to uphold the Kashmir issue, which it felt was being sacrificed by the Nawaz Sharif Government. And later in 2003, it was the prospect of peace with India seemed to have bailed General Musharraf from the domestic political during the debate in the Parliament on the controversial nature of his position vis-à-vis the constitution. In nutshell, Pakistan defines its security as the ability to stave-off a military threat from India and there are two supporting pillars of this peculiar approach :

(a) building national military capability with the objective of challenging India's military might and providing for an effective defence; and

(b) searching for military-oriented alignments, which can assist primarily in dealing with New Delhi.[296]

Nuclear tests by India and Pakistan which was followed by a conventional war between the two at Kargil sector had totally changed the security context and made them defence scarced. In a radically different situation it became urgently necessary for both to abandon the mindset of yesterday in bilateral and multilateral negotiations relating to political and security concerns. For India before any serious talk of far-reaching global arms control, it has to ensure acceptance of minimum nuclear deterrence. In the sphere of deterrence still India faces three challenges in achieving its desired goals. First, the country's small reserves of weapon-grade plutonium and limited financial resources dictate that it can only have puny nuclear forces. Secondly, India has to build a credible minimum deterrent in a global environment, openly hostile to further overt weaponisation, particularly by a new nuclear weapons state. And third, India is still at some distance from acquiring the technical capacity to terminate Chinese nuclear threat and needs plug this vulnerability on a war footing.[297] On the basis of mutual deterrence established, it was hoped that India and Pakistan would settle down to hold talks and sort out the various problems.

With the nuclear explosions equating India plus one Islamabad, had hoped to settle down the serious problems of Indo-Pak relations including the issue of Jammu and Kashmir. Much before the tests Mirza Aslam Beg, former Chief of Pakistan Army, had said that minimal nuclear and missile deterrence should be kept intact as they were the cheapest options for peace and had helped maintain peace between India and

Pakistan. Dr. Abdul Qadir Khan, the Pakistani nuclear scientist had also expressed the belief after the tests on May 31, 1998 that the tests were a peace guarantor and would improve relations between India and Pakisan.[298] However, the overall picture emerging from Pakistan was not encouraging as Pakistan's Foreign Minister Gohar Ayub Khan had said that his country is getting ready to equip Ghauri missiles with nuclear warheads. He also dismissed India's offer of no first strike treaty on the plea that the strike time for missiles either way was a matter of minutes and that the question of first strike or second strike was meaningless as it would be difficult to find out who struck first.

The post-nuclear II phase witnessed a changed and charged atmosphere in relations between the two countries. The decision to launch Operation Badr, a codename for the operation, across 160 km of the Line of Control in Kargil sector was taken soon after General Pervez Musharraf took over as the Pak Army Chief in October 1998. An old contingency Plan 2 was updated, and after carrying out detailed preparations during winter, the operation was launched to coincide with the melting of snow and the opening of India's National Highway IA linking Srinagar to Leh via Kargil. The military objectives of the whole preparations were to :

(a) occupy approximately 700 sq km area on the Indian side of the LoC in Kargil-Turtuk Sector;

(b) interdict Srinagar-Kargil-Leh Road;

(c) capture Turtuk and cut off Southern and Central Parts of Siachin Glacier Sector, and

(d) intensify militants activities in Jummu and Kashmir, which had received a setback after the State Assembly and National Parliament elections in 1997-98.

The war at Kargil was preceded by a bus journey to Lahore of Atal Bihari Vajpayee, the Prime Minister of India, in February 1999. Apparently when Prime Minister Nawaz Sharif was giving warm welcome to Indian Prime Minister, secretly Pakistani regulars and other intruders were busy occupying the Kargil heights on Indian side of Line of Control as Vajpayee said later, 'while he took message of goodwill and friendship, Pakistan stabbed India at its back.[299] Within three months of the Lahore Declaration, a limited conventional war broke out between India and Pakistan in the Kargil sector. Earlier too in reply to a question George Fernandes, India's

Defence Minister, said in the Lok Sabha on March 18, 19991, 'Pakistan's ISI agents in Kargil are suspected to be behind the accuracy of Pakistani firing in the Uri-Kargil sector recently.' The picture became clear soon and the government belatedly accepted that the intrusion of Afghan militants was noticed as early as the first week of May 1999.[300]

The Pak Army, taking advantage of the terrain and the extreme climatic conditions, achieved a tactical surprise but could not cope with the subsequent Indian military reaction. The Indian military had the formidable challenge of getting the Pak intrusion vacated under the most adverse conditions of terrain. This adversity was further compounded by the political mandate that the LoC should not be violated. However, it had to maintain a strategic balance and a deterrent posture all along the Indo-Pak front on the ground, air and sea – should there be a sudden escalation. A deliberate decision was taken to continue the political and military level dialogue. The politico military strategy made it clear that although India was a victim of intrusion, and exercising maximum restraint, it was determined to get the intrusion vacated. All the calculations of Pakistan and its army in the war went completely wrong when in May 1999 Indian army, supported by the air force, launched 'Operation Vijay and finally defeated the enemy decisively. The war ended on 26 July 1999 when all Pakistani troops were finally evicted from our side of the LoC. During the war, 473 Indian soldiers were killed : Pakistani casualties were estimated to be over 700. In the background of Kargil conflict India had prepared itself to face any consequences of development in Pakistan. An event of immense significance took place in October 1999 when General Pervez Musharraf sacked the elected government of Nawaz Sharif and once again Pakistan witnessed the failure of democracy.

For the Government in India, the Pak intrusion after its Lahore initiative was a serious political setback. Kargil was an unusual aggression in as much as it was engineered largely by the dynamics of the internal power structure in Pakistan. Among the factors two were significant as having caused the aggression. First, the desire of the army to acquire renewed importance in the governance of the country. Second, the salience acquired by Islamic militants in the political system of the country through their successes in Afghanistan and their strong nexus with ISI, the army, and the political class. The Kargil war, fought at the turn of the century, has been a major turning point in Indo-Pak security relations. After Kargil India emerged from the war with enhanced capacity for negotiation and compromise while Pakistan stood with this capacity almost destroyed. It has left a deep impact. Its lessons are indeed important and are a useful input when we discuss Indo-Pak relations, or peace and stability in South Asia.

Further the tragic events of September 11, 2001 in the USA that shown that terrorism represents most serious threat to the world have also affected the security perceptions of India and Pakistan. Although the attack was not the beginning of terrorism, it however, has brought about the recognition that the issue has become a global phenomenon with links among various terrorist groups and organisations and therefore called for global response. In this context New Delhi stressed that Pakistan should dismantle its terrorist infrastructure and stop cross-border terrorism. India asserted the point that if the US wants to overcome terrorism, it must realise that the focus should be on Pakistan and not on Jammu and Kashmir and that the military fundamentalist character of states like Pakistan must change. Indian President A. P. J. Abdul Kalam and Home Minister L.K. Advani have also highlighted the issue and urged the international community to take serious note of it before it costs dearly to the world. On the other the terrorist attacks exposed America's military might, its foreign policy bankruptcy along with its unilateralist postures and expansionist designs which it had continuously nourished since the collapse of the USSR.[301] But the 11 September attacks shattered the military preponderance of America, dashed its economic might and questioned its political authority in ways which will continue to be analysed for all time to come.

In post-September 11 periods Pakistan's traditional security perception of threat from India, a rival neighbour did not seem to have changed. The recent threat was posed by non-state actors based locally appears to be a new and far more serious problem. As earlier the non-state actors or the large number of militants present within its boundaries were raised and nourished by the military establishment to fill the conventional military gap via-a-vis India. While not being able to force a military solution of Kashmir on New Delhi, the militants were viewed as a cost-effective option. The policy did not go out of control because of the involvement of these very same militants in Afghanistan and their engagement in sectarian killings inside Pakistan. General Pervez Musharraf after September 11, 2001, aimed to change only this portion of policy, except relating to militants involvement in Jammu and Kashmir.

Tension on Indo-Pak border spread as a result of militant attack on Jammu and Kashmir's State Assembly in October 2001 and later in December on Indian Parliament. In relations between the two countries the year 2002 started on a very disappointing note– Pakistan demanding the solution of Kashmir problem and India asking Islamabad to stop cross-border terrorism. The recent violent terrorist attacks sponsored by Pakistan has left India with no option but to take retaliatory action. Keeping the background of India-Pakistan relations in view New Delhi in January 2002 tested a variant of the Agni-1 missile with a range of 700 km. The launched missile was a part of the country's indigenous Integrated Guided Missile Development Programme (IGMDP) and was 'non-provocative' and not directed at any country. The new missile was expected to bridge the gap between the short-range Prithvi (150 km) and the intermediate range Agni-2 which has a range of 1500 km. Although before the test India has informed the five permanent members of the UN Security Council – US, Russia, UK, China and France along with others as Germany, Japan, EU President and Spain, the Pakistan's foreign office statement said, 'We hope the international community will take note of this Indian behaviour which is prejudicial to the pursuit of stability in our region, especially during the current situation.[302] On India's part it was said that the test has no political significance or relationship to any event. It was a well thought-out step in consonance with our security and defence postures, including our declared doctrine of no first use. India has always stressed that our missile programme is not country specific. Our aim is really to ensure that we have the indigenous capability to guarantee the credibility of our minimum nuclear deterrent.

This phase of war like situation continued for the coming days but received a halt when the United States of America exerted pressure to stop cross-border terrorism and initiate a dialogue with New Delhi. On the other the US also assured India on Pakistan's part and convinced the former to start talks with Islamabad in the interest of peace and stability in the region. In afterwards the two countries signed a four year ceasefire agreement along the international border, the Line of Control and the Actual Ground Position Line in Jammu and Kashmir on November 23, 2003. Apart from this several confidence building measures were initiated between the two countries to ease tension on borders and establish an atmosphere of peace and mutual confidence. It included the decision of India and Pakistan to establish a 'dedicated and secure' hotline to prevent misunderstandings and reduce nuclear risks.[303] The experts of India and Pakistan met in June 2004 and after talks for two days issued a seven point joint statement in which, among other things, each side reaffirmed its unilateral moratorium on conducting further nuclear explosions unless, in exercise of national sovereignty, it decides that extraordinary events have jeopardised its supreme interests. It also said that both countries would continue to engage in bilateral discussions and hold further meetings to work towards implementation of the Lahore Memorandum of Understanding reached between the two Prime Ministers in February 1999.

REGIME OF UNITED PROGRESSIVE ALLIANCE

Premiership of Manmohan Singh (22 May 2004 - 22 May 2009)

In May 2004 as a result of the general elections the BJP-led coalition lost power in India and was replaced by a coalition led by Indian National Congress whose leader Manmohan Singh became the new Prime Minister. The change of guard at New Delhi did not witness any change in its policy towards Pakistan and the earlier efforts initiated by the previous government continued further. The entire series of misunderstandings reveals how difficult it has become for governments to make radical departures of policy in the information age. Today neither the Indian nor the Pakistani government enjoys the freedom to broker deals that they would have enjoyed half a century ago. In the situation the visit of President Musharraf to India in April 2005, the opening of Munabao-Khokrapur rail link, promise to reopen trade consulate at Mumbai and Karachi, reviving of Joint Economic Commission of 1983, linking of religious places through bus route, holding of talk for Indo-Iranian gas pipeline, reduction of troops and ceasefire in Jammu and Kashmir, the launching of Srinagar-Mujaffarabad bus service, the exchange of visits by both the foreign ministers, the talks for nuclear risk reduction measures etc are the indications of changing thrust in India-Pakistan through Confidence-Building Measures (CBMs). The CBMs are regarded as the harbinger of peace. Treaties, agreement and pacts can generate confidence and create an atmosphere of peace, friendship and cooperation if they are implemented with full vigour and zeal.

Hence at the start of the new dispensation both India and Pakistan appeared seeking ways of achieving and sustaining détente with each other. Islamabad too is eager for normalization of relations, or even that such sentiments weigh with Pakistan's rulers or that they now see a danger to their power from the fanatics they had thought they could use against New Delhi.[304] After a month of government formation on June 28, 2004, the foreign secretaries of India and Pakistan met in New Delhi and issued a joint statement to mark the resumption of the dialogue. It recalled the reassurance contained in the joint press statement of January 6, 2004 and they exchanged views on carrying the process forward in an atmosphere free from terrorism and violence. In a major breakthrough the Indian Prime Minister Manmohan Singh and General Pervez Musharraf met in Newyork on September 25, 2004 and agreed to explore options. This is a quest that goes beyond a Kashmir solution. It concerns the future of Indo-Pak relations. It was the high point of the initiative in which Indian Prime Minister assured Musharraf that India would consider virtually any solution that did not involve a redrawing of boundaries in Kashmir. He apparently explained that a change of boundaries would amount to a second partition on religious lines and could upset the social balance in the country. After the meeting both emerged looking relaxed and relieved. In response to talks held between them in early October India submitted a 72-point agenda for confidence building which was later minimized to 30 points and Pakistan agreed to examine the proposals.

It followed the visits of Pakistan's Foreign Minister and Prime Minister to India. Khurshid Mahmood Kasuri, the Foreign Minister of Pakistan, although failed to unfreeze the deadlock over Kashmir, yet the meeting did, however, lead to a further easing of visa restrictions, an agreement to increase the number of crossing points and, perhaps most promising of all, an agreement by India in principle to share a gas pipeline from Iran with Pakistan, On November 23-24, 2004, Pakistani Prime Minister Shaukat Aziz paid a visit to India. After reaching New Delhi Aziz made it clear that he had not come with any concrete proposal on Kashmir, and that Musharraf had been speaking informally to a Pakistani audience in order to get a feedback. He confined the larger part of his discussions to promoting closer economic relations between the two countries. But Aziz's visit failed to come to an agreement on the opening of the Srinagar-Muzaffarabad road. India agreed that there would be no need for visas and that an entry permit on a separate paper would suffice, but insisted that this should be accompanied by a passport, as proof of identification. It also insisted that the road should be open to use by non Kashmiri from both countries who had the necessary visas. On the other Islamabad was adamant that passports should not be used and that a certificate from the district magistrate should suffice as it used to before 1953. Further as a gesture of goodwill India decided to ease visa rules for senior citizens and young persons from Pakistan with an expectation of reciprocity.[305]

Diplomatic understanding between India and Pakistan strengthened further in April 2005 when President Pervez Musharraf paid his second visit to India. At New Delhi the leaders of the two countries discussed entire gamut of Indo-Pak relations and at the end a joint statement was issued. The latest joint statement brings out a different, more collaborative spirit that has now begun to suffice the India-Pakistan diplomatic discourse. The references to the duties and obligations of one or the other party have now been replaced by shared constructs. This is all the more remarkable because each word and sentence that appears in the document had been subject to intense discussion and negotiation. As the statement observed both sides 'agreed to continue these discussions in a sincere and purposeful way.' They also jointly pledged that they would not allow terrorism to impede the peace process.[306] On the basis of subjects covered in the statement there is no wrong in assuming that the underlying theme of the agreements on expanding trade, people to people contacts and promoting more CBMs is that the two sides have finally agreed on a joint strategy of moving ahead their agenda of normalizing relations. Earlier in the same month, as a follow up of the decision taken in February 2004 in course of the visit of K. Natwar Singh, India's Minister for External Affairs to Pakistan Srinagar-Muzaffarabad bus service was started from April 7, 2005. In line India and Pakistan also resumed train services after 40 years on February 18, 2006.

Later Pranab Mukherjee, India's Minister for External Affairs paid a visit to Islamabad to invite Pakistan for the 14th SAARC Summit on 3 and 4 April. It was also aimed at to push forward the peace efforts that were a halting process due to several reasons at different times. In the past few months the two countries had come closer as India adopted a three-pronged strategy of involving Pakistan, political parties in Jammu and Kashmir and separatists in talks. During the visit, Pakistan for the first time, softened its attitude and was hopeful of resolving the Siachen issue. In response Mukherjee went a step ahead and said that all serious efforts were being made to resolve all issues. He referred to the talks held earlier between Manmohan Singh and President Pervez Musharraf which contained the theme that all issues should be discussed and that we are prepared to discuss each and every idea to find a solution.[307] In addition the two ministers agreed to liberalise visa regime in February 2007 and set up a committee of retired judges of the senior judiciary on both sides to visit jails in the two countries to ensure humane treatment of each other's nationals and expedite their release. The statements made soon after showed that the peace process is firmly on track. The two countries were willing to put terrorism at the back burner to give priority to close economic and trade links. For the first time the political and military leaders of Pakistan were talking of enduring peace and friendship between India and Pakistan. They seem to be realising that peace is essential for the survival of the two nations.

The year 2007 witnessed political instability in Pakistan that brought several changes of immense significance in the country. Political uncertainty prevailed till the formation of a duly elected democratic government. The emergency rule declared on November 3, 2007 highlighted more questions to Pakistan's political stability than providing any solution. In sequence the declaration of emergency was followed by the suspension of the Constitution, mass detentions of activists and lawyers, the clampdown on the Pakistani media, forbidden to express any opinion prejudicial to the ideology of Pakistan or its integrity and the summary removal of the feisty Chief Justice of the Supreme Court Iftikar Chaudhary who had been spiritedly resisting the attempts to curb the independence of the judiciary, were chilling signs that the dreaded days of military rule are back. The general had now been revealed in his true colours as a ruthless military dictator.[308] Further General Musharraf had stepped down from the position of being an Army Chief and had moulded himself as a civilian President on November 29, 2007. In an unprecedented event the legend of voice of democracy in Pakistan its former Prime Minister and present chairperson of Pakistan's People's Party Benazir Bhutto was assassinated in the last week of December 2007. Indian leaders in general expressed the shock and dismay over her assassination and termed the happening a negation of democracy. Expressing shock and horror Indian Prime Minister Manmohan Singh said, 'it was a reminder of the common danger that our region faces from cowardly acts of terrorism and of the need to eradicate this dangerous threat'.[209] Not only India but leaders of the world have also condemned her brutal killing.

As a result of the general elections held in Pakistan a new government of Pakistan People's Party with coalition partners was formed and its leader Yousuf Raza Gillani became the Prime Minister of the country. On his assumption Indian Prime Minister Manmohan Singh, while congratulating expressed his wish for India-Pakistan ties to become the 'best ever'. This time in particular there is more than one reason to believe that things would improve. First bilateral relations are clearly better than ever before, with more interaction between people across the border. Intellectuals, academics, think tank, and artists are increasingly talking to each other. Second the post- poll scenario in Pakistan, it is for the first time that the military is on the back- foot. As an institution the army stands to lose its credibility and hold over the polity.[310] However, even at the time the statement of Asif Ali Zardari, who later became the President of Pakistan, that a consensus exists on the Kashmir issue and that the Pakistan Army was committed to the cause in line with the aspiration of the people, made the move in positive direction almost difficult.

After the formation of a new democratic government in Pakistan its Foreign Minister Shah Mahmood Qureshi came to New Delhi in July 2008 and discussed several bilateral aspects of their relationship in a climate conducive for strengthening bilateral ties and resolving age-old dispute by dialogue. According to the joint press statement the two sides agreed to maintain and enhance peace, friendship and harmonious relations particularly through augmenting of mutual cooperation in economic and trade sectors and people to people contacts. Their discussions took around a wide range of issues comprising Kashmir, trade, infrastructure projects, mobility of more trains, interaction on anti-terrorism issues, liberalisation of visas and IPI gas pipeline among others. In the talks Islamabad stressed on New Delhi to deal Kashmir issue seriously, the latter reminded the former of its commitment on terrorism, 'No matter what our political differences, we have to fight terror unambiguously'. They both felt that they have been blessed with the unique opportunity conducive as all major political players in both countries are in support of establishing normalisation – whether it is the ruling Congress and Pakistan People's Party or the chief opposition BJP and major opposition parties in Pakistan.

In modern Indian history November 26, 2008 would be considered as the saddest day. On this day, Mumbai, the financial capital of India, faced the brazen terrorist attack by ten professionally trained men of Pakistani origin which represent the gravest provocation to the Indian states in decades. The devastating terror attack was made at Hostel Taj, Nariman House, Hotel Trident Oberoi and other places in the city. It took about two hundred precious lives, and left over 300 people severally injured. The casualties included Indians, foreigners, police personnel, NSGs and others. It was the worst ever terror attack in India which lasted for about 60 hours in which nine terrorist were gunned down and one was caught alive. In the operation against the terrorists 20 policemen and 2 NSG Commandos were killed. Among the dead 23 were of foreign nationals. The recent terrorist attack on Mumbai was in several respects very different from those in the past.[311] It was a bold, brave frontal, ferocious attack in which terrorists were well prepared. Once again the attack demonstrated how incapable India is as a nation to prepare itself to fight against terrorism. It not only shocked the nation, but also gave us an impression that we can only boast of preparedness, but the reality is altogether different. Our intelligence agencies are not as alert and fast as the terrorist are. Now, after six decades, the state can not even perform its basic function of protecting its citizens, never mind giving them a better life.

The recent terror attack in Mumbai at different places in the city had furthered India-Pakistan relations in all spheres near collapse and created a war-like situation between the two countries. For a long Islamabad refused the truth that the attackers were Pakistani nationals, it however, lastly accepted the fact that they were our citizens and attack's plan was prepared on Pakistani soil. In an atmosphere of anger and sorrow Indian Foreign Minister Pranab Mukherjee was of the view that the terror strikes have kept recurring because the 'puppet masters' have been assured 'immunity from prosecution is unimpeachable. What the democratic regime in Pakistan needs to realise is that, given the gravity of the latest affront to the Indian state and the public mood in India, the Manmohan Singh government has shown exemplary restraint. In post-attack phase the tragic deterioration of India-Pakistan relations continued because of inflamatory statements from the two countries and reached a stage of not-too-happy.[312] But the two countries must not stop here. They should rapidly evolve positive measures to create a scenario of peace, justice, trust and finer fraternity amidst Indo-Pak humanity. They should do this with a profound feeling of good neighbourliness. In May 2009 Asif Ali Zardari, the President of Pakistan, made the optimistic remark that peace process with India halted after the November 2008 Mumbai terrorist attack could resume after the Indian general election.[313] Once the formation of government is settled, the new dispensation would need to think urgently about going back to the table with Pakistan, and to do so without setting pre-conditions.

Developments on Jammu and Kashmir

At the time the new government headed by Manmohan Singh took over in India the composite dialogue on the issue of Kashmir was already under way and it decided to go along broadly with the schedule and sequence of issues for discussion. Earlier an optimism was raised over the issue as a result of the January 2004 agreement in which Islamabad committed not to permit any territory to be used to support terrorism. It was a breakthrough in India-Pakistan relations which paved the way for strengthening relations between the two countries. Viewed in larger perspectives, the agreement between India's new Prime Minister and president Musharraf to continue talks on all contentious issues including Kashmir had inspired optimism about reduced tensions in South Asia. For the first time the Lahore Declaration defined only one issue by name as an outstanding dispute : Jammu and Kashmir. By June 2004, in the foreign secretary level talks, India had committed itself to a peaceful negotiated final settlement on Kashmir and juxtaposed the UN Charter with the Simla agreement. In the meeting India's recognition of Kashmir as an unsettled issue resolvable through 'give and take' represented to the Pak military establishment half a success. Most of us consider keeping the dialogue going on as more important than achieving concrete, enduring results. Even the then process was founded on conflicting presumptions. India's premise has been that the process would persuade Pakistan to cease sending extremists into India and start building goodneighbourly ties. On the other Pakistan has viewed the process as a means to nudge India to make progress on Kashmir, a euphemism for Indian concessions.[314] However, if Pakistan is unwilling to give up cross-border terrorism and its blinkered approach of holding the larger relationship hostage to a final settlement of Kashmir, India should not accept a timetable for a new cycle of talks. After all, talks can not be continued for talks, sake.

Often we seek resolution and solution of the problem of Jammu and Kashmir but there is a political distinction between the two terms. Here the word 'resolution' is more of a long term concept and is an improbability at this stage. It could mean settling of all claims on Kashmir of all the actors, once and for all. From the beginning the people of India, Pakistan and Jammu and Kashmir have grown up on a diet of vicious rhetoric and hostile folklores and seen the bloody manifestation in terms of violence. Bitter peoples, competing in bitterness, are the most unlikely settings for a resolution. Hence in the interim period we would have to look for a solution, a short term concept whose aim should primarily be to set the stage for an era of uninterrupted peace and reconciliation of realities. It would entail concessions, bold decisions resorting to the unthinkable and yet not threatening geography.[315] Related to it is the status quo and the three slogans, accession to India, accession to Pakistan and an independent Kashmir, depict the problem. The short-term concept of solution would have to rule out all these options.

In the circumstances summits and hyped bilateral talks need to make way for a feeling of a solution having been reached. The process of confidence building measures initiated by India and Pakistan is a step in right direction. But there is a persisting and bothersome difference between the Indian and Pakistani approaches to their dialogue that officials on both sides seem to be glossing over. India sees the confidence building measures as a means to facilitate the settlement of their most difficult problem Jammu and Kashmir while Pakistan sees it as a technique of evasion.[316] Islamabad has to be persuaded that the resolution of outstanding issues between the two countries requires a two-track approach. The first, to immediately begin the process of mitigating the difficulties of ordinary folk-whether they are people under detention, travellers to each other's countries or families divided by partition and war.

India and Pakistan committed themselves to a 'composite dialogue' in 1997 in which all issues would be dealt with simultaneously. This process was revived in 2003 but since Kashmir is by far the most complex and sensitive of all issues, whatever little progress there has been, has taken place on other issues. Still they maintained their earlier stark opposition in which Pakistan has held that Kashmir is the core issue and must be dealt first while India is of the view that other issues should be resolved first, in order to create an atmosphere conducive to the resolution of the Kashmir dispute. The change in the stated position began when in September 2004, Musharraf met Manmohan in Newyork and the latter had hold the former unambiguously that a change in borders was not possible. The Indian Prime Minister laid out an alternative approach to resolving the Kashmir dispute and appealed President Musharraf to keep the dialogue alive.

The alternative approach that they gradually learned to resolve the Kashmir issue was a people-centered approach. The new concept had shifted the emphasis from demarcating territorial boundaries to increasing the freedom and welfare of the Kashmiris. It required a progressive softening of the LoC and progressively removing consular and other barriers that prevented Kashmiris in both parts of the old state from meeting, trading and discussing common problems with each other. Perhaps as a follow up of the view in active consideration India and Pakistan agreed to commence a Srinagar-Muzaffarabad bus service from April 7, 2005. But every step towards the normalization of relations without a direct engagement on Kashmir reinforced fears in the Pakistani security establishment that India was trying to make it accept the LoC by the backdoor. This is why Musharraf before coming to New Delhi in April 2005, made it clear that he wanted to establish a time- frame for the resolution of the Kashmir issue. In his meeting with Musharraf Indian Prime Minister apparently convinced the general that there could be no time-frame for the resolution of the dispute because it was a process.[317] Each step in it depended upon the completion of the previous step and there was no way of accurately predicting how long that would take. As part of India's new Kashmir policy Monmohan Singh announced in May 2006, the creation of five working groups – a mechanism so far commonly used only in bilateral diplomacy based on the most pressing aspects of the Kashmir problem. Unlike the NDA government Manmohan Singh also took a tough stand on violence and emphasised that New Delhi would only talk to militants once they shun the path of violence.

The problem of Jammu and Kashmir also figured further when India's Minister for External Affairs Pranab Mukherjee paid a visit to Islamabad. Apart from discussing the issue with Khurshid Mehmood Kasuri, his Pakistani counterpart, both made serious efforts to address the terrorist issue and give joint mechanism against terrorism a fair trial. They seem to be serious in making the experiment successful so that it can become an effective instrument to combat terrorism. In the meeting Mukherjee agreed with Kasuri to have the first meeting of the two Foreign Secretaries on anti-terror mechanism on March 13 and 14, 2007. In June-July 2008, the two foreign ministers met and discussed the issue of Kashmir and the last one was held after the restoration of democracy in Pakistan.

Economic Relations

When the government headed by Manmohan Singh took over in India in May 2004 the ranking of the two countries on international comparisons of social well being was not quite so high. The United Nations Development Programms' 2004 Human Development Report placed India at number 127 out of a total of 177 nations, while Pakistan was at an even more dismal 142. In present day Pakistan economy witnesses a sign of gradual worsening. Inflation has gone over the roof and trade and fiscal deficit are widening. Forex reserves have depleted and the rupee recently touched an all time low. In the circumstances Pakistan while talking peace with India remained loath to establish normal trading ties with New Delhi. Islamabad in the hope of earning hundreds of millions of dollars in annual fees, it wanted India to accept the overland

Iranian gas pipeline project proposal. New Delhi too must keep on pushing the gas pipeline even as a 'stand alone' proposal requiring no reciprocity, since the very establishment of a pipeline would change the dynamics of India-Pakistan trade and make Pakistan's position redundant.[318] However, in recent past India's exports to Pakistan and its imports from Pakistan has been growing at an average rate of 62% and 65% since 2002-03 until 2007-08. As a result the two-way trade its growth would stay around US$ 5 billion and the process of composite dialogue would be responsible for it as its continuation would open up the borders of trade that remained closed for many decades. The bilateral trade between the two countries swelled from $235.74 million in 2001-02 to around $ 2 billion in 2007-08. The share of Pakistan's exports to India in total exports also remained on the rise from 0.5% in 2001-02 to 1.8% in 2005-06. However the balance of trade continued to be in India's favour.

Naturally the economic relations between India and Pakistan improved and reached broader as a result of the visit of political dignitaries and interaction between the two governments at different levels. During his visit to India on November 23-24, 2004, Pakistani Prime Minister Shaukat Aziz apart from SAARC issues, confined the larger part of his discussions to promoting closer economic relations between the two countries. In particular, he made it clear that Pakistan would welcome Indian participation in the gas pipeline project, although it was prepared to go it alone if India decided to stay out. This visit, too, produced little more than an agreement to keep talking. India wanted Pakistan to offer Most Favoured Nation treatment to Indian exports, in exchange for participating in the pipeline project. Later New Delhi reduced its demand to being allowed transit access for Indian goods to Afghanistan through Wagah and Lahore. But the Pakistani Prime Minister dug his heels in and insisted that the pipeline project had to be a stand alone project, while the other issues were a part of the composite dialogue. Likewise the visit of President Pervez Musharraf which took place in April 2005, although yielded no major breakthroughs, but it provided a rich harvest of small and incremental steps especially in trade and the opening up of the borders that will eventually aggregate to that big step which would scale the impossible heights that divide India and Pakistan today.[319]

Economic cooperation between India and Pakistan in diverse fields continued further in 2007 and 2008. In sphere of financial assistance the two countries had consented to cooperate each other as informed by Pawan Kumar Bansal, India's Minister of State for Finance, in a written reply to the Lok Sabha in May 2007 that Reserve Bank of India and State Bank of Pakistan have agreed to open two branches across the countries. The RBI has proposed the name of two leading banks, SBI and Bank of India, to open two branches in two major cities of Pakistan. At the sametime, the State Bank of Pakistan has proposed the name of three major Pak banks to open their doors for Delhi and Mumbai, the chief metropolitan cities in India. Now they will review the respective regulatory policies and procedures and with mutual consent provide licences to banks in both countries, to open branches on reciprocal basis. In order to build economic ties the commerce secretaries of the two countries met on August 2-3, 2007 to discuss further liberalization. They reached the significant decision of increasing bilateral trade from $ 1.7 billion to $ 10 billion by 2010. The two countries further decided to improve transport links, expand the trade basket, reduce tariffs on a larger number of products and assist each other in capacity building. In June 2008 the Foreign Ministers of India and Pakistan met at New Delhi to strengthen mutual bilateral relations in all specific areas and they discussed, among other things, trade and infrastructural projects in particular. In the talks the IPI gas pipeline project was also at the core of the discussion and viewing the soaring energy price Pakistani Foreign Minister told his Indian counterpart to move quickly on gas pipeline project. Thus economic relations between the two countries have moved towards normalization even though officially Pakistan sticks to the stand that relations can not be normalized without solving the Kashmir issue.

Defence Understandings

Understanding between India and Pakistan gained in sphere of politics and economy spread to defence area and with the change of government in May 2004 the two countries began to discuss their security aspects. Background for sound defence relations had already been prepared by the several visits, summits and interaction at various levels between the two countries. In May 2004 a foreign secretary level meeting was held in Islamabad in which they discussed a five-point agenda and a path was drawn with a view to normalise relations between the two countries. It was agreed in the meeting that the future bilateral dialogue would include Siachen, Wullar Barrage/Tulbul Navigation project, Sir Creek, terrorism and drug trafficking, economic and commercial cooperation and promotion of friendly exchanges in various fields along with constant dialogue on Kashmir. They also agreed that the upper echelon of both the nations defence forces would constantly meet to create a better understanding and avoid any untoward incidents in the future.

India's Minister for External Affairs K. Natwar Singh paid a visit to Pakistan in October 2005 and with his counterpart Khurshid Kasuri signed an agreement for notify each other before testing ballistic missiles. Along with mutual agreements and meets an agreement was reached on the establishment of hot line between the two maritime security agencies of India and Pakistan to facilitate early exchange of information regarding apprehended fishermen who inadvertently stray into the other side's territorial waters. Again coming to Lahore MoU, the Foreign Secretaries also promised unilateral moratorium on further nuclear testing provided that the sovereignty and integrity of both the nations is not threatened. They also reaffirmed their commitment to avoid all incidents in the sea. Side by side they vowed to carry out negotiation process in future and establish communications.[320] Further, they declared for bilateral consultations on security, disarmament and non-proliferation issues in the context of the future multi-lateral summits, conferences and negotiations.

In May 2006 the 10th round of defence secretary level talks of India-Pakistan Joint Task Force was held to resolve the Siachen dispute. It ended inconclusively amid hints that a political nudge was now needed to stitch up an agreement. They decided, however, to strengthen a 19-month old ceasefire holding in the hostile snow clad battlefield. Pranab Mukherjee, the Indian Defence Minister, shortly before a joint statement was issued, said the main obstacle was mapping bases and the frontline in the hostile region. 'Perhaps there can be forward movement in another round of discussions. In this round of discussions, we could not make any breakthrough.[321] Further in February 2007, India and Pakistan signed an agreement on 'Reducing the Risk from Accidents Relating to Nuclear Weapons'. However, improving mutual confidence and trust in the political domain is the first order of business for creating effective CBMs. Establishing even a medium of trust is necessary in order to stabilize their adversarial relations.

References

1. Kalim Bahadur, 'India and Pakistan", Bimal Prasad, ed., International Studies, Vol. 17, (Vikas Publishing House, New Delhi, July-December 1978), p. 517.
2. The Hindustan Times (New Delhi), April 2, 1977.
3. Bhabani Sen Gupta, "A Deeply Divided Nation", Contemporary Pakistan-New Aims and Images, Prem Chopra, ed., (Vikas Publishing House, U. P., India, 1983), p. 83.
4. Pakistan Economist (Karachi), February 2, 1978.
5. Pakistan Times, April 19, 1978.
6. The Dawn (Karachi), November 2, 1978.
7. The Pakistan Economist, March 31, 1979.
8. The Hindu, April 15, 1977.
9. M. S. R. Khemchand, ed., Asian Recorder, A Weekly Digest of Asian Events, Vol. XXIII (Recorder Press, New Delhi, September 17-23, 1977), p. 13937.
10. Ibid., p. 13944.
11. The Amrit Bazar Patrika (Calcutta), February 6, 1978.
12. The Patriot (New Delhi), February 7, 1978.
13. S. C. Gangal, "A Successful Visit", The Indian Express (New Delhi), February 14, 1978.
14. The Amrit Bazar Patrika, February 11, 1978.
15. Robert Fraser, ed., Keesings Contemporary Archives, Vol. XXIV (Longman Group; Scotland, 9 June 1978), p. 29018.
16. S. C. Gangal, op.cit.
17. Robert Fraser, op.cit., p. 29018.
18. Jayanta Kumar Ray, "A View from Outside", op.cit., p. 390.
19. Lok Sabha Debates, Vol. XII, 21-23 March 1978, cols. 254-56.
20. Ibid., vol. XXIII, 5-9 March, cols. 141-42.

21. Robert Fraser, op.cit., p. 29701.
22. Vijay Dutta and Sevanti Ninan, "The Route of Discontent", India Today, Aroon Purie, ed. (Living Media, New Delhi, 16-31 July 1978), p. 16.
23. Nazir A. Kamal, "Karakoram Highway-A Nation Building Effort", Strategic Studies-Quarterly Journal of the Institute of Strategic Studies, S. Irtiza Hussain, ed., Vol. II, no. 3 (S. Irtiza Hussain on behalf of the Institute of Strategic Studies, Islamabad, spring, 1979), p. 16.
24. Vijay Dutt and Sevanti Ninan, op.cit., p. 16.
25. Nazir A. Kamal, op.cit., p. 16.
26. Robert Fraser, Vol. XXV, 6 July 1979, p. 29701.
27. When Vajpayee visited China in February 1979 he took up the matter with the Chinese Government. The Government of India made their position known to the Chinese that they considered the construction of the Karakoram Highway as 'illegal' as it had been constructed in a territory which was an integral part of India and that the Government of India could not acquiesce in the legal implications of the construction of this road. Lok Sabha Debates, Vol. XXVIII, 9-13 July 1979, col. 50.
28. Reported by Girilal Jain at a Seminar at Columbia University, November 1982. Referred in W. Howard Wriggins, "Pakistan's Search for a Foreign Policy After the Invasion of Afghanistan", Pacific Affairs, Vol. 57, no. 2 (The University of British Columbia, 1984), p. 285.
29. Quoted in Bimal Prasad, "India and the Afghan Crisis" International Studies, Vol. 21 (Vikas Publishing House, New Delhi, 1980), p. 636.
30. The Hindu, December 31, 1979.
31. Ibid.
32. Ibid.
33. Benazir Bhutto, Foreign Policy in Perspective (Agha Amir Hussain, Lahore, 1978), pp. 32-33.
34. Dieter Bram, "Changes in South Asia Intra-regional and External Relationship", Liliana Brisby, ed., The World Today, Vol. 34 (Royal Institute of International Affairs, London, October 1978), p. 393.
35. Bhutto, reacting to a statement of Vajpayee made on 4 April 1977 suggesting a no War-Pact between the two countries, said that Pakistan could consider the proposal only if the question of Kashmir was settled. See the Bangladesh Observer (Dacca), April 9, 1977; General Zia, reacting to a statement of India's Minister for Defence Jagjivan Ram that the

Kashmir problem had already been settled made it clear that unless the Kashmir problem was solved friendship between the two countries would not be real. See The Pioneer, January 26, 1978; General Zia raised the question of Jammu and Kashmir at the Havana Conference of Non-Aligned Nations held in the first week of September 1979, and said that his country sought the solution of the problem in accordance with UN resolutions and Simla Agreement. The Indian Express (New Delhi), September 7, 1979.

36. Robert Fraser, op.cit., p. 29018.
37. Ibid.
38. The Times, April 13, 1978.
39. The Indian Express, September 7, 1979.
40. Ibid.
41. P. R. Chari, "India's Nuclear Policy", Janata's Foreign Policy, K. P. Mishra, ed., (Vikas Publishing House, New Delhi, 1979), p. 57.
42. Pramod K. Mishra, South Asia in International Politics (Udh Publishers, Delhi, 1984), pp. 72-73.
43. Ibid., p. 98.
44. The Times of India (New Delhi), June 22, 1977.
45. Ibid., June 25, 1977.
46. Robert Fraser, op.cit., Vol. XXV, 6 July 1979, p. 29701.
47. The Hindu, August 16, 1979.
48. The Indian Express, September 8, 1979.
49. In an interview, given to Chatan (Lahore) and Nawa-i-Waqt (Islamabad) in February 1984, Dr. A. Q. Khan, Chief of Pakistan's nuclear plant at Kahut, claimed that Pakistan had left India behind by many years in uranium enrichment and that Pakistan had acquired the capability of producing the atom bomb. The Times of India, 15 September 1986.
50. Quoting US defence intelligence sources, woodward, a leading American columnist, revealed in *The Washington Post* in a leading article on 3 November 1986, that Pakistan had conducted two series of tests that year of an explosion trigger device for its nuclear weapons programme, the second series was conducted in the third week of September, and that it had enriched uranium 235 to 93.5 per cent (only a 90 per cent enrichment level is required to make a bomb). *The Times of India* (Patna), very appropriately commented on 5 November in its editorial that these facts

make it abundantly clear that Pakistan has now well and truly become a nuclear weapon power in all but the name". See *The Times of India*, 3 and 5 November 1986. J. A. Naik is of the opinion that Pakistan has attained adequate nuclear capability. It has the capacity to make the bomb at reasonable notice. See J. A. Naik, The Pak Bomb And Rajiv's India (National Publishing House, New Delhi, 1986).

51. Manorama Kohli, "Foreign Policy Initiatives of the National Front Government in India", Ramakant (ed.), South Asian Studies, Vol. 25, no. 1 & 2 January-December 1990 (University of Rajasthan, Jaipur, 1990), p. 141.
52. The Hindu (Madras), January 15, 1990.
53. The Times of India, February 2, 1990.
54. Ibid., February 3, 1990.
55. Manorama Kohli, op.cit., p. 141.
56. The Times of India, August 9, 1990.
57. Dileep Padgaonkar, "Pak Crisis and India's Choices", Ibid., August 6, 1990.
58. Foreign Affairs Record, Vol. XXXVI, no. 5, May 1990, p. 108.
59. The Hindu, January 12, 1990.
60. Ibid, January 22, 1990.
61. Foreign Affairs Record, no. 58, p. 109.
62. The National Herald, January 22, 1990.
63. Ibid., January 23, 1990.
64. The Statesman, January 25, 1990.
65. The Indian Express, February 1, 1990.
66. Rajendra Sareen, "Dimensions of Turmoil", The Tribune, February 5, 1990.
67. The Statesman, February 6, 1990.
68. Ibid.
69. The Times of India, February 9, 1990.
70. The Hindustan Times, February 11, 1990.
71. Ibid.
72. The Times of India, February 11, 1990.
73. The Statesman, February 12, 1990.
74. Bhabani Sen Gupta, "How to Avoid War with Pakistan", The National Herald, February 13, 1990.

75. Ibid.
76. Bhabani Sen Gupta, "Global Change Cripples Pakistan", Ibid., February 22, 1990.
77. The Times of India, February 22, 1990.
78. S. Nihal Singh, "Edging Back from the Brink", The Tribune, April 17, 1990.
79. The Times (London), April 14, 1990.
80. Ibid.
81. S. Nihal Singh, op.cit.
82. The Times of India, April 22, 1990.
83. The Hindustan Times, April 23, 1990.
84. The Indian Express, April 26, 1990.
85. The Hindu, April 27, 1990.
86. The Patriot, May 4, 1990; See also The Indian Express, May 12, 1990.
87. The Statesman, May 12, 1990.
88. Cecil Victor, "Busting Terrorist Bases no Solution", The Patriot, May 18, 1990.
89. The Hindu, May 15,1990.
90. Nikhil Chakravartty, "Foreign Ties : Why so Formal ?" The Times of India, June 10, 1990.
91. Foreign Affairs Record, op.cit.
92. Ibid., p. 109.
93. The Hindustan Times, January 26, 1990.
94. The Indian Express, February 4, 1990.
95. The Hindustan Times, February 11, 1990.
96. The Hindu, March 1, 1990.
97. The Indian Express, February 17, 1990.
98. The Patriot, January 29, 1990.
99. The Times of India, February 1, 1990.
100. The National Herald, February 21, 1990.
101. Inder Malhotra, "China's Stance on Kashmir", The Times of India, February 22, 1990.
102. The Indian Express, February 12, 1990.
103. The Times of India, February 20, 1990.
104. Ibid., February 22, 1990.

105. Moonis Ahmar, "The Role of CBMs in the Post-Cold War Era", ACDIS, Occasional Paper (Department of International Relations, University of Karachi, Pakistan, October 1993), pp. 9-12.
106. The Hindustan Times, June 8, 1990.
107. The Patriot, June 8, 1990.
108. The Statesman, June 7, 1990.
109. The Patriot, June 11, 1990.
110. Nikhil Chakravartty, op.cit.
111. The National Herald, June 30, 1990.
112. The Hindustan Times, July 18, 1990.
113. Ibid., July 19, 1990.
114. The Indian Express, July 20, 1990.
115. Moonis Ahmar, op.cit., p. 12.
116. Ibid.
117. The Patriot, August 12, 1990.
118. Ibid.
119. The Times of India, September 26, 1990.
120. The National Herald, September 28, 1990.
121. The Times of India, October 1, 1990.
122. The Hindustan Times, January 1, 1991.
123. Pran Chopra, "Talking to Pakistan", The Hindu, January 18, 1991.
124. Ibid.
125. Ibid., January 26, 1991.
126. Ibid.
127. The Times of India, February 3, 1991.
128. The Hindustan Times, June 12, 1991.
129. Foreign Affairs Record, vol. XXXVII, no. 3, March 1991, p. 40.
130. Ibid., p. 41.
131. Ibid., no. 4, April 1991, p. 62.
132. The Statesman, June 13, 1991.
133. Foreign Affairs Record, Vol. XLII, no. 6, June 1996, pp. 97-98.
134. Ibid., p. 98.
135. Sreedhar, "Indo-Pak Relations in Post-Benazir Period", Strategic Analysis, Vol. XIX, no. 12, March 1997 (Institute for Defence Studies and Analysis, New Delhi, 1997), p. 1695.
136. Indian Recorder, A Weekly of Events and Happenings, Vol. III, no. 29, July 15-21, 1996, New Delhi, p. 2078.

137. Sreedhar, op.cit., pp. 1695-96.
138. Indian Recorder, August 12-18, 1996, p. 2182.
139. Sreedhar, op.cit., p. 1696.
140. Ibid.
141. The Hindustan Times, October 27, 1996.
142. Indian Recorder, December 16-22, 1996, pp. 2468-69.
143. Ibid.
144. Ibid., December 23-31, 1996, p. 2487.
145. Ibid, January 1-7, 1997, p. 2502.
146. Ibid., March 5-11, 1997, p. 2645.
147. Ibid., March 12-18, 1997, p. 2658.
148. Ibid., March 26-April 1, 1997, p. 2690.
149. Ibid., April 9-15, 1997, p. 2725.
150. Ibid., April 16-22, 1997, p. 2738.
151. Ibid., 30 April-6 May, 1997, p. 2769.
152. Ibid.
153. Ibid., 7-13 May 1997, pp. 2790-91.
154. Ibid., 22-28 July, 1996, p. 2134.
155. Ibid.
156. Ibid., 12-18 August, 1996, p. 2182.
157. Ibid., 7-13 October, 1996, p. 2310.
158. Ibid., 12-18 March, 1997, p. 2658.
159. Ibid.
160. Ibid., 19-25 March, 1997, p. 2669.
161. Ibid., 15-21 July, 1996, p. 2115.
162. Ibid., 22-28 July, 1996, p. 2134.
163. Ibid.
164. Ibid., 4-10 November, 1996, p. 2372.
165. Ibid., 25 November – 1 December, 1996, p. 2418.
166. Ibid., 26 March-1 April, 1997, p. 2690.
167. Ibid.
168. Ibid.
169. Ibid., April 9-15, 1997, p. 2726.
170. Ibid., April 23-29, 1997, p. 2756.
171. Ibid., July 15-21, 1996, p. 2116.
172. Ibid.

173. Ibid.
174. Ibid., p. 2117.
175. Sreedhar, op.cit., p. 1696.
176. Ibid.
177. Indian Recorder, 9-15 December, 1996, p. 2458.
178. Ibid.
179. Ibid., 16-22 April, 1997, p. 2740.
180. Ibid., 9-15 April, 1997, p. 2726.
181. Ibid., 28 May – 3 June, 1997, p. 2838.
182. Ibid., 4 June – 10 June, 1997, p. 2854.
183. Apratim Mukarji, "Friendliness is not Weakness", The Hindustan Times (New Delhi), October 6, 1997.
184. Ibid., March 6, 1998.
185. Ibid., July 22, 1997.
186. Ibid., July 26, 1997.
187. Ibid., August 22, 1997.
188. Ibid., September 1, 1997.
189. Ibid., September 15, 1997.
190. Ibid, September 19, 1997.
191. Ibid., (editorial), September 20, 1997.
192. Ibid., September 25, 1997.
193. Ibid., October 26, 1997.
194. Ibid., February 4, 1998.
195. A. N. Dar, "Need for a Cautious Approach in Kashmir", Ibid. August 27, 1997.
196. Ibid, August 23, 1997.
197. Ibid., September 9, 1997.
198. Ibid., October 19, 1997.
199. Ibid., March 17, 1998.
200. Ibid., (editorial).
201. Ibid., September 3, 1997.
202. Ibid., (editorial), August 31, 1997.
203. Ibid., September 3, 1997.
204. Ibid., September 14, 1997.
205. Ibid., October 9, 1997.
206. Ibid., November 19, 1997.

207. Ibid., February 15, 1998.
208. The Times of India, July 26, 1997.
209. Ibid.
210. The Hindustan Times (editorial), August 27, 1997.
211. Ibid., September 24, 1997.
212. Ibid, September 28, 1997.
213. Ibid., (editorial), September 30, 1997.
214. Ibid., October 16, 1997.
215. Ibid., November 25, 1997.
216. Ibid., editorial, October 19, 1998.
217. J. N. Dixit, "Signs of Progress", Ibid, October 28, 1998.
218. Mahendra P. Lama, "Boosting Indo-Pak Trade", January 1, 1999.
219. Ibid.
220. Ayesha Siddiqa, 'Pakistan's Security Perspective : Problems of Linearity', P. R.. Kumaraswamy, ed., Security Beyond Survival (Sage Publications, New Delhi, 2004), p.172.
221. The Hindustan Times, October 14, 1999.
222. Ibid.
223. Veena Kukreja, Contemporary Pakistan, Political Processes, Conflicts and Crisis (Sage Publications, New Delhi, 2003), pp. 166-67.
224. Asian Recorder, New Delhi, 1999, p. 28554.
225. Veena Kukreja, op. cit., p.275.
226. J. N. Dixit, 'In the General's Own Words', The Hindustan Times, February 2, 2000.
227. Ibid, December 10, 1999.
228. Sugata Bose and Ayesha Jalal, Modern South Asia – History, Culture, Political Economy, Second edition, (Oxford University Press, New Delhi, 2004), pp.191-92.
229. Brahma Chellaney, 'Hard Words, Soft Actions', The Hindustan Times, February 29, 2000.
230. Ibid.
231. Ibid., June 20, 2000.
232. Kalim Bahadur, 'Pakistan Journey to Nowhere,' World Focus, Vol. XXI, nos.10-11-12 (October-November-December 2000), p. 32.
233. Dhrubajyoti Bhattacharjee, 'India-Pakistan Relations, A Troubled History with A Bright Future?', Dr. Subhash C. Kashyap, ed., South Asia Politics, Vol.6, no-9, January 2008, New Delhi, pp. 29-30.

234. Ibid.
235. Veena Kukreja, op. cit., p.290.
236. The Hindustan Times, January 1, 2002.
237. Ibid., January 6, 2002.
238. Ibid., January 14, 2002.
239. Ibid.
240. Brahma Chellaney, 'Pakistan's Janus Face', Ibid., February 20, 2002.
241. Ajoy Bagchi, 'The General Just Cannot Deliver', The Pioneer (New Delhi), January 26, 2002.
242. The Hindustan Times, May 19, 2002.
243. Stephen Philip Cohen, 'Indo-Pak Track-II Diplomacy : Building Peace or Wasting Time', P. R. Kumaraswamy, ed., op. cit., p.215.
244. Ravi Pratap Singh, 'India-Pakistan Conflict-Analysis Through the Lenses of Conflict-transformation Theory', Dr. Subhash C. Kashyap, ed., Vol.8, no. 9, February 2009, New Delhi, 2009, p. 30.
245. Ibid.
246. Ibid., p. 28.
247. Ibid.
248. Y. C. Halan, 'Peace Prospect Possibility in Indo-Pak Relations', Ibid, Vol. 5, no. 11, March 2007, New Delhi, 2007, p. 18.
249. Rajkumar Singh, Indo-Pak Nuclear Tension 1974-1998 (Samiksha Prakashan, New Delhi, 2001), pp. 103-04.
250. The Times of India, June 9, 1998.
251. Ibid., (editorial), August 4, 1998.
252. Rajkumar Singh, op. cit., pp. 106-07.
253. The Times of India, October 19, 1998.
254. V. N. Khanna, Foreign Policy of India (Vikas Publishing House, New Delhi, 2004), p. 101.
255. As Quoted in Ibid., pp. 103-04.
256. The Hindustan Times (editorial), June 15, 1999.
257. Rajkumar Singh, op. cit., pp. 131-34.
258. Ibid., pp. 198-207.
259. Prem Shankar Jha, 'Where Next With Pakistan?,' The Hindustan Times, February 12, 2000.
260. Ibid.
261. Brahma Chellaney, 'A Perilous Course', Ibid., January 11, 2001.

262. J. N. Dixit, 'Slowly But Surely', Ibid., May 10, 2001.
263. Ibid.
264. Ibid., July 11, 2001
265. Ibid., August 17, 2001.
266. Kanwar Sandhu, 'Why Are We Tongue – tied?', Ibid., August 1, 2001.
267. Dhrubajyoti Bhattacharjee, op.cit., pp.29-30.
268. Sugata Bose and Ayesha Jalal, op, cit., p.197.
269. Anand K. Sahay, 'Kashmir As General Fodder', The Hindustan Times, January 29, 2002.
270. Ibid.
271. Ashok K. Mehta, 'A Borderline Case', Ibid., August 6, 2003.
272. Joginder Singh, 'India's Response to Pakistan's Terrorism', vol. 8, no. 9, February 2009, New Delhi, 2009, pp. 8-9.
273. Bir Good Gill, 'India and the Problem of Cross-Border Terrorism: Challenges in Kashmir', Mahavir Singh, ed, International Terrorism and Religious Extremism (Anamica Publishers, New Delhi, 2004), pp. 275-76.
274. Ibid.
275. Riyaz Punjabi, 'The Concept of an Islamic Caliphate : The Religious and Ethnic pulls of Kashmir Militant Movement', Journal of Peace Studies, Vol. 1, no. 1, November-December, 1993, p. 42.
276. K. Warikoo, 'Religious Extremism and Terrorism in Kashmir', Mahavir Singh, ed., op. cit., pp. 257-60.
277. Rajkumar Singh, Past, Present and Future of Kashmir (Gyan Publishing House, New Delhi, 2008), pp. 275-76.
278. Sumantra Bose, Kashmir-Roots of Conflict and Paths to Peace (Vistaar Publications, New Delhi, 2003), pp. 140-47.
279. Bir Good Gill, op. cit., p. 276.
280. Prem Shankar Jha, 'Nightmare Begins', The Hindustan Times, September 21, 2001.
281. Veena Kukreja, op. cit., p.288.
282. Pankaj Vohra, 'Strike at Parliament is Attack on India's Sovereignty', The Hindustan Times, December 17, 2001.
283. Brahma Chellaney, 'Flailing in the Shadows', Ibid., October 3, 2001.
284. Ibid., January 9, 2002.
285. Ibid., editorial.

286. Ibid., January 15, 2002.
287. B. Raman, 'Attack of the Clones', Ibid., January 5, 2004.
288. Ibid.
289. Shahidur Rehman, 'In a Hole, and Digging', The Hindustan Times, June 24, 2001.
290. Ibid.
291. Ibid., December 28, 2001.
292. Ibid., editorial, January 5, 2002.
293. Ibid., November 8, 2001.
294. Rajkumar Singh, op. cit., p.143.
295. Pervez Iqbal Cheema, 'Security in South Asia : An Approach' Shelton U. Kodikara, ed., External Compulsions of South Asian Politics (Sage Publications, New Delhi, 1993), pp. 42-43.
296. Ayesha Siddiqa, op. cit., pp. 165-69.
297. Rajkumar Singh, op. cit., pp. 84-85.
298. Ibid., p. 87.
299. V. N. Khanna, op. cit., p. 105.
300. Rajesh Ramachandran, 'War as Politics', The Hindustan Times, June 7, 1999.
301. Michael Cox, 'American Power Before and After 11 September : Dizzy With Success?', International Affairs (London), 78 (2), 2002, p.68.
302. The Hindustan Times, January 26, 2002.
303. The Times of India, June 21, 2004.
304. K. Shankar Bajpai, 'Three in This Marriage', Ibid., March 15, 2005.
305. Ibid., editorial, December 30, 2004.
306. Ibid., editorial, April 19, 2005.
307. Y. C. Halan, op. cit., pp. 18 and 21.
308. The Hindu, editorial, November 5, 2007.
309. Ibid., December 28, 2007.
310. Rajkumar Singh, India and Pakistan, Social, Political and Military Perspectives (Regal Publications, New Delhi, 2009), p. 289.
311. The Hindu, editorial, December 27, 2008.
312. V. R. Krishna Iyer, 'Statesmanship, the Need of the Hour', Ibid., December 21, 2008.
313. Ibid., editorial, May 9, 2009.
314. Brahma Chellaney, 'LoC Stock and Barrel', The Hindustan Times, August 31, 2004.

315. Sajad Lone, 'Exile on Main Street', Ibid, November 1, 2004.
316. Ibid., editorial, December 30, 2004.
317. Prem Shankar Jha', A Question of Trust', Ibid., April 22, 2005.
318. Ibid., editorial, December 30, 2004.
319. Ibid., April 18, 2005.
320. Duryodhan Nahak, 'Necessity of CBMs in Indo-Pak Relations During Post-Pokhran II period and Visions for the Future', Subhash C. Kashyap, ed., South Asia Politics, Vol. 6, no. 4, August 2007, New Delhi, pp. 40-41.
321. Dhrubajyoti Bhattacharjee, op. cit., p. 31.

2

India-Nepal Relations

REGIME OF JANATA PARTY

Premiership of Morarji Desai (24 March 1977-28 July 1979)

The 1977 elections in India were fought on the crucial issue of democracy versus authoritarianism, which aroused keen public interest in the neighbouring countries. The victory of the Janata Party was hailed by the Nepalese elite which implied an indirect criticism of the political system of Nepal itself.[1] A section of it felt that it must have its impact on their neighbouring country. The Janata Party and its leadership had received critical comments during the elections from the Nepalese press for demanding the release of B.P. Koirala and his associates and for raising the question of human rights and democracy in Nepal.[2] For all these reasons therefore, the Nepalese authorities had the apprehension, notwithstanding Janata party's declaration in its Election Manifesto that its government "will consciously promote a good neighbourly policy"[3], that the new Indian Government might not be favourably disposed towards the government in Nepal and that Koirala and his colleagues might receive support from the ruling Janata Party.

Nevertheless, the two leading newspapers of Nepal. '*The Rising Nepal*' and '*The Gorkhapatra*' in their editorials congratulated Desai on his assumption of the office of Prime Minister and hoped that this would facilitate the opening of a new chapter in the close and meaningful relations between the people and Governments of the two neighbouring countries.[4] *The Rising Nepal* hoped that Indo-Nepalese ties would continue to develop and flourish in the years ahead, where *The Gorkhapatra* hoped that the change of political leadership in New Delhi would not bring about change in India's permanent foreign policy.[5] Tulsi Giri, the Nepalese Prime Minister, hoped that the recent changes in India would not make any difference to Nepal as the changes had taken place in the government and not in the political system itself.[6]

In the first week of April 1977 King Birendra paid an unofficial visit to India to attend the World Conference on Religion, Philosophy and Culture. He was anxious to be assured of the attitude and policies of the new Indian Government.[7] He stopped over for a day in New Delhi and took the opportunity to hold wide-ranging discussions with Desai, Vajpayee and Jagjivan Ram on various issues of mutual interest, including the need to conclude a new treaty of trade and transit as soon as possible and to conduct negotiations to that end.[8] At this time Desai's Government was only a week old and the King's visit to New Delhi happened to be the first visit of any head of state since the Janata Party's assumption of power.

The King returned reassured that the relations between India and Nepal would continue to be friendly. Krishna Raj Aryal, Nepal's Foreign Minister, who accompanied the King, termed the visit as "successful" and said that the new administration in India was looking forward to having "very good relations with Nepal" and that was what Nepal wanted.[9] However, before any progress could be made for strengthening the ties between India and Nepal a controversy arose which cast dark shadow over their relations and it appeared that improvement of relations between them would not be easy.

On 9 April, 34 members of the Lok Sabha belonging to the Janata party made an appeal to the King of Nepal to release Koirala. The appeal stressed the point that it should not be interpreted as 'an interference in the internal affairs of Nepal".[10] This appeal was followed by an appeal by Jaya Prakash Narayan on 11 April. He appealed to the King to release Koirala and initiate the process of democratisation in his country. He said that Koirala symbolised the democratic forces in the country and that his release would be a good gesture by the King to bring about a political settlement.[11]

The statements produced sharp adverse reactions in Nepalese ruling circles. Nine members of the Rashtriya Panchayat of Nepal in a statement issued on 12 April bitterly criticised the statement issued by the Indian Members of Parliament terming it as an interference in the internal affairs of Nepal and saying that such statements would "only Jeopardise the growing friendly relations between India and Nepal".[12] At a Press Conference on 24 May 1977 Tulsi Giri said that "a full speed hate-Nepal campaign" showing undue concern for the political system of Nepal had been launched in responsible circles in India. He said that the Indian press and other media of communication and prominent leaders of the erstwhile Socialist Party had shown undue concern for the political system of Nepal. No self-respecting country would tolerate interference from external resources in matters of domestic jurisdiction, he asserted. He said that friendship and good relations between two sovereign countries could not flourish in such a climate.[13] Nepalese press was equally vehement in criticising India.[14]

On India's part, Chandra Shekhar, who later became the Chairman of the Janata party, was sent to Kathmandu on 27 April as an emissary of Jaya Prakash Narayan to intercede with the King for Koirala's release. But he was not permitted to see Koirala and returned after having an audience with the King.[15] The matter complicated further when on 9 May 1977 at a Press Conference at Gwalior Vajpayee said that India wished democracy to flourish all over the world and that, India being a democracy, people were free to express their views on issues including the detention of Koirala. On 10 May clarifying Government of India's stand Vajpayee repeated that he had said at Gwalior about India being a democracy and its people being free to express their views on issues including the issue of Koirala's detention but, at the same time, asserted that far from interfering in the internal affairs of other countries, his Government would maintain friendly relations with all countries and that its relations with the countries in the neighbourhood of India would be brotherly.[16] *The Gorkhapatra* welcomed Vajpayee's statement as timely and illustrative of the anxiety of the Government of India to strengthen Indo-Nepalese ties.[17] The newspaper's assessment was correct but Government of India's clarifications failed to convince Nepal.

On 25 May an spokesman of the Ministry of External Affairs expressed regret and unhappiness at Giri's statement. He said that India was surprised "that the Prime Minister of Nepal should characterise expressions of anxiety expressed by the free press in India as a kind of deliberate hate Nepal campaign". He reiterated that India would continue to work towards the development of healthy and good neighbourly relations with Nepal notwithstanding the statement made by Giri.[18] Obviously this alone could not have satisfied Nepal and Desai, with a view to pacify the ruffled feelings of Nepal, clarified that Jaya Prakash Narayan was not the Government of India and that the policy of the Government of India was based on non-interference in the internal affairs of other countries.[19] But even Desai's clarification failed in dispelling misgivings in Nepal against the Janata Party and its Government and the newspapers in Nepal continued to make adverse comments on India.[20]

However, soon thereafter Koirala was released on parole on grounds of ill-health for treatment abroad. Government of Nepal announced that it would bear the expenses incurred on the treatment of Koirala and he stayed for a few days in New Delhi en route to the United States.[21] Whatever might have been the motives of Nepal in releasing Koirala but obviously it responded to India's opinion though it tried to show otherwise.

Meanwhile, addressing the Royal Commonwealth Society of London on 10 June 1977 Vajpayee reiterated his Government's intention "to pursue even more vigorously than its predecessor the policy of friendship and understanding between India and its neighbours"[22] Having perhaps the recent controversy with Nepal in his mind, he said that there was in India "the greatest goodwill and friendship for Nepal and, therefore, such minor difficulties as may arise from time to time can be settled easily".[23] But Nepal continued to have misgivings about India to which the King gave oblique vent when on 15 June, addressing the National Panchayat of Nepal, he reiterated his determination to develop relations with friendly countries "on the basis of equality, non-interference in internal affairs and respect and understanding for each other's political systems and aspiration".[24] Read in the context of Nepal's complaints against India, the meaning of King's statement was obvious. Perhaps the King did not want to aggravate the controversy by himself making direct reference against India. As such, he referred to his discussions with the new leaders of the Government of India which, as he said, had further promoted mutual understanding between India and Nepal.[25]

On 29 June initiating the debate on the demands for grants of the Ministry of External Affairs in the Lok Sabha Vajpayee explained India's neighbourhood policy at some length in which he disavowed any intention, on India's part, to pose any threat to its neighbours, national personalities and recognised their (neighbours) "right to determine their separate national fulfilment". Such declarations of pious intentions failed to remove Nepal's misgivings as was clear from Giri's address to the Rashtriya Panchayat on 3 July. He said that India was indulging in "hostile activity" against Nepal by permitting its press, radio and television to indulge in "undesirable propaganda against our system and the supreme institution.[26] Nevertheless, Koirala's release created a thaw in the relations between the two countries.

Vajpayee succeeded in allaying Nepal's suspicions when he paid a visit to Kathmandu 14-16 July 1977. Nepal had a lingering suspicion, further strengthened by the controversy over the release of Koirala, that the new Government in New Delhi, like its predecessors, would take it for granted and have an overbearing attitude towards it. Vajpayee tried to remove misunderstandings and reinforce trust and confidence between the two neighbours. He showed ample awareness to the sensibility and psychology of India's small neighbour which had been keen for the recognition of its distinct identity and personality and for being treated on equal footing. But India by its omnipresence cast a long shadow over its cherished desire. Vajpayee in his speeches in Nepal repeatedly referred to Nepal's independent status in the comity of nations, disavowed, on India's part, any interest to interfere in its affairs, conveyed India's desires to have friendship on the basis of equality, and showed interest in Nepal's economic development and mutual beneficial co-operation.

In reply to a calling attention motion on his Nepal visit Vajpayee informed the Lok Sabha on 26 July that while he reiterated his government's commitment to the democratic way of life in India, at the same time, he "also pointed out that the Government of India would not interfere in the internal affairs of Nepal or for that matter, of any other country".[27] Earlier in his banquet speech in Nepal he had said that he felt "at home in the independent Kingdom of Nepal". That India and Nepal were two "independent" nations and that India had been "the first to rejoice in the development of Nepal's role in international affairs". That India recognised that Nepal had now "an honoured place in the brotherhood of nations and a diversity of international friendship". That the two countries should never "cease to respect each other, or to take each other for granted". He referred to India's repeated declarations that it would not interfere in the internal affairs of its neighbours as also to India's vision of destiny which was never of conquest but of friendship and equality with other nations and expressed new Government's determination to be true to that tradition. He had left no doubt in what India valued friendship with Nepal. As he said.

> with Nepal our experience and our goals are turned to furthering of our friendship. In friendship, we are and must be equals. Given friendship, India will consider it a privilege to make sacrifices without demanding equal benefits in return.[28]

Vajpayee discussed with his Nepalese counterpart all matters pertaining to India-Nepal relations in friendly and cordial atmosphere. However, two of them require special mention because of their overriding significance. The first of these was Nepal's proposal that it be declared a Zone of peace. Vajpayee clarified that his Government's stand in this regard was that the entire subcontinent should be an area of peace. He informed the Nepalese side that his Government was taking steps to improve relations with all of India's neighbours. As far as Nepal was concerned, he indicated that, in keeping with the friendly relations between the two countries, India would consider any suggestion from the Government of Nepal with an open mind.[29] At the same time, he also affirmed that there was a Treaty of Peace and Friendship between India and Nepal which accepted that both countries would live in perpetual peace and that this treaty and India's subsequent actions fully reaffirmed the independence, sovereignty and territorial integrity of Nepal.[30] The second issue was the question of a new Treaty of Trade and Transit between the two countries, which had been pending since 1976. Both sides stated their respective positions and agreed to "give careful consideration" to each other's point of view.

With his eloquence characterised by frankness and sensibility alike and with his willingness for pragmatic accommodation, Vajpayee succeeded in removing misunderstandings and in reinforcing trust and confidence between the two countries. Nepal welcomed the change of style in New Delhi of which Vajpayee gave ample proof.[31] "Even before Vajpayee left for Kathmandu both sides were aware that many of the problems had been blown out of proportion resulting in mutual suspicion."[32]

Vajpayee's visit to Kathmandu was followed by Desai's visit in December 1977. Desai was accompanied by his Foreign Minister Vajpayee. His visit to Kathmandu was the part of the new government's strategy to extend the hands of friendship and co-operation to the countries of the subcontinent in the hope that by living in harmony the nations of the subcontinent would gain stature in world forums.[33] Desai's visit to Nepal took place in a very congenial atmosphere and raised high hopes of a more amenable era of relations between the two countries. On his arrival in Kathmandu he said India's relations with Nepal will go on getting strengthened not only for mutual advantage but for the good of the whole neighbourhood. In reply to a question from a press reporter he said in his characteristic style that there was going to be complete co-operations between the two countries. There was no question of discussions about it.[34] He conveyed to the Government and people of Nepal that India cherished friendship with them and sought to promote relationship in a manner which respected the independence of both, advanced mutual interests and brought benefit to both[35]. Wide ranging discussions were held and mutually advantageous agreements reached which had earlier been settled between Vajpayee and Nepalese leaders.

The joint communique issued at the end of Desai's visit noted that the measures of identity of their views led the two Prime Ministers to believe that based on goodwill and trust a new chapter could be opened in relation between the two countries. They recognised the need to strengthen their economic co-operation on the basis of equality and mutual benefit. Desai affirmed India's determination to continue to participate fully in the developmental programmes of the Himalayan

Kingdom. It was in this spirit of understanding that they agreed to give priority to projects on the rivers linking the two countries for multiple benefits and the Devighat Power Project to which the Government of Nepal attached great importance.

On his return from Kathmandu, Desai told the Parliament in a statement on 12 December 1977 that the decision to have two treaties and separate agreement was a reflection of the spirit in respect of each other's independence as well as sensitivity that each country's economic policies did not harm the other.[36] Nepal could not have expected any more from the visit and it was not surprising, therefore, that the Nepalese considered the joint communique issued at the end of the visit "a significant enough gesture." They also noted Desai's willingness to accommodate their point of view as far as was possible[37] though he had not agreed to accept the proposal to constitute Nepal into the Zone of Peace.

Following the visit the atmosphere was one of expectancy of the opening of a more amenable era of relations between the two countries. Desai drew the right conclusions when he said that his visit, the discussions which he had and the general atmosphere of warmth and cordiality led him to believe that apprehensions and misgivings about India's attitude had been removed.[38] It was evident from the fact that when, on his return from the US, Koirala was again arrested and Jaya Prakash Narayan again made an appeal to the King for his release, it did not spark off, as in the past, a furore of anti-India sentiment in Nepal. Qualitative improvement of relations between the two countries appeared to have become steady.[39]

Development on Pending Projects

During the visit the two sides felt the necessity to remove bottlenecks in the execution of pending projects and agreed upon specific measures to set in motion the process of expeditiously executing four projects on the rivers Karnali, Mahakali, Rapti and Trisuli[40]. The Karnali Project was to be finalised entirely by international agencies including the United Nations Development Programme (UNDP). The project with an ultimate installed capacity of 4,000 MW was to be one of the biggest of its kind in the subcontinent.[41] The Pancheshwar Hydro-electric Project, proposed to be built on river Mahakali in Western Nepal, was equally ambitious and envisaged to generate 1,000 MW of electricity on completion. It was to be financed entirely by India. The two Prime Ministers agreed to nominate the representative of their respective country within three months to start joint investigations about this project.[42]

On the multi-purpose project on river Rapti at Bhalubhang it was agreed that experts of the two countries should meet within one month to finalise arrangements and prepare detailed project estimates within two years. As for the Devighat Project, India was to take it up as a turn-key project and it was agreed that a formal agreement to enable commencement of the work should be signed a soon as possible. The project, for which the Government of India was to provide Rs. 30 crores, was expected to meet the growing power needs of the Kathmandu Valley where Nepal was making an ambitious bid to set up several industrial units.[43] As to the Dolaghat-Dhankuta road in the mid lands in eastern Nepal, it was agreed that detailed ground surveys should be undertaken in as efficient and expeditious a matter as was possible.

An agreement was signed between the two governments on 7 April 1978 for the renovation and extension of the Chandra Canal System, construction of a pumped canal from Western Kosi Canal for lift irrigation and construction and distribution system from Western Kosi Canal in Nepal. Together these projects were expected to benefit a total area of 34,690 hectares in Nepal and were estimated to cost Rs. 12.45 crores. The planning and execution of these works were to be undertaken by Nepal. The agreement further paved the way for better co-operation between the two countries for the utilisation of water resources.

It was evident from the outgoing discussons that the climate of relations between the two countries had considerably improved since the formation of Janata Government in India. The Nepalese Prime Minister K.N. Bista who visited India 15-20 April 1978, termed it as "remarkable" and "tremendous"[44]. The ties between the two countries were further cemented as a result of his visit. He appeared to be assured of India's goodwill for Nepal, its disinclination to interfere in the internal affairs of its neighbours, and its desire to live in peace and harmony with Nepal and spoke eloquently about India's major role in generating a new climate of peace in the subcontinent.

Trade Treaties and Industrial Development

The Treaties pertaining to trade and transit could not be signed during Desai's visit as the documents were still being examined by experts of the two countries.[45] These could be signed in March 1978. Two treaties and an agreement of co-operation were signed in New Delhi on 17 March. The two treaties, the Treaty of Trade and the Treaty of Transit replaced the Indo-Nepal Treaty of Trade and Transit of 1971 which had expired in August 1976. Valid for a period of five years from the date of signing, the treaty of trade provided that India would assist in the industrialisation of Nepal by enlarging the scope of preferences for Nepalese manufactured products in the Indian market, that the two countries would give preferential treatment to each other's primary products on a reciprocal basis, and the necessary arrangements would be made to maintain supplies of essential commodities needed by each other.

Since the early 1960s when, as a counter-measure to its economic overdependence on India, Nepal embarked on the course of diversifying its trade with third countries and started demanding transit facilities at Radhikapur on erstwhile East-Pakistan-India border.[46] But India viewed the demand as motivated by political considerations as it would draw in a third country in a bilateral arrangement and thereby could enlarge the area of conflict[47]. The new Transit treaty threw upon the use of overland routes for the export of Nepalese goods to Bangladesh as also for Nepal's trade with third countries through Bangladesh. It thus conceded a long standing Nepalese demand for an alternative transit route for goods originating from and destined to Nepal. But it should be noted here that the situation had changed considerably since the emergence of Bangladesh as an independent country. It was expected that the procedures prescribed in the treaty would considerably facilitate the traffic-in-transit for Nepal's cargo. The new facilities included movement of bulk cargo both by rail and road.[48]

Considerable economic benefits for Nepal resulted from Bista's visit to India. The visit marked the beginning of India's involvement in the industrialisation of the Himalayan Kingdom. India's interest in the industrialisation of Nepal could be traced back to April 1976, or even earlier, when in course of Nepalese Prime Minister Tulsi Giri's visit to this country, the idea of India co-operating in setting up joint enterprises for Nepal's industrial development had been mooted.[49] But areas suitable for such enterprises could not be identified so far. This was done during this visit and it covered the fields of cement production, paper and pulp industries, fruit processing and canning.[50]

Wide ranging and encompassing discussions were held between the two sides which were marked by complete understanding and shared perception on both bilateral and international issues. A notable area of discussion was the economic, technical and ecological aspects of the various river projects for harnessing the waters of the tributaries of Ganges in Nepal with Indian assistance. These discussions were related to the progress of the projects that were already under construction with Indian collaboration and others that were now under active consideration. The talks reflected the keenness of the two sides for a periodic review of the ongoing projects and an early commencement of the feasibility studies of the others to draw up a time bound programme for their completion. In a joint communiqué issued on 17 April 1978 the Prime Ministers of the two countries expressed their hope that the draft agreement on the Devighat hydro-electric project would be signed soon. Bista, on his part, expressed his happiness at India's decision to increase its commitment for the renovation of Chandra Canal, construction of Pumped Canal and the distribution system of the Western Kosi Canal in Nepal.

Bista stressed Nepal's policy of self-reliance in economic development. Desai pledged India's continued assistance in various fields of Nepal's scientific, technical and infrastructural development. Both expressed that India's contribution had been beneficial to the development of Nepal.

In pursuance of the decision taken in April 1978 in course of Bista's visit to New Delhi a high powered multi-disciplinary team of senior Indian officials led by V. Krishnamurthy, Secretary, Department of Heavy Industry, Government of India, visited Nepal 26-30 July 1978[51]. A Memorandum of Understanding on Industrial and Economic Co-operation was signed at Kathmandu on 30 July 1978 by D.P. Koirala, leader of the Nepalese delegation and Secretary in the Ministry of Industry and Commerce, Government of Nepal, and Krishnamurthy. The Memorandum envisaged new dimensions of economic and industrial co-operation between the two countries. It opened a new chapter of close partnership in respect of joint projects covering the large, medium, small scale, cottage and agro-industrial sectors.

Among the large projects considered, the more important were related to a cement plant at Udaypur and the development of paper and pulp industry for export to India and third countries. Other large projects to be taken up as joint ventures were related to magnetite, zink, lead and iron and steel. It was agreed that a diesel pumping set project would be established in Nepal for the manufacture of five HP diesel pump sets.[52] Joint ventures in the implementation of large industrial projects were considered with a view to reducing the trade deficit between the two countries and subserving other objectives of Nepal's industrial policy. Co-operation was also established in the area of promotion of small and cottage industries which included extension and establishment of industrial estates, entrepreneurship development programmes, deputation of technical personnel, training of technical personnel and provision of credit.

It was decided to share India's experience with Nepal in upgrading skills and expertise of artisans, craftsman and technicians. India's Hindustan Machine Tools organisation was to extend its expertise towards setting up a regional training institute to serve the needs of western and far-western regions of Nepal and a functional industrial estate at Butwal which was to comprise several light engineering industries with the Common Facilities Centre. The HMT was to be associated with the setting up of a production-oriented polytechnic in the central region which, in addition to courses in civil, mechanical and automobile engineering, was to provide training facilities to skilled workers.

In view of several large projects which were to be set up envisaging exports to India and third countries, it was recognised that infrastructure relating to rail links would be required to be developed. A quick assessment was to be made for the establishment of railway lines and railway sidings which was crucial in enhancing the feasibility and viability of large projects in such areas as cement, pulp, paper, magnesite etc. Financial arrangements regarding joint ventures were also discussed. Time bound schedules were provided for the implementation of the decisions taken at the meetings between the two delegations.

George Fernandes, Minister for Industries. Government of India, visited Kathmandu 24-26 September 1978 for, as he said, "formalising" the understanding and decisions arrived at earlier in giving shape to bilateral discussions during the past few months particularly in respect of joint industrial ventures.[53] Ground had already been cleared during the official level talks ten days earlier in New Delhi in respect of a large cement factory and a large paper factory with Indian collaboration and minority equity participation. He signed a Memorandum of Understanding with his Nepalese counterpart. In terms of the Memorandum, feasibility studies were to be conducted by the Government of India regarding railway links among others, for the Udaypur cement project, the pulp and paper project and for transit of goods from Dhulabari in eastern Nepal to Calcutta.[54] Following the signing of the agreement, Fernandes told that India would involve a total investment of 180 crores in these industries which would be set up jointly in Nepal. These industries were expected to provide employment to 10 thousand people and reduce Kingdom's adverse trade balance which stood at Rs. 100 crores. He also announced that India would provide a package grant-in-aid assistance of Rs. 9 crores to be given over a period of two years. India was also to provide 3.5 crores for financing the purchase of capital goods required for the development of small scale industries.[55]

Fernandes utilised the opportunity to discuss the problem of the control of floods and the plans to use river water resources for irrigation and power generation. He found the Nepalese response to the Indian viewpoint of joint control of floods "very positive" and was appreciative of Nepal's gesture of help and sympathy towards flood victims in India.[56] It emerged from the discussions that the members of the Planning Commission of both the countries should hold a meeting with the energy experts to formulate plans to use river water resources for irrigation, power generation and flood control. Fernandes was satisfied with the discussions and said a "deep understanding" had been reached".[57]

On his way back from Havana after attending the Non-aligned Summit King Birendra paid a six-day official visit to India 19-24 September, 1979. Vast changes had occurred in India in the last few months. Janata Government of Morarji Desai had collapsed. The leader of the break away faction, Charan Singh, had taken over as the Prime Minister of India, who, having failed to win the confidence of Lok Sabha, had announced elections to be held in January 1980. As such, Charan Singh's Government was only a caretaker Government. Serious discussions could not be held under the circumstances. Moreover, no outstanding bilateral problem existed between the two countries at this time. So the talks perhaps did not go beyond the exchange of greetings. Meanwhile, a referendum had been announced in Nepal to be held in may 1980 to decide the issue of retaining the existing partyless governmental system or to adopt multi-party democratic system. This raised high hopes in India in view of its people's and government's known preferences for a democratic system of government based on people's will.

Unauthorised Trade Across the Border

The joint communique, issued at the end of Desai's visit to Kathmandu stated that the two countries also discussed problems relating to the unauthorised trade across the border. It included the open common border between the two countries across the problem of unauthorised flow of goods. By the late 1950s re-export of goods from Nepal into India imported by the former from third countries took place on a cosiderable scale. It became a major irritant in India-Nepal economic relations and it was stipulated in the Treaty of Trade and Transit of 1960 that Nepal would ensure that there was no re-export into India of goods imported by it from third countries.[58] However, inspite of the treaty provision the evil, instead of being eliminated, went on increasing. This issue was discussed and it was decided that "a separate agreement should be reached which would embody effective measures to control such flows across (our) open border."[59]

In pursuance of the decision arrived at between Desai and Bista to curb unauthorised flow of goods across the open border between the two countries an agreement of co-operation was signed to ensure that the economic interests of either country were not adversely affected through unauthorised trade between the two countries.[60] The two countries also agreed to consult each other regularly to facilitate effective and harmonious implementation of the Treaties and Agreements with a view to promoting closer economic co-operation between Nepal and India and for the harmonious working of the two. It was agreed that an inter-governmental committee would meet regularly every six months alternately in Kathmandu and New Delhi.

Following the signing of the treaties. The *Times of India* (New Delhi) commented in its editorial that New Delhi viewed the signing of the separate trade and transit treaties as a magnanimous gesture by a big country towards a small neighbour designed to make relations friendlier than before. It regretted that Kathmandu did not view the Treaties that way and considered it as a victory.[61] Nevertheless, there was no doubt that relations between the two countries had become extremely happy and the benefits flowed to Nepal.

Basic Issues Remained Unresolved

The Janata Government in New Delhi appeared to have largely succeeded in "winning the confidence and trust of the authorities in Kathmandu through a process of give and take."[62] Kathmandu appeared to have shed its earlier prejudices to co-operate with India in a big way. But Nepal did not give up the stance of viewing itself as a buffer between India and China, notwithstanding the qualitative improvement in the relations between the two countries which was now characterised by trust and confidence. Bista gave expression to this anxiety of Nepal when, in his address to the Indian Council of World Affairs on 16 April 1978 said that in situations when it became difficult for India and China strive for peaceful co-existence, a small country like Nepal could not influence the course of events by taking side in such situations.[63] Kathmandu's efforts to seek the involvement of China in the affairs of the subcontinent under the guise of regulating the use of the eastern rivers also betrayed the same anxiety. Nor did it give up the idea of Zone of Peace which was based, as Bista said, on its realisation that it could not seek comfort by walking on a razor's edge all the time for avoiding involvement in conflicts of big power interests working at cross purposes. Thus the basic cause of difference between India and Nepal remained unresolved. In view of India's sensitivity and known stand on these issues Nepal simply chose to play them down and to work with patience which had paid it in the immediate past.[64] In less favourable circumstances these issues could erupt to mar Indo-Nepal relations.

REGIME OF NATIONAL FRONT

Premiership of V.P.Singh (1 December 1989-7 November 1990)

As a result of the general elections held in November 1989, with the support of the Bharatiya Janata Party and the Left Front, Vishwanath Pratap Singh became the new Prime Minister of India. Although the election was fought on domestic issues, the Indo- Nepal relation received adequate publicity in the speeches of the political leaders. The National Front Manifesto had referred to India's relations with Nepal and stated that "negotiations will be started on all issues of contention to find an amicable solution" and also help "strengthen the economy of Nepal and honour her self-respect"[65]. V.P. Singh, the Prime Minister of India, after taking over the office, expressed his government's keenness to take all possible steps to improve the relations with Nepal.[66] On 2 December 1989, in an interview he said that an "undue shock was given to Nepal and the trauma, which Nepal had to undergo due to the deadlock in Nepal-India trade and transit relations, is quite unnecessary."

Kathmandu too, welcomed the change of guard in New Delhi and Prime Minister Marich Man Singh Shrestha, in his message of congratulations to the new Indian Prime Minister, had said that he was encouraged by the latter's reported statement to improve relations with Nepal and assured his full co-operation and support towards improving the traditional, close and friendly relations between Nepal and India to the mutual benefit of the peoples of both countries. *The Rising Nepal*, in its editorial, while welcoming the new dispensation stated that everyone was wishing Singh's success in his endeavours, hoping that Nepal's position in favour of dialogue to end the unfortunate statement in Nepal-India relations would be reciprocated and that definite steps would be taken earlier towards improving the bilateral relations.[67]

But as far as the basic content and substance of the foreign policy was concerned, V.P. Singh soon realised that there was no scope for a sharp divergence or major departure. While answering a question he conceded that foreign policy is not partisan. It meant that it does not belong to a single party. It is dictated by geo-political considerations.[68] He elaborated this idea in course of an interview to a foreign media when he said that in relation to Nepal security issue between the two countries needed to be settled early. The National Front Government did not bring about a drastic change in India's Nepal Policy. In the circumstances, Shailendra Kumar Upadhaya, the Nepalese Foreign Minister visited New Delhi 2-5 January 1990 for talks on the Indo-Nepal trade and transit dispute.[69] The talks were held, according to a foreign policy spokesman, in a cordial and friendly atmosphere, covered the entire gamut of relations and were aimed at achieving understanding on broad components of bilateral relationships.[70] However, no breakthrough came as a result of these negotiations. Despite the fact that New Delhi was willing to accommodate Nepal, it was not willing to surrender its security and other concerns while negotiating with Nepal. India was not prepared to give security a back seat while talking to Nepal. Hence it belied the hopes of several people, particularly in Nepal, that with the change in government things would get normalised. The strategic perceptions of the new government were not substantially different from their predecessors.[71] As a follow up of this visit official level talks were held in New Delhi 3-5 Februrary 1990 between delegations led by the foreign Secretaries of the two countries.

The success of V.P. Singh in building an anti-Congress front in India in 1989, showed that the centrist and leftist parties could join hands politically for a clearcut objectives. The year also witnessed a common objective for the Nepali Congress and the leftist parties in the Himalayan Kingdom. The common approach was to have a multi-party political system in Nepal in place of the Partyless Panchayat System. Thus a new political grouping was intended to organise a political struggle for democracy. In the new system King Birendra was bound to appoint the leader of the majority party as his Prime Minister. On 18 February 1990 the movement for democracy was started. Ultimately the revolution in Nepal celebrated its victory on 19 April 1990 by the swearing-in of a new ministry, with Krishna Prasad Bhattarai as the Prime Minister. Bhattarai, in a letter to the Prime Minister of India on 30 April 1990 said, "I am deeply grateful for you friendly sentiments and encouraged by your expression of desire to resolve Nepal-India relationship and strengthen it in all areas. I fully reciprocate your friendship and wish to assure you of my whole-hearted effort to that end.[72] He also proposed a meeting at the highest level with India for a political settlement and added that for him there was no prestige issue on such a vital matter which was affecting the entire Nepalese people and also the Indian people living on the other side of the border.[73]

As the Interim Government in Nepal led by Bhattarai was more responsive to Indian initiatives and sensitivities, Inder Kumar Gujral, India's Minister for External Affairs, said in an interview with *The Rising Nepal*, a government-owned English daily, that India was willing to "accommodate the economic aspirations of the Nepalese people".[74] He hinted that India was disturbed about "security concerns" and discrimination of Indian nationals in Nepal. "If these two things are sorted out there will hardly be anything which can keep us away from co-operation.[75] It was an opportune moment and in a bid to minimize the economic problems of the people of Nepal as well as widen his political support, Bhattarai came to India and negotiated with it in June 1990. The understanding reached between the two governments brought an end to almost a year long stalemate. Government of India's agreement to open all the traditional points of transit for trade purposes and a few more to allow foreign tourists to visit Nepal had indeed been widely acclaimed in Nepal.[76] The acrimony and suspicion that marked Indo-Nepal relations during the past two years or so had given way to a new phase of mutual understanding and goodwill.[77] As a follow up, the accord implementation was reviewed in August 1990 when Inder Kumar Gujral paid a three-day official visit to Kathmandu.[78] The Indian Foreign Minister also met King Birendra, who expressed the desire that india should play a major role in the regional development of South Asia through SAARC. The situation on both the sides became favourable to a point that Kathmandu turned to India for expert advice and friendly consultations for Constitution Recommendation Committee and, New Delhi, in response, made available the services of Dr. Laxmi Mall Singhvi, eminent constitutional expert and jurist together with Bombay-based leading lawyer and writer on constitutional issues, A.G. Noorani.[79]

Economic Issues

The National Front Government inherited a tense Indo-Nepal relations. It was on account of the lapse of the trade and transit treaties signed in March 1978. This treaty continued until 1988 and was extended twice for the period of six months each, continuing till March 1989. When the Trade and Transit Treaty actually expired, it brought the bilateral trade relations to a grinding halt and putting the Nepalese to great inconvenience. One of the principal differences between New Delhi and Kathmandu which persisted since March 1989, was that the former insisted on having one integrated treaty covering both trade and transit while the latter wanted two separate treaties.[80] It seemed possible that the new National Front Government in New Delhi headed by V.P. Singh might dilute the stand of the earlier government on this issue and thus pave the way for a resolution of the problem. Already the new leadership had made it clear that improvement of relations with neighbours would be their endeavour and that Nepal and Sri Lanka will be its immediate concern[81] But why did things reach such an impass? Leadership in New Delhi blame Kathmandu for adopting a partisan attitude towards the Indian people and trade, whereas the Nepalese leadership has no definite version to defend the action. Perhaps this seemed to be the reason that it is playing the rhetoric of so called imposition of economic blockade by India. However, the balance of trade of the decade, under reference, indicated that trade went up from 21.00 million dollars to 52.00 million dollars. Even on 23 March, 1989 when trade relations got scrapped, the import and export of Nepal with India were 31.3 per cent and 41.2 per cent of the total. Hence, it may be wrong to suggest that Nepal had an unfavourable trade with India and, therefore, whatever steps it has taken recently in relation with India's trade may be considered as a biased action. Some were also of the view that the crux of the present crisis lies elsewhere. To pressure India for the acceptance of the Zone of Peace' proposal and to extract some more benefits on the trade front, Nepal as usual, not only preferred to criticize India but treated the Indian people and trade against all treaty commitments.[82]

Sensing the good gestures of the new regime Shailendra Kumar Upadhaya, the Foreign Minister of Nepal visited New Delhi 3-5 January 1990 to discuss the entire gamut of Indo-Nepal relations. The fruitful talks held during the visit and as a follow up India-Nepal official level talks were held in New Delhi and Kathmandu respectively at the Foreign Secretary level. In between a meeting of Indo-Nepalese Co-operation in Energy and Civil Aviation was held in New Delhi and represented by Nepalese Ambassador to India Smt. Bhinda S. Shah. Referring to the bilateral co-operation in energy India's Minister of Energy and Civil Aviation Shri Arif Mohammed Khan said that a number of irrigation and power projects had been set up with Indian assistance in Nepal. These include Kosi Barrage and Western Kosi Canal, Gandak Barrage, Chatra Canal, Trishuli and Devighat Hydroelectric Power Projects and Chandra Canal modernization and Pump Canal.[83] Several rounds of talks were held between India and Nepal which covered subjects of mutual interests, trade transit, economic co-operation and security matters. The talks contributed to greater mutual understanding of each other's serious concerns and sensitivities and registered a definite progress towards a comprehensive solution of all outstanding problems.[84] Inder Kumar Gujral, India's Minister for External Affairs admitted in a statement in Lok Sabha on 30 March, 1990 that significant progress had been achieved towards understanding and resolving outstanding problems with Nepal.[85]

New Delhi and Kathmandu had a major breakthrough in its relations in June 1990 when Nepal's Prime Minister Krishna Prasad Bhattarai came to India and discussed the whole gamut of Indo-Nepal relations with his Indian counterpart, Vishwanath Pratap Singh. On the eve of his visit, India's Foreign Minister Inder Kumar Gujral expressed his country's willingness to "accommodate the economic aspirations of the Nepalese people". In an interview to the government-owned English daily *The Rising Nepal* he also revealed that New Delhi attached considerable importance to the forthcoming visit of Nepalese Prime Minister.[86] Bhattarai was also hopeful and before he left for New Delhi, in Kathmandu said that his mission was to reopen his country's trade life line through India.[87] Two rounds of exhaustive talks between the two Prime Ministers were marked by "particular warmth and cordiality and resulted in restoring by 1 July, 1990, trade and transit ties between the two countries.[88] The non-renewal of the trade and transit treaties had seriously damaged the economy of the Himalayan Kingdom.[89]

ANNEXURE-1

Steps to be taken by the Government of India.

Trade

1. Import of primary products from Nepal to be exempted from basic customs duties as well as from quantitative restrictions.

2. Provide access, free of basic customs duties and quantitative restrictions, for all manufactured articles containing not less than sixty-five per cent of Nepalese materials or Nepalese and Indian materials, on a case-by-case basis, keeping in mind the need for expeditious clearance.
3. Allow fifty per cent tariff concession of MFN rate of import duty, where value of Nepalese and Indian materials and labour added in Nepal is at least forty per cent of the ex-factory price, on a case-by-case basis, keeping in mind the need for expeditious clearance.
4. Export to Nepal of quota goods, namely, those that are either restricted or canalized for export from India.
5. The refund of Indian Excise Duty to Nepal under the Duty Refund Procedure should be such as to cover, but not to exceed, the basic and additional customs duties levied on similar goods imported from third countries.
6. Supplies of coke and coal to Nepal under quota will be resumed. Prices and supply schedules will be subject to agreement between the MMTC and the Nepal Coal Limited.
7. Canalizing of exports of POL products to Nepal through IOC, and Agreement between IOC and NOC for product exchange between the two organizations.
8. Restoration of the standby credit facility to Nepal at the enhanced level of Indian Rupees 35 crores.

Transit

9. Notification under section 7 of the Customs Act, 1962, restoring the 22 border points covered under GOI Notification No. 73/ Customs/F.No. 552/58/78-LCI and 238/Customs dated 19.5.1984, and the routes specified therein as Land Customs stations for the movement of goods between India and Nepal.
10. The 15 points earlier designated as Transit Points for Nepal's transit trade, through India, with third countries will be reinstated.

Others

11. Restoration of the movement of Nepalese trucks to and from the nearest railway heads/terminals.
12. Once a joint venture is approved by the two Governments, the Government of India would allow the movement of capital as per the terms agreed upon in the joint venture.

13. Restoration of the three earlier immigration points on the Indo-Nepal border for the movement of tourists.

ANNEXURE-II

Steps to be taken by His Majesty's Government of Nepal.

Trade

1. Restoration of tariff preferences to Indian goods by inter alia, exemption of additional customs duty.
2. Exemption of basic customs duty on imports of primary products from India as provided for similar products from Nepal imported to India.
3. Tariff preferences for third country goods should not be such as to be detrimental to the tariff regime for Indian exports.
4. Valuation of Indian goods exported under CRP for the assessment of Basic Customs duty will be made on the basis of ex-factory/ex-depot price excluding any element of refundable Indian duties and taxes but including transport and insurance charge, where applied.

Indian Nationals

5. Removal of Indian nationals from the ambit of the Work Permit Scheme.
6. Indian nationals employed in schools in Nepal will be placed on the same footing as Nepalese nationals as regards the terms and conditions of employment.

Other Matters

7. Removal of restrictions on the movement of Indian currency between Nepal and India on the basis of reciprocity.
8. Restoration of facilities for Indian nationals to have their vehicles registered in Nepal on the basis of reciprocity.

Consequently, India will once again import raw material without imposing any duty and Nepal will reciprocate by abolishing the additional imports it had levied on goods from this country.[90] The acrimony and suspicion that marked Indo-Nepal relations during the past two years or so have given way to a new phase of mutual understanding and goodwill.[91] The happy turn of events has shown that a sense of goodwill and trust have been restored. This breakthrough gave substance to the National Front Government's bid to improve the political environment in the region[92]

With a view to review the implementation of the accord signed by V.P. Singh and K.P. Bhattarai, India's Minister for External Affairs Inder Kumar Gujral paid a three-day visit to Nepal 5-7 August 1990.[93] During the visit, in course of the talks with prime Minister K.P. Bhattarai it was agreed to open three additional entry points along the Nepal-India border in the interest of overseas tourists.[94] Another positive development was an agreement for a team of Indian experts to arrive here (in Kathmandu) shortly in connection with preparing a project report on the proposed Raxaul-Kathmandu railway (route). Probe is to be made into the possibilities of laying up railway network in other parts of the country.[95] In Kathmandu, Gujral took the opportunity to address Nepal Chambers of Commerce on 5 August 1990 and Nepal Council of World Affairs on 6 August respectively. He advocated on the occasion for the establishment of a South Asian Free Trade Association or a common market for the region and suggested that the South Asian Association for Regional Co-operation is obvious framework within which it could be done.[96]

Defence

Security perception of India's new government was not substantially different from their predecessors. The National Front Government did not bring a drastic change in India's Nepal policy. It refused to give security a back seat while talking to Kathmandu as indicated by Vishwanath Pratap Singh, in one of the interviews to foreign media that security issue between the two countries needed to be settled early.[97] Actually, what made Indian attitude stiff towards the treaty of trade and transit leaving Kathmandu to face a lot of difficulties, was Nepalese purchase of ground to air missiles and other military hardware from China. India, however, did not press this issue openly. But Article five, six and seven of the Treaty of Peace and Friendship (1950) says that the Government of Nepal shall be free to import from or through the territory Indian arms, ammunition or warlike material and equipment. This arrangement shall be worked out by the two governments acting in consultation.[98] The purchases were also against the 1965 exchange of letters in which the Nepalese ambassador confirmed that these letters constituted an agreement between the two countries. The understanding was that India would supply the entire requirement of the Nepalese army to the best of its ability, with Britain and the USA being allowed to step in only when India was unable to do so. Moreover, the agreement further stipulated that even when British and US arms were permitted, they would have to be routed to the land-locked Kingdom only through Indian territory. Thus, arms purchases from China without India's knowledge and approval were implicitly ruled out.

The visit of Nepalese Foreign Minister Shailendra Kumar Upadhyaya to New Delhi in the first week of January 1990, followed by Foreign Secretary level talks between the two countries, failed to resolve the deadlock. New Delhi, perhaps not being satisfied and in cognizance with its security threats and perceptions, had sent a draft proposal to Nepal in March 1990, which dealt with provisions relating to social, economic and political issues. Part II of the proposal dealing with defense co-operation stated that India would provide arms, ammunition, military training and assistance in the raising of additional units of the Royal Nepal Army. Article IV of Part II made it binding on Nepal to consult India before entering into any alliance with a third country on import of arms, ammunition or military training. By the proposals India desired to restrict Nepal procuring arms from China in 1988 which was considered by India to be against the spirit of the 1950 Treaty and 1965 Agreement.[99]

On 19 April 1990, an Interim Government was formed under the premiership of the Nepali Congress leader Krishna Prasad Bhattarai. The new leadership in Nepal should be given the credit for recognizing the Indian understanding, Indian susceptibilities. One of the first indications to come out of Nepal after the Bhattarai Government took over to make it known that the arms deal with China would not be carried further. Bhattarai made the right gesture before coming to India when he announced that the next shipment of arms from China was being deferred.[100] His visit to New Delhi took place in June 1990 and discussed with the Indian counterpart several issues including security. In the joint communiqué, issued at the end of the visit on June 10, both countries agreed to respect each other's security concerns and pledged not to allow any activities on their soil directed against the other. Once again, it was agreed to have "prior consultations with a view to reaching mutual agreement on such defence-related matters which in the view of either country could pose a threat to its security"[101]. By accepting the security concerns of India, an implicit assurance was elicited from Nepal that it would not use a policy of equidistance, violating Indian security interests, and this included not granting the Chinese projects in the Terai and importing arms from China. In an interview, Bhattarai had assured that Nepal would take care of Indian susceptibilities on security matters and would not allow Nepal to be a base for any anti-Indian activity.[102]

During his visit to Kathmandu, Inder Kumar Gujral met King Birendra in August 1990. In their 30-minute talks both underlined the necessity that Nepal and India should seriously consider reduction of military expenditure and more meaningful diversion of resources for the economic development of the region.[103] Gujral, while addressing to the Nepal Council of World Affairs, drew Nepalese attention to the grave limitations of the pursuit of security through military means and said. "The real threat to our domestic social order, as well as to the international order, today stems from the non-military threats to security- the degradation of the environment; the distortions which excessive military expenditure have introduced in the global economy and the way they are crippling the national economies of major military spenders; inequality among nations; and above all the denial of social justice within nations.[104] After the fall of the present government, the former Ambassador to Nepal. Lt. General S. K. Sinha claimed that relationship of India with Nepal was never as good as it became during the Janata Dal Government led by V.P. Singh. He added further that Indian Government being the biggest military power in the Indian subcontinent should understand the viewpoints of Nepal, if the relationship has to be cordial. The V.P. Singh's Government instilled confidence among the Nepali rulers by assuring non-interference in Nepal's internal affairs.

Chandra Shekhar
(10 November 1990-21 June 1991)

In place of V.P. Singh, Chandra Shekhar became the Prime Minister of India with the support of the Congress Party. The present Prime Minister had been, in particular known to be a champion of the pro-democratic forces in Nepal. The first country, the new premier liked to visit was Nepal in February 1991 at a time when the country were going to embark on the great democratic exercise of universal adult franchise with a view to institutionalizing parliamentary democracy. In Kathmandu Chandra Shekhar discussed with Bhattarai, his Nepalese counterpart, in an cordial atmosphere. He sought to dispel misconceptions in Nepal that India being much bigger in size would try to dominate Nepal's economy but suggesting that the two economies were characterized by a relationship of inter-dependence rather than of dependence.[105] The multi party elections under the new constitution were held on 12 May, 1991 and Chandra Shekhar sent the warmest felicitations and good wishes to Girija Prasad Koirala on assumption of Prime Minister's office of the Himalayan Kingdom.[106] Because the new regime of India was supported by Rajiv Gandhi it was apprehended that Chandra Shekhar may be under pressure to follow the former Congress (I) Government's policy towards Nepal. This may again lead to a worsening of bilateral relations.[107] But it did well to follow the wise policy of the National Front Government towards Nepal. The essential ingredients of that policy were a scrupulous respect for Nepal's sovereignty and sensitivity, avoidance of any action that might even remotely appear as interference in Nepal's internal affairs and magnanimity in providing economic and other assistance.[108]

The visit of Chandra Shekhar to Kathmandu began on 13 February 1991 and it was viewed variously in political circles. The anti-Nepali Congress groups were of the view that the Indian Prime Minister is coming basically to indicate in no uncertain terms his solidarity with the Nepali Congress. They contended that the Indian leader had timed the visit to tell the Nepalese voters that as one of the "architect of Nepalese democracy" it is his wish that the Nepali Congress is voted into power in the elections. The Himalayan Kingdom can expect to get almost everything it wants from India. While, on the other were the ones who presented a more "balanced and realistic" view that soon after assuming office of the PM Chandra Shekhar had said that his first official visit would be to Nepal, a close and friendly neighbour with whom India's relations have indeed been varied and wide ranging from time immemorial.[109] This school of thought claimed that Chandra Shekhar is visiting Nepal to keep his own words.

In the background of a very cordial relations brought about by the National Front Government, Chandra Shekhar was bound to receive a tumultous welcome and more so in the case of the present Prime Minister, in view of his personal relations with the Nepali Congress leaders. On the eve of his visit to Nepal a spokesman said that Chandra Shekhar's visit was expected to strengthen the unique and exceptionally close relationship between the two countries.[110] His Nepalese counterpart K.P. Bhattarai hosted a banquet in honour of the visiting guest and took the opportunity to recall, "we both realise that there is the necessity to strengthen economic ties between our two countries. It is not only the compulsion of geography that dictates closer links, though that itself is no less vital. He expressed sincere gratitude to the Government and people of India for the generous help and assistance that they have extended to us.[111] Chandra Shekhar had wide ranging discussions with his Nepalese counterpart and other political leaders but the visit failed to remove the air of suspicion to an extent, an overhang of the past is nurtured by the Big Brother Syndrome under which official Nepal continues to labour vis-a-vis India.[112]

But the visit was a success from the economic point of view. According to a decision taken during the visit a high level delegation went to Kathmandu, led by the Secretary, Department of Power, Sri S. Rajgopal to attend the meeting of the Karnali Co-ordinating Committee. The Karnali Project, located in Western Nepal on the Karnali river known as Ghagra in India, would have an installed capacity of 10,8000 MW, the second largest in the world. The Project envisaged the construction of the 270 mt. high Rockfill dam, the third highest in the world.[113] As a follow up of the visit the second meeting of the Indo-Nepal Sub-Commission on Water Resources[114] began in the middle of April 1991 in New Delhi. The Indian delegation was led by Dr. M.A. Chitale, Secretary, Water Resources and Nepalese delegation by B.K. Pradhan, Secretary, Water Resources, Government of Nepal. During the four day discussions they discussed the development of common water resources including that of taming of Kosi river and other mega projects like Karnali and Pancheshwar. The meeting was being viewed as that of great importance in this background and was expected to draw an action plan and time frame for different activities of mutual interest to both the countries.

REGIME OF UNITED FRONT

Premiership of H.D. Deve Gowda (1 June 1996-21 April 1997)

H.D. Deve Gowda, as a leader of the United Front (a coalition of thirteen political parties) took the oath of Premiership of India on 1 June

1996. Soon after his assumption of office the King of Nepal in his message of greetings maintained that it carries Kingdom's sincere good wishes for your successful tenure along with our hope that the age-old relations between our two neighbouring countries would be further strengthened during your tenure of governance.[115] In July 1996, the Communists in particular became critical in Nepal inside and outside parliament over the news that India had encroached Nepalese territory in the east. On 3 July the border officials of the two countries after an understanding decided to identify boundary pillars on the basis of the old map of 1874. The agitation in Kathmandu was pertaining to the controversial junge pillar built across Mechi river in 1818. Although the Indian Embassy in Nepal, in a strong worded press release on 25 July said, "There is no question of the boundary pillar being manipulated to the advantage of either Nepal or India. Far less are the possibilities of forcible alteration of any of the border lines.[116] Prakash Chandra Lohani, the Nepalese Foreign Minister said, "The newly built markers in Jhapa are in line with the 1816 Sugauli Treaty and they were constructed only on being approved by the joint field team representing both Nepal and India."

For the last several years Nepal had been facing the problem of Bhutani refugees of the Nepali origin who were driven out by Bhutan and were now attempting to cross the border from the Indian side. In the two-days meeting of Nepalese Foreign Minister, P.C. Lohani with Indian leaders in August 1996 Kathmandu sought India's direct intervention in the matter because Bhutan and Nepal had held eight round of talks on the issue, but without success. The Government of India viewed it a bilateral issue and the dispute should be resolved between Kathmandu and Thimpu. Inder Kumar Gujral, the Minister for External Affairs under the new dispensation, made it clear that both Bhutan and Nepal continue to be India's neighbour. New Delhi would not like to get involved in any controversy between the two.[117] Apart from this, Lohani said that India had agreed in principle to allow Nepal alternative transit routes through Kakar Bhitta, Phulbari and Banglabandh points to take its goods to Bangladesh. He also disclosed that on the Indo-Nepalese treaty both sides have agreed to review it at the "appropriate" level and time. It went to the credit of the coalition Government in Nepal to have the Mahakali treaty ratified on 20 September 1996, by an overwhelming majority in the joint session of Parliament. The ratification paved the way for foreign investment in Nepal. Had the treaty been rejected in Parliament it would have led to a serious crisis in the government.[118]

Inder Kumar Gujral
(21 April 1997-19 March 1998)

In a significant political development in India, Inder Kumar Gujral replaced H.D. Deve Gowda as the Prime Minister of the country on 21 April 1997. The new Prime Minister went to Nepal in June 1997 and discussed the matters of mutual interest in a cordial and co-operative atmosphere. The two sides took a number of decisions and in pursuance of that, senior officials from the Home Departments of the two countries held their first meeting at Kathmandu in July 1997 which continued for three days. At the end of the talk it was stated that the two sides have agreed to evolve a mechanism to enhance co-operation to check the infiltration of terrorists smuggling of arms and ammunition, trafficking of girls and crimes on both sides of the 1750 kms, open border.[119] Man Mohan Adhikari, as a gesture of goodwill congratulated the people of India, President of India and Prime Minister on the Golden Jubilee Celebration of India's independence and referred to the fact that several Nepalese politicians made their contribution in the freedom struggle.

With the visit of Indian Prime Minister to Kathmandu most of the suspicions existed between the two countries had been evaporated. In the two day talks between India and Nepal at the Foreign Secretary level concluded in August 1997 both sides agreed that a final decision on granting long term transit trade rights to Nepal would be taken after India examined the security concerns. In the discussions the main focus was on the Treaty of Peace and Friendship which was found as a bedrock of a "special relationship" binding the two countries. Of course, Nepal had been particularly keen to see the treaty changed and had raised the issue time and again. The Indian side made it clear that New Delhi's attitude on the treaty issue had been marked by a certain hesitancy in the past, partly because Kathmandu, while pressing for change did not appear quite clear about the content of such change. It would certainly help the officials of the two sides if the political parties in themselves were persuaded to evolve some kind of consensus on the issue.[120]

In the first week of October 1997 the six month-old coalition Government was voted out of power in Nepal and in place of Lokendra Bahadur Chand, Surya Bahadur Thapa became the new Prime Minister of the country. Like many Nepali Congress stalwarts, 69- year old Thapa had graduated from the Allahabad University and had done several stints as minister under different governments. In an interview given to *The Hindustan Times* he admitted that India is our close neighbour and none can change this geography. Keeping in view the problem of mass poverty in Nepal he laid emphasis to take advantage of the proximity with India and execute the hydel projects to advance on the path of progress. Under the Mahakali Treaty signed in June this year India and Nepal would jointly execute Pancheshwar project and in pursuance of the decision taken, the high level delegations from India and Nepal had made reasonable progress in sorting out the irritants to finalise the detailed project report (DPR) of Pancheshwar hydel project. However at the close of the year a reported reference, the Jain Commission's interim report said quoting a Research and Analysis Wing (RAW) letter stating that "the queen of Nepal has asked Major General Aditya Shamsher Jang Bahadur, an honorary aided camp to King Birendra, to arrange for the assassination of Rajiv Gandhi", for which Rs. 10 crore would be made available.[121]

As the news came the Nepalese authorities have taken strong exception to the unsubstantiated references to queen Aishwarya in the Jain Commission report. India regretted aspersions cast on Nepal royalty and described it as "groundless and misguided". The External Affairs Ministry spokesman said, "India holds their Majesties the King and Queen of Nepal in the highest esteem and deeply cherishes her traditional friendly relations with Nepal.[122] In the meantime, in the Jain Commission's report controversy between United Front and the Congress Party, Gujral Government resigned. Because Political parties failed to form viable combination, on 4 December 1997 Indian President K.R. Narayanan dissolved 11th Lok Sabha and the new House was to be constituted by 15th March 1998.

Economic Issues

Inder Kumar Gujral's visit to Kathmandu undertaken in June 1997 witnessed a major breakthrough in Indo-Nepal relations. In course of the visit as a major give-aways the two countries signed Mahakali Treaty under which India and Nepal would jointly execute Pancheshwar Project and estimated cost may be about Rs. 20 crores. It was decided to finalise the parameters of the detailed project report (DPR) within six months. In pursuance of the decision, the high level delegation from India and Nepal met in the middle of November 1997 and made reasonable progress in sorting out the irritants to finalise the DPR. The two Prime Ministers during the visit had agreed to open the Phulbari route and accordingly on 1 September, 1997 New Delhi allowed an alternative transit route through Phulbari to connect Nepal with Bangladesh.[123] Speaking on the occasion K.V. Rajan, India's Ambassador to Nepal, said the opening of the Phulbari route to Bangladesh is yet another milestone in India-Nepal relations. He hoped that this would lead to an expansion and diversification of trade and economic relations within the region.

As a follow up of the decision taken in Male in May 1997 by the Heads of States an inter-governmental group from seven SAARC countries met in Kathmandu in August 1997 and agreed to give a thrust on the process of the implementation to create the free trade area zone with zero duty by 2001. U.S. Bhatia, led the Indian delegation and chaired the first meeting of third round of South Asia Preferential Trading Arrangement (SAPTA). He said later that India had shown its readiness to accept the proposal of giving the tariff concessions on product to product basis or sectorally. India was also ready to go ahead in the manner which would be beneficial to all SAARC countries. India did not have problem with Nepal and Bhutan who have got access to Indian markets. Bilateral negotiations were also held before agreeing on the common approach. Regarding performance in the meeting he made it clear that we had been successful in convincing other states about our intentions to create South Asia Free Trade Area (SAFTA) within time framework and there was no intention to dominate anyone in the region. Further in the last week of November 1997 the Foreign Ministers of South Asian countries met in Maldives to review and discuss ways to speed up regional trade liberalisation. It would also take up the progress made so far in expediting trade liberalisation and setting up a Free Trade Area, the target year for which is 2001. In the meeting India was represented by Minister of State for External Affairs Salim I. Shervani.

In a significant development as a follow up of the Mahakali Treaty signed in June 1997 the high level delegations from India and Nepal made reasonable progress in sorting out the irritants to finalise the detailed project report (DPR) of Pancheshwar hydel project. Ramesh Chandra, Chairman Central Water Commission led the delegation from India whereas Vijay Shankar Shreshtha, Director General Development Centre headed the Nepalese side. According to sources, both sides were successful in agreeing on several points which included height of the dam (300 metres) peaking capacity (about 6,000 MW) and storage capacity of the main dam i.e. 6.5 billion cubic metres. The irrigation facilities from the project would be available in abundance of India and Nepal besides huge power share.

Defence

India and Nepal had reached an understanding on security matters during I.K. Gujral's visit to Kathmandu in June 1997. The two Prime Ministers agreed to direct the officials from the Home Ministries to discuss the security matters within one month and as a follow up senior officials of the two countries met in July 1997.[124] In the meeting New Delhi and Kathmandu have agreed to evolve a mechanism to enhance co-operation to check the infiltration of terrorists, smuggling of arms and ammunition, trafficking of girls and crimes on both sides of the 1750 kms. open border. At the end of the talks, as disclosed by V.S. Mathur, Special Secretary, Home Ministry, Government of India, that there was unanimity over the proposal to start joint patrolling by officials from the customs and Police Departments on both sides of the border. They felt that it would contribute in checking infiltration by the terrorists and smuggling of arms and ammunition. On the other hand, Karan Dhoj Adhikari who led the Nepal side told the correspondent of *The Hindustan Times* that it was a good beginning, which would yield a positive result in future. He admitted that security matters were of equal concern in both countries. The two sub-groups would submit the details of the procedures and modalities to enhance co-operation on border, supervise management in future. In the talks held in August 1997 at the Foreign Secretary level between the two countries Nepal seemed keen to see the treaty (1950) changed and had raised the issue time and again. India had equal reason to see that an updated treaty that took into account its concerns over security and related issues was put in place. The easy trans-border access provided under the provisions of the 1950 treaty had at times been used by terrorists, arms smugglers and other out laws as an escape route.[125] The other important decisions taken in the talks included that a final decision on granting long term transit rights to Nepal would be taken after India examined its security concerns. On the matter of territorial dispute over Kalapani, which lies in the Uttara Khand region, Nepal had already submitted its maps on the basis of which it claims that the area belongs to it. India had promised to examine them and also other evidence Nepal has provided in support of its claim.

For the last some years the people of Nepal are terror-stricken. They were subjected to inhuman atrocities at the hands of United Marxist Leninist Communist Party (UMLCP). As reported, about five hundred Nepali citizens have taken refuge in several villages along the Indo-Nepal border in East Champaran (Bihar). An MP and District President of Nepali Congress (Rothat) Md. Aftab Alam has urged the Government of India to hold talks with Nepal Government and help Nepali people in solving the crisis. Maoists are reportedly having links with LTTE and ULFA. In the circumstances Kathmandu proposed to purchase arms from India when latter's Chief of Army Staff, General V.P. Malik went to Nepal on a six-day official visit. General Malik discussed with General Dharampalbir Singh Thapa, his Nepalese counterpart about the common problem of terrorism faced by India and Nepal and there was unanimity over the enhancement of co-operation to tackle such problem. He said Indian army was ready to impart the training to Nepalese officials to deal with terrorists. Both sides also agreed to enhance army to army co-operation in future.[126] Having found satisfactory the level of understanding between the two countries, Kamal Thapa, the Nepalese Foreign Minister told newsmen in Calcutta after attending the Indo-US investment summit that his country would not allow any subversive activity on its soil against India and called for a fresh Indo-Nepal treaty in the present day context.

REGIME OF NATIONAL DEMOCRATIC ALLIANCE

Premiership of Atal Bihari Vajpayee (19 March 1998 - 12 October 1999)

The result of the general elections held in India, in March 1998, went in favour of Bharatiya Janata Party and it emerged as a single largest party in the Lok Sabha. An alliance of eighteen political parties under the premiership of Atal Bihari Vajpayee formed the Government at the centre who took the oath of office on 19 March 1998. A simultaneous change of premiership took place in Nepal and a new coalition led by Nepali Congress president Girija Prasad Koirala succeeded Surya Bahadur Thapa in April 1998. The new Indian regime, in its foreign policy pronouncements said that it would emphasise the importance of bilateral diplomacy and because it happens to be the larger country it would be all the more responsive to the aspirations and needs of small neighbours. However, the nuclear blasts by India on 11 and 13 May, quickly followed by Pakistan, was criticized by Nepal and Kathmandu held the view that it would increase arms race in the region.

In the circumstances three-day visit of K.R. Narayanan, the President of India, to Nepal took place. It was understood that following the five underground nuclear tests, India was in a position now to further press its calls which earlier had gone unheeded. On 28 May King Birendra hosted a state banquet in his honour and the Indian President pointed out that since India's independence, it had advocated and striven for peace and co-operation in Asia and the world. "India was the first to call for a ban on nuclear testing in 1954, for a non-discriminatory treaty on 'non-proliferation' in 1965, for a treaty on non-use of nuclear weapons in 1978, for a nuclear freeze in 1982, and for a phased programme of complete elimination of nuclear weapons in 1988". He also referred to the present state of Indo-Nepal relations and said that bilateral relations between the two countries had offered a model for the multipolar pluralist world that was emerging as a result of the ongoing worldwide phenomenon of liberalisation, economic reforms and opening up to the world. President Narayanan appreciated the initiatives taken by Nepal for sub-regional co-operation under the auspices of South Asian Association for Regional Co-operation (SAARC) but, at the same time called upon Nepal to ensure that "misgivings and apprehensions" did not come in the way of realising the larger and nobler objectives of bilateral co-operation.[127]

In Kathmandu, speaking at a civic reception accorded to him the President remembered with deep gratitude the support that India received during its freedom struggle from Nepali leaders and the people of Nepal. He said on the occasion," I believe that it is a symbol of the openness that characterises the relationship between our two countries, there are no doors or walls between India and Nepal. There is, instead, an open border between us, across which our people move and mingle without hinderance.... "Narayanan visited the famous Pashupatinath Temple, one of the most important pilgrimage sites for Shiva devotees but the highlight of his visit was that he was being honoured with D.Litt. by the Tribhuvan University, the oldest in Nepal. Speaking at the convocation ceremony of the University the President expressed confidence that the "recent confusion and sound and fury" caused by the nuclear tests by India and Pakistan will pass and the normal processes of peaceful dialogue will go on in the region. He said that in South Asia, New Delhi had initiated a new policy of improving relations with all neighbours. To ease the tension in the area Girija Prasad Koirala offered Kathmandu as a venue for Indo-Pakistan talks when he met Atal Bihari Vajpayee at the 10th Summit of the South Asian Association for Regional Co-operation held recently in Colombo.

A six-day return visit was paid by King Birendra to New Delhi and apart from attending the 50th Republic Day celebrations as the Chief Guest the Nepalese Monarch took the opportunity to discuss long-term bilateral relationship of mutual benefit on the basis of a series of treaties renewed and signed by the two sides in recent years. In New Delhi King Birendra met several leaders including President and the Prime Minister and leader of the Opposition Sharad Pawar. The Republic Day initiation, in itself, has reflected the 'high esteem' in which New Delhi held the monarchy in Nepal. Despite the frequent political changes in both the countries, India gave credit to the King for the "significant upgradation" of bilateral relations as symbolised by milestone agreements on water resources co-operation, trade and transit, investment, power trade and civil aviation. These treaties represented the continuity and the sense of direction in Indo-Nepal relations. Further, as part of collaborative efforts, India and Nepal in March 1999, had agreed to link trans-border protected areas through eco-corridors to help provide genetic continuity for animals across the border. According to a declaration signed after a two-day trans-border meeting of wild-life experts from India and Nepal, it had been decided to set up and maintain linkages between Royal Bardia National Park in Nepal and Katarniaghat Wildlife Sanctuary in Uttar Pradesh. The two sides have also agreed by consensus to promote bilateral co-operation on the issue of trans-boundary protected areas system and control of illegal trade in flora and fauna. This was the second meeting of this kind in two years, the first such held in Kathmandu in June 1997.

However, the trans-border smuggling from Nepal into Bihar has assumed alarming proportions. It has been learnt from the reliable sources that the ISI (Pakistan's Intelligence Agency) is desperately trying to broaden its base along the Bihar-Nepal border areas following the near decimation of its network by the Indian security forces in Jammu and Kashmir and Punjab. The sources claimed that the ISI has been supplying sophisticated weapons to the outlaws and private armies operating in different parts of the state. King Birendra of Nepal when visited New Delhi in January 1999, conveyed to legitimate concerns over the matter. It followed the Nepalese assurance that it would not allow its territory for activities inimical of India's interest. Jaswant Singh, India's Minister for External Affairs, in a written reply to the Rajya Sabha said, "Centre is engaged in a dialogue with the Nepalese territory against India's interest. Suitable mechanism, such as, the joint working group on border management and regular home secretary-level interactions between India and Nepal have put in place to prevent misuse of the open border between the two countries."[128]

Claim on Kalapani

Nepal's claim for the Kalapani, a strategically important tri-junction has assumed frightening dimensions and is likely to snowball into a major controversy. It surfaced first during the Sino-Nepal Border Agreement (1961), Sino-Nepal Border Protocol (1963) and in the subsequent 1979's Border Protocol. The claim spread over all the areas east of the Lipu Gad, the rivulet that joins the river Kali at its border tri-junction with India and China. Of late, in the light of its domestic intra-party political pressure the claim may trigger a fresh row between the two countries. The Communist Party of Nepal, both UML and ML factions have been mobilising public support over the issue as a part of their Indian hegemony insinuations. A 60-member All Nepal National Free Student's Union (ANNFSU), the student wing of the CPN (ML) was flagged off at Kathmandu by the Party general secretary Bam Dev Gautam and was escorted by the Nepal Police up to the Nepalese side of the Kalapani border. It was preceded by a 'Kalapani March' by the CPN(ML) cadres near Changru in Dharchula district of Kalapani junction.

According to Article 5 of the Sugauli Treaty (1815), Nepal had renounced all claims to areas 'lying west of the river Kali'. The Kali (now Mahakali) river thus evolved into a well-identified border demarcation in the west. Significantly, as against other neighbouring countries, India's borders with Nepal have for long been clearly demarcated since the earlier phase of the British rule. Despite this fact seventy square kilometres of the Kalapani area in Pithoragarh district is claimed by Nepal. It says that according to the 1815 Sugauli Treaty between the British Government and the Kingdom of Nepal, this area, which lies at the junction between the Tibet region of China, India and Nepal, belongs to the Kathmandu regime and that India is illegally occupying it.

The dispute over this territory was officially taken up by Nepal during former Prime Minister I.K. Gujral's visit to Kathmandu in June 1997. Gujral had told the Nepal Government that it could send maps and other papers relating to its claim to the Government of India for examination. However, India has contradicted this position saying that the river Kali begins only from the meeting point of the Lipu Gad with the stream from Kalapani springs. In the survey of India maps, the border thus leaves the mid stream of the Kali river below Kalapani turning eastwards away from the river, to follow the high watershed. It is important to mention here that the first regular surveys of the upper reaches of the Kali river were conducted during the time of British India in 1870s. Such a map of 1879 vintage shows the whole Kalapani area as part of India. Even a fresh set of surveys conducted by the Nepalese surveyors in the 1920s, confirmed the 1879 border alignment. Apart from this official sources claim that administrative and revenue records dating back to 1830s (available with the UP State Government), show that Kalapani area has traditionally been administered as part of Pithoragarh district.

The issue of Kalapani was raised by Girija Prasad Koirala, the Prime Minister of Nepal, when his Indian counterpart met him at Colombo on the eve of 10th Summit of the South Asian Association for Regional Co-operation. Referring to the meeting Koirala said in Kathmandu, in the first week of August 1998, that he told Vajpayee to settle the Kalapani border issue as early as possible on the basis of historical documents and other valid paper. He also added that unless India could come up with new valid papers or valid historical documentary proof about Kalapani, it belongs to Nepal. Further, in a 25-point programme signed by the ruling Nepali Congress president and Prime Minister Girija Prasad Koirala and Sahana Prashan, CPN(ML) President, a new found partner-in-governance, the two parties expressed their commitment to ending the border dispute through dialogue while reaffirming that the Kalapani area belonged to Nepal and that Indian troops should vacate it. Differences over the issue continued when King Birendra visited New Delhi in January 1999.

Even in a recently published Nepalese map, the Indo-Nepal border has been depicted, falling along the Lipu Gad right up to the main Himalayan crest-even as the river has been named as Mahakali. Following its border agreement with China, Nepal has suggested that the sensitive western extremely along the junction be discussed trilaterally between China, Nepal and India, adding yet another dimension to the dispute. It was feared that the continuing border dispute may endanger the safe movements of traders and pilgrims along the strategically-located Lipu Lekh Pass–the all weather and reliable entry point into Tibet from Almora. Following the general elections held in May 1999, the clear majority gained by Nepali Congress has raised the hope of better understanding between New Delhi and Kathmandu. The 75-year old Krishna Prasad Bhattarai was administered the oath of office as the new Prime Minister of the Kingdom on 31 May 1999 by King Birendra at Narayanhity Royal Palace.

Further Developments

While a fresh general election was held in Nepal on May 3 and 17, 1999, in a surprise development earlier in April 1999 Prime Minister Atal Bihari Vajpayee's government lost the confidence of the Lok Sabha by the razor-thin margin of one vote which followed Vajpayee's resignation soon thereafter, he however was asked by the President to continue in office in a caretaker capacity till alternative arrangements were made. On April 26, 1999 President K. R. Narayanan dissolved the 12th Lok Sabha on the recommendation of Union Cabinet. The Rashtrapati Bhawan communiqué noted that the ruling coalition had lost its majority because of a lack of cohesion within its ranks and those who voted out the alliance showed the same lack of cohesion when trying to form an alternative government. In an another announcement M. S. Gill, the Chief Election Commissioner of India, announced that having consulted nation's political parties, the poll dates for the 13th Lok Sabha would be in September-October and the new House is to be constituted before October 21, 1999.

The new ruling dispensation of Nepali Congress and K. P. Bhattarai, the new Prime Minister of Nepal, had hoped a better understanding between the two neighbours. He, in a talk to the correspondent of *The Times of India* at Kathmandu spoke of Indo-Nepal relations and said that relations between them are closer than two independent countries which are neighbours can hope to have. Under these circumstances, he explained, the old issues where there is a difference of perception can be sorted out through quiet discussions. These include the border dispute in the Kalapani area and on the origins of Mahakali river.[129] He expressed satisfaction on the position of India-Nepal trade treaty which allows anything manufactured in Nepal, regardless of the local content, to be exported to India. Transit facilities provided by India through the Chicken's Neck to reach Bangladesh despite the security problems involved are also appreciated.[130] In course of the talk he even became philosophical at a point and when asked to comment on the recent developments in Kargil he said that a practical solution would have to be found to settle the outstanding disputes between India and Pakistan. He was more optimistic on the issue because of the international atmosphere which was rapidly changing in favour of peace and prosperity.

Even in the period of caretaker government of Atal Bihari Vajpayee relations between India and Nepal strengthened further as a result of the visits undertaken by both sides. Nepalese Foreign Minister Dr. Ram Sharan Mahat visited India August 17-19, 1999 for consultations prior to the forthcoming SAARC Summit in Kathmandu. During the visit Foreign Minister Mahat called on President and Prime Minister, besides meeting the India's Minister for External Affairs. Although the visit was primarily in context of SAARC, it provided the two neighbours, an opportunity for discussions on several issues of mutual concern.

A return visit was paid by Jaswant Singh, India's Minister for External Affairs, to Nepal in September 1999 and attended a function in which the B. P. Koirala Institute of Health Sciences (BPKIHS), Dharan, was inaugurated and dedicated to the nation by the Prime Minister of Nepal. During the inauguration the External Affairs Minister of India announced to extend the facility support to BPKIHS for an additional 5 years till 2009 on the basis of the request received from the Government of Nepal. Later this project was completed on schedule without any cost over runs, even though the civil works in the project were increased by ten per cent. It is now making a very significant contribution in the health care sector for the entire Eastern Region of Nepal and a large number of patients from India are also benefiting from the facilities. By the India's Minister for External Affairs an assistance was also extended to the Paropakar Maternity Hospital in Kathmandu for procuring sophisticated medical equipment to facilitate the setting up of Maternity and Neo-natal Intensive Care Units at the Hospital. The ICUs were formally inaugurated and handed over to the Hospital authorities on September 10, 1999 during this visit. The Government of India had been extending assistance to this hospital since its inception in 1959.

Second Term of Atal Bihari Vajpayee (13 October 1999-22 May 2004)

As scheduled in the elections of 13th Lok Sabha out of 537 seats for which elections were held, 182 were won by the BJP and 112 by the Congress and the results dented the all India national pretensions of both alike. More than 250 seats were bagged by a variety of regional parties and again with its coalition partners which covered a wide shades of regional parties including of the South, the Bharatiya Janata Party formed the government at the centre and Atal Bihari Vajpayee became the Prime Minister of India who took the oath of office on October 13, 1999.[131] However, in contrast in the period the political situation in the Himalayan Kingdom remained unstable and witnessed a series of change in the premiership of the country. The ruling Nepali Congress which formed the government in May 1999 became a victim of factionalism and K. P. Bhattarai was replaced by Girija Prasad Koirala as the new Premier of Nepal in early 2000. In the name of younger generation another change also took place and G. P. Koirala was replaced by Sher Bahadur Deuba in July 2001. On the other the Maoist People's War which was launched in 1996 assumed alarming forms adding confusion in the democratic politics of Nepal.

Anticipating a constitutional crisis in the background the Government of Sher Bahadur Deuba in May 2002 recommended the dissolution of the Parliament but found it difficult to hold elections because of the Maoist insurgency. The new King Gyanendra who was coronated after the royal massacre of June 2001, seized this opportunity and invoked Article 127 of the Constitution to dismiss the Prime Minister and his cabinet for 'incompetence' in October 2002. He nominated Lokendra Bahadur Chand to head a nine-member interim government in order to restore law and order, hold mid-term elections and elections to the local bodies which were dissolved in July that year, solve Maoist insurgency, implement development works and stop the economy sliding further downhill. Major political parties were critical of the King's action and refused to participate in the interim government. Further in March the main stream forces of the country forged an alliance and finalized a 18-point common minimum programme and launched a movement against the monarchic takeover.

India's understandings with the Himalayan Kingdom strengthened further when latter's Foreign Minister Chakra Prasad Bastola visited New Delhi from May 7-9, 2000 and held useful discussions with his Indian counterpart Jaswant Singh, Home Minister and Water Resources Minister, besides calling on President and Prime Minister of India. Soon thereafter, a return visit was paid by Lalit Mansingh, India's Foreign Secretary to Nepal 19-21 May 2000. In course of the visit entire gamut of bilateral issues were discussed. He was also called on Prime Minister, Home Minister and Water Resources Minister of Nepal, besides the Leader of Opposition. Despite political confusions prevailed in Nepal, it continued its bilateral contacts at practically all levels. In June 2000 the two countries conducted successfully the High Level Task Force Meeting which was led by India's Principal Secretary of the Prime Minister and included among others Finance Secretary and Secretary, Water Resources along the representatives of Ministry of Commerce and Surface Transport. In the meeting the two sides discussed a number of new projects and reviewed the projects already completed.

In a sudden and surprise event King Birendra and Queen Aishwarya alongwith other family members was gunned down by the Crown Prince Dipendra on the bloody night of June 1. 2001. India expressed shock at the tragic and untimely demise of Nepal's King and the Queen and declared three-day State mourning across the country. In a resolution passed at an emergency Cabinet meeting convened by the Indian Prime Minister, the Government of India termed the demise as a 'very great tragedy and an irreparable loss to Nepal and its people. It stated that as a neighbour and close friend, we share the feelings of immense sorrow and pray that the mourning nation and its citizens are bestowed the strength and courage to bear this irreparable loss.[132]

After the death of Birendra, his younger brother Gyanendra became the King of Nepal. About dealing with the new King the Indian government remained in a dilemma – what it should or should not do? At the juncture the Indian government was not worried about King Gyanendra's record of hostility toward New Delhi, it however, caught in the cleft of a legitimacy crisis. In view of King's rejection by the mob the greater fear expressed by India was that there would be no government at all. If the new King failed to win the confidence of the people Nepal's fragile democracy would not survive. The polity then will polarized between a military autarch and urban mobs backed by Maoist guerillas. Thus New Delhi was keeping a low profile about the developments in Nepal. By the time Gyanendra inherited the throne in 2001, the country was at war with itself.[133] Had he been wise, he would have realized that the Maoist insurgency was the product of Nepal's feudal economy and social structure and that only an inclusive, democratic revolution could save the country from bloodshed.

In fact Gyanendra's coronation was marked by popular protests and it was believed that the King would rely heavily on the army to contain public hostility. Both needed each other in this hour of crisis – King Gyanendra would need the army to consolidate his position and the army would depend on the palace to hold together a socially diverse country. On the other the elected government had mobilized the Army against Maoist insurgents. Hence, as said by a senior Marxist-Leninist leader, 'it is going to be a tight rope walk for the new King. Although containing the Maoist revolt remained a top priority of the new King, many of us including Lok Raj Baral, Professor of Political Science at Kathmandu's Tribhuvan University held the view, Gyanendra is mature and shrewd. He will try to adjust to the situation'. India remained conscious about the current situation because one of the central planks of the Maoists is to break Nepal's close ties with India. In post-massacre period the Maoist rebellion had gained a considerable social support and self confidence to challenge the Kingdom's armed forces. The primary target of the Maoist continued to be monarchy, but to tap nationalist sentiment, they also inveighed against Indian 'hegemonists' who allegedly prop up the oppressive system.[134]

From strategic points of view India's political relations with Nepal received a sudden, severe jolt with the Palace Massacre which happened on the night of June 1, 2001. The turn of events in Nepal as believed by official circles in India, has not only anti-India mindset but is also believed to have patronized the elements having close links with Pakistan. 'It is really a pity that Gyanendra has been installed as King. It does not bode well for Indo-Nepalese ties.[135] However, some others including Bimal Prasad, a noted scholar and former Indian Ambassador to Nepal, did not share King Gyanendra's alarmist appraisal who said, 'I did not find any indication of hostility towards India in my interaction with Gyanendra'. He continued the impression even now about the king, 'Indo-Nepal relations will operate on the same wave-length in which they existed. There is every likelihood that the old policy will continue.[136] His assessment was based on two counts. One, that Gyanendra was closely associated with the late monarch and agreed with his policies and two, relations between countries are not determined by the predelictions of one individual but strategic interests. Just because there is a change in monarch, it does not mean there will be a change in policy.

In a further news analysis it was made clear that India's enemies would benefit the most from Nepal's chaos. The two democratic parties, the Marxists and the Nepali Congress refused to let the other rule for even a month in peace. The ruling Koirala Government was hanging by a thread. Hence in the period of the new King the primary beneficiaries would be forces inimical to India. In line the first is a Maoist insurgency that now controls about half the country at that time. In past the Maoist guerillas had penetrated Kathmandu Valley whose slogan is Kathmandu first, New Delhi next. The second beneficiary is Pakistan and the Inter Services Intelligence. The ISI has found Nepal a useful base for two reasons. One a porous border with India. Two, a growing militant Islamic presence in southern Nepal. India can get Nepal to sign agreement after agreement but Kathmandu is almost beyond the ability to enforce them.[137] A vacuum exists in Nepal and the new regent is expected to see this as an opportunity. Exactly the same as estimated by the analysts, in post-massacre phase Nepal's mutual understanding with China had strengthened further through exchange of visits and fruitful cooperation achieved in various fields.

However, despite the dilemma on Indo-Nepal political relations, the progress in economic relations between the two continued as earlier and in February 2002 they renewed the protocol to the India-Nepal Treaty of Trade which strengthened further relations between them. All 12 Articles of the Treaty had been renewed unchanged. As per terms continued access was provided to the Indian market for Nepalese manufactured goods on non-reciprocal preferential, duty-free basis. In its revised form the treaty is proving to be an effective instrument in providing a strong impetus to industrial growth and economic development in Nepal and in expanding bilateral trade ties with India. In the year 2001-2002, 60.7% of Nepal's overall exports were to India and 42.5% of Nepal's imports were from India. Thus, in spite of hectic developments in Nepal relations between the two continued as earlier. But the negative aspect of the treaty were highlighted later and the *Weekly Telegraph*, wrote, The Treaty was renewed in 2002 with specific modifications comprising value addition requirements of 30 per cent, quantitative restrictions on export for vegetable, ghee, acrylic yarn, copper and zinc oxide, and existence of a negative list. These conditionalities disrupted efforts towards industrialization in Nepal. The issue of quantitative restrictions on specified items on the pretext of import surge in India from Nepal could be neutralized through regulating deflection of trade at the border.[138]

Among other developments the trans-boundary conservation efforts between India and Nepal began in 1997 with the hosting of a trans-boundary consultative meeting in Kathmandu. This was followed by mid-level meetings in 1999 and 2002 between the two countries, and exchange of visits of parks wardens, officials, and scientists from adjoining park areas. The process has also raised awareness among the local community in the proposed scheme. Trans-boundary exchanges between all three countries during 1997 and 2003 have further strengthened relationships among professionals and have started to address specific livelihood issues identified at the local level.[139] From the start ecotourism and improving the livelihood of the people have been the major thrusts among the local border communities within the area.

With the passage of time the number of deaths due to the Maoist insurgency went on rise unexpectedly. Between 1996-2001 the conflict had claimed 2,700 lives. In 2002 alone, over 4,300 people were killed in a staggering period of heightened escalation. It compelled popular demand for peace intensified as the death toll mounted. Especially after a disastrous 2002, the involved parties ceased killing in January 2003 to return to the negotiation table at the urging of Western nations and King Gyanendra. It was believed that the struggle had reached a point of 'strategic equilibrium', a state where both parties recognized they could not defeat their adversary through military means[140] leading up to the January 29, 2003 cease-fire, the monarchy did receive substantial pressure from the European Union, the US and India to find a political solution to the mounting rebellion in the region.[141] According to the British Embassy in Kathmandu at the end of February 2003, the United Kingdom appointed a representative, Diplomat Sir Jeffrey James, to coordinate UK and international efforts in support of the ceasefire and emerging peace.

In the Premiership of Atal Bihari Vajpayee the foreign policy makers and politicians as well remained throughout in a dilemma regarding New Delhi's approach in the Himalayan Kingdom. It chanted the ideal of constitutional monarchy and lent almost total support to the King's authoritarian moves. Behind the policy was India's somewhat imprudent and unrealistic dislike for corrupt and power hungry political leaders as well as its near hatred for the Maoists who were seen as a supporters and abettors of the Naxalite and insurgent groups in India.[142] Apart from this a section of opinion in India was pleading for the direct and active military support to the Royal Nepal Army against the Maoists. Countries like the US might welcome such a daredevil course, but that would be a foolhardy, if not suicidal, move.[143] Government of India's confusing approach was also reflected in its dealings with Pakistan, its sponsored terror. Vajpayee had remained obsessively fixated on this semi-failed neighbour, sometimes vowing a fight to the finish and at other times exuding love.[144] His policy pendulum feverishly swings from one extreme to the other, even as cross-border terrorism in his reign had morphed from hit- and-run attacks to daring suicide attacks on army camps and national emblems of power like Parliament and Red Fort.

At the juncture and over the developments in Nepal what India really needed to do was to work as a quiet and honest facilitator. It should try and set a sincere peace process, involving all the three major players, moving in the Himalayan Kingdom. Towards that end, it had to lean heavily on the King to make him accept the role of a genuine constitutional monarch. India, at the time also needed to engage constructively with the political parties as well as the Maoists without prejudice. But the then Indian government had not only failed to capitalize on the boost provided by India's new nuclear state stature, but it had also acted in ways to erode the country's self-esteem which giving vent to the self-importance.

Economic Relationship

The signing of the India-Nepal Treaty of Peace and Friendship 1950 established the framework for the unique ties between the two countries. Since then India has contributed significantly to Nepal's economic development. Its assistance has done a lot in the development of the economic infrastructure in Nepal. In fact the Himalayan Kingdom is a land-locked country, surrounded by India in the east, south and west. It has a population of around 29 million with the GNP per capita of approximately USD 226. It is among the world's poorest countries and its economy is pre-dominantly agricultural. Agriculture accounts for 40% of GNP and 80% of labour force. Nepal's industrial sector is small, manufacturing activity provides employment to about 1% of the labour force. Water is its biggest natural resource, followed by forest.

From economic point of view the installation of multiparty system in 1990 was a boon for Nepal as it initiated and carried forward the enhanced structural adjustment facility (ESAF) of the International Monetary Fund (IMF) with the objective of a 5 per cent increase in the GDP growth. In the light of new ideas and guidance the Eighth five year plan (1992-97) set the target of bringing the level of poverty from 49 per cent to 42 per cent. It also drew a long-term perspective plan for agricultural development, sustainable development, reduction in regional imbalances and resource conservation. During the Ninth five year plan (1998-2002) the structural changes initiated in the previous plan were continued. In the age of globalization several long-term ambitious and developmental plans were brought about to make Nepal competitive, competent and technologically perfect. However, during the period political instability and the violence unleased by the Maoist insurgency move had adversely affected the development in all sectors.

In Vajpayee's dispensations, the Government of India as part of its continued policy not only assisted Kathmandu in the development of its infrastructure but also increased the quantum of help over the years. Since 1997 annual Government of India's disbursement has been around Rs. 70 crores. Major Indian projects have been completed or are due to be completed. In March 1998 the Government of India provided financial assistance to cover costs of technical inputs and materials in connection with the Sri Krishna Mandir Conservation Project at the Patan Durbar Square, Lalitpur, which is one of the monuments in the World Heritage List of UNESCO. Likewise, in the year 1999-2000 it granted assistance to Nepal Netra Joyti Sangh, Malangwa, Chanidanda Madhyamic Vidyalaya, Syngja and Nepal-Bharat Friendship School, Pokhra. In addition India and Nepal discussed their bilateral relations and exchanged views on matters of mutual interest when King Birendra and Queen Aishwarya of Nepal paid a State visit to India January 24-29, 1999. They agreed to emphasise in particular the potentials for long term bilateral cooperation in core sectors including water resources, trade and transit and tourism. It should be noted here that Nepal has an estimated potential to generate 83,000 MW of electricity, which remains untapped due to resource constraint.

The treaties signed between India and Nepal relating to bilateral trade are a symbol of the very special relationship on non-reciprocal basis which offer extremely beneficial terms to Nepal. The formal trade treaty signed in 1951 was renewed later in 1961 and 1971 and incorporated provisions regarding transit facilities extended by India for Nepal's trade with a third country. In 1978 in lieu of this single treaty, three different agreements were signed and modified thereafter in 1991. After the advent of democratic government in the Himalayan Kingdom these treaties were modified significantly to provide unilateral concessions. In December 1996 the treaty was renewed for a further five years with the provision of automatic renewal of the Treaty every five years.

As an important further step in this regard the Protocol to the India-Nepal Treaty of Trade was renewed with some modifications in February 2002. Modifications have been made in certain clauses of the Protocol with the given salient features :-

- detailed Rules of Origin incorporated to encourage genuine industrialization in Nepal and to provide greater clarity and transparency;
- value addition norm-a very low value addition percentage has been agreed to by India of a maximum ceiling for third country inputs fixed at 75% for 1 year from 6th March 2002 and 70% thereafter;
- certain sensitive items will be allowed continued entry into India free of customs duty on the basis of a special and liberal quota. No ceiling prescribed for imports of these items into India on Most Favoured Nation (MFN) basis; and
- safeguard clause introduced with provisions for the affected country to take appropriate remedial measures only if joint consultations on surge do not yield results.

Even earlier and during the period India's share in Nepal's exports, imports and total volume of trade over the years has been on rise as reported by Nepal Rashtra Bank is being given below :-

Nepal's Export, Import and Volume of Trade

	1998-1999	*1999-2000*	*2000-2001*	*2001-2002*
Nepal's exports	35.5%	42.8%	46.7%	60.7%
Nepal's imports	34.9%	34.8%	39.0%	42.5%
Total volume of trade	35.0%	37.2%	41.8%	48.1%

In general, both imports and exports of Nepal have increased over the years. In the year 2000-2001, Nepal's global imports were worth Nepalese Rs. 113 billion, of which Nepalese Rs. 46 billion were from India, i.e., around 41%; and Nepal's global exports were around Nepalese Rs. 57 billion of which around Nepalese Rs. 27 billion worth were to India, i.e., nearly 47%. In the year 2001-02, 60.7% of Nepal's overall exports were to

India and 42.5% of Nepal's imports were from India. The figures from Nepal Rashtra Bank for the Nepalese fiscal years 1998-99, 1999-2000 and 2000-2001 registered a surge in Nepalese exports to India amounting to 42.5%, 80.5% and 28.7% respectively. Nepalese exports to India increased by five times from 1996 to year 2001 from exports worth Rs. 5 billion to exports worth Rs. 27 billion. Even in the first six months of the year 2002-03 witnessed exports from Nepal to India worth Rs. 12.9 billion.

Among the reasons for India's substantial favourable balance of trade with Nepal and Kathmandu's underdeveloped industrial base, narrow range of exports, facility of easy import of daily use items from India, including import of inputs for some of Nepal's major exports such as readymade garments, and unauthorized trade through the long and open border. As a positive implication the new Trade Treaty has widened the basket of Nepalese export commodities to India. The traditional Nepalese export to India have been jute goods, pulses ginger, oil cakes, cardamom, rosin, skin etc. As a result of the new treaty provisions the new items, such as vanaspati, toothpaste, acrylic and polyester yarn, Ayurvedic medicines, soap, copper wire and other copper products have been added to the Nepalese export basket. In 1999-2000 only three items-vanaspati, toothpaste and soap were exported to the tune of Nepalese Rs. 2.7 billion, 2.2 billion and Rs. 1.08 billion respectively.

In sphere of joint venture and Foreign Direct Investment due to its proximity and the Trade Treaty the two countries have manifested themselves, inter-alia, through Indian investment and joint ventures in Nepal. At present there are hundreds of approved Indian joint ventures in Nepal in which over hundred are operational, with a cumulative total Indian investment amounting to between 36-40% of the total Foreign Direct Investment in Nepal. The total cost of approved projects is around 28.5 billion, with fixed investment amounting to Rs. 21.9 billion and the foreign investment component amounting to Rs. 7,427 billion. The joint ventures are in practically every sector, including tourism, infrastructure, consumer durable and non-durable and export oriented industries like garments and carpets. The Government of India has established a special 'Nepal Window' to facilitate approvals for Indian investment in Nepal.

From the beginning the Government of India has helped Nepal in diverse fields. In sector of surface transport a bilateral agreement for the construction of 22 bridges on the Kohalpur-Mahakali sector of the East–West Highway was signed in February 1996 during the visit of Nepalese Prime Minister Sher Bahadur Deuba to India. With the signing of this agreement Nepal had become operational even during monsoons and had opened up this part of Nepal bordering India to new possibilities in trade, investment and economic growth. Apart from this development of tourism and industrial activities in this region are sure to get a boost as a result of this project. Under the Mahakali Treaty signed earlier between the two countries the construction of Tanakpur-Mahendranagar Link Road is one of the obligations of the Government of India and a joint on-site inspection to finalise the alignment of the proposed 14.5 km. link road was constructed in February 1999 and the modalities for the project were firmed up in subsequent discussions with the representatives of the Department of Roads, Government of Nepal. For the construction of Raxual / Birganj Broad Gauge Rail Link under the Indian assistance was formalized through the exchange of letters during Indian Prime Minister's visit to Nepal in June 1997. The work on the rail link had commenced in November 1999.

In addition, the Government of India has been deeply involved in other development-related aspects such as health, education, duty refund programme, welfare activities for Indian Armed Forces ex-servicemen of Nepal, pension payment etc. Particularly in health sector the Prime Minister of India during his visit to Nepal in June 1997, laid the foundation stone of the 200–Bed Emergency and Trauma Centre, which would be an extension of the existing Bir Hospital set up by India in the 1970s. In this regard a team of architects from Central Design Bureau of the Ministry of Health visited Kathmandu in February and September 1998 to prepare the project design and parameters. Further a four-member experts group led by Dr. P. K. Dave visited Kathmandu from May 31st to 4th June 2000 for holding discussions with Bir Hospital authorities and the Government of Nepal to firm up the project parameters.

China and Pakistan Factor

Sandwiched between two giant neighbours, the main challenge that Nepal is facing is to maintain an equidistance between India and China. Undoubtedly, it is an arduous task which needs distancing away from the preponderant Indian influence. China encourages Nepal to be more independent, but in contrast to what many Indian analysts believe, does not intend to build a military alliance with Nepal. The geostrategic location of Nepal makes it imperative for China to maintain an intimate relationship with Nepal in order to protect its southwestern border.[145] So far as the policy of Nepal is concerned it has been experienced by New Delhi that Nepalese autocrats, in general, had played a China-card effectively in the regional politics for continuing their unjust and undemocratic regimes. Whenever Nepal had democratically elected governments, the Chinese autocrats lost the partners in autocratic governance giving way to the democratic countries such as India, the US, the UK and other European democratic governments to have more influence on the elected governments in Nepal than the Chinese government. Naturally, often the Chinese Autocratic Proletarian Government got sidelined, and found ignored by the elected governments in Nepal tended to loosen their control over the Tibetan refugees in Nepal and let them freely travel and engage in their activities for freedom in Tibet. Therefore, the Chinese autocratic proletarian government always found democracy in Nepal as a threat to their oppressive rule in Tibet.

From 1996 onwards Nepal faced a serious internal problem when the Maoists presented their 40-point demands before the Nepali Congress Government. As we are aware the success of the Chinese revolution had a profound impact on the world, creating a wave of joy amongst the oppressed countries in South Asia on the one hand and sending shivers down the spine of the developed capitalist countries of Europe and especially America on the other. Chinese revolution served as the required fuel to ignite the hidden passions of freedom for many a third world countries.[146] The Himalayan Kingdom was no exception to this where Maoism took birth and reached to political power with the active and open support from the Chinese. The Maoists in Nepal had demanded several basic changes in Nepalese political system including the abolition of monarchy which had continued for centuries and establishment of a federal democratic republic.

Since 1998, the Nepal Army has sent officers and soldiers to study in Chinese military universities and military relations and cooperation between China and Nepal have experienced continuous development.

Nearly all the former Army Chiefs and Defense Secretaries of Nepal have visited China. The Defence Minister and the General Chief of Staff of China have also visited Nepal. China has rendered help and assistance to Nepal within its own capacity. The two armies have conducted good cooperation in personnel training as well. Although considerable weitage was given to security issues by both sides, they also strengthened their relations in other spheres. In order to sustain the deep rooted cultural relations at present times, the two countries have reached an agreement on cultural cooperation in 1999. It followed various cultural programmes and activities. In 2001, the two countries signed the Memorandum of Understanding on Tourism Cooperation, including Nepal into the list of the tourism destination for outbound Chinese travellers. Relations between the two also strengthened when Zhu Rongji, the Premier of China, visited Nepal in May 2001.

Exactly the same as estimated by the analysts in post-massacre phase Nepal's mutual understanding with China had strengthened further through exchange of visits and fruitful cooperation achieved in various fields. In April 2002 Nepalese Foreign Secretary Achariya visited China and briefed the Chinese side on the latest developments in Nepal. The same year in July Nepalese King Gyanendra paid a state visit to China and met the President, Vice-President and Premier of the country. They spoke highly of Sino-Nepalese neighbourly friendship and cooperation and reached broad consensus on further deepening and expanding exchanges and cooperation in various fields. Both sides also signed agreements of mutual interest in course of the visit. In 2004 Nepal and China also signed Air Service Agreement according to which China opened a direct air link with Nepal by route of Chengdu-Lasha-Kathmandu.

The Himalayan Kingdom had leaned more towards the People's Republic of China than to New Delhi in the period of King Gyanendra. In addition as Beijing is a permanent member of the United Nations Security Council, Nepal is of the conviction that only with the meaningful role of China, the acts and decisions of the UN achieves greater support from the world community. The responsible role being played by China to maintain international and regional peace and achieve a harmonious world will always be laudable for Nepal. With the change of time across the globe they both concluded that peace, stability, cooperation and development are the calling of the period and the common aspiration of the mankind. They felt by seizing this opportunity, the two neighbouring countries should build on past achievements and push ahead to bring China-Nepal good-neighbourliness, friendship and cooperation to a new heights.

On a number of issues of mutual interest both China and Nepal have supported each other in recent past. For over a decade Nepal has been affected by conflicts and instability. As an immediate neighbour and close friend of Nepal China had shown great concern. It tried its level best to play a constructive role in urging all sides in Nepal to solve problems through dialogues and talks. The Chinese Government and people respect political system and road of development chosen by Nepalese people and sincerely hope that all constitutional forces in Nepal will set store by the fundamental interest of the country and people and seek to appropriately settle the current difficulties and problems through dialogues, based on the maintenance of Nepal's independence, sovereignty and national integrity. On the other Nepal has also recognised Tibet and Taiwan inalienable part of People's Republic of China. In this connection, the Nepal government has unequivocally supported the anti-succession legislation enacted by the National People's Congress in 2005. Nepal has also appreciated 'one country two systems' principle as enunciated by China and applied successfully in Hong Kong and Macao in the form of special administrative regions. Exchange of bilateral visits immensely contributed to further nurturing Nepal-China relations and promoting the understanding between the two countries.

Next to Beijing Kathmandu had made Islamabad its strategic partner keeping in view latter's tense relations with New Delhi. It used Pakistan as a less important pressuring tool because Islamabad had till date fought four declared, unsuccessful wars with India. In the early 1980s, Nepal started sending officers for military training to China and Pakistan, and in 1988 it imported anti-aircraft guns from China, contravening the 1950 agreement stipulating that arms were to be imported only from or through India.[147] In succeeding and particularly from the early 1990s the activities of Pakistan's Inter Services Intelligence (ISI) have increased in India through the tacit support of Nepalese authorities and a section of the people as well. A large number of underworld ganglords and criminals have been arrested in Nepal who were on the 'most wanted' list of Indian police. Normally Pakistan supported elements who were assigned to do destructive activities on Indian soil come through Nepal and after doing their jobs returned to Nepal as there is a open boundary system between India and Nepal. Several criminals and terrorists have confessed, during interrogations, their links to the officials of Pakistan's embassy in Kathmandu where they get cash, training, travel documents and explosives. Security agencies of India have long been warning of ISI activity in Nepal, which started operations there during the Punjab crisis.

After all, on the basis of facts India took its first diplomatic initiative in 1997 when the Prime Ministers of the two countries met and an Indo-Nepal joint working group was established. Later Nepal assured that it would not allow its territory for activities inimical to India's interest. It was told by Jaswant Singh, India's Minister for External Affairs in the Rajya Sabha, in a written reply, that the two countries are continuing cooperation in this regard to prevent misuse of the open border between India and Nepal. 'Centre is engaged in a dialogue with the Nepalese Government following reports about ISI of Pakistan misusing Nepalese territory against India's interest. Suitable mechanism such as the joint working group on border management and regular home secretary level interactions between India and Nepal have been put in place to prevent misuse of the open border between the two countries.[148] Following the reports of increase in infiltration by Pakistan-trained militants, ISI agents and also large scale illegal trade in select goods, commodities and narcotics New Delhi had decided to upgrade vigilance across its free borders with Nepal. In addition an action plan was also under active consideration under Union Home Ministry to streamline the existing security network with active involvement of four States – Uttar Pradesh, Bihar, West Bengal and Sikkim who shared the 1751 km. along border with Nepal.[149] However, the new security network was to be within the confines of the Indo-Nepal Treaty of 1950. The issue of ISI agents' activities in Nepal was also raised in September 1999 when Jaswant Singh, India's Minister for External Affairs, visited the Himalayan Kingdom and King Birendra came to New Delhi as chief guest of the Republic Day celebration in January 1998.

Despite Indian efforts and Nepalese assurance that it would not allow any anti – Indian ISI activities on its soil, gradually security system of Tribhuvan international airport at Kathmandu became non-existent as reported by a correspondent of *The Hindustan Times*, a daily newspaper, in December 1999. Kashmiri militants came to Kathmandu in flights from Islamabad and they are taken care of by ISI officials who are part of the Pakistani embassy in Kathmandu. These militants stay for a few weeks in Kathmandu and then they go to Nepalgunj where some Muslim families make arrangements for them. Then they easily cross over to India and travel to their destination.[150] The Indian government, however, had always raised this issue during dialogue with successive Nepalese Prime Ministers who have always denied the existence of such activities. Thus, Nepal has never admitted the role of the ISI behind this racket in Kathmandu. With this soft attitude on the part of Nepalese authorities, the ISI has never faced any problem in sending Kashmiri militants to India to create troubles in Jammu and Kashmir.

Nepalese security lapses at Tribhuvan international airport and soft handling of ISI agents activities became public on December 24, 1999 when the hijackers of Indian Airlines IC - 814 easily boarded Kathmandu airport and then went to Kandahar (Afghanistan) and put their initial demands through the Taliban. The incident along with others that happened earlier had worried New Delhi which India continued to furnish Nepal with incriminating evidence on Pak-backed anti-India operations from its soil. One of the reasons for this, as held by many and intelligence sources is that in long precious years the ISI has reported to have managed a great deal of influence amongst its resourceful politico-business circles. Apart from this Nepal had also maintained total silence over India's offer on entering into two bilateral treaties – Mutual Legal Treaty in Criminal Matters and Memorandum of Understanding for Combating International Crime and Terrorism. Two proposals were put forward by New Delhi in August-September 1998 and in early March 1997.[151] On the issue of hijacking Atal Bihari Vajpayee, the Prime Minister of India, wrote to K. P. Bhattarai, his Nepalese counterpart, in the aftermath and drew attention to the major security lapse despite oft-repeated promise of checking anti-Indian activities on its soil. Visibly lapses on the part of Kathmandu had left India unhappy. Earlier on two occasions in 1986 and in 1996 New Delhi had made security-related offers to Nepal but failed to get any answer.

The Joint Working Group (JWG) of India and Nepal met at Kathmandu in February 2000 and discussed the issue as focal point. In the meeting Indian side was represented by a Home Ministry Special Secretary with inputs from a delegation of civil aviation security experts that had just returned from Nepal after studying the security arrangements at Tribhuvan airport. In previous meetings India had also raised the introduction of a passport-visa regime, patrolling of Indo-Nepalese border by para-military forces and tightening of custom controls as safety measures. The Indian delegation pointed to their Nepalese counterpart the need for effective sharing of intelligence between the two countries and review of the effectiveness and adequacy of the existing arrangements for exchange of information on criminal and terrorist activities.[152] In course of the discussions New Delhi also expressed its readiness to provide help in the form of sharing expertise on counter-terrorism and to impart training to Nepalese police and security forces for tackling left-wing extremist violence. Further Nepal's security nexus with Pakistan-backed ISI gained its base stronger in the Himalayan Kingdom in post-Palace Massacre period which took the life of king and queen along other members of the royal family on June 1, 2001.

Maoism and Indo-Nepal Relations

The Maoists of today were once a part of the mainstream politics under the banner of United Peoples Front of Nepal (UPFN) led by Baburam Bhattarai. In a split in the Party, the Baburam faction failed to get the recognition of the Election Commission to participate in the mid-term elections in 1994. This group joined hands with the Communist Party of Nepal (Maoists). The declared aim of the Maoists is to establish a People's government through peoples' war that is inspired by Marxism-Leninism-Maoism. In 1996 the Maoists launched the 'Peoples Movement' or Jana Andolan by carrying out attacks in different parts of Nepal. Indeed they launched insurgency after the state repeatedly ignored their demands and received support from the population ignored by the state. Like other Leftists, the Maoists of Nepal considered the states as a semi-feudal organization and held it responsible for the prevailing socio-economic ills within the country. The Maoists of Nepal have also projected India and the US as the imperialist powers trying to subvert the interests of the people of Nepal by aligning with the rightist forces within Nepal.

The latest struggle for ideological and political control of the Kingdom of Nepal officially commenced on February 13, 1996, when the CPN-Maoists, commonly referred to as the Maoists, issued a charter of forty demands that were submitted to then Prime Minister Sher Bahadur Deuba. The submitted demands sought to; (a) Abrogate all unequal agreement with India including 1950 Peace and Friendship Treaty; (b) Control and regulate Nepal-India open border; (c) Close Gorkha Recruitment Centres and create dignified employment within the country; (d) Provide employment to all Nepalese, and employ the foreigners if unavoidable only under work permit system; (e) Stop imperialistic and expansionist culture; (f) Establish a constitution through elected representatives; (g) Abolish the privileges of the King and the royal family; (h) Establish control of the people over army, police and administration; (i) Declare Nepal a secular state; (j) Allow a share of the paternal property to daughters; (k) Distribute the land to the tillers and excess land to the landless; (l) Confiscate the property of the exploiting capitalistic class for ultimate nationalization etc.[153] Apart from this some other high profile Maoist demands were also made such as the drafting of a new republican constitution, radical distribution of land and property, and the removal of the monarchy from power. However, it is a long accumulated overall dissatisfaction and what exists beneath these issues – the underpinning 'drivers' of the conflict – are sources of popular unrest fueled by decades of political instability, extreme poverty and social stratification.[154] These issues represent the fundamental causes for what has culminated into the 'People's War'.

The Maoists stood first in the mobilization of the rural poor and their issues. They canvassed the countrysides of the Western and Midwestern Nepal to stir the impoverished and disenfranchised in a play to seize control. The involvement of such a sizable portion of the Nepalese population has transformed the Maoist establishment from an ideological platform for governance into a social movement spearheaded by armed guerillas to overwhelm government security forces stationed in the countryside. The resolve of this movement has amassed enough strength for the Maoists to seriously contend with military forces and threaten the demise of incumbent institutions including the monarchy.[155] In the Himalayan Kingdom no political party or movement had mobilized the rural people more than the Maoists. This is significant because the mainstream movements and political parties, despite their claim of representing the rural people, were mostly led by urban and rural elite. If the mobilization of hitherto largely neglected people is a contribution towards democratization, the Maoists have played a significant role.[156] But the violent methods adopted by them undoubtedly undermined electoral democracy and put a question mark on the future of democracy.

By the time the Peoples Movement was started by the Maoists the systems of the country as whole provided them a convenient phenomenon. With the democratic politics in Nepal being extremely factionalised successive governments in Nepal found it difficult to implement governmental policies and programmes. One result of this was the rate of economic growth was modest but it did not match the rate at which population grew. Particularly in the Ninth Plan (1998-2002) which was planned to make Nepal a competitive, competent and technologically oriented society failed to achieve the target due to the violence unleashed by the Maoists insurgency. The Peoples Movement cast a dark shadow on the development in all sectors. It resulted in massive unemployment and illiteracy in a society that had an ethnically and religiously fragmented population. It all favoured the Maoists because those who often seek resources or comfortable policies from the state. This situation helped them in intensifying conflict among groups who control the state and its resources and those who want a voice in the state and a share of its resources. The Maoists used terror tactics to spread their influence in the rural areas and taken effective control of administration in several districts. By the end of 2000, the Maoists were active in over two-thirds of the 75 districts of Nepal. They had setup Peoples government in five districts of Western Nepal. In the areas under their control, the Maoists do local policing, settle local disputes, collect levies from the people and even setup banks.

In the early years of the Maoists movement, Nepalese politicians belonging to the leftist camp displayed a fraternal resistance to taking any harsh measures toward the Maoists. The Communist Party of Nepal Marxist-Leninist, the third largest political party in Nepal, openly endorsed the aims of the Maoists even while disapproving of its working style. The majority ruling party, the Nepali Congress, beset with internal problems, could not take concrete action to deal with the Maoist problem. The Maoist insurgency added confusion in the democratic politics of Nepal that was already reeling under factionalism which ultimately led to a constitutional crisis. The key problem for Nepal at the time was the absence of linkage between the people at large and their government. Consequently the formation of a healthy civil society in Nepal has been held in check. The conflicts in Nepal have been the outcome of incongruence between societal aspirations and state institutions.[157]

The Maoists of Nepal took maximum benefit of the prevailing political instability of the Kingdom and from 2001, onwards began to dominate the politics and political events of the country. It assumed grave proportions became number one problem of Nepal and government's measures such as, force, persuasion and negotiation to tackle the Maoist problem proved both useless and counterproductive as well. Since March 2001, several rounds of peace negotiations have been held between the government and the Maoists. But due to irreconcilable differences and mutual suspicion, these efforts have not borne results. Terror and violence by the insurgents continued and the security forces have stepped up counter insurgency operations. However, the Maoists activities had restricted the democratic rights of the common people even when they were conducted in the name of protecting democratic rights. The most well-known public protests were the bandhs which called for closure of markets, town, cities or the whole country. Those who dared to continue with regular activities were often violently stopped. The common people were thus denied their fundamental political rights and civil liberties.

For long the Maoists of Nepal had held the normal political processes under seize as prescribed in the constitution of 1990. In May 2002, the Deuba government recommended the dissolution of the Parliament but found it difficult to hold elections because of the Maoist insurgency. Taking advantage of the situation King Gyanendra invoked Article 127 of the Constitution to dismiss the Prime Minister and his cabinet for 'incompetence' in October 2002. He nominated Lokendra Bahadur Chand to head a nine-member interim government but in March 2003 the mainstream forces of the country launched a movement against the monarchic takeover. Since then a tripartite power struggle has dominated Nepali politics, between the King, the mainstream political parties and the Maoists. Even during this period the Maoists remained adamant in their demand for the creation of a Constituent Assembly to draft a drastically revised constitution. As the Maoist insurgency raged, the King declared a state of emergency on February 1, 2005, arresting mainstream political leaders and assumed absolute power.

REGIME OF UNITED PROGRESSIVE ALLIANCE

Premiership of Manmohan Singh (22 May 2004-22 May 2009)

Amidst the political instability in Nepal a change of guard took place in India and in place of Atal Bihari Vajpayee, Manmohan Singh became the new Prime Minister of India in which the Indian National Congress replaced earlier BJP – led coalition in May 2004. The rising Maoists threats in the country had, in fact, left political activities to zero level and at the juncture New Delhi was in dilemma on how to tackle the situation in favour of Nepalese people and India-Nepal relations as well. Earlier the several rounds of peace negotiations have been held between the government and Maoists but due to irreconcilable differences and mutual suspicion, these efforts were miserably failed in giving desired results. Terror and violence by the insurgents continued and the security forces have stepped up counter insurgency operations. On the other hand in March 2003 the mainstream political forces in Nepal forged an alliance and finalized an 18-point common minimum programme and launched a movement against the Monarchic takeover of October 2002. According to official sources, by early 2004, the fight against the eight year Maoist insurgency has claimed nearly 8,000 lives on both sides, including 2,800 security force personnel.

In a significant political development King Gyanendra, firing the democratically elected government on February 1, 2005, took over the executive powers imposing emergency rule and vowing to tackle the Maoist uprising. The army had expressed its readiness to take on the Maoists militarily. The King's coup with restrictions on fundamental rights and freedom, media and communications, national and international human rights watchdogs, and political parties and activities, has created desirable conditions for the army to run riot in Nepal. As said by Brigadier General Deepak Gurung, the Chief RNA spokesman, now we can solely go after the Maoists in a single minded manners without having to worry about what is going to happen on the streets.[158] But at the sametime the efforts to keep the political leadership on the run and the cadre confused and directionless may prove to be counterproductive. It was widely believed in academia and in a large section of the people in and outside the Kingdom. On the happenings in Nepal India, the US, the UK and the international community as a whole condemned and suspended the military supplies to the Royal Nepal Army. The King could not convince the international community that his army would not use the arms and ammunition against the people fighting for fundamental rights and democracy in the country.

When King Gyanendra decided to dismiss the Government of Sher Bahadur Deuba and declare emergency in the Himalayan Kingdom in 2005, it was clear that his days were numbered. Although the country was passing from the worst form of political instability and dilemma, dismissing the government was not the best option. The Maoists have been able to grow, in part because of the factious nature of the mainstream parties but a major share of the blame surely rests on the King who had not given any administration in Kathmandu and room for negotiation.[159] The King had also betrayed the expectations that the country had from him following his incarnation in 2001. To falcify the King's calculations the Maoists and the democratic forces joined hands together and after a nineteen days mass demonstration in April 2006 the King had to left his executive powers and agree to work with an interim government. In a grand alliance of seven parties and the Maoists, the latter had consented to join the interim government. This grand alliance was entrusted to conduct elections to a Constituent Assembly. The interim government would have also to administer the country till the formation of a new government elected on the basis of the Constitution which will emerge from the Assembly's deliberations.[160] The 8-point agreement between Seven Party Alliance (SPA) and the Maoists explicitly provided for the United Nations to help in the management of arms and armed personnel of both the sides and to monitor it in order to conduct elections for the Constituent Assembly in a free and fair manner.[161] It was the best chance ever provided for the peaceful democratic change in the Himalayan Kingdom.

As monarchy was battling the last war for its survival in Nepal

King Gyanendra, in a calculated move, before the take over had shut down the offices of representatives of Dalai Lama and of Tibetan refugees in the country. Obviously, this was done to keep the Chinese Government happy. The Nepal government also issued a statement in which it reiterated its support for Beijing's 'One China' policy that recognizes Tibet and Taiwan as integral parts of China. In return, China, as an honest strategic partner, described the developments in Nepal as an internal matter and refrained from taking any stand on King Gyanendra's take over. The occasion reminded the events of the sixties when King Mahendra played a China–card effectively for suppressing the opposition political activities on the borders with India, expressed obligations for Indian efforts and said Shriman Narayan, the then Indian Ambassador to Nepal, 'On my part, I and my government have now decided to request China to abandon the eastern sector of the East-West Highway and initiate a fresh survey for another road somewhere in the middle regions of Nepal.[162] Even at that time, he also suppressed the voices of Tibetan refugees in Nepal, and stopped any political activities of them from Nepal against the People's Republic of China in 1960s.

In the year of take over King Gyanendra visited China and perhaps, in response, Nepal received 18 truckloads of arms and ammunition according to media reports in November 2005. Supplying lethal weapons to Nepal, China had not only demonstrated its disregard for suppression of democracy, civil liberties and human rights but also added fuel to the further bloodshed in Nepal. India's daily newspaper, *The Indian Express*, in its observation, wrote, 'the continuing Chinese arms supply to Kathmandu is more than a tactical threat to India's attempt at promoting democracy and stability in Nepal. The time is running out for the Indian government to get its Nepal act together and compel King Gyanendra to pay the costs of the China-card he has chosen to play against India. Unable to engineer a split in the coalition between India and the Anglo-American powers, King Gyanendra has put all his eggs in the China basket.[163] Shyam Sharan, India's Foreign Secretary, on his return from a three-day visit to Nepal in December 2005, also called on China to stop supplying arms and ammunition to Nepal and join international efforts to force King Gyanendra to restore democracy.[164] However, China continued its moral and material support to King Gyanendra's regime and in early

2006 the Chinese Ambassador to Nepal said that his country accorded a high priority to the construction of the proposed Koshi-Lhasa Highway linking Nepal's eastern zone with China's Tibet Autonomous Region.[165] King Gyanendra toyed with a plan to let China and Pakistan open consulates in the sensitive Indo-Nepal border areas and the Indian Government had already communicated its strong displeasure to Kathmandu.

Turn of events moved fastly in Nepal and King Gyanendra's activities had left no option but to form an alliance of the two opposite forces – the Maoists and the Nepali Congress in the larger interest of the nation. The first such effort was made in November 2005 when they signed the 12-point agreement which paved the way for second understanding between the SPA and the Maoists in March 2006. As a result of their mass movement in April 2006 the King's absolute rule ended that led to the reconvening of Nepalese Parliament, suspended in 2002. The two fighting forces of the country entered into a grand alliance in November 2006 and the Maoists joined the interim government.

As scheduled the election to the members of Constituent Assembly was held on April 10, 2006 that saw more than 60 percent participation of the 17.5 million-strong electorate in 21,000 polling centres. In results the Nepali citizenry surprised itself and the world on occasion with a show of people's will that was unprecedented and path-breaking. It had fought a rebel force barely out of the jungle into the driver's seat of national politics. The Maoists has achieved a massive win over its rivals, the Nepali Congress and the mainstream left Communist Party of Nepal (UML). By voting in the Maoists as the single largest party, the electorate has sent a clear message that it favoured the new. But voters tempered this message by denying the former rebels an absolute majority of their own. Under the rules of Nepal's interim constitution a two thirds majority was needed for any major decision, including the election of Prime Minister and President. By giving the Maoists a little more than one-third of the seats, the electorate said that it wanted the Maoists to keep alive the principle of consensus that had served Nepal's parties so well in the struggle against the monarchy.

Several factors seem to explain the crushing success of the Maoists in Nepal. To begin with, the Maoists win is the result of a well oiled campaign machinery worthy of a politico-military organisation. There was country wide deployment of threat and intimidation during the run up to the elections, which demoralized competing party activists and civil servants alike. A major reason for the win seems to be voter's desire to keep the Maoists from returning to the People's War and suffering attendant miseries. The imperfect peace process, made so by the absence of the rule of law and state administration over the last two years, left the population beleaguered and worried of a return to that horrific period. It is said that urban people were convinced of the Maoists' popular promise in a country whose workforce continues to migrate in massive numbers to India and overseas because of high levels of poverty. The Maoists projected themselves as true agents of change.[166] Lastly they also filled their candidates from the members of the deprived communities, including the Dalits, the Janajati ethnic category and women. They laid claim with justification to having introduced all the salient issues that had been placed before the electorate, including the demands for inclusion, federalism, secularism and an overturning of economic relations to serve the underclass.

Emergence of the Maoist as the single largest party had paved the way for formation of a Maoist-led coalition government in Nepal. Having confirmed that he would lead the Maoists in the government Pushpa Kamal Dahal 'Prachanda' began to speak on its relations with neighbouring countries and at the same expressed his party's vision of a new Nepal. Apart from underlining his desire to follow the policy of 'equidistance' in relationship with giant neighbours India and China,[167] he also wanted to change the image of the Maoists among the middle class in Nepal and among the international community. There was some suspicion about the Maoists' intentions, given their background as insurgents against the monarchy and it was thought that they would be autocratic when they assumed power. Initially there were doubts whether they would participate in the democratic process of elections as it was assumed their strength lay only in the power of arms. After emerging as the largest party there was still some concern that would turn autocratic, Prachanda emphasised that they would again proved the critics wrong by demonstrating their commitment to multi-party democracy and democratic rights and freedoms.[168] However, with some delay in forging the alliance the Maoists had reached an understanding with the

Communist Party of Nepal (UML) and Madhesi Janadhikar Forum (MJF), the two major parties, to support Prachanda's candidacy first and later the government. In afterwards his candidacy was also backed by other small parties. He took the oath of office of the Prime Minister with eight ministers in the third week of August 2008.[169] Now the time has come to rectify the past misdeeds and address the question of disjunction with utmost care and importance.

The victory of Prachanda in Nepal represented the ultimate win of sobriety, accountability, and morality over the politics of cynicism and distrust.[170] Although governing Nepal at a time of global economic uncertainty will be challenging, the most important task before him is to lead the writing of a new constitution. The key challenges will be here to articulate robust mechanisms for the exercise of citizen's political, social, cultural and economic rights, working out a federal structure that can address the needs and aspirations of different ethnic groups, including the Madhesis; and ensuring that the army remains subordinate to civil authority.[171] The new government and constitution are likely to place Nepal's relations with the outside world and with India on a sounder footing. But the change in Nepalese political system did not carry any change in its leaning towards the People's Republic of China in spite of earlier assurance to maintain equidistance in relation to two giant neighbours – India and China. Prachanda also took the opportunity to clarify the exact meaning of equidistance and said, 'It is to have good relations with both the neighbours', but at the sametime showing favour to China added that the Maoist-led government would take strong measures against anti-Chinese activities in Nepal where Tibetan activists had been staging protests against Chinese rule in Tibet.[172] He had also undertaken his first visit to Beijing within a week of taking the oath of office and discussed with Chinese leaders issues of mutual interest.

Perhaps with a view to strengthen Kathmandu's relations with India Pushpa Kamal Dahal, Prachanda, the new Prime Minister of Nepal, came to India on a four-day official visit in September 14-17, 2008, and held wide ranging discussions with Indian leaders. According to official sources India had decided, even before the visit, to respond positively to any proposal for revising the much-talked Indo-Nepal Treaty of 1950. India was also looking forward to the visit of Prachanda as it would provide an opportunity for New Delhi to establish a political equation with the new Maoist-led dispensation in the Himalayan republic. On the Nepalese side, its Foreign Minister Upendra Yadav, who accompanied the Prime Minister in his visit to India, in an interview to *The Rising Nepal* disclosed, 'we have already prepared a draft which I am carrying to India. He did not stick to the point that India should accept his proposed draft but was of the view that it should be done in such a way that all matters be included in the treaty are worked out following the formation of a task force of the officials of the two countries.[173] However, he added that during the visit primary focus would be to remove the crisis of confidence between Nepal and India at a political level. A policy document was also released in Kathmandu which focussed that Nepal needed India's creative responses were counted as; political stability of the coalition regime, culmination of the peace process through security sector reforms, timely conclusion of the Constitution drafting and implementation of the vision of 'economic revolution' in a decade.[174] The Nepalese Prime Minister on 15 September 2008 described his country's relations with India as unassailable and said that it can not be compared with any other country.

At the end of the visit a joint statement was issued which covered a wide range of subjects discussed by the leaders of the countries during the four-day official visit. According to it India and Nepal would undertake mega projects, including for infrastructural development. Kathmandu will provide conducive environment for Indian business, which has complained of security issues and labour problems. On its part New Delhi will seek to reverse the erosion of gains to Nepal under the 1991 trade treaty. It will undertake a comprehensive review of the existing trade and transit arrangements with a view to promoting industrialization in Nepal.[175] On India's part, traditional attitude towards Kathmandu should be left behind because peace and political stability in Nepal are in India's genuine interests. The successful visit, to a large extent, has been able to remove suspicions and misunderstandings towards each other.

References

1. L. S. Baral, "India and Nepal", Bimal Prasad, ed., India's Foreign Policy Studies in Continuity and Change (Vikas Publishing House, New Delhi, 1979), pp. 175-76.

2. Ibid., p. 174.
3. Janata Party Election Manifesto, 1977 (New Delhi, 1977), pp. 23-24.
4. The Times of India, March 28, 1977.
5. Ibid.
6. The Hindustan Times (New Delhi), April 3, 1977.
7. The Indian Express (New Delhi), April 4, 1977.
8. The Hindu (Madras), April 4, 1977.
9. Ibid.
10. Ibid., April 13, 1977.
11. Jaya Prakash Narayan's appeal was released at a press conference on 11 April 1977 by Krishnakant and Ram Dhan, two leading members of Parliament of Janata Party. The Conference was also addressed by G. P. Koirala, the younger brother of B. P. Koirala, who claimed to have received reports from Kathmandu to the effect that B. P. Koirala had been sentenced to death after a secret trial. See The Indian Express, April 12, 1977.
12. The Hindu, April 13, 1977.
13. Ibid., May 26, 1977.
14. Naya Samaj (Kathmandu), May 25, 1977; Gorkhapatra, May 26, 1977.
15. The Times of India, April 30, 1977.
16. The Hindu, May 10, 1977.
17. The Times of India, April 30, 1977.
18. The Hindu, May 26, 1997.
19. L. S. Baral, op.cit., p. 183.
20. Ibid., p. 184.
21. Ibid.
22. S. C. Gangal, Indian Foreign Policy-A Documentary Study of India's Foreign Policy Since the Installation of the Janata Government on 24 March 1977 (Young Asia Publications, New Delhi, 1980), pp. 158-59.
23. Ibid.
24. Gorkhapatra, June 16, 1977.
25. Ibid.
26. Ibid., July 4, 1977.
27. S. C. Gangal, op.cit., p. 280.
28. Atal Bihari Vajpayee, New Dimensions of India's Foreign Policy (Vision Book, New Delhi, 1979), p. 207.
29. The Hindu, July 17, 1977.

30. Ibid.
31. L. S. Baral, op.cit., p. 187.
32. Aruna Asaf Ali, ed., Link, vol. 19, no. 50, 24 July 1977, p. 1.
33. Ibid., vol. 20, no. 18, 11 December 1977, p. 23.
34. The Hindu, December 10, 1977.
35. S. C. Gangal, op.cit., p. 283.
36. Ibid., p. 284.
37. Aruna Asaf Ali, 18 December 1977, op.cit., pp. 22-23.
38. S. C. Gangal, op.cit., p. 255.
39. L. S. Baral, op.cit., p. 189.
40. S. C. Gangal, op.cit., p. 284.
41. The Hindu, April 17, 1978.
42. For the Joint Communique Ibid., December 10, 1977.
43. Ibid., April 17, 1978.
44. Ibid., April 16, 1978.
45. Aruna Asaf Ali, op.cit.
46. Ibid, op.cit., p. 1.
47. Ibid.
48. S. C. Gangal, op.cit., pp. 286-87.
49. The Financial Express (New Delhi), April 9, 1976.
50. See the Joint Communique in Asian Recorder, 21-27 May 1978, p. 14318.
51. S. C. Gangal, op.cit., p. 289.
52. Ibid., p. 290.
53. The Times of India, September 25, 1978.
54. Asian Recorder, 26 November - 2 December 1978, p. 14625.
55. Ibid.
56. The Times of India, September 26, 1978.
57. Ibid.
58. S. C. Gangal, op.cit., p. 284.
59. Ibid., pp. 286-87.
60. The Times of India (editorial), April 19, 1978.
61. Ibid., September 30, 1978.
62. The Hindu, April 17, 1978.
63. L. S. Baral, op.cit., p. 191.
64. Manorama Kohli, "Foreign Policy Initiatives of the National Front Government in India". Ramakant, ed., South Asia Studies, vol. 25, no. 1

& 2 January-December 1990 (University of Rajasthan, Jaipur, 1990), p. 139.

65. The Times of India (New Delhi) , December 13, 1989.
66. The Rising Nepal, December 4, 1989.
67. The Times of India, December 16, 1989.
68. The Hindustan Times, January 1, 1990.
69. The Hindu, January 4, 1990.
70. The Times of India, December 13, 1989.
71. Avtar Singh Bhasin, Nepal's Relations with India and China Documents 1947-1992, vol. I (Siba Exim, Delhi, 1984),. P. 471.
72. The Times of India, April 23, 1990.
73. Ibid., June 2, 1990.
74. Ibid.
75. Jagat Mehta, "Blazing a New Trial", The Indian Express (Chandigarh), August 31, 1990.
76. The Patriot, June 12, 1990.
77. The Times of India, August 4, 1990.
78. The Hindustan Times, August 10, 1990.
79. Monorama Kohli, op.cit., p. 139.
80. R. L. Varshney and Raj Kumar, Foreign Affairs Report, vol. XXXIX nos. 1 & II, January-February 1990 (Indian Council of World Affairs New Delhi, 1990), p. 17.
81. S. K. Chaturvedi, "Indo-Nepal Relations : Tension Areas", Vol. XXXIII, no.5, May 1989, Ibid., p. 77.
82. Foreign Affairs Record, Vol. XXXVI, no. 1, January 1990, p. 12.
83. Avtar Singh Bhasin, op. cit., p. 469.
84. Ibid., p. 468.
85. The Times of India, June 2, 1990.
86. The Hindustan Times, June 8, 1990.
87. Ibid., June 11, 1990.
88. The Hindu, June 11, 1990.
89. The Tribune, June 12, 1990.
90. The Patriot, June 12, 1990.
91. The Times of India, June 11, 1990.
92. Ibid., August 4, 1990.
93. The Indian Express, August 6, 1990.

94. Avtar Singh Bhasin, op.cit., p. 503.
95. The Statesman, August 7, 1990.
96. The Hindustan Times, December 20, 1989.
97. S. K. Chaturvedi, op.cit., p. 76.
98. Sangeeta Thapliyal, "Nepal in India's Security parameters", Strategic Analysis, Vol. XVIII, no. 9, December 1995 (Institute for Defence Studies and Analysis, New Delhi, 1995), p. 1201.
99. A. N. Dar, "Mr. Bhattarai Plays it Right", The National Herald, June 16, 1990.
100. The Times of India, June 11, 1990.
101. Ibid.
102. The Hindustan Times, August 7, 1990.
103. Avtar Singh Bhasin, op.cit., p. 499.
104. The Hindu, February 14, 1991.
105. Avtar Singh Bhasin, op.cit., p. 515
106. S. K. Sinha, "Value of National Front's Policy", The Statesman, February 11, 1991.
107. Ibid.
108. The Times of India, February 4, 1991.
109. Ibid., February 12, 1991.
110. Avtar Singh Bhasin, op.cit., p. 507
111. The Hindu, February 14, 1991.
112. Foreign Affairs Record, vol. XXXVII, no. 3, March 1991, p. 35.
113. The sub-commission on water resources is one of three headed by Ministers of External Affairs of the two countries and was constituted in August 1988. The first meeting of the sub-commission was last held at Kathmandu in December 1988. See, Foreign Affairs Record, Vol. XXXVII, no. 4, April 1991, p. 56.
114. Foreign Affairs Record, Vol. XLII, no. 6 June 1996, p. 107.
115. Indian Recorder, September 23-29, 1996, p. 2279.
116. Ibid.
117. Ibid.
118. The Hindustan Times, July 22, 1997.
119. Ibid., editorial, August 24, 1997.
120. Ibid., December 5, 1997.
121. Ibid., September 3, 1997.

122. Ibid., July 22, 1997.
123. Ibid., editorial, August 24, 1997.
124. Ibid., November 28, 1997.
125. Ibid., May 29, 1998.
126. Ibid., March 4, 1999.
127. Ibid., March 5, 1999.
128. Ibid., August 4, 1998.
129. The Times of India, August 4, 1999.
130. Ibid.
131. Sugata Bose and Ayesha Jalal, Modern South Asia-History, Culture, Political Economy (Oxford University Press, New Delhi, 2004), pp. 190-91.
132. The Times of India, June 4, 2001.
133. The Hindu, editorial, May 30, 2008.
134. Manoj Joshi, 'A Tale of Two Countries", The Times of India, February 5, 2005.
135. The Hindustan Times, June 4, 2001.
136. Ibid.
137. Ibid.
138. The Weekly Telegraph, September 1, 2004
139. Kavita Arora, 'Trans-boundary Forest Management in South Asia-Geopolitical Concerns for India', Dr. Subhash Kashyap, ed, South Asia Politics, Vol. 5, no.12, April 2007, New Delhi, 2007, pp. 29-30.
140. Ganga Bahadur Thapa, 'The People's War of Nepal', in Ibid, Vol. 3, Issue.6, October 2004, New Delhi, 2004, p. 26.
141. Ibid., p. 28.
142. S. D. Muni, 'On a Hot Tin Roof', The Hindustan Times, August 30, 2003.
143. Ibid.
144. Brahma Chellaney, 'Closet Nehruvian', Ibid., August 7, 2003.
145. Mahinda Werake, 'China and South Asia in the Eighties', Shelton U. Kodikara, ed., External Compulsions of South Asian Politics (Sage Publications, New Delhi, 1993), p. 90.
146. Uddipan Mukherjee, 'Maoism and Its Future in India', Subhash C. Kashyap, ed., South Asia Politics, Vol. 7, no. 3, July 2008, New Delhi, 2008, pp. 26-27.

147. Verghese Koithara, Society State & Security, The Indian Experience, (Sage Publications, New Delhi, 1999), p. 72.
148. The Hindustan Times, March 5, 1999.
149. Ibid., August 6, 1999.
150. Ibid., December 27, 1999.
151. Ibid., January 6, 2000.
152. Ibid., February 6, 2000.
153. Ganga Bahadur Thapa, 'The Peoples War of Nepal', Subhash C. Kashyap, ed., South Asia Politics, Vol. 3, no. 6, October 2004, New Delhi, 2004, p. 25.
154. Ibid.
155. Ibid., p. 28.
156. Raj Kumar Kothari, 'Democratic Transition in Nepal Banes and Boons for India', in Ibid., Vol. 7, no. 2, June 2008, New Delhi, 2008, pp. 24-25.
157. Ibid., p. 26.
158. S. D. Muni, 'The Hand, Great Monarch' The Hindustan Times, February 9, 2005.
159. Ibid., editorial, February 2, 2005.
160. Siddharth Varadarajan, 'In Nepal Time to Check the Dangerous Drift', The Hindu, September 20, 2006.
161. Ibid.
162. Shriman Narayan, India and Nepal : An Exercise in Open Diplomacy, New Delhi, 1971, p. 124.
163. The Indian Express, November 28, 2005.
164. The Financial Times, December 14, 2005.
165. Xinhua, January 3, 2006.
166. Kanak Mani Dixit, 'Enter Nepal's Maoist Establishment', The Hindu, April 14, 2008.
167. Ibid., June 14, 2008.
168. Ibid., June 30, 2008.
169. The Times of India (Nagpur), August 23, 2008.
170. The Hindu, editorial, August 16, 2008.
171. Ibid.,
172. Ibid., June 14, 2008.
173. Ibid, September 14, 2008.
174. S. D. Muni, 'Dealing With a New Nepal', in Ibid., September 15, 2008.
175. Ibid., September 18, 2008.

3

India-Bangladesh Relations

REGIME OF JANATA PARTY

Premiership of Morarji Desai (24 March 1977-28 July 1979)

Assumption of power by the Janata Party's Government in New Delhi in March 1977 brightened the prospect for the resolution of outstanding issues and improved relations between the two countries. The new party gave thought to the problem of India's foreign policy. Its election manifesto issued on 10 February took note of it and declared among other things that its government would strive to resolve such outstanding issues as remained with some of India's neighbours and would consciously promote a good-neighbourly policy.[1] In his inaugural address to the Conference of Foreign Ministers of Co-ordinating Bureau of Non-aligned Countries in New Delhi on 7 April 1977, Desai expressed his government's determination to make every effort so that India's relations with its immediate neighbours improved on the basis of dignity and mutual interest.[2] On another occasion addressing the Royal Commonwealth Society of London on 10 June 1977, Atal Bihari Vajpayee, the Minister for External Affairs, under the new dispensation, reaffirmed that his Government would pursue the policy of friendship and understanding between India and its neighbours.[3] A change of regime almost simultaneously took place in Bangladesh and Ziaur Rahman took over as the President on 21 April 1977. He received a massive mandate in a referendum in May 1977 which finally established him as the ruler of his country.

There was a radical shift in India's Bangladesh policy. The Janata Government adopted an attitude contrary to that adopted by Mrs. Gandhi's Government. The new government promptly stopped giving aid and succour to pro-Indian Bangladesh rebels.[4] The BSF began to co-operate with the BDR in combating the insurgents. Information about activities along the border where the BDR could not penetrate were conveyed to them by the BSF. The insurgents who had taken shelter in India were forced to leave. About 1,500 insurgents, including sick and wounded, were handed over to BDR. Virtually a joint operation was conducted by India and Bangladesh to crush the armed struggle led by the indomitable freedom fighters of 1971 fame, Kader Siddique.[5]

The Farakka Tangle

The Farakka Barrage[6] accord which was signed in November 1977 could also be cited as an instance. The problem of sharing the Ganga waters had been plaguing the relations between the two countries since 1951 when preliminary investigations of the project had started and with it the inter-governmental consultations and negotiations. In a joint declaration in May 1974 the Prime Ministers of the two countries agreed that a mutually acceptable allocation of waters available during periods of minimum flow in the Ganges should be arrived at before commissioning the barrage. Following the commissioning of barrage the two countries signed an interim agreement in April 1975, covering the flow of the Ganges during the lean period from 21 April to 31 May. But unfortunately no agreement could be reached for the dry season of 1975-76 and thereafter. It made Bangladesh anxious and it even started moves to internationalise the issue. Consequently, differences between the two countries continued. Bangladesh government wanted that India should completely stop withdrawal of water at Farakka pending an agreement. It was not acceptable to India. The Government of India viewed Bangladesh's demand that withdrawal of water at any time of the year should have its prior approval, was unjustified and, as such, refused to entertain. As the 1976 lean season approached, India repeatedly called for talks on the Farakka issue, while Bangladesh kept insisting on pre-conditions.[7]

In pursuance of its declared policy of friendship and understanding the new Indian Government moved to remove the irritants in its relations with Bangladesh. The first such irritant was the issue of sharing the waters of the Ganges at Farakka. Jagjivan Ram, a very senior member of Desai's Government, led a delegation to Dacca 15-17 April 1977 for talks on the issue. Besides Ram, the delegation included Prakash Singh Badal, Minister for Agriculture, Jagat Mehta, Foreign Secretary, and other senior officials of the Ministries of External Affairs, Agriculture and Irrigation. The great importance that India attached to the Farakka issue as well as to the over all problem of normalisation of relations with Bangladesh was evident from the very composition of the delegation. Ram used the opportunity to assure his host of his government's desire to have friendly relations with all of India's neighbours.[8] Ziaur Rahman, Chief Martial Law Administrator of Bangladesh, said to Ram, when the latter called on him, that he expected India to appreciate the sufferings of Bangladesh and hoped for a comprehensive agreement.

Both the countries attached significance to the issue from their own point of view and as such, in course of the discussions at times acrimonious exchanges also took place. Nevertheless, Ram succeeded in persuading Ziaur Rahman that in setting the modalities of sharing the lean season flow the two sides should evolve an agreed framework for tackling the long-term aspects, preferably through Indo-Bangla Joint Rivers Commission (JRC) that was already in existence.[9] It could be noted here that this commission was established in the year 1972. The two delegations jointly announced at the Dacca airport that a preliminary understanding had been reached and that details had been left to be worked out by the officials of the two countries in New Delhi. Referring to the understanding reached between India and Bangladesh on the issue of sharing waters of the Ganges at Farakka, Ram said that it would go a long way in restoring and further strengthening the friendly relations between the two neighbouring countries. He hoped that the understanding reached would remove suspicion of each other and restore confidence between the two neighbouring countries.[10]

The Working Groups of the two countries met in New Delhi 7-11 May 1977 and went into the details of the draft proposed by the two sides. An official statement, issued at the end of six-day discussions said that the talks were held in a cordial and friendly atmosphere and covered considerable ground on the various aspects of an agreement on the sharing of the Ganges waters at Farakka and on long term solutions.[11] It was agreed to resume talks in Dacca on mutually convenient dates to settle the remaining points of differences in their respective approaches.

At the Commonwealth Conference of Heads of Government, held in June 1977 in London Desai and Ziaur Rahman established personal rapport which helped them in preparing fresh ground for improving relation between the two countries. They discussed some of the outstanding issues between the two countries such as the Farakka issue and the question of rebels from Bangladesh being given asylum in India.[12] On the latter question Desai told President Zia, *inter alia*, that those who wanted to would go back if assured of safety and equality of treatment, but that he would not pressure those who did not want to.[13] Zia accepted this position. Following his talks with Desai, he said in London on 10 June that his talks with Desai on problems confronting the two countries were taking a "positive shape".[13] There were indications that both the sides were willing to strengthen the relations between the two countries by removing misunderstandings and irritants.[14]

A change in the attitude of the Government of India could easily be discerned hereafter. In reply to the debate on demands for grants of the Ministry of External Affairs in the Lok Sabha on 29 June 1977, Vajpayee, while reiterating Government of India's known stand that Bangladesh nationals seeking asylum in India would not be pushed back, stated at the same time that they would not be allowed to indulge in hostile activities against Bangladesh - "a friendly country".[15]

Following the second round of talks held in Dacca on Farakka from 29 July to 6 August, a joint statement announced that the differences had been further narrowed down.[16] Both the sides appeared to be optimistic and Jagjivan Ram informed the Indian parliament on 10 August 1977 that in the larger interest of friendship and sympathy for the weaker party an agreement would be reached for six to eight weeks of the year when there was not enough water and that India would get less than

40,000 cusecs which it had demanded.[17] However, an understanding on the issue could only be reached at the third round of official level talks which was held in New Delhi 29-30 September 1977. It finally culminated into the famous Farakka accord. The understanding reached at this time contained interim arrangements for sharing of the Ganges waters at Farakka and for finding a solution to the long-term problem of augmenting its flow.[18] India reduced its earlier demand of 40,000 cusecs of water to only 20,000 cusecs. Bangladesh also cut down its demand from 49,000 cusecs to 34,700 cusecs during the lean summer season.[19] The two sides also agreed to resolve the differences bilaterally that might arise in the interpretation of the agreement. The historic Farakka agreement was formally signed in Dacca on 5 November 1977 by Surjit Singh Barnala. India's Minister for Agriculture and Irrigation, and M. H. Khan, Advisor to the Bangladesh President on Flood Control and Irrigation.

The agreement ended the dispute over the issue between the two countries. The agreement was initially for a period of five years, subject to review at the end of an stipulated period of the three years and every six months thereafter in the light of proposals submitted by Joint River's Commission.[20] The agreement contained fifteen articles divided into three parts. The first part covered Articles I-VII and dealt with the terms and conditions of the sharing of the Ganga waters during the lean season. Article II of the agreement provided for the sharing of waters from Ist of January to 31st of May every year which was to depend on the availability of waters at the barrage. It also gave a guarantee to Bangladesh of 80% of its share for 10 days from April 21 to April 30th. Articles IV-VII were related to the setting up of joint committees of the representatives nominated by the two governments to observe and record the daily flow below the Farakka barrage and in the feeder canal as well as at Hardinge bridge. The Committee was to be responsible for supervising the implementation of the short-term aspects of the agreement relating to the division of the available waters during the lean season.[21]

The Joint Rivers Commission was reactivated with a view to finding a long term solution of the problem during the dry season in accordance with the provisions of Part II of the agreement. The Commission was to "carryout investigations and study of schemes" relating to the augmentation of the flow proposed by either side and "work out an economic and feasible" scheme acceptable to the two governments.[22] The third part (Articles XII-XV) dealt with the provisions of review and duration of the Agreement.

Divergence in Perception and Approach

Desai and Vajpayee made an official statement in the Lok Sabha and the Rajya Sabha respectively on 14 November 1977 on the Agreement. The statement noted that the agreement had to be based on the principles of shared sacrifices and mutual accommodation without affecting the right and entitlement of either country as during the lean season there was not enough water to meet the requirement of both the countries. It drew the attention of the members to the political imperative of improving relations with India's closest neighbour. It said that the Agreement was an acid test of the effectiveness and credibility of India's entire foreign policy and for that matter of the principles which it had always advocated and which should guide relations among nations. It noted that the agreement contained best possible arrangement for realising the objective of the Farakka Project and at the same time meeting the requirements of Bangladesh during the period of distress. It expressed Government of India's view that with the signing of the Agreement and its simultaneous coming into force a major problem which had bedevilled relations between the two countries and vitiated the political atmosphere in the sub-continent for over 25 years had been resolved. It also expressed its hope that the agreement would not only lead to a solution of the long-term problem of augmenting the flow of the Ganges, but would also pave the way for the optimum utilisation of the water resources of the region as a whole. It also hoped that the activisation of the Joint Rivers Commission under the terms of the Agreement should result in increasing co-operation between India and Bangladesh for flood control and in other problem areas affecting the interests of the other party. It noted Government of India's hope that the approach and spirit which made the Agreement possible, if applied to larger spectrum of India's relations with Bangladesh, should lead to an ever-widening cooperation between the two countries, both bilaterally and in multilateral forums. It also noted that the Agreement should also contribute to the furtherance of India's objectives of promoting peace and development in the sub-continent and of working together towards a better world order. The statement appealed to the members not to treat the Agreement as a partition issue and view it in the wider perspective of the overall objective of India's foreign policy and specifically the well being of the two countries.[23]

In course of the consideration of the statement in the House, the Agreement drew critical references from some of the leading members of the Lok Sabha, particularly those from the state of West Bengal. Samar Guha termed the statement as "nothing but an apologia for a political agreement entered into with the intention of appeasing a military regime." He charged the government that it had never consulted a single hydrological expert whereas Bangladesh was each and every time assisted by hydrological experts and scientists. In his view the Agreement was not a sincere agreement based on technological and scientific data. He called it a bankruptcy of our intelligence.[24] Saugata Roy criticised the agreement mainly on the ground that the interests of the port of Calcutta has been compromised. He called the agreement a sell out for political purposes.[25] Somnath Chatterjee criticised the Government for not consulting the Government of West Bengal.[26] P. K. Kodiyan criticised it for sacrificing the interests of our country.[27]

With the hope of finding a long-term solution of the problem the Government of India decided to show maximum generosity to Bangladesh in the matter of allocation of Ganges waters during the lean season. But India's efforts of finding a long-term solution of the problem did not fructify as Bangladesh had an entirely different approach to the problem. It wanted to politicise and internationalise the issue by involving not only third countries (Nepal) but also the World Bank.[28] Ziaur Rahman visited Kathmandu 18-19 December 1977 and discussed with King Birendra and his Prime Minister Kirtinidhi Bista the possibility of a tripartite agreement between India Bangladesh and Nepal on co-operation in the development of water resources. From Kathmandu Rahman came straight to New Delhi. As he said he held fruitful talks in New Delhi covering various aspects of the relations between the two countries. It was agreed to raise the Joint Rivers Commission to ministerial level and to have its meetings as early as possible to discuss the question of a long-term solution for the augmentation of waters in the Ganges as laid down in the Farakka Agreement. Bangladesh wanted to have the facilities of an overland route connecting Bangladesh and Pakistan and this issue was also discussed.[29]

On the otherhand, the Indian side raised the issue of minorities in Bangladesh and politely explained to Rahman that although the minorities were the citizens of Bangladesh, the problem of their security tended to have ramification on bilateral relations. The Indian leaders expressed the hope that the Bangladesh Government's efforts would give the minority a greater sense of security. It was also conveyed to him that the incidence of influx of the minorities from Bangladesh to India, though not large, did cause concern. Rahman, however, maintained that his government did not believe in communalism.[30]

A joint communique was issued at the end of Rahman's visit which recognised that the Agreement on sharing of the Ganges waters had paved the way for wider co-operation between the two countries, particularly for the optimum utilisation of the water resources of the region as a whole. It noted that the two leaders (Desai and Rahman) attached importance to a speedy solution of the long-term problem of augmenting the flow of the Ganges which was essential for adequately meeting the requirements of both the countries. It also noted that they regarded the Agreement signed in Dacca in November on sharing the Ganges waters at Farakka and on augmenting its flow as of historic significance and that the accord could be possible because of the spirit of mutual accommodation and understanding shown by the leaders of the two countries.

The joint communique stressed the bonds of geography, tradition and culture and recognised the need for maintaining close and friendly relations between the two countries. Reiterating their commitment to non-alignment, the two leaders reaffirmed their determination to develop and strengthen these relations on the basis of equality and non-interference in each other's internal affairs. The communique noted the conviction of the two leaders that such an approach would contribute to the consolidation of the emerging edifice of peace in the region and the promotion of peace and stability in the world at large.

Improvement in the Climate

Though finding a long-term solution to the problem of allocation of the Ganges waters at Farakka still eluded, Rahman's visit to India proved helpful in facilitating co-operation between the two neighbours by improving the climate of relations between them. It should be noted here that the relations between 'the two countries had not been very cordial since the assassination of Sheikh Mujibur Rahman in August 1975. President Rahman's visit left behind a distinct impression in India and signs of change for the first time appeared on the scene. *The Pioneer* (Lucknow) described the visit as "well timed"[31] and *The Statesman* (Delhi) saw in Rahman's visit "a genuine desire to restore the rapport that once existed between the two countries."[32]

The positive impact of improved climate could be seen on India's commercial relations with Bangladesh. The trade between the two countries was governed by an agreement signed in 1973 which provided for an annual trade review. Talks were held in New Delhi 25-27 February 1978 for the year 1978-79. In the talks the Bangladesh delegation stressed the point that India should step up its imports from Dacca to reduce its large trade surplus. At the conclusion of the talks India agreed to purchase 10,000 tonnes of newsprint, 200 tonnes of Neptha, 60,000 tonnes of furnace oil, 15,000 tonnes of steam coal from India and also to consider purchasing 75,000 tonnes of Assam coal.[33]

Government of Nepal and the Government of Bangladesh had entered into a Treaty of Transit in 1976 providing for use of Bangladesh ports to facilitate Nepal's oversea's trade. It was agreed under the provisions of Indo-Nepal Treaties and Agreement of 17 March 1978, through an exchange of letters, that to enable Nepal to make use of this facility over land routes would be provided to Nepal for its trade with Bangladesh as also for Nepal's trade with third countries through Bangladesh. The procedural arrangements to facilitate this was left to be worked out by the Government of India with the Bangladesh Government.

An Indian delegation visited Bangladesh 11-14 August 1978 to conclude arrangements and procedures with the Bangladesh to facilitate Nepal's trade with it and with third countries through the territories of India and Bangladesh. The talks were held in a cordial and friendly atmosphere and resulted in the signing of a Memorandum of Understanding which provided for the expeditious and smooth movement of "Traffic in Transit" through the agreed rail route of Radhikapur in India and Biral in Bangladesh and for the related customs and other procedures.

Both the delegations agreed that the procedures as applicable under the protocol and memorandum to the Indo-Nepal Treaty of Transit 1970, should apply to Nepal's "Traffic-in-Transit" in the territory of India. Similarly, the procedures as envisaged in the protocol to the Bangladesh-Nepal Transit Agreement 1976, was to apply to Nepal's "Traffic-in-Transit" in territory of Bangladesh. The agreement reached between Bangladesh and India also provided for periodical consultations between officials of the two governments to ensure smooth and speedy movement of goods in transit.[34] The procedures and arrangement envisaged in the Memorandum of Understanding which came into force on 15th September 1978 were expected to facilitate Nepal's overland trade with Bangladesh.

As a part of Janata Government's drive to improve relations with India's neighbours Desai paid a visit to Bangladesh 17-18 April 1979. He was accompanied by his Foreign Minister Vajpayee. The invitation had earlier been extended in course of Rahman's visit to New Delhi in December 1977. Desai's statement at a press conference at Dacca on 17 April 1979 gave indications to India's attitude and approach to the problem of normalisation of relations between the two countries. He referred to the all sorts of proximities between the two countries, their intertwined destinies, and regretted that situations should have arisen in the past which kept the two countries apart. However, he hearteningly noted that the past was buried and that the leaders of the two countries had dedicated themselves to the future of friendship, understanding, co-operation and closeness between the two countries.[35]

The joint communique issued at the end of Desai's visit noted that outstanding bilateral, regional and international issues were discussed in a spirit of great cordiality and understanding was reached on some of the issues. Thus, the two leaders felt that they should co-operate in improving communications between the two countries—both telecommunication and road transport. They agreed to explore the possibilities of co-operation in diverse fields like economic co-operation, establishment of joint ventures and co-operation in the field of science and technology with particular reference to the development of solar energy. In that context some specific export-oriented projects, such as, the manufacture of cement, sponge iron and urea (fertilizer) were identified. The two sides expressed the need for augmenting and diversifying trade between the two countries and also to reduce existing trade imbalance. In order to reduce the imbalance which existed in the trade between India and Bangladesh it was decided that the infrastructure facility such as transport and telecommunication should be improved. The two leaders also discussed the lapses of Boundary Agreements signed in 1974. It was agreed that the two sides would resume negotiations at an early date to resolve the question of maritime boundary on a mutually satisfactory basis.[36]

While reviewing the international situation the two leaders emphasised that peace and stability could be ensured only by a strict adherence to the purposes and principle of the United Nations' Charter. They reiterated their belief that respect for sovereign equality and territorial integrity, non-interference in the internal affairs of other country and abandonment of the use of force for the settlement of disputes should be practised in bilateral relations.

The joint communique revealed the common desire of the two sides to consolidate and further strengthen the existing friendly relations between the two countries.[37] In course of the talks the two leaders affirmed that the role of non-alignment movement was an important factor in promoting peace and understanding among the nations. In this respect they stressed the need to preserve the unity and solidarity of non-aligned countries. The Farakka water dispute was also discussed and the two leaders reiterated their firm commitment to make all possible efforts for the optimum utilisation of water resources for the betterment of the conditions of the people of the two countries.

The visit was publicised as fruitful one. Before leaving Dacca, Desai told newsmen that India and Bangladesh had reached understanding on many important problems and were now ready to explore new fields of co-operation and mutual assistance.[38] Commenting on Desai's visit to Bangladesh, Ziaur Rahman said that relations between Bangladesh and India had improved since the Janata Government came to power in India and added that Desai's visit would "undoubtedly strengthen the relations between the two countries."[39] However, these reactions were somewhat premature and over-optimistic. At this stage it could not be said with any certainty that all misunderstandings between the two countries had been removed. *The Times of India* made a correct assessment of the situation in its editorial on 20 April 1979 and said that the joint communique was more a declaration of intention than a plan of action to solve outstanding problem between the two countries.[40] The basic difference over the distribution of water at Farakka remained, Desai taking the stand that the issue should be taken bilaterally while Bangladesh insisting on third party involvement.

However, it should not be concluded from the outgoing comments that the visit was all futile and achieved nothing. It marked an earnest effort to bury the unsavoury past.[41] An important gain of the visit was the establishment of personal rapport between Desai and President Rahman and also a better understanding by each side of the views of the other on a wide range of subjects of mutual interest. By the discussions some of the misunderstandings had changed the atmosphere of suspicion and mistrust prevailing since the assassination of Sheikh Mujibur Rahman.

Claims and counter-claims over about 50 acres of land that had surfaced on the River Muhuri in the Balonia sector between eastern Bangladesh and north-eastern Indian state of Tripura led to border troubles, and even to border skirmishes by the end of 1979. Several rounds of talks between the two sides at the lower appropriate levels led to no results and both the sides blamed each other for taking unreasonable and rigid stand.[42] Undoubtedly, the border troubles resulted in some tension in the relations between the two countries. But it could not be said to be so acute as during the days of Indira Gandhi. Despite the border skirmishes and conflicting claims over territory, there were encouraging signs for establishing good relations since Desai 'Government's attitude towards India's small neighbours was significantly different from that of the previous government. Dacca, on its part, too, appeared to be keen to respond.[43] Thus, though the period ended on a more or less hopeful note for relations between the two countries, the basic differences remained unresolved.

REGIME OF NATIONAL FRONT

Premiership of V. P. Singh (1 December 1989-7 November 1990)

As a result of the general elections held in November 1989, the second non-Congress Government of National Front, headed by Vishwanath Pratap Singh was formed in India who succeeded Rajiv Gandhi on 1 December 1989. By the time the new Indian Government came, the international political scene had gone a sea change which characterized by both hope and despair. Hope lies in the acknowledgement of the futility of war as an instrument to influence or change international political processes. There is Glasnost and Perestroika through which ideological distortions, socio-political and economic bureaucratisation of society and polity are sought to be put an end to. But these hope-generating phenomena are not unmixed blessings. Despair, in some way also emanating from these very phenomena, and their subjective interpretations, too, is fast engulfing the psyche of the international world. Despair overtaking the hope remains very much in the realm of possibility.[44] The developing world's concern for socio-economic development and equality in the international world should not be allowed to be over-shadowed by euphoric assertion of the superiority of the capitalist model.[45] In the circumstances, the new Indian Prime Minister V. P. Singh, while campaigning for his Jatana Dal during the February 1990 election for the State Assemblies, declared that the Government has chalked out a fresh foreign policy. The Prime Minister elaborating his fresh perspective on foreign policy, stated that henceforth the objective would be strengthen the bonds of friendship with the like-minded world powers and neighbouring countries.[46]

Major problems between India and Bangladesh are the Ganga water dispute, the Ghakma refugees, Teen Bigha and illegal migration across the international border. These problems are exploited by Bangladesh authorities for generating anti-Indian feelings and are convenient in their hands to perpetuate their anti democratic rule. Soon after the new regime assumed office President Ershad addressing the winter session of the Parliament said, "We hope it will be possible to peacefully and rapidly settle all our outstanding problems including the sharing of Ganga Water."[47] Leaders of two main opposition parties Sheikh Hasina Wajid, President of Bangladesh Awami League and Begum Khalida Zia, Chairperson of Bangladesh Nationalist Party and some other opposition leaders representing different political opinions have congratulated V. P. Singh on his assumption of office as new Indian Prime Minister.[48] In response, the Indian Prime Minister in a letter to Ershad, the President of Bangladesh, expressed the belief that the friendly relations between the two countries must be nurtured and diversified further. The new Prime Minister said he was looking forward to working with him in resolving the outstanding problems in a manner which would safeguard the legitimate interests of both the countries on the basis of equality and equity.[49]

The National Front Government as part of a new peace-offensive to promote good relations with the neighbouring countries, sent Inder Kumar Gujral, the new Minister for External Affairs on a three-day visit 16-18 February, 1990 to Bangladesh. The visit, being somewhat of an exploratory exercise had revived optimism that some of the outstanding problems would receive immediate attention.[50] At the Dhaka airport, Gujral said that bilateral problems between India and Bangladesh could be sorted out in a spirit of friendship and cooperation. His Bangladeshi counterpart Anisul Islam Mahmud hosted a banquet in honour of the visiting guest in which he sought India's co-operation in the fields of industry and technology. In a reply speech, Gujral, apart from reiterating his government's policy towards neighbours reminded that the National Front government wanted South Asia to be an area of friendship and peace. Obviously, referring to the improvement in the relations between the two superpowers. Gujral said, "the situation should change in the same way in South Asia, the way the whole world has changed."[51]

Gujral, while leaving from Dacca, expressed satisfactory over the talks he had with the Bangladesh during his three-day stay and stressed the need for fostering co-operative spirit needed for the South-Asia region. In South Asia peace, co-operation and friendship should be the platform for the building up of new structures. He discussed with Bangladesh leaders bilateral, regional and international issues in a friendly and cordial atmosphere and mentioned specially the burying of cold war and a new atmosphere changing the global scenario.[52] The goodwill trip to Dacca resulted in two major gains. First, two foreign ministers of South Asia for the first time agreed that not only relations between their countries but the entire fabric of regional relationship be turned to the central thrust of global change. This thrust was defined by Gujral and his Bangladeshi counterpart, as a shift from confrontation to dialogue, from conflict to peaceful coexistence from antagonism to co-operation. Together with a commitment to resolve all disputes and differences through peaceful constructive negotiations. Secondly, for the first time an Indian foreign minister declared categorically that Indian territory would not be allowed to be used for action aimed against Bangladesh.[53] At least, the job of initial familiarisation has been done and emphasis should be laid for close interaction, particularly at the political and intellectual levels. At the moment, there is also enough scope for an active relationship at the non-official level, particularly in the context of a powerful democratic movement in Bangladesh with the tradition of friendly relations with India.[54]

Water Problem

Distribution of Ganges water had been a bone of contention in Indo-Bangladesh relations. With the coming of V. P. Singh Bangladesh expressed its desire to improve relations with New Delhi and hoped that all outstanding problems including the sharing of Ganga water would be resolved. Gujral's visit to Dacca in February 1990 did not carry any solution but only the discussion on the issue. The only gain of the visit was that both the leaders agreed to reactivate the Joint Rivers Commission and the task force constituted on flood and the latter would submit its report expeditiously.[55] Further the two sides discussed the latest position on water sharing and on the Teen Bigha enclave in course of the Indo-Bangla Economic Commission, particularly India's offer of Rs. 30 crore credit.

The 31st meeting of the Indo-Bangladesh Joint Rivers Commission was held at Dacca on 21 and 22 June, 1990. The Indian delegation was led by Manubhai Kotadia, Minister for Water Resources and Bangladesh side by A. B. M. Ghulam Mostaffa, Minister of Irrigation, Water Development and Flood Control. In a text of press release, issued in New Delhi, on 19 June, 1990 it was stated that this would discuss the action taken on the finalisation of the Task Force Report on Flood Management. Some of the issues likely to be covered include exchange of information of flood levels of flashy rivers and trying up of river embankments at the border.[56] Taking these all as the gestures of goodwill, Ershad, the President of Bangladesh, was happy over progress in ties with India.[57] It appeared that the waters of hope of rivers Ganga. Brahmaputra, Teesta and Meghna could remain as waters of despair as long as Bangladesh stuck to its intransigent demand.[58]

The other economic gains during the premiership of V. P. Singh was the supply of portable bridges to Bangladesh. The Indian Railway Construction Company Limited (IRCON), a public sector unit under the Ministry of Railways had bagged a contract for supply of portable steel bridges to the Roads and Highways Department, Government of Bangladesh. The order valued at 2.12 million US dollar and under the contract, IRCON would supply the latest state of art technology by adopting the "Quadricon System."[59] In May 1990 the second rail link was established between India and Bangladesh. The two countries discussed modalities for reopening of the new broad gauge link that would provide an alternative interchange point to the existing rail link between the two countries. It would also enable transport of massive quantities of boulders and stone chips to Bangladesh for Jamuna bridge project and other construction works in that country. A decision to reopen the second rail link between the two countries was announced after the visit of the External Affairs Minister Inder Kumar Gujral to Bangladesh in February this year.[60] India also participated in the 13th session of the International Jute Council of International Jute Organisation being held at Dacca from 9th to 13th of May 1990. The Indian delegation was led by L. V. Saptarishi, Joint Secretary, Ministry of Textiles and other senior member of the delegation was S. Ahmed, Director, Ministry of Textiles.[61]

Defence

Inder Kumar Gujral paid a successful visit to Bangladesh in February 1990 and it appeared that the solution of all the problems were on the card. Since the National Front government besides being benevolent, was exclusively concerned with the rulers of Bangladesh and would do nothing that could annoy them. Even moral support to democratic movement will not be forthcoming. Bangladesh, instead of being accommodative towards India's overtures, had been emboldened to adopt even tougher attitude on the issues besetting Indo-Bangladesh relations. Not only this, the position of Bangladesh with regard to bilateral Indo-Pakistan problems, had undergone significant shifts from neutrality to a tilt in favour of Pakistan on Kashmir issue. In a significant development after the visit of Gujral Pakistan's Foreign Minister Yakub Khan came to Dacca and reportedly, urged Bangladesh to raise the Kashmir question at the forum of the Organization of Islamic Conference.[62] Bangladesh had flouted the norms it had itself set for good neighbourly relations by expressing concern at what it had alleged the oppression of Muslims of Kashmir. President H. M. Ershad issued a call for stopping "oppressive measures" when he met a group of editors in Dacca. The country had chosen to move away from its position of neutrality between India and Pakistan over the Kashmir question to a stance of clear support for Islamabad. However, the development should not be treated as a post-Gujral's visit approach. Even before the visit General Ershad viewed threats only from India as he said in London that the defence strategy of his country "sees India as its only adversary and possible source of threat". He disclosed that Bangladesh intends to raise one more division, which will complete the minimum defence requirements. Dacca "had very close defence collaboration with Pakistan including frequent exchanges of delegations and it has also received some equipment from Pakistan. Ershad stated that most of our equipment is from China and our officials also receive training there".[63] It was a known fact that General Ershad was a good friend of Pakistan's Chief of Army Staff General Mirza Aslam Beg.

Chandra Shekhar
(10 November 1990-21 June 1991)

The new Prime Minister found Indo-Bangla relations not up to the mark. The long standing problems were not resolved and pro-Pakistan gesture was surfaced in recent months. In despair the only ray of hope was the declaration of Parliamentary elections of 27 February 1990, and it was hoped that the return of democracy in Bangladesh would serve India a golden opportunity for sorting out the differences with the new government.[64] New Delhi, as a gesture of goodwill on its part, signed a contract agreement for provision of modern facilities for modern training in railway operation in Bangladesh. The agreement was signed on 14 January 1991, at Dacca by M. D. Khattar, Managing Director, Indian Railway Construction Company and Nurul Momin, Secretary, Ministry of Communications, People's Republic of Bangladesh. In line with the growing trends of regional co-operation between India and Bangladesh a sophisticated Railway Working Model Facility will be provided to Bangladesh Railway by the Government of India in furtherance of the training of their Railway personnel.[65] The project with an over all cost of Rs. 65 lacs' was being rendered as a gift to the Bangladesh Railway as a goodwill gesture to the people of Bangladesh. This training facility which was being provided as a measure of technology transfer will help supplement the training of Railway personnel with the necessary practical training in safe and efficient train operations using working models.[66]

India expressed happiness over the results of the general elections that led to the establishment of democracy in Bangladesh. Khalida Zia became the new Prime Minister of the country who, even before the elections stated that Bangladesh would strive towards friendly ties with her neighbours. She reiterated the desire after assuming the office that the two countries would come closer once again and overcome various problems that have come in the way of amicable relations between the two nations.[67] The Indian spokesman, commenting on the report that the relationship between the two is expected to be "correct but cool" said, "we have enjoyed the friendship of relations with our neighbour Bangladesh. We have no reason to apprehend any dimination in the mutual regard and affection in which the peoples of the two countries hold each other. It was said when the results of the elections were announced. We have expressed our hope and intention to work with Bangladesh, to strengthen our bilateral relations based on our mutual national interest.[68] On 10 May, 1991 the Educational Consultant India[69] had been entrusted with preparation of a detailed project report for setting up an Open University in Bangladesh. The project was awarded to EPCIL by the Asian Development Bank against stiff international competition from organisations like Open University, UK, UNESCO, France and Department of Education, Australia.

The real test of friendship and co-operation between the two countries came when in May 1991 Bangladesh was facing the post-cyclone sufferings. In this hour of turmoil the then Prime Minister of India Chandra Shekhar paid his three-hours visit to Bangladesh on 12 May 1991 and expressed India's solidarity with that country. India pledged all possible assistance to Bangladesh to help her cope with the havoc wrecked by the cyclone. Rice, the staple diet of the Bangladeshis, was being supplied by India in 10 tonnes trucks via the road network. It had also set up a Bangladesh Relief Contribution Fund as a long-term measure to help

Bangladesh in its hour of crisis.[70] Apart from these all, the Government of India sent a railway expert to assess the damage and the assistance required by Bangladesh. It had also offered training facilities to Bangladesh personnel in weather forcasting as a measure within the framework of the SAARC Charter. India's gesture and assistance was apprcciated by Bangladesh President Shahabuddin Ahmed and Prime Minister Khaleda Zia have said that six Indian helicopters for the relief operations were doing good job and are regularly dropping food in the cyclone-affected areas.[71] Thus, at the moment, Indo-Bangladesh relations were on an optimistic point.

REGIME OF UNITED FRONT

Premiership of H. D. Deve Gowda (1 June 1996-21 April 1997)

Even during the 13 days premiership of Atal Bihari Vajpayee (May 16-28, 1996) New Delhi did not miss the occasion to convey deep sympathy on behalf of the Government and people of India for the victims of the tornado which struck Tangail district and neighbouring areas on 14 May, 1996.[72] The release also stated that the Government of India stands ready to assist the Bangladesh Government in its relief and rehabiliation efforts that are underway.

H. D. Deve Gowda succeeded Atal Bihari Vajpayee as the leader of United Front and became the new Prime Minister of India on 1 June 1996. Inder Kumar Gujral, India's new Minister for External Affairs under the new dispensation, sent a message to his Bangladeshi counterpart Abdus Samad Azad and Sheikh Hasina Wajed, the Prime Minister of the country felicitating the assumption of office had expressed the confidence that India and Bangladesh would develop relations of great co-ordiality, friendship and co-operation, to the mutual benefit of both our countries.[73] In an another press release H. D. Deve Gowda, the Indian Prime Minister, felicitated Sheikh Hasina Wajed on her assumption of the office of the Prime Minister of Bangladesh and expressed the confidence that Bangladesh would make progress towards greater prosperity and harmony under her leadership. He stated that her appointment provided an opportunity to deepen and expand ties between the two nations.

The understanding between the two democratic governments grew further when Salman Haider, India's Foreign Secretary, visited Bangladesh in July 1996 as Prime Minister's special envoy to deliver the PM's message to Sheikh Hasina. During the visit Haider met the Prime Minister, Foreign Minister and Foreign Secretary of Bangladesh. Sheikh Hasina, in response to the sentiments and greeting of Indian Prime Minister said that Bangladesh would like close and friendly relations with India and all bilateral issue between the two countries need to be resolved. Responding with happiness to the message from the Indian External Minister Abdul Samad Azad described India as an "old friend" of Bangladesh and underlined his desire to resolve outstanding issues between India and Bangladesh and work for constructive co-operation between the two countries.[74] The Indian Foreign Secretary also held discussions with his Bangladeshi counterpart in which both sides agreed to take steps to intensify dialogue between the two countries on all issues in the bilateral relationship. It was agreed that expeditious action would be taken to convene the Indo-Bangladesh Joint Commission and promote media exchanges, interaction between business communities, and to increase cultural and sporting exchanges.

The dividends of good understanding between the two countries started. Bangladesh, perhaps, as a gesture of goodwill changed its earlier stand on Kashmir and had cold shouldered a Pakistani request to politically support Islamabad's stand on Kashmir. The request was conveyed to Bangladesh Prime Minister Sheikh Hasina Wajed by a letter from Benazir Bhutto which was handed over to the new Bangladeshi leader by the visiting Pakistani Foreign Secretary Najmuddin Shaikh in August 1996.[75]

The four-day visit of Inder Kumar Gujral, India's Minister for External Affairs, to Bangladesh in September 1996 came as a major breakthrough in relations between the two countries, particularly on the sharing of Ganga waters. The Indian Foreign Minister, as a result of a 90-minute talks with his Bangladeshi counterpart Abdus Samad Azad, the two sides on 7 September agreed on the "broad principles" to resolve the issue of sharing Ganga water. Experts from both sides would workout of the details on the quantum of water sharing and the mechanism for the purpose would be set in motion soon.[76] The water sharing issue was discussed "to the satisfaction of Bangladesh side and in the talks priority was given to the issue as Dacca expected a solution to the problem before the onset of the coming lean season in January. As Gujral said almost all the pending issues between the two countries, such as, strengthening of trade relations, repatriation of Chakma refugees to Bangladesh from Tripura, demarcation of land boundary and security figured at the talks. On 29 October 1996 a fresh request to finalise the renewal of the bilateral agreement on sharing of Ganga waters was put forward by visiting Bangladesh Water Resources Minister Abdur Razzak, in a meeting with India's Water Resources Minister Janeshwar Mishra. Razzak was leading a delegation of senior officials of Foreign Affairs and Water Resources to resume talks on the sharing of Ganga waters and find a solution to this long-standing problem.[77]

Historic Agreement

In pursuance of the principle of "equity and fair play" the two countries signed a historic agreement on 12 December, 1996 on sharing of Ganga water. The treaty was signed by Sheikh Hasina and her Indian counterpart H. D. Deve Gowda, at Hyderabad House. West Bengal Chief Minister Jyoti Basu who played a key role in the negotiations was present with Foreign Minister I. K. Gujral. The treaty will be valid for 30 years with provisions for review after every five years or earlier. Provisions have been made to take care that neither Bangladesh nor India or more precisely West Bengal is at a disadvantage. The signed treaty provided that if the availability of water at Farakka is 70,000 cusecs or less, it will be shared between the two countries on 50-50 basis. If the quantum is between 70,000 and 75,000 cusecs, Bangladesh will get 35,000 cusecs, while India will retain the rest. If the quantum rises above 75,000 cusecs, India will retain 40,000 cusecs while the rest will go to Bangladesh. The lean period for both the countries starts in the first week of January and lasts 150 days. But the leanest period is between the middle of March to the first week of May. In addition, the 10-day hydraulic cycles giving the advantage to India and Bangladesh alternately, ensures that neither side will face a crisis during the period.[78]

The signing of the treaty was welcomed in New Delhi and Dacca. In a joint press statement at Vigyan Bhawan. New Delhi, Deve Gowda declared, "It is a matter of profound satisfaction for me in finding a solution to this problem."[79] Sheikh Hasina Wajed, the Prime Minister of Bangladesh, responded to the treaty with equal warmth and said. "It is a moment of high emotion for me. The treaty is of great significance and will influence bilateral relations between the two countries for many years to come." Soon after signing the treaty, Gowda went to Parliament and read out its broad outlines in both houses. Though most parties, seemed happy about the outcome of the week-long negotiations, the Bharatiya Janata Party raised objections. But the Left Front Government of West Bengal was happy with the treaty and said that it was in both countries best interest. Asim Dasgupta, the Finance Minister, viewed it as an improvement of the 1977 arrangement and hoped, "There is no threat to Calcutta port. Instead, seven out of 15 hydraulic cycles, under the alternate advantage formula, has ensured that 40,000 cusecs of water is kept for maintaining navigability of the port." It was also resolved that the pact, which has been the bone of contention bedevilling bilateral ties, would be used as a stepping stone for co-operation in other areas.

Exchange of Visits

In the background of hopeful relations between New Delhi and Dacca H. D. Deve Gowda went to Bangladesh in the first week of January 1997, the first Indian Prime Minister to visit Bangladesh on a bilateral level in over two decades. In Dacca, he was accorded a rousing reception on arrival. In a rare gesture, four fighter jets escorted the Prime Minister's plane soon after it entered the Bangladesh air space. On 6 January, Sheikh Hasina hosted a banquet in honour of the visiting Prime Minister and in her address said, "we remember with gratitude the co-operation and support extended by the Government and people of India during the war of our liberation. We have also not forgotten that the bilateral relations between us blossomed in the early years of our independence under the dynamic and visionary leadership of Bangabandhu Sheikh Mujibur Rahman."[80] In a reply speech, Deve Gowda observed that the liberation of Bangladesh was achieved "through unique joint endeavour". He also referred in the speech, the recently concluded treaty and said.: "The historic treaty on sharing Ganga waters.... is a landmark in our bilateral relations because it provides a just, equitable and lasting solution to an issue which is of vital importance.

In course of Deve Gowda's visit to Bangladesh the two countries discussed in detail ways to counter across the border terrorism, especially in view of the stepped up insurgent activity in the North-East. The Indian Prime Minister said, "Over the years, due to a variety of factors, violent and illegal groups have been able to establish themselves and find sanctuary and access to arms and weapons in the territory of some of our neighbours. We are deeply conscious of your commitment and that of the government to end violence in your country and to ensure that the soil of Bangladesh will not be available to such negative elements. It is a pressing priority for us to ensure that actions on the ground are taken to put an effective check to this menace. On 7 January 1997, Deve Gowda addressed a meeting of businessmen in Dacca and said, "I ...look forward to establishing a long term partnership between our two countries .... I look forward to an enduring friendship with the business community.[81]

Encouraged by the positive attitude of the Government of India, Dacca sought stronger ties with New Delhi. In February 1997, Sheikh Hasina Wajed, the Prime Minister of Bangladesh, came to New Delhi, to attend the International Parliamentarian's Conference and in a series of meetings with Indian officials discussed the measures to strengthen the bilateral economic ties. Inder Kumar Gujral, India's Minister for External Affairs, called on her and their numerous interactions were part of the minister's pursuit of the "Gujral doctrine wherein India has been addressing bilateral issues without expecting" reciprocity in the pursuit of better relations. In the talks, the two sides have also proposed to review the Joint Rivers Commission which was set up in the 70s to review Indo-Bangladesh water sharing. Security and border trade was also discussed by the two sides.[82] Recently, a high-level team from Bangladesh comprising Government officials and representatives of the tanners visited effluent treatment plants operating in different tanning clusters in Tamil Nadu and in Bangalore and for tackling such problems in Bangladesh as disclosed by K. Azharul Haq, Managing Director of the Dacca Water Supply and Sewerage Authority.[83]

Inder Kumar Gujral
(21 April 1997-19 March 1998)

Inder Kumar Gujral, the Minister for External Affairs under Deve Gowda dispensation became the new Prime Minister of India on 21 April

1997. With this coming, it was hoped that the pace of development in relations between the two countries would continue as earlier. The problems were best known to the new incumbent and understandings received further encouragement. The two sides strived to find an amicable solution to the pending issues, such as, problems of Chakma refugees, trade, defence etc. As a follow up of the decision taken earlier the 32nd ministerial level Indo-Bangladesh Joint Rivers Commission (JRC) was held on July 19 and 20, 1997. The Indian side was attended by the Union Water Resources Minister Sis Ram Ola. The JRC meeting agreed that the joint committee of experts under chairmanship of the secretaries, Water Resources Ministers of the two countries would be immediately reactivated to discuss the issues of sharing of water of Teesta river and other common rivers. The meeting also discussed the issue of immediate revival of the standing committee and local level committees to resolve pending issues.[84] At the JRC meeting it was decided that the standing committee and the local level committee headed by the respective members of the Joint Rivers Commission of the two countries would immediately meet at Teesta border to discuss the fying of embankment for an early solution. The two sides appreciated the need to remove the "bottlenecks" in the implementation of Ganga Water Treaty. In September 1997, when the Bihar Government sought some clarifications regarding the treaty, the centre had, in a written undertaking to Bihar, "freeing it from any responsibility to maintain the water level required at the Farakka barrage as per the Indo-Bangla Treaty on the Ganga sharing signed in December 1996.

Problem of Chakma Refugees

The decision of the Pakistani Government in 1964 to remove the curbs on the plains people to settle in the tribal areas created an atmosphere of fear and mistrust among the Chakmas. Being Buddhists, they also had genuine fears on account of the Islamisation drive. Chakma tribals fled from Bangladesh 11 years ago when the country decided to become an Islamic state. The Chittagong Hill Tracks are full of thick forests where the land-man ratio has been much lower than the rest of Bangladesh. The tribal refugees took shelter in South Tripura since April 1986 following massacres, armed clash and violence in various parts of the CHT. At one time during 1989-90 the number of refugees had gone up to 72,000. The Bangladeshi tribal refugees sheltered in six South Tripura camps for the last 12 years. The Ziaur Rahman Government, in fact, followed a well-calculated policy of encouraging the plains people to settle in the tribal land. The Khaleda Zia's regime obviously could not discontinued such a policy despite assurances given to the Indian Government. The repatriation of refugees first began in February 1994. Since then 11,900 refugees have gone back to their homes in three phases. The last batch left for Chittagong in April 1997.

The smooth repatriation of Chakma refugees in their homeland in the Chittagong Hill Tracks (CHT) is a welcome sign of fast improving relations between Dacca and New Delhi. In March 1997 Bangladesh and Chakma refugee leaders signed an agreement for the repatriation of refugees, sheltered in six camps in Tripura for the last 11 years.[85] On 7 August 1997, a six-member high powered Bangladesh delegation led by ruling Awami League tribal MP Kalpa Ranjan Chakma arrived Agartala to persuade 44,000 tribal refugees, mostly Buddhists, to return home. The delegation held a series of meetings with the refugee leaders for the three days but the refugee leaders were unwilling to return home until their five point demands were met. After a marathon seven-hour-long meeting with refugee leader and former Bangladesh Parliament member Upendra Lal Chakma, who led a nine-member refugee delegation in the meetings with Bangladesh Government delegation, said that the Bangladesh Government had failed to implement the provisions of the 20-point economic package and bipartite agreement signed between the Bangladesh Government and the refugee leaders.

With a view to finalise the modalities for the fourth phase of repatriation a five-member high level Bangladesh official team arrived at Agartala on 13 November 1997. Sheikh Hasina Wajed, the Prime Minister of Bangladesh, assured the refugee leaders that her government would implement the 20-point economic package and provisions of the agreement.[86] The present delegation would hold meetings with the task force headed by the tribal MP Kalpa Ranjan Chakma and the 20-point implementation Committee headed by Nutan Mohan Chakma. These meetings would scrutinise the implementation of the 20-point economic package and rehabilitation of the refugees. Still the Chakma refugees were not sure of their safety and security that they want to be ensured. The refugee leaders, in general, felt that if the Indian Government wanted the refugees and tribals to live in CHT of south east Bangladesh with dignity, the problems of tribal masses could be solved easily. New Delhi should apply its influence on Dhaka for the betterment of the CHT people. However, the Bangladesh Government has assured refugee leaders that it is committed to provide economic package to the tribal and has urged the Indian Government to send all the Chakma tribals in one go to settle this problem permanently and without any delay. But the Chakma leaders want to return in batches and have decided to send another group of refugees to Bangladesh.[87] The resumption of the repatriation process after a gap of seven months is indeed heartening. This will create a favourable atmosphere for the scheduled meeting between the Bangladesh Government and Shanti Bahini leaders on 26 November 1997. The two sides are expected to sign an agreement to end tribal insurgency. Such an agreement would have a sobering effect on Tripura's militant groups.[88]

In a significant development, the Awami League Government signed a peace pact with Shanti Bahini, an armed wing of the Parbatya Chattagram Jana Samhati Samity (PCJSS). The two sides have arrived at a formula to end the insurgency which has claimed about 25,000 lives. According to the provisions of the pact the Shanti Bahini guerillas surrendered before the Bangladesh Government on 9 February, 1998 at Khagra Chari Stadium and it would be completed in three phases, the last phase would be on 28 February 1998. Although the accord has been criticised by the Bangla National Party, Begum Khaleda Zia had charged that the deal would help New Delhi gain control over the territory of greater Chittagong up to Feni (Begam Zia's) constituency. But a senior official maintained that despite objections by the Bangladesh opposition parties to the signing of the peace accord with the tribal leaders, the refugees began returning home after the Bangladesh Government's assurance about security of their life and property and satisfactory implementation of the economic package.[89] As far as India is concerned, the Chittagong Peace Pact will have a solutory impact on insurgency movements in the North-East, much will, of course, depend on Dhaka's attitude. New Delhi will have reason to be happy about the deal for it removes a major irritant in Indo-Bangla relations.

Economic Issues

Under the new dispensation the Indo-Bangla economic relations improved considerably. In the field of transport the two countries agreed to sign a "Motor Vehicle Agreement" which would introduce the operation of a direct Bus service between Calcutta and Dhaka. The agreement, coming as it will close on the heels of inauguration of the road transit between Nepal and Bangladesh through 51 k m. of Indian territory, is in the spirit of the Gujral doctrine of good neighbourhood. The negotiators of both the countries are also making fast progress towards the conclusion of a water-sharing agreement of the Tistha river and likely to be finalised soon.[90] The two sides took stock of the progress of the bilateral relations when the Prime Minister of Bangladesh Sheikh Hasina came India to attend the funeral of Mother Teresa at Calcutta. Dhaka's trade with Kathmandu also received a boost when India allowed a route through its territory.

As a major breakthrough in India's economic relations with Bangladesh and Pakistan, the Prime Ministers of these countries met at Dhaka in January 1998 to discuss the ways of improving economic ties among them. At a banquet speech hosted by Sheikh Hasina, the Prime Minister of Bangladesh, Gujral underlined the significance of the coming together of the three Prime Ministers in Dhaka in subregional context and observed that going by the enthusiasm and expectations among the business delegations such occasions would multiply in the coming years. He also lauded Sheikh Hasina for her leadership and understanding of the Indo-Bangladesh issues and said that both the countries would have to implement the agreements in good faith and this required wisdom and political will.[91] In response, the Prime Minister of Bangladesh paid personal tribute to Gujral's role in reducing tensions in South Asia in her speech at the banquet. She said that his initiatives have brought out a qualitative change into the politics of South Asia and it has also given the politics of this region a moral fabric that will contribute to sustain peace and stability for the country's economic development.

Inder Kumar Gujral, in his address to the first trilateral business summit was in the form of elaboration of a new vision of South Asian economy in the new century but even then he did not forget to mention that the private sector industrialists of the three countries must take the lead in evolving concrete proposals for mutually beneficial business co-operation, looking beyond a free trade area towards a South Asian Economic Community with the free movement of capital goods and service within the region. Sheikh Hasina, the Prime Minister of Bangladesh, went a step further and suggested some machinery for interaction between private and public sectors of the three countries since specific issues pertaining to private sector initiatives in certain areas could be discussed that will provide further inputs for negotiations at the inter-governmental level.[92] In the summit Indian business delegation led by FICC President K. K. Modi did extremely good work at the summit by making a solid presentation of the fruits of co-operation among the three countries in the energy sector.

The Indian Prime Minister, as a special gesture expressed his readiness to lift quantitative restrictions on agreed items of interest for Bangladesh and other least developed SAARC countries. He announced that the Indian negotiator would also have the requisite mandate to reduce tariffs insignificantly with deeper cuts for Bangladesh and the least developed SAARC countries as part of the latest round of trade preference talks. Gujral laid special emphasis on investment possibilities in the region and declared that the Indian Government had decided to double the ceiling for overseas Indian investment under the fast track in this region.[93] However, apart from all these, the tension between India and Pakistan had its echo in the trilateral business summit, when the leader of the Pakistani business delegation dubbed Inder Kumar Gujral as the caretaker Prime Minister and tried to minimize the importance of his announcements at the summit. The trilateral business summit has achieved at least one objective. All the three Prime Ministers have agreed on increasing the role of the private sector in fostering regional economic co-operation in the coming years.

Defence

The security of Bangladesh and India is inter-linked as close neighbours in the region. The two countries had military co-operation from the earlier but during the visit of General Shankar Roy Chowdhury, the Indian Chief of Army Staff, both expressed the desire to have a developed relationship in this regard.[94] He said that the existing level of co-operation covers the training of officers of one country in another country's military academy. The General in an interview, ruled out a drastic cut in defence budget unless there is a radical change in the security system. In a significant development, at a five-day meeting of Border Security Force and Bangladesh Rifles held at Dhaka 14-18 October 1997, the two sides agreed to maintain status quo in the disputed border areas till the final decision on the issue. The disputed areas are identified along the 856 km. long Indo-Bangla border with Tripura. These are Muhuri Char, Khowai, Feni and Juleya in south and west Tripura district.

REGIME OF NATIONAL DEMOCRATIC ALLIANCE

Premiership of Atal Bihari Vajpayee (19 March 1998-12 October 1999)

With the help of pre and post election alliances of political parties Bharatiya Janata Party succeeded in forming the government at the centre and Atal Bihari Vajpayee became the Prime Minister of India who took oath of the office on 19 March 1998. The new regime inherited a tension-free Indo-Bangladesh relation except minor differences on some bilateral issues. Vajpayee's assumption of office was welcomed in Bangladesh. Extending the heartiest felicitations and warmest greetings Sheikh Hasina, the Prime Minister of Bangladesh, hoped that he will no doubt bring to the august office a new vision that will see his great country reach a new and higher level of overall development. She expected that "we have no doubt that as neighbours, we too will immensely benefit from your acumen and your leadership in our common cause to further strengthen and consolidate our bilateral relations." Referring to her 21-months regime she said, "We are now on a steady course of development of our bilateral relations to the mutual benefit of our peoples." The new Prime Minister, in his first foreign policy pronouncement maintained that his regime will "strain every nerve" to accelerate the process of building better ties with neighbours. He laid special emphasis on the importance of bilateral diplomacy.

Sheikh Hasina, the Prime Minister of Bangladesh, paid a goodwill visit to New Delhi in June 1998. On the eve of the visit it was made clear that it would be to foster the bilateral ties between the two countries and ruled out Dhaka's mediation to defuse Indo-Pak tension over the nuclear tests, "we are not going to mediate. We want India and Pakistan to talk to each other and settle their differences. We have not ambition or intention to play any role in Indo-Pakistan bilateral dialogue.[95] At New Delhi, the two Prime Ministers held wide-ranging talks on matters of bilateral and mutual interest to further promote better and warmer ties between the two neighbours. This was followed by delegation level parleys on issues covering trade, investment, tariff concessions and co-operation in various fields. Sheikh Hasina had also a meeting with former Prime Minister Inder Kumar Gujral and is understood to have discussed issues relating to Indo-Bangladesh relations.[96]

The visit had an added importance because it was the first tour by a foreign dignitary after India exploded its nuclear device on May 11 and 13. The Prime Minister of Bangladesh, in course of her talks with the Indian counterpart appreciated India's security concerns and the rationale behind the nuclear tests. It was significant for the fact that she is representing a Muslim majority neighbour and is fighting a bitter battle in her own land against the fundamentalist forces who are essentially anti-India. New Delhi has also reasons to be happy because, despite the tremendous political pressure after the Pokhran blasts came out against India on the nuclear issue, she restrained herself and accepted the sovereign right of India to take appropriate measures based on its own security perceptions. Sheikh Hasina had excellent rapport with Prime Ministers H. D. Deve Gowda and I. K. Gujral and if this first meeting after the coming of the B.J.P. Government could establish a personal equation between the two, it should be a welcome development.

To facilitate greater trade with India, Bangladesh's Prime Minister, on 23 June 1998, inaugurated Bangabandhu Bridge, South Asia's longest bridge built at an estimated cost of $ 1 billion over river yamuna in Bangladesh. India supplied the largest quantum of boulders needed for river-training before construction of the bridge work for which had started in October 1994. Officials are hopeful that the bridge would make transportation of goods to and from northern Bangladesh, which has a number of official trade outlets with India, faster and less cumbersome compared to movement of riverine transport. Emphasising the importance of the bridge. M. Thambidurai, Minister for Law, Justice and Surface Transport, Government of India, told reporters that it would facilitate transport of goods to India's north east when Dhaka allows New Delhi transit facilities through its territories.[97]

Sheikh Hasina, within a week of her visit to New Delhi went to Islamabad, accompanied by Abdul Samad Azad, the Foreign Minister of Bangladesh. Her visit took place despite Vajpayee's reiteration to a Dhaka-based weekly *Economic Times* that "Even now having become a nuclear weapon state, there is no dilution in India's commitment to the goal of nuclear free world. We are ready to engage in meaningful negotiations on the progressive and total denuclearisation. The Indian Prime Minister made it clear that India's nuclear tests were a reaction to the deteriorating security environment and asserted, "We are not a threat to any nation and do not wish to target any nation". Even before the visit, as stated by a senior official in Dhaka, regional and bilateral issues were likely to dominate the meeting between Sheikh Hasina and Nawaz Sharif, her Pakistani counterpart.[98]

As the visit took place in the background of tense Indo-Pakistan relations, analysis of Dhaka's motives and designs were natural. Two reasons were being cited by the cynics to explain her visit to New Delhi and Islamabad. One is to save the Clinton visit to Dhaka, now that India and Pakistan legs have become uncertain in the wake of the nuclear tests. The other is to impress upon the US and others that by imposing economic sanctions smaller nations of South Asia are being victimised by them. It is also vehemently denied by the officials that Sheikh Hasina is motivated by any pressure that Bangladesh must act, being a signatory to the NPT and the CTBT. The visiting Prime Minister had, herself emphasised that Bangladesh did not wish to "take advantage of the difficulties that may confront India and Pakistan in the wake of the sanctions. As indicated by an official "We want to prove our worth as a genuine friend with genuine concern about an arms race in the subcontinent. India and Pakistan can not be left to themselves as there will be no talk in the current mood. We want to show that when others are imposing sanctions and saying angry words, as a responsible SAARC member we are ready to stand by and be of some help, and not treat anyone as pariah."[99]

The two Prime Ministers discussed bilateral issues including trade and the long standing issue regarding repatriation of nearly 2.5 lakh Bihari Muslims stranded in Bangladesh since 1971. Bangladesh want Pakistan to accept those Biharis who are living in refugee camps for more than 25 years. As they associate themselves with Pakistan, Islamabad, has, in principle, agreed for their repatriation. At the end of Sheikh Hasina's visit to New Delhi and Islamabad, Bangladesh issued a statement which stated that her approach at both was even-handed. She listened to Sharif, just as she listened to Vajpayee. At both places she expressed concerns but stopped short of reiterating her strong opposition to any weaponisation on the nuclear front, as would only be expected of a CTBT signatory. She made it a point to explain, however, why Bangladesh had signed NPT and CTBT to countries who have refused to do so. She reiterated the principle of bilateralism of Indo-Pak issues. While Sharif talked of Kasmir as the "core issue" she shared with him, "thoughts on peace and security in South Asia and the urgency of finding a solution to the Kashmir problem.

Further, in January 1999 the Calcutta book fair was inaugurated by the famous poet from Bangladesh, Samsur Rahman. Sheikh Hasina, the Prime Minister of Bangladesh, attended the fair on the inaugural day and took the opportunity to discuss the issues of mutual concern, particularly co-operation in the energy and transit and transport sectors with Jaswant Singh, India's Minister for External Affairs. Describing the meeting as "very good", the External Affairs Minister said that Sheikh Hasina wanted discussion between the two sides to be followed up by prompt actions. The two had also discussed the Dhaka-Calcutta and Dhaka-Tripura bus services. Jyoti Basu, the Chief Minister of West Bengal, in his inaugural address said that India cherished the desire of having friendly relations with all the neighbouring countries, including Pakistan.[100]

Another landmark in the development of mutually beneficial relations was the signing the agreement on 18 February 1990, to begin a thrice-weekly bus service between Calcutta and Dhaka. It would be valid for two years initially and subject to renewal. It was decided to run three buses from either side every alternate day.

Regional Co-operation

The two-day meeting of first-ever SAARC Information Ministers' was held in Dhaka and inaugurated by Sheikh Hasina who in her address, stressed continued expansion of close co-operation through unfettered flow of information aiming at overall development of the SAARC region.

She said the seven SAARC countries could have their further development through exchanging information on agriculture, health, education, industry, commerce, tourism and culture. Hasina referred to the cardinal principle of SAARC that aimed to promote harmonious relationship and co-operation among the member countries. The region, she said, abounds with enormous resources with which we can overcome our resource constraints if we can make planned utilisation of resources for the welfare of the people on the basis of co-operation. However, Mushahid Hussain, Pakistan's Information and Media Development Minister, during a closed door session, referred to Kashmir as a flash point in the region because of the unresolved dispute between his country and India. He also called for an early settlement of the dispute to boost regional co-operation. Sushma Swaraj, India's Minister for Information and Broadcasting, reacted sharply to the remarks made by Pakistani minister and demanded its deletion. Despite protests from Pakistani delegates, Bangladesh Information Minister Abu Sayeed who was presiding over the session said anything contrary to the regional spirit would be automatically deleted from the meeting proceedings.

The Indian Minister, in her address, stressed the need for creating an information order that can facilitate better understanding and strengthen the bonds of friendship among the member countries of the SAARC. "The better way to achieve this is pooling our resources and acting the concert" she added. She also had an opportunity to speak at the working session of the SAARC Ministers in which special emphasis was given on the need to evolve mechanism for information sharing. At the end of their two day meeting the SAARC plan of action on media and information with the avowed objective of promoting peace, progress and co-operation in the region was adopted. Known as the Dhaka communiqué, the plan of action outlined the goals and objectives under a comprehensive strategy for co-operation stressed greater flow of information in the SAARC region on all issues of common concern. The Ministers agreed that an appropriate mechanism should be set up to oversee the implementation of the SAARC plan of action on media and information. Apart from the objectives, the communique further said that member countries will work to generate, disseminate and exchange information materials on all SAARC initiatives in important areas with development, functional co-operation, environmental protection and human resource development.

The relations between the two countries strengthened further when Foreign Secretaries of India and Bangladesh met in Dhaka in June 1998 and stressed the need for closer co-operation in all fields of economic activity by taking necessary steps for the mutual benefit of the two. Mustafizur Rahman, the Foreign Secretary of Bangladesh said that the talks were a steps forward in strengthening our bilateral ties. Replying to a question the secretary said that we had no issue of conflict but we have issues of mutual interests being looked into our relation with the present Indian Government is as good as it was before. The Indian Foreign Secretary K. Raghunath too claimed that the talks were useful, productive and fruitful with two sides exchanging views candidly on all issues concerning them. On nuclear issue he said that the Indian stand is well-known. India wants a universal, comprehensive, non-discriminatory nuclear disarmament.[101] He added that the Bangladesh shares Indian perception for a nuclear-free world. People want everything solved in a quicker pace so that people of both the countries get benefited.

India and Bangladesh took in November 1998, steps to improve the ties between the two countries. In a spirit of cordiality, B. P. Singh, India's Home Secretary and his Bangladeshi counterpart Safiur Rahman signed the agreed minutes that would help the two countries take positive steps on the plaguing issues like insurgency, cross-border smuggling, terrorism, illegal, migrants and trafficking in women and children. Both the countries expressed their firm commitment to stamping out the problems of terrorism and insurgency through mutual co-operation. They expressed thier confidence that, as very close neighbours having very friendly relations, would co-operate with each other to solve the problems bilaterally through dialogue. Home Secretaries of the two countries expressed happiness after signing the minutes and termed it "very very positive and constructive dialogue to resolve the issues." Further two-day SAARC Commerce Ministers' meeting was preceded by the 10th meeting of the commerce secretary-level committee on economic co-operation under SAARC and was organised by Bangladesh. The meeting was inaugurated by Tofail Ahmed, Industry and Commerce Minister of the country, who, in his address, said that the South Asian regional economic integration should be faster for creating new opportunities for regional development. The Commerce Secretaries in their deliberations, would review the progress of the implementation of the decisions taken at the previous meeting and the decision of the second SAARC Commerce Ministers' meeting held in Islamabad last year. They also reviewed the progress of the implementation of the SAARC Preferential Trading Arrangement (SAPTA). P. P. Prabhu, India's Commerce Secretary attended the meeting and said in his address that greater economic co-operation in the region would help bring about a success of the SAPTA since all the countries of South Asia were in favour of a close economic integration among themselves.[102] In a significant decision, India and Bangladesh agreed to enforce the 1991 agreement which stipulated that any person declared to be Bangladeshi national by the court, illegally staying in India would be sent back.

Commerce Secretary level committee's meeting was followed by the two-day SAARC Commerce Minister's meeting aimed at augmenting intra-regional trade and investment through exploration of new areas of co-operation. Inaugurating the meeting Sheikh Hasina, the Prime Minister of Bangladesh emphasised harmonious and coordinated approach to develop economies of SAARC countries in a spirit of co-operation. She referred to the immense possibilities of investment covering the fields of hydro-power, communication, infrastructure, sea port gas and energy. On the issue of trade and investment, Hasina stressed the need for intra-SAARC investment flow to the benefit of the countries of the region. She laid emphasis on the South Asia Quadrangle created within the SAARC framework to harness the untapped resources of Bangladesh, Nepal, Bhutan and the North-Eastern part of India for mutually beneficial purposes. Due to preoccupation at home, India's Commerce Minister could not attend the meeting and was represented by the Commerce Secretary, P. P. Prabhu. Thus, the co-operation between India and Bangladesh seemed to touch a new height under the new dispensation.

Defence

Early the year 1998 the US activities in Bangladesh increased disproportionately. It sent a draft proposal for Status of Forces Agreement (SOFA) with the United States to pave the way for increased military co-operation between the two countries. The proposed SOFA envisaged a special status to the entry of US armed forces in Bangladesh in connection with the non-combatant joint exercise, relief operation and imparting training on UN peace keeping. If signed as per US proposal, would enable US troops and their equipment enter and go out of the country without immigration and custom formalities. The proposal was followed by visit of Bell Richardson, US Ambassador to the United Nations, to Bangladesh in April 1998, who, in course of the tour said that US wanted to build stronger ties with the South Asian region. In reply to a question he disclosed that US is interested in energy and power sectors and hoped that Bangladesh would actively consider US firms. He even did not miss the moment to praise Bangladesh when met with Sheikh Hasina and said, "Bangladesh can be cited as a model for the Third World Muslim countries where Islam and democracy are going side by side. As a step further, in July 1998 Bangladesh and United States signed a memorandum of understanding to implement US peace corps programme in the country. US Ambassador John C. Holzman signed the MoU on behalf of his Government. The first batch of 25 peace corps volunteers who would come to Dhaka, would be engaged particularly in the fields of education, rural development, housing, health, agriculture, environment and in other areas to be mutually agreed upon by two sides.

The added fear to country's defence was due to expanded activities of Pakistan's ISI who had been bold enough in the pursuit of its anti-India agenda and it had opened an office-cum-transit centre in a well-known locality in Dhaka. The ISI centre in Dhaka had plans to despatch more mercenaries to Kashmir. In fact the Pakistani trained militants and mercenaries had been under pressure in the valley for sometime and now they could use the Dhaka route for the purpose. In February 1999 a Bangladesh youth, named Sayed Abu Nasir had been arrested in this connection with a plot to blow up the American consulates in Calcutta and Chennai and had confirmed to US Federal Bureau of Investigation (FBI) agents that he was on ISI's pay-rolls. India's Home Secretary B. P. Singh raised the issue in his meeting with US Attorney General Janet Reno and requested him to speed up the ratification of the Indo-US extradition treaty. Even for the Bangladesh government there are obvious limitations. Earlier attempts by the Sheikh Hasina government to close the ISI backed centres providing sanctuary to the north eastern rebels had not gone very far because of the indifferent attitude at the lower levels of the administration. It would be more difficult in future in view of the fact that Sheikh Hasina's government had come under more pressure following the formation of a joint front by the three main opposition parties along with the fundamentalist Jamait-e-Islam, that might curtail her ability to take decisive action in the matter. In the circumstances, New Delhi would need to think out its own strategies to foil attempts at trans-border terrorism.

Second Term of Atal Bihari Vajpayee (13 October 1999-22 May 2004)

Like earlier the poor performance of the Congress Party in the general election of 1999 created the conditions for the formation of a BJP-led coalition government at the centre. Having continued as a caretaker Prime Minister from 17 April 1999 to 12 October 1999, in a hattrick Atal Bihari Vajpayee, the moderate face of the BJP became the new Prime Minister of India and took the oath of office on 13 October 1999. In the Lok Sabha, out of 537 seats for which elections were held, 182 were won by the BJP and 112 by the Congress. More than 250 seats were bagged by a variety of regional parties. On the side of the ruling coalition were parties like the Telegu Desam of Andhra Pradesh; the Dravida Munnetra Kazhagam of Tamil Nadu; the Samata party of Bihar; Trinamool Congress of West Bengal and many others. Earlier BJP had agreed to place the Ayodhya issue as well as its demands for a uniform civil code and the scrapping of Article 370 for Jammu and Kashmir.[103] In the election campaign the regional parties emphasised on local issues and sought more autonomy for the states and a legitimate share of power at a more federal and less unitary centre. Similarly, Vajpayee during his campaigns went to the extent of saying that in a country as diverse as India it would be patently undemocratic to have a single party government.[104] He added further that even if the BJP won a majority on its own, he would form a coalition.

In Bangladesh there is an intense and at times violent political rivalry between the country's two main political parties – the Bangladesh National Party (BNP) and the Awami League (AL), and the presence of radical Islamist parties and groups have defined the further political course of the country in recent years. The BNP and the AL are headed by Khaleda Zia, the widow of former President and military strongman Ziaur Rahman, who was assassinated in 1981, while the AL by Sheikh Hasina who is the daughter of Bangladeshi independence leader and first Prime Minister Sheikh Mujibur Rahman, killed in 1975. As a general feature both when out of power, have devoted their energies to Parliamentary boycotts, demonstrations, and strikes in an effort to unseat the ruling party. Bangladesh witnessed last parliamentary elections in June 1996 and the chosen government continued till 2001. In this election the victory was won by Awami League under the captainship of Sheikh Hasina who although got 147 seats, with the cooperation of the Jatiyo Party (31 seats) and the Jama'at-e-Islami (3 seats) formed the government. The main opposition party led by Khaleda Zia also won a respectable 116 seats despite serious charges of corruption, her BNP party protested vote rigging by the AL and as a result the tenure of Sheikh Hasina was marked by frequent boycott of Parliament by the BNP, demonstrations and strikes. Gradually the political condition of Bangladesh deteriorated and in early 1999 a four party opposition alliance was formed to boycott the Parliamentary by–elections and local government elections. In July 2001 the Awami League Government stepped down to allow a caretaker government to preside over parliamentary elections scheduled in October. Earlier the constitution was duly amended to provide for such an arrangement. Elections in Bangladesh are to be held every five years but as per the provision the President has been assigned to appoint an interim government in the immediate lead-up to polls in order to prevent the incumbent government from using the power of office to unfair political advantage.[105]

There is a 300-seat unicameral national Parliament in Bangladesh known as Jatiya Sangsad. The general election as scheduled held on October 1, 2001, and in the results, the Bangladesh National Party led by Khaleda Zia emerged as the single largest party getting 193 of its own. It, alongwith alliance partners which included the Jamaat-e-Islami (JI), the Islamiya Okiya Jote (IOJ) and the Jatiya Party (JP) Manzur Faction, won 41% of votes. The Awami League of Sheikh Hasina won 58 and the number of seats gained by other parties were as follows : JI:17, JP (Ershad Faction):

14, IOJ:2, JP (Manzur Faction):4, and others:12.[106] Khaleda Zia took the oath of office as the 11th Prime Minister of Bangladesh on October 10, 2001. Although observers declared the poll generally free and fair, the Awami League of Sheikh Hasina refused to accept the result of the 2001 election and called for a programme of national resistance against the government and immediately announced a boycott of the eighth Parliament. It claimed that the elections were rigged but after boycotting the first two sessions of the Parliament the Awami League announced that it was forming a shadow cabinet and ended its boycott of Parliament on June 24, 2002, entering the parliamentary debate on the national budget. However, since then the Awami League had regularly boycotted most Parliamentary sessions or walked out of sessions in protest.[107] Later the ruling Bangladesh National Party had published a white paper on the misuse of power, mismanagement and corruption allegedly committed during the period of Awami League rule. The AL had expressed concern over the inclusion of Jamaat-e-Islami Party which wanted to make Bangladesh an Islamic republic.[108]

The crisis in governance is not unique to Bangladesh. In its case it is the result of the circumstances in which the new nation was born. In Pre-independence days the undivided Pakistan's inability to come to terms with the electoral verdict exposed the flaws in the political system. Mujib's own authoritarian tendencies led to unrest and dissatisfaction with the masses, military rule and the elections that lacked legitimacy further exposed the weakness of constitutional government. In recent years the rivalry and competitive politics of the two major parties under Sheikh Hasina and Khaleda Zia resulted in frequent hartals and strikes, disturbing civic life. Low literacy and state controlled media forces the opposition parties to take the issues to streets to mobilise masses to win their support to their programmes. As Patricia Butenis, the former US Ambassador stated that Bangladeshis 'have suffered because the political parties could not agree on the basic rules of game ... the hard part is actually creating political parties that are genuinely democratic in practice and outlook, parties that focus on issues and the national interest instead of personalities.[109] The situation has given small Islamist Parties, some of which have ties to violent Islamist radicals, a disproportionate voice in Bangladesh's government and politics. Islamists support the imposition of Sharia law in Bangladesh where Islam has served as a legitimizing political force in Bangladesh which is 88% Muslim. Bangladesh's status as a secular and moderate state, as well as its democratic process,, has been jeopardized as a result of the approach taken by the two main political parties. It is also a question that should Bangladesh become a failed state or a state with increased influence by Islamist extremists, it could increasingly serve as a base of operations for terrorist activity.

India's links with Bangladesh, like with her other South Asian neighbours, are civilizational, cultural, social and economic. There is much that unites the two countries – a shared history and common heritage, linguistic and cultural ties, passion for music, literature and the arts; with Bangladesh, India shares not only a common history of struggle for freedom and liberation but also enduring feelings of both fraternal as well as familial ties. This commonality is reflected in multi-dimensional relations with Bangladesh at several levels of interaction. High-level exchanges, visits and meetings take place regularly alongside the wide-ranging people-to-people interaction. India's missions in Bangladesh issue about half a million visas every year and thousands of Bangladeshi students study in India on self financing system and over 100 annual Government of India scholarships. The exchanges and interactions undertaken during the premiership of Atal Bihari Vajpayee after his taking over in October 1999 serve as an important adjunct to the official-level interaction.

The theoretical proposition that first appeared in the government of Morarji Desai in 1977, was later developed and encapsulated in the Gujral doctrine. It has been interpreted variously and at one extreme, generosity confined to rhetoric, through unilateral accommodation, where possible, in neighbours interests without demanding reciprocity to, at the other extreme, giving away more than is reasonable. It sent a message to the neighbours that in every issue India should given more than it gets in order to demonstrate that it is, indeed, not a bully out to dominate the region. However, despite India's willingness to cooperate with Bangladesh, the latter had failed to be responsive with New Delhi's sensitivities. Ever since the BNP government came to power in 2001, Indian commentators, especially those from West Bengal, have shackled that government with radical Islam, anti-Indian sentiments and actions, anti-secularism, anti-democracy, and pro-China policies. These shackles have become stronger with the years, regardless of the facts. Not only Indian but analysts all over the world have perceived this change and a Hong- Kong based weekly noted that a revolution is taking place in Bangladesh that threatens trouble for the region and beyond if left unchallenged. Islamic fundamentalism, religious intolerance, militant Muslim groups with links to international terrorist groups ... are combining to transform the nation. Another comment appears more suitable; fundamentalism seems to have won the first round in Bangladesh. This development in the society and politics of Bangladesh has over shadowed the relations, political in particular, between the two friendly neighbours. For centuries enjoy so much intimacy and widespread mutual goodwill as India and Bangladesh do; yet New Delhi and Dhaka are finding it impossible to sustain a serious political dialogue to solve bilateral problems.

Relations with New Delhi and Dhaka have been strained as Indian officials have accused Bangladesh of harbouring both agents of Pakistan's intelligence service and separatist militants fighting the New Delhi government in India's north-eastern states, such as the All Tripura Tiger Force.[110] Dhaka has denied the accusations as totally baseless and irresponsible. Acrimony over migration issues led to periodic and lethal exchanges of gunfire between the border security forces of India and Bangladesh.[111] Even at the end of Vajpayee's regime there are several political issues which yet to be resolved satisfactorily : Ulfa camps inside Bangladesh's border; illegal migration of millions of Bangladeshis to India; India's decision to fence the border and the host of associated issues it has raised has bedevilled India's relations with Bangladesh.[112] However, the gradual changing in Bangladesh's society was largely responsible for the rise in terrorist incidents, which New Delhi, on its part, has made a precondition for improving its relations with Dhaka.

Changed Social Setup and Terrorism

Bangladesh is the largest Muslim country in the world with over 85% of its population being the followers of Islam. It is a multi-religious society constituting about 12% Hindus, 1.2 Buddhists and .01 Christians. Muslims are dominant in all parts of the country, excepting Chittagong Hill Tracks where Buddhists are pre-dominant. In general Hindus are present in all regions, though they constitute a majority in some parts of

Khulna division. Religiously, Sufism is essentially a popular movement in Bangladesh with its three orders– The Qadiri, Naqshbandi and Chishti. The beliefs and practices of the first two are quite close to those of orthodox Islam, the third founded in Ajmer, India, is peculiar to the subcontinent and has a number of orthodox practices. In spite of being a Muslim country it emphasised secularism in the Constitution of 1972 but after the assassination of Sheikh Mujibur Rahman in 1975 the new rulers turned towards Islamisation of the nation and in order to establish its Islamic credentials, inserted an invocation on the top of the Constitution adding new articles and clauses. In 1988, General Ershad inserted an article in the constitution which declared that 'the state religion of the Republic is Islam, but other religions may be practised in peace and harmony in the Republic. As a result a number of religious parties have emerged which press the government to implement Islamic principles in governance. The political scenario in Bangladesh indicates that religious fanaticism is on rise and the development has affected socio-economic life of the country.[113]

Other countries alike the foreign policy and relations of Bangladesh is very largely shaped by domestic political change and the changes that are taking place in the country are steadily eroding even the fragile equilibrium of the present day society. In over three decades, millions of its workers have returned from West Asia infected by the austere Sunni and Wahhabi Islam they found practised there. About three million Bangladeshis work there and a large proportion come back changed almost beyond recognition : They go as ordinary men but come back completely different. They wear different clothes, cut their beards differently, put their women in burqas and profess an intolerant Wahhaby type of Islam that is completely alien to other countrymen.[114] The percolation of this imported Islam into Bangladeshi society has turned the Jamaat-i-Islami into a potent political force. An allied cause of this is the failure of the State education system. This has sent more and more children to Madrasas, which are founded by private donations, and by liberal inflows of funds from religious trusts in Saudi Arabia and other West- Asian countries.[115] These changes have led to the emergence of an intolerant, aggressive, messianic fringe of reformed Sunni Muslims, who are bent upon purifying Bangladesh on the lines of the Taliban in Afghanistan.

Frank Pallone, the Democratic Congressman from New Jersey in May 2004 also drew attention of the US House of Representatives to the plight of the Hindus whom he called a disappearing minority' and it was confirmed by electronic media and the US State Department as well.

Religious fundamentalism and effects of the outside Muslim world gave birth to several terrorist and militant extremist groups in Bangladesh that include Harkat ul Jihad Al Islami (HuJI), Jagrata Muslim Janata Bangladesh (JMJB), and Jamaatul Mujahideen Bangladesh (JMB). In this context it is the general view of analysts and media observers that the presence of two Islamist parties, the Islamiya Okiyya Jote (IOJ) and the Jamaat-e-Islami as a coalition partner in the former ruling Bangladesh National Party (BNP) had expanded Islamist influence in the country and created space within which terrorist and extremist groups could operate. Islami Okiyya Jote is thought to have ties to the radical Harkat-ul-Jihad-al-Islami (HuJI).[116] Another coalition partner the Jamaat-e-Islami has also ties to Harkat-ul-Jihad-i-Islami which has ties to Al Qaeda and the former's leader Fazlul Rahman signed an Osama Bin Laden holy war declaration in 1998.[117] The JMB seeks the imposition of Sharia law for Bangladesh and is thought responsible for the widespread and coordinated August 2005 bombings, while HuJI has been implicated in the January 2002 attack on the American Center in Calcutta, India. HuJI is on the US State Department's list of 'other terrorist organizations' and has links to Pakistani militant groups with a cadre strength of several thousand of its own. The JMJB is an unabashedly terrorist organization in Bangladesh which claims more than 10,000 full-time cadres and 300,000 part-timers and helpers in the country and has been killing cadres of extremist groups like the Purbo Banglar Communist party, whom the police has not been able to control. By doing these the organization is gaining a spurious legitimacy with not only the key members of the BNP but also the police. It has openly modelled itself on the Taliban and claims that its aim is to build a society based on the Islamic model laid out in the Holy 'Quran-Hadith'.[118]

In the meantime these terrorist and extremist groups of Bangladesh have got not only social but political base in the country and now they are a permanent factor in the politics. For them which party rules the country is a secondary matter and this is true of the Awami League government under Sheikh Hasina as it is of the BNP government of Begam

Khaleda Zia. Bangladesh's creeping estrangement from India is rooted in an attempt by its political leaders and elite to shield their secular heritage from the creeping Islamisation of their society. The fear that these fundamentalists would succeed in enlisting Bangladeshi nationalism to overwhelm its secular polity is the main reason why every government in Dhaka has felt obliged, at least in public, to adopt a less than cooperative attitude to India. For example in 1997, the Awami League government agreed to close down the Ulfa camps in Bangladesh. But after closing down around 50 of them, it found that it could not go any further because of determined resistance from within the Bangladesh army. Since 2001, most of these camps have been reopened.[119] One may easily think in the circumstances that if cooperation with India is depicted as both a surrender of national sovereignty and a betrayal of Islam, then withholding it becomes one way of preventing the fusion of the two ideas. As we are aware an attitude of non-cooperation accounts for the steady accumulation of unresolved issues among the nations of the world.

For the present Bangladesh's political parties and intelligentsia as well are trying to ride the tide. In comparison to Awami League of Sheikh Hasina the reportcard of BNP headed by Begam Khaleda Zia is painful. Under the BNP Bangladesh has recognised the ubiquity of the madrasas and opted to recognise their degrees and to modernise their curricula. Recognising the growing strength of a terrorist organisation and realising that it is concentrated in the western border belt alongside India, the BNP was quick to form an alliance with it. And BNP's alliance played a decisive role in its stunning and unexpected victory in 2001. At the time Awami League leader Sheikh Hasina had accused the government of 'letting loose communal extremist forces'. It is also reported that some international extremists are using Bangladeshi passports and that some are obtaining them with the assistance of sympathetic officials at various Bangladesh Embassies.[120] However, the BNP government of Bangladesh had also taken some steps against the terrorist and extremist groups, but the opposition leader Sheikh Hasina stated, 'militants are partners of the government ... the government catches a few militants whenever foreign guests visit Bangladesh'. She charged that the Jamaat has 15,000 guerillas and its own training camps. 'Steps are only the tip of the iceberg'.[121]

The foundation of terrorist and extremist groups in Bangladesh gradually became a concern for the world in larger context. Selig Harrison, a prominent South Asia Analyst expressed his view and noted in August 2006 that 'a growing Islamic fundamentalist movement linked to Al-Qaeda and Pakistani intelligence agencies is steadily converting the strategically located nation of Bangladesh into a new regional hub for terrorist operations that reach into India and Southeast Asia. He quoted that Prime Minister Khaleda Zia's Bangladesh National Party's coalition alliance with the Jamaat-e-Islami party of Bangladesh led to a 'Faustian bargain' that brought Jammat officials into the government. These official, he argued in turn have allowed Taliban-styled squads to operate with increasing impunity, Jammat's entry into the former BNP government also reportedly led to fundamentalist control over large parts of the Bangladesh economy, Islamist Madrassa schools that act as fronts for terrorist activities.[122] The facts and views on the issue failed to convince the US authorities and the State Department continues to consider the government of Bangladesh as working to thwart terrorist activities.

Terror and Security Concerns

Notwithstanding India's attempts to improve and consolidate its bilateral relations with Bangladesh, the latter continues to indulge in hostile acts that compromise India's security and territorial integrity. Despite the assertions by India's Border Security Force (BSF), backed by concrete evidence, Bangladesh is not willing to concede that it is hosting militants having inimical designs on India. Bangladesh does not accept that any military camps are functioning on its territory. But facts remain that some 172 training camps belonging to different insurgent groups have operating in Bangladesh for a long time. The BSF has been submitting lists of such camps at annual border meetings with its counterparts the Bangladesh Rifles (BDR) since the late 1990s. According to the 1996 accord between them, both countries were expected to disallow such bases on their side of the border, however, Bangladesh did not keep its word as is obvious from the experience to the contrary. From the recent past Dhaka deliberately ignores the disruptive activities of Pakistan's Inter Services Intelligence which is out to destabilise India's North-East as part of its long-cherished desire to bleed India through a thousand cuts and eventually dismember the state. Rajnath Singh, President of Bharatiya Janata Party has called on the Indian Government to pressure

Bangladesh to dismantle terrorist training centres in Bangladesh[123] and stated that the country had become a centre of Islamic fundamentalist forces.

In the Indian view there is no doubt that terrorist groups, largely those which target India, do get support in Bangladesh; that a number of terrorist actions from the neighbourhood against Indian states have been planned and carried out by such groups; and that the government has, to say the least, done much less than it could have to control all this. The Government of India, from time to time has been providing list of terrorist and anti Indian activities to its Bangladeshi counterpart. But the attitude of the Bangladeshi has been lack luster and in clear indications that they are not at all interested in handing over them to India. Although the fact can not be denied that, Bangladesh has played a significant role in international peace keeping activities. Several thousand Bangladesh military personnel are deployed overseas in different nations on peace keeping operations.

However, the heart of the matter lies elsewhere. Bangladesh is less than helpful on the issue of terrorism because of the control of the armed forces over such operations. Every government after 1975, including post-1991 governments, has tried to ensure that the armed forces are kept reasonably well funded and equipped. But the justification for well-equipped forces can only be the threat from India. Military exercises in Bangladesh are traditionally conducted against a fictitious 'Wolf land', a thinly disguised name for India. Of late a retired senior military officer described India as Bangladesh's greatest enemy, while another said the claim of Bangladesh to India's northeast was greater than that of India; and there are serving officers who in published articles have recommended support for insurgents fighting in the north east. There was a time when this enemy image attached to India acquired political resonance, helping the armed forces to stay in power; and that was the time a variety of operations against India were put into planning, some of which were initiated. As a party initiated by the armed forces, and which is still manned by a large number of retired officers – the Bangladesh National Party who came in power with coalition partners in 2001 continued this thinking prevailing in the country. In its view as Morshed Khan, the Foreign Minister of Bangladesh, said to a group of journalists in Dhaka on 7th

September 2004 that India's Northeast was Bangladesh locked and that Dhaka could easily end India's trade surplus by banning Indian goods.

The 4096-kilometer long India-Bangladesh is one of the most difficult area to patrol because of the hostile topography, riverside patches, dense forest hills, arable lands and dense human settlements. The porous border has led to numerous trans-border problems, including infiltration into the Indian side mainly Assam and West Bengal, smuggling of arms and drugs contraband goods, illegal movement of persons, and common crimes such as kidnapping for ransom, cattle lifting, extortion etc. It is a known fact that Bangladesh's cooperation in this regard would help in tackling the long festering problem of illegal immigrants from Bangladesh. One section of opinion has also suggested for opening the borders with Bangladesh, as is the case with Nepal and Bhutan. The measure would help in effective monitoring of inter-border movements of citizens and ensure issue of work permits for citizens on both sides of the border. Such a bold step would also pave the way for better political relations due to the positive spin-offs of improved economic ties.

Behind this a basic background works related to India's size and potential. There is no dearth of commentators who have stressed that India's regional supremacy has played a central role in the development of Bangladesh's foreign relations. For each of the smaller South Asian states, India's intentions are of great concern, but particularly to Bangladesh because it is 'almost surrounded by India' and it lacks the military strength and extra-regional alliances to withstand a serious challenge. Geography compounds the impression of size since India seems to surround that country. Tabarak Hussain, a former Bangladesh foreign secretary, writes : 'Bangladesh's neighbourhood is dominated by India's presence. A sense of its pervasiveness seems to prevail. Heavy imbalance in the power equation between the two countries compounds the situation. One set of aspects which runs like a common thread in the practice of international relations in South Asia is the intimacy and intricacy with which domestic and foreign policies interact. There is a long-term sense in which this is true for foreign policy in general. The classic writings on international relations tell us that national power, national ideology, geography, economic strength are among a large number of factors that influence foreign policy decisions. Thus foreign policy is not created from vacuum and grounded on a country's strengths and weaknesses. It is also an extension of domestic policy, through which objectives of domestic policy are to be pursued robustly and achieved ultimately.

With the coming of BNP government headed by Begam Khaleda Zia in 2001 there has been a new foreign policy and political dynamics in Bangladesh. Earlier Dhaka's relations with Pakistan strengthened since the advent of military rule in Bangladesh. This understanding between the two continued to remain positive and has been an incremental phenomenon, responsive to Bangladeshi threat perceptions and interests.[124] As India looms large in Bangladesh's foreign and security policies as a potential threat, Dhaka needs to counter balance the potential threats it perceives with equations with countries like China and Pakistan. Apart from grievances on economic front with India Dhaka also kept political issues in active consideration in her dealings with New Delhi. The closer integration of the Northeast into the rest of India, which the transit facility would promote, is something China does not want. This became particularly clear when in June 1987 Chinese Vice-Premier Qiao Shi said in Dhaka that China had apprehensions about the proposal; President Ershad was in China the following month and assured his Chinese hosts that Bangladesh would not allow India to move military hardware across Bangladesh into the Northeast. Further Bangladesh and China signed a Defence Cooperation Agreement in December 2002.[125] Even today when the relationship between India and China has changed profoundly, development in the last one decade suggests that China's attitude towards the more intensive integration of the Northeast with the rest of India is less than positive.

Bangladesh's intention and need to counter-balance its relations with India was a product of Dhaka's geo-strategic location and the memories of India's support to Bangladesh's freedom struggle. Therefore Dhaka believes in cultivating close relationship with Pakistan to redress to over-arching geographical presence of India. On the other Pakistan is equally interested in creating a subcontinental balance of power vis-à-vis India. It was in this background that Pervez Musharraf visited Bangladesh in course of his journey to Sri Lanka and China in the last week of July 2002. He was the first military head of State and government from Pakistan to visit Bangladesh after its liberation in December 1971.

Although Zulfiquar Ali Bhutto went Bangladesh in July 1974 but he had not expressed any regret and it was with reluctance that he visited the martyrs' memorial at Savar near Dhaka. In contrast the year 2002 visit of Musharraf officially regretted the tragic violence in Bangladesh preceding and during the liberation war.

In course of the visit two agreements were signed between the two countries on cultural and technological cooperation. The cultural agreement by implication means Pakistan acknowledge the separate ethno-cultural identity of Bangladesh. It also emphasised links between Bangladesh and Pakistan as Islamic countries – a measure that would counter the influence of Hindu India. Another agreement signed on technological cooperation was an umbrella under which Pakistan can be of assistance to Bangladesh for defence supplies. There are defence technology capacities in Pakistan which Bangladesh cannot get from other countries unless it is willing to pay very high prices.[126] In a joint security measure Bangladesh and Pakistan expressed the agreements with the US for location of American forces in their respective territories. It was resulted in an unarticulated security arrangement. However, they avoided any overt political or security agreement in apprehension of a critical response from India which at least, Bangladesh did not want for the present. In order to survive and to ensure peaceful co-existence Bangladesh must desist from emulating Pakistan in harbouring anti-India elements.

Economic Relationship

The political relationship between India and Bangladesh may not be very encouraging, but the economic relationship has recently improved in favour of Bangladesh. It was in the year 1991 under the Bangladesh Nationalist Party of Begam Khaleda Zia that it had embarked on an economic programme aimed at promoting budget discipline and export-led growth. As a result significant progress was made in reducing the budget deficit, increasing foreign reserves, and attracting new foreign investment. Despite infrastructural bottlenecks, the market oriented reforms have resulted in substantial increase in the flow of FDI in the 1990s. It increased from $60.27 million in 1990 to $804 million in 1993-94 and to $2,119 million in 1999-2000. Most of the FDI was in the form of joint ventures. A number of multinational companies collaborated with local investors to start joint ventures. Sheikh Hasina's Awami League government (1996-2001) continued to pursue economic reforms, making some headway in improving the investment climate. However, bureaucratic delays and labour union resistance have hindered implementation of many reforms, including major privatisation efforts. But in general the economy of Bangladesh has been described as mostly unfree as a result of high levels of trade protectionism and regulation, and an extensive black market economy.[127] Prime Minister Begam Khaleda Zia who took over the reign of administration in 2001 also called for faster and deeper economic integration for the member states of the South Asian Association for Regional Cooperation.

Bangladesh is one of the poorest and most densely populated countries of the world. The annual per capita income is about $2,300 in purchasing power parity. The agricultural sector employs approximately 63% of the workforce and accounts for 19.9% of GDP while industry employs 11% and contributes 20.6% of GDP.[128] Services account for 26% of the labour force and 59.5% of GDP. The major crop is rice, in which Bangladesh is nearly self-sufficient. Industry is centered mainly on cotton textiles, jute manufacturing and food processing. Readymade garments and knitwear are important exports for Bangladesh. Foreign exchange earnings from remittances by Bangladeshis working abroad is another key source of wealth for Bangladesh.[129]

Bangladesh's trade and its imbalances with India, from the start remained at the top of Dhaka's agenda. India is an important trading partner of Bangladesh and bilateral merchandise trade between the two has been growing steadily in recent years. There has been a massive increase in the exports of Bangladesh to India. It has risen by 68 per cent, amounting to $241.96 million in fiscal year 2005-2006. In the preceding year, they stood at $143.66 million only. This increase in exports has largely been to north-eastern states. On the other hand, according to the statistics provided by Export Promotion Bureau (EPB) of Bangladesh its imports from India have dropped by around 8 per cent, totalling $1,868 million in the last financial year from $2,025.78 million in fiscal year 2004-2005. As a result of the rise in exports and decline in imports the trade deficit of Bangladesh with India narrowed by around 14%. The trade deficit of Bangladesh with India had ballooned to a record $2,003 million in 2003-2004. However, it came down to $1,882 million in the following year and $1,626 million in fiscal year 2005-2006. According to Mir Sahabuddin, the Vice-chairman of Export promotion Bureau, exports to the north eastern states of India have increased substantially because of change of policy of the Government of India which has facilitated the work of businessmen. Though Bangladesh has a trade deficit with India, it is surplus with the north-eastern states. It has made sustained effort to increase its exports to India. Position of merchandise trade between the two countries is given below during the year 2001-2002 to 2004-2005 issued by Bangladesh Bank and Export promotion Bureau in US $ million.

Trends in India-Bangladesh Trade

	2001-2002	*2002-2003*	*2003-2004*	*2004-2005*
Bangladesh exports to India	50.28	84.08	89.27	114.20
Bangladesh imports from India	1,011.84	1,354.98	1,599.46	2,030.00
Total Trade	1,062.12	1,439.06	1,688.73	2,174.20

However, despite this jump in exports, Bangladeshi exporters are still complaining that some non-tariff barriers like mandatory testing required by India, inadequate banking facilities and poor infrastructure at the land ports are hindering Bangladesh's export growth to India. They also claim that India deliberately tries to stall imports from Bangladesh, as its land customs officials are not informed about the preferential market access given to Dhaka by New Delhi. Earlier Bangladesh has not been able to export to India because it had a very small export basket. Besides, its products were not very competitive internationally. As a result they have not been able to penetrate into Indian economy that is increasingly getting globalised. India has been trying to help Bangladesh and is willing to relax restrictions for Bangladesh even in the area of restricted categories like readymade garments for which Bangladesh has been insisting. Apart from this many members of the intelligentsia also urged India to give preferential, or free, market access to Bangladeshi consumer goods. This would help Bangladesh to reduce its large trade deficit with India and easier for it to lift various non-tariff barriers to improve from India. The step would create a strong businessmen's lobby in favour of closer relations with India which would also act as a counterweight to the fundamentalist forces in the country.[130] It is an undeniable fact that with its creation in 1971 Bangladesh's economy suffered a severe blow for it lost both its market and sources of food grains and raw materials in erstwhile West Pakistan.

But for Bangladesh the issue of trade and the deficit thereof has been a matter of political use and accusation. It has consistently used the trade deficit for political purpose, the usual accusation being made by either of the two main political parties that the other has 'sold out' the economy to India, or acquiesced in India converting Bangladesh into a 'captive market'. The second fact is that given the diversity of India's productive capacity and the limits of that of Bangladesh, the trade deficit would continue, perhaps in unabated form. The reason behind this situation is that the country has not developed an efficient and dynamic manufacturing sector. Industrial activity is minimal if not stagnant and of the products 75% comprises textiles and garments.

Not only in politics but in trade too Bangladesh is playing 'China Card' against India. From the side of Bangladesh no sign of cooperation has been seen and the country has been following policies which discourage imports from India. In the past, India has been the largest trading partner of Bangladesh. Now that is not the case and according to the data released it had indicated that China has replaced India as its largest trading partner. Easily understandable point in this is that Bangladesh has an almost equally large trade deficit with China and it is not complaining and what it wants from India is specific concessions. On the other India had also linked the trade with transit which Dhaka is not willing to provide. This would be a even more political issue for a large cross section of leaders in Bangladesh who believe and proclaim that the grant of transit facilities would endanger independence and national sovereignty; that this would be an Indian corridor cutting Bangladesh in two; and lastly that India would transport arms as result of grant of the facility leading to a military threat to Bangladesh.

Arguments for deficit of trade and concession on the part of Bangladesh apart it seemed doubtful that India could grant all the facilities asked for. It has been calculated that even if India gives totally customs free access to the exports of Bangladesh the loss of revenue would be less than one percent of the total. And the result would be, given the high import intensity Bangladesh's exports, a further increase of India's exports to that country; higher income there would further increase the market for India's products. In general it would give a considerable boost to bilateral trade and to the goodwill that undoubtedly exists in Bangladesh, and create a strong support base among commercial circles there for the development of yet closer relations. Thus, if India accepts Bangladesh's request for export concessions, this would cost little and go a long way to show that it is prepared to go the extra mile. The future of Bangladesh is inextricably intertwined with India and the latter is the natural market for most, if not all of Dhaka's products. Therefore, Bangladesh is affected by virtually every decision that India takes in fields as diverse as energy, ecology and economic policy and unfortunately it has no capacity to modify them to minimize their impact upon its economy.

Energy or sources of energy is another sphere that India and Bangladesh want to resolve amicably without third party involvement. Energy-security is a challenge for meeting the developmental needs of Bangladesh. India is coal-rich, Nepal is rich in hydro-power and Bangladesh is gas-rich. Cooperation in having a common regional energy grid is called for.[131] The Fifth Five Year Plan (1995-2000), elaborately described the goals and objectives for the sustainable development and gave priority to oil and gas sector, recommended for the establishment of a 'Green Fund' to facilitate investment in clean technology for pollution control. In 1995 National Energy Policy was announced with the objective to ensure optimum development of all the indigenous energy sources; ensure rational use of all potential energy source with balanced energy mix. A regional security collaboration is necessitated as India has been looking eastwards to the extensive natural gas reserves of Bangladesh and Myanmar, which have become vital for India's economic growth. The geographic proximity of the two to India makes the import of gas not just convenient, but an economically attractive proposition. To encourage natural gas exploration, the Government of Bangladesh opened the natural gas sector to foreign investments in 1993. However, internal opinion in Bangladesh is divided over the quantum of gas available for domestic consumption and exports but Indian observers are hopeful that someday Bangladesh would supply its own gas to India by joining on existing trans-national pipeline.

Unwillingness on the part of Bangladesh in agreeing to supply natural gas to India is viewed by a section of people in the country as a sign of evil intentions towards New Delhi. The Islamist forces in Bangladesh are against any policy, especially of an economic nature, that would benefit India. They argued that Bangladesh policy-makers would not grant India rights of passage for a trans-national pipeline because such a decision/policy will be blocked by Jamaat-influenced senior military and political officials. Now the issue of natural gas between the two has become a political matter as, in its place, Bangladesh is demanding non-tariff barriers block access of Bangladesh products, not only to Indian market, but also to Nepal. If India wants Bangladesh to deliver on the Myanmar-Bangladesh-India gas pipeline project, it should be willing to grant trade concessions to Bangladesh by lifting such barriers. Bangladesh has said that it will consider allowing a pipeline originating from Myanmar if India allows Dhaka a free trade corridor to Nepal and accompanying trade benefits. It has also asked India to remove barriers that exist in trade between the two countries.

These conditions have further complicated negotiations over the laying of the pipeline, as free trans-national movement through the sensitive 'Siliguri Corridor' is not acceptable to India. The Government of India has held the view that Bangladesh has shown a lack of commitment in entering into a treaty for providing a transit route for Indian goods, including the Myanmar-India gas pipeline, through their land, forcing India to consider other circuitous and uneconomic options.[132] In this connection Christina Rocca, US Assistant Secretary of State during her visit (11-13 March 2002) remarked, 'it is in the interest of Bangladesh to make a positive decision on gas export to broaden its investment base and woo US entrepreneurs.[133] Therefore, it was felt that effective and appropriate regional cooperation could thus be one possible means to ensure long term energy security for the South Asian region in general and Bangladesh in particular.

In addition as a measure to address the problem the Government of Bangladesh stressed on harnessing non-conventional energy sector like solar, wind and hydro-electricity that could lessen burden on fossil fuels for generation of energy. Under an arrangement made between India and Bangladesh there is a provision for exporting the surplus power from the eastern states of India to deficient western region of Bangladesh and in turn surplus power from eastern part of Bangladesh would be exported to the north east states of India.[134] To most Bangladeshis, it is Farakka that symbolises their inability to control their destiny. It has a super-abundance of water that comes from a single three month monsoon that regularly causes the Brahmaputra to flood a third of the country. It is, therefore, adversely affected by almost every hydel project on the Ganges or one of its tributaries that reduces the flow of water in the river as it enters Bangladesh. As a result the Government and people of Bangladesh is fully conscious on the issue of water-related management. It reacted sharply when in the year 2003 the Atal Bihari Vajapayee government had announced its ambitious river-linking project without even a token discussion with Bangladesh, despite the fact that it involved building a link canal from the Brahmaputra to Ganges and up to six dams and barrages on the tributaries of the former in Assam and NEFA. Perhaps it is the single issue that could drive the two countries irrevocably apart.

As an integral part of economy degradation of environment poses security risk for Bangladesh. In 1998, Bangladesh suffered its worst flooding of the 20th century which lasted for three months and covered two-thirds of the country. Change in the pattern of monsoon, increase in the frequency of floods and drought, rise in sea level by 15 cm in past few decades and rising at least by 3 mm every year, increase in temperature by 0.60^{0} over the Twentieth Century, year 1998 and decade 1990-2000 as the warmest in human history have strengthened the belief that global climate is gradually changing. In the situation particularly the survival of Bangladesh is at stake due to its geographical location since most parts of it have an elevation of less than 10 metre above sea level. Flat terrain, low economic growth, high population density, intensive dependence on agriculture, lack of infrastructure combine to make the country vulnerable to any variation in climate and sea level. According to United Nation Environment Programme (UNEP) Bangladesh comes in the list of ten most vulnerable countries.[135]

Acknowledging the growing concern for occurrence of natural disasters, the Government of Bangladesh had till 2002, ratified or acceded to more than 44 multilateral environmental treaties, conventions and protocols. At the domestic level it has carried out some of the earliest studies on assessing green house gases emissions, vulnerability to climate change and lately to assessing adaptation options. Apart from Five Year Plans in the annual budget for 1999-2000, a project at a cost of Taka 82.29 crore for preservation of biodiversity in the Sunderban had been undertaken with the assistance of the Asian Development Bank. The Department of Environment had also undertaken a project at a cost of Taka 30.25 crore for the management of air quality. At world level the Bonn Agreement of July 2001 had incorporated afforestation, reforestation projects to be eligible under Clean Development Mechanism (CDM) in non-annex countries. It has created three new funds for developing countries : Special Climate Change Fund; Least Developed Countries Fund; and Adaptation Fund. If Bangladesh plays its cards right, it can raise funds and technical assistance that would help in sustainable development programme by restructuring its energy, industry and forestry sectors. Earlier in 1996 India and Bangladesh had signed a 30-year agreement on distribution of water at Farakka, however, major water management issues – including hydro electric power, deforestation, and water storage remain to be addressed.

Issue of Migration

The continuing illegal immigration from Bangladesh into India remains a serious issue. The long and porous borders, socio-economic pressures coupled with ineffective border controls have been major contributory factors. The high population density, endemic poverty and vulnerability to the vagaries of nature exacerbate the flow of illegal immigration to India. They have come in search of employment and have settled down mostly in slums. Some non-Muslims have been illegally coming as refugees because of occasional communal tensions.[136] The notion of refugee, when associated with humanitarian aims, differs from that used in international arguments. However, all refugees have common characteristics viz. natural calamities, religious and political persecution, which have been creating continually a class of dispersed persons who are uprooted from their native homelands. This class of displaced and uprooted persons is referred as to refugees.[137] The refugee is an involuntary migrant and in the sense every refugee is naturally a migrant, but not every migrant is a refugee in order to settle elsewhere either in his own or in another country. The presence of refugees creates several problems in social, cultural, political and economic spheres, both for the host country and the refugee.[138] In 20th century, India since independence has perhaps witnessed the world's largest refugee influx from East Pakistan, now Bangladesh.

The migration of persons from East Pakistan and then Bangladesh into India has been substantial. And most of the migration among both Muslims and Hindus is for economic reason due to flood or drought or lack of employment opportunities, though some of the latter, sporadically and in small numbers is due to violence against the minorities. Although initially there has been some exodus among both Hindus and Muslims due to tacit encouragement from India, especially in the late 1960s and early 1970s, but it stopped thereafter. The issue first became politically active when the All Assam Students Union started agitating in the mid 1970s against the Central government for what Assamese saw as a policy of liberally allowing and even encouraging Bangladeshis to enter India to increase the number of votes for the Congress Party. Later it came to the fore when the 1981 census results showed that in West Bengal and Assam in particular, but also in Tripura, the over all population increase was three times the national average, and that the growth of the Muslim population in particular was too high to be explained by natural causes.

The issue of migration became sensitive as large number of Bangladeshi nationals, who entered into India illegally, have spread all over the country causing socio-economic problems, rise in crime and is causing change in demographic pattern in certain areas. Apart from the usual suspects, the militants and economic migrants, the recent political turmoil in Bangladesh has also resulted in many Bangladeshi political dissidents and people from the religious minorities attempting to sneak into India to avoid political and religious persecution. Various reports also certify that the large number of sophisticated arms and ammunition are being smuggled to north eastern parts of India from Bangladesh. In addition the porous nature of the border and the constant flow of people have also made it easy for Indian insurgents groups (IIGs) to cross over into Bangladesh, where they have set up safe houses and training camps under the benign eyes of Pakistani and Bangladeshi intelligence services.[139] Harbouring of Indian insurgents inside Bangladesh is causing a serious threat to the integrity and sovereignty of India.

In that kind of situation, the hitherto neglected border along Bangladesh is gradually getting the attention of the Central government, bringing with it much needed money and manpower. To meet the challenge posed by the issue of migration the Government of India adopted a two-pronged strategy – to initiate dialogue at political level to settle the problem and strengthening of border management including the wire-fencing. India from the start had raised the issue with the Bangladesh government which steadfastly denied about such movement but admitted in the early 1990s and agreed that large scale illegal immigration was a problem that needed to be solved. For India this cannot be a straightforward issue of sending back illegal immigrants/infiltrators and stopping any more from coming in. The Hindus could not; they were regarded as refugees rather than immigrants. Of the Muslims many had settled in states far from the border; the population figures showed high increases in Bihar and even further away in Delhi. Most seemed to have documents proving that they were Indian citizens, given to them when they were being encouraged to vote. They had been there for two or even three generations. The policy of sending back resulted only in a few incidents in each of which some dozens were pushed back; this only led to border incidents, and those pushed back re-entered by another route. India's concerns over the magnitude of the problem are regularly conveyed to Bangladesh, including at the highest level. Discussions have been held and there are some signs that they will lead to better security along the border, but the long term solutions lies in more jobs and better living conditions in Bangladesh.

Border-security related other measures like the raising of additional Border Security Force battalions, construction of more Border Out Posts (BOPs), building of roads along the border and acquiring new equipment and erection of barb wire fences are being undertaken for improving vigilance along the border to check infiltration. Recently an institutional framework has been established for discussion on border management through the meetings of Home Secretaries and the Director General level talks between the Border Security Force and the Bangladesh Rifles. These have been taking place regularly. As to the fencing of 4096 km. long border, it started in mid 1980s and about a third has been fenced. It is being built along the border in order to ensure better border management and to check illegal cross-border movement. However, erecting the fence along the border has not been without its problems. The inhospitable terrain, the largely un-demarcated border area and consequent border disputes, the non-cooperative attitudes of the various state governments and also that of the Bangladesh Rifles are all hurdles in the way of effective fencing the border.[140] India and Bangladesh are also poles apart on the issue and the former is getting stiff resistance from the latter. Bangladesh objects on the ground that the construction of any defensive structure within 150 yards of the international boundary is not permitted under guidelines agreed to in 1975. On the other hand, India maintains that it is demolition of defensive structures and not construction of fences that forms part of 1975 guidelines.

In the present circumstances to have a constructive cooperation India needs to take certain types of steps and Bangladesh needs to take some others. If India accepts Bangladesh's request for export concession, this would cost little and go a long way to show that it is prepared to go the extra mile. On the problems of land and maritime border which are more difficult, Bangladesh needs only assurance that India is serious in expediting settlement, not a specific deadline by which this will be done. Equally Bangladesh, on its part, must take concrete measures against the insurgents camps that have been established in its territory. As Dhaka's flat denial aroused suspicions in India, it needs to be assuaged. It also has to take measures to reassure the minorities on regular basis.

REGIME OF UNITED PROGRESSIVE ALLIANCE

Premiership of Manmohan Singh (22 May 2004 - 22 May 2009)

In pursuance of the results of general election held in India in May 2004, the Indian National Congress emerged as the single largest but due to the lack of majority of its own, formed the government with the support of the communists and other allies. Prime Minister Atal Bihari Vajpayee was replaced by Dr. Manmohan Singh who became the new Prime Minister of the country. Unlike India, Bangladesh did not witness any change of guard and Begam Khaleda Zia of the BNP who took over the premiership of Bangladesh in 2001 continued till 2006 but as a follow up of the provision in the constitution at the close of this year she handed over the reign of administration to a caretaker government to conduct a free and fair national election scheduled in January 2007. The ruling regime of BNP under Khaleda Zia (2001-2006), particularly its alliance with the Jamaat-e-Islami repelled moderates, liberals, and secularists in town and countryside alike. In this period Begam Zia wooed the fundamentalist fringe and ended up having to tackle Islamist militants of various hues.[141] The last two years of her regime also witnessed a rise in political violence that has become a part of the political landscape in Bangladesh. On August 21, 2004, grenades were hurled in an apparent political assassination attempt on opposition leader Sheikh Hasian at a political rally in Dhaka which killed 22 persons. The Finance Minister of previous Awami League government A.M.S. Kibria and four others were killed in a bomb attack at a political rally of the Awami League on January 27, 2005, claimed 26 lives and injured dozens were the most notable happenings in recent years.

Thus, the rising graph of political violence in preceding years of the scheduled poll of January 2007, marred the future of a fair election in the country. The United Kingdom Parliamentary Human Rights Group reported in October 2006 that prospect for a free and fair election in Bangladesh looked bleak. Manipulation of voters lists, rampant and escalating political violence, the assassination of former finance minister, the attempt on the British High Commissioner's life, grenade attacks against AL leader Sheikh Hasina, the suicide bombing of two judges, the simultaneous bombings across the country in August 2005 and killings by the elite Rapid Action Battalion have been identified as sources of instability and reasons for pessimism on the democratic process in Bangladesh.[142] Others have agreed with this assessment. Sheikh Hasina, the leader of Awami League with her alliance had also threatened to boycott the January 2007 elections and held large scale demonstrations in December 2006 to highlight their demands which included a revision of the voter list.[143] Sheikh Hasina's charges of irregularities were also confirmed independently by the National Democratic Institute (NDI) who found the voters' list of 93 million names as substantially inconsistent with the 2001 census data and agreed that the voting age population was approximately 80 million people.[144] In the circumstances the scheduled general election of January was postponed and by declaring emergency, a military-backed caretaker government headed by Fakhruddin Ahmed was installed on January 11, 2007.

India as earlier, continued to constructively engage the caretaker government in Bangladesh that assumed office after the imposition of emergency in the country on January 11, 2007. On February 19, 2007, Pranab Mukherjee, India's Minister for External Affairs, visited Bangladesh and extended an invitation to Bangladesh to participate in the 14th SAARC Summit in New Delhi. In course of the visit he held detailed discussions with President Dr. Iajuddin Ahmed, the Chief Advisor of the Caretaker Government, Dr. Fakhruddin Ahmed and Foreign Affairs Advisor Dr. Iftekhar Ahmed Chowdhury. In Indian context it appeared that the military-backed Interim Government of Bangladesh had shown an inclination to improve relations with India as informed to the media by Iftekhar Ahmed Chowdhury, 'let me say unequivocally that this caretaker government wishes to place Bangladesh's relations with India on a firm footing so that future governments of both countries can build on the progress we make'.[145] In terms of bilateral relations, both sides agreed to take steps to place bilateral relations on an 'irreversible higher trajectory'. Indian Prime Minister Dr. Manmohan Singh also met Bangladesh Chief Adviser Dr. Fakhruddin Ahmed on April 2, 2007 in New Delhi during the 14th SAARC Summit and the two leaders held discussions on all major bilateral issues.

At the invitation of Bangladesh Foreign Secretary for holding the Foreign Office Consultations (FOCs) the Foreign Secretary of India paid an official visit to Dhaka June 24-27, 2007, and the two Foreign Secretaries held constructive and forward looking discussions on issues relating to security, peaceful management of borders, water resources, economic and trade matters and regional cooperation. The Indian Foreign Secretary was also called on Chief Adviser, Foreign Affairs Adviser and Chief of Army Staff and held useful discussion with them. In July 2007 Jairam Ramesh, India's Minister of State for Commerce, went Dhaka to inaugurate India-Bangladesh Chamber of Commerce and Industry. During the visit he was called on President Dr. Iajuddin Ahmed. It followed the Home Secretary level talks of the two countries in New Delhi on August 2-3,

2007 during which they discussed bilateral security issues at length. Again India's Foreign Minister Pranab Mukherjee visited Bangladesh on December 1, 2007 to support and announce India's help in the wake of Cyclone Sidr and made New Delhi's decision known to Dhaka.

In 2008 after the gap of a decade Bangladesh's Chief of Army Staff General Moeen U. Ahmed visited India during February 24-March 1, 2008 at the invitation of Indian Army and discussed the issues of bilateral nature. In a significant development the Foreign Secretaries of India and Bangladesh in July 2008 at New Delhi discussed a wide range of subjects covering terrorism, economy, security and other issues of mutual interest. They described terrorism as a global problem and added that the governments of both countries have been discussing counter-strategies to neutralise this menace at both the bilateral and multilateral levels. Addressing a joint press conference they said, 'we are convinced that our security is interlinked and that terrorism will have to be tackled resolutely'.[146] India's Foreign Secretary Shivshankar Menon took the opportunity to reiterate that India and Bangladesh share a common cultural heritage and historical bonds, and therefore, New Delhi would always remain committed to strengthening its relationship with Dhaka. We had a very good discussion toady where we discussed our trade and economic relations, our political relations, common security issues, water issues and the other aspects where we would like to carry our relationship forward.'[147]

Economic Relations

In economic sphere India and Bangladesh took exchange of views on several aspects and the issue of water management between the two countries was one of them. On the sharing of river waters the two countries have a bilateral Joint Rivers Commission (JRC) that was established in June 1972 to maintain liaison between the two countries to maximize benefits from common river systems, formulation of flood control works, formulation of proposals on advance flood warnings, flood forecasting and cyclone warning, as also study of flood control and irrigation projects. In post-Vajpayee period a meeting of Joint Rivers Commission took place in Dhaka in September 2005. In September 2006, the Water Resources Ministers of both the countries jointly visited some river sites in both countries and discussed issues relating to riverbank protection, minor lift irrigation and drinking water schemes. Apart from this on assistance side, India, as always, had stood by Bangladesh in its hour of need with aid worth over Taka 250 crore to help it cope with natural disasters and flood in the year 2007-2008. India is working with Government of Bangladesh for rehabilitation of ten cyclone-affected villages in the southern part of Bangladesh.

Likewise the two countries discussed their problems of trade at the fourth meeting of the Indo-Bangladesh Joint Working Group (JWG) which was held in Agartala on 5-6 July 2006. M.V.P.C. Shastri, joint secretary in the commerce ministry, headed the Indian delegation while the Bangladesh team was led by Elias Ahmed, additional secretary in the commerce ministry. Senior officials of the commerce and industries department of the five bordering states – West Bengal, Assam, Meghalaya, Mizoram and Tripura also participated in the meeting. In this meeting India and Bangladesh had decided to modernise and upgrade existing infrastructure, including roads, to boost their bilateral trade especially between the north eastern states of India and Bangladesh. Once again the issue of huge bilateral trade gap existing between the two countries discussed and Shastri, who led the 16-member Indian team said, 'The north-eastern states of India have huge resources and raw materials and these can be exported to Bangladesh. After due processing, the finished products can be made available to the people of the region at much cheaper rates. But unfortunately the attitude of cooperation has not been seen from the side of Bangladesh. The country has negative trade balance with most countries and uses remittances from expatriate Bangladeshis to finance its imports. Bangladesh appears to be obsessed with the trade gap, which it has with India. As a result, the country has been following policies which discourage import from India.

Despite unwillingness on the part of Bangladesh to cope with the trade gap between the two, India has considered the country an important trading partner and its trade had grew with Bangladesh by 145% in the last five years from about USD 1 billion in 2001-02 to USD 2.55 billion in 2006-07. While Bangladesh's imports from India grew by 124% in the last five years (2001-2007), its exports to India grew by 480% in the corresponding period. As a part of goodwill gesture India extended zero duty excess/tariff concessions to Bangladesh under SAFTA, SAPTA and APTA. It was provided with effect from January 1, 2008 and in pursuant to the announcement made by the Indian Prime Minister at the 14th SAARC Summit held in New Delhi in April 2007. The facility was to be applicable to the products originating from SAARC, LDCs, including Bangladesh, except for some items in the sensitive list.

Furthermore, with a view to address trade imbalance India has agreed to extend duty free access to eight million pieces of readymade garments from Bangladesh every year under SAFTA. A Memorandum of Understanding on procedural arrangements was signed in Dhaka in September 2007, and customs notification issued by Indian Department of Revenue on April 21, 2008. However, the present trading arrangements are governed by the revised India-Bangladesh Trade Agreement signed in March 2006. As a further step an India-Bangladesh Chamber of Commerce and Industry (IBCCI) has been set up in July 2007 which has become a useful platform for exchange of information, promoting greater interaction between business communities from both sides. And in sequence in November 2007, the Government of India has removed the prohibition on investment into India by citizens of Bangladesh or entities incorporated in Bangladesh, allowing investments that have prior approval of the foreign investment policy board of the Government of India. In a development a total 181 FDI and joint venture investment proposals from India worth of USD 435 million have been registered with the Board of Investment, Government of Bangladesh in sectors such as agro-industry, textiles, chemicals and engineering industries.

The economic relations and trade in particular between India and Bangladesh suffered because of poor infrastructural facilities. The infrastructural bottleneck between the two countries was also highlighted by the multilateral donor agency World Bank. It felt that an inter-country railway link between Bangladesh and India would accelerate economic growth of the two countries. Speaking at a press conference in Dhaka on July 3, 2006, Christine I Wallich, the World Bank Country Director, said, 'when I first came to Bangladesh, I had visited some border areas and found the possibility of such a railway linkage'. At another occasion the issue of infrastructure was raised by Indian High Commissioner Veena Sikri when Bangladesh Commerce Minister Hafiz Uddin Ahmed tried to highlight the issue of trade gap while inaugurating the Indian Cotton Yarn and Fabric Show 2006 at a hotel in Dhaka on July 9, 2006. Sikri suggested that Bangladesh develop its Mangla port and link it with haldia port in West Bengal to accelerate trade and reduce the trade gap between the two countries. She stressed the need for increased direct transport links with Bangladesh. Faster and deeper economic integration was also called by Begam Khaleda Zia when the Foreign Ministers of SAARC countries met in Dhaka at the end of July 2006 to discuss security and trade issues.[148] Later in November 2007 a Sub-Group under the Joint Working Group on Trade was set up to look into ways and means of strengthening border trade infrastructure in a more coordinated way.

In the background of above facts and opinions, several ways were envisaged to improve transit facility and people to people contact between the two countries. Earlier, the direct bus service between Dhaka and Kolkata started in 1999 and Dhaka-Agartala since 2003. However, giving a major breakthrough to the purpose the direct passenger train service was resumed between Kolkata and Dhaka Cantonment station in April 2008. It was inaugurated as a follow up of an agreement signed between India and Bangladesh and many people expected that the train service would substantially contribute to consolidating ties between the two neighbours.[149] The caretaker government's council of advisers decided on February 24, this year to clear the ways and approved the Indian proposal and with this the 'Maitree Express' – a friendship train backed on the rails after a gap of forty-three years. Even prior to 1947 there was a regular overnight railway service from Kolkata to Dhaka, it however, was ceased to operate after the Indo-Pak war of 1965.[150] The railway service between the two neighbours, as is expected, would expand mass transportation, result in greater interaction between the people not only in tourism terms but also in terms of trade, commerce and cultural exchanges. It has opened a new chapter in India-Bangladesh relations.

Immigration and Security Concerns

There are also some developments on issues such as immigration and border management. The presence of illegal Bangladeshi immigrants in large numbers posed a grave threat to India's internal security. In reference to the measures taken by the Home Ministry to tackle illegal immigration a Parliamentary Standing Committee on Home Affairs was constituted under the leadership of Sushma Swaraj. The 25-member committee in its observation also reported that certain Bangladeshi insurgent groups were involved in the terrorist incidents in our country.[151] In its report the Committee recommended the fencing of the border, floodlighting and laying of roads to enable effective patrolling assignment of the border guarding duties to a single force, reduction of gaps between the border outposts, provision of modern surveillance and other equipments gadgetry to the Border Security Force. As an effect of the report instructions have been given to the State Governments and Union Territories to take sustained action to detect foreign nationals including Bangladeshis, staying illegally in the country. Lal Krishna Advani, the Leader of Opposition, while addressing a BJP rally in Guwahati at the close of September 2008 also noted the flood and infiltration as the two major challenges faced by the people of the State and called for pushing back the illegal Bangladeshi infiltrators.[152]

The boundary between India and Bangladesh is looked after by a Land Boundary Agreement (LBD) signed between two in 1974. Recently in December 2001, the two countries established a bilateral mechanism called the Joint Boundary Working Group (JBWG) to make some recommendations to settle the outstanding issues. The JBWG has so far held several meetings and involved aspects were discussed in detail in order to have a satisfactory solution. In March 2006 India and Bangladesh signed a bilateral Agreement on Mutual Cooperation for Preventing Illicit Trafficking in Narcotic Drug and Psychotropic Substances. Further the Home Secretary level talks were held in New Delhi on August 2-3, 2007 while the Director General level talks between BSF and Bangladesh Rifles were held in New Delhi on April 7-12, 2008.

With a view to strengthen border management New Delhi and Dhaka conducted two-day Home Secretary level talks in Dhaka in August 2008. The 14-member Indian team was led by India's Home Secretary Madhukar Gupta while the leader of 18-member Bangladesh team was Abdul Karim. In the meeting the two sides agreed to take action against militants and insurgent outfits, smuggling of arms, ammunition, explosives and fake currency and bring the culprits to justice.[153] Both sides agreed that there was a strong need to identify the racketeers engaged in human trafficking especially in women and children, and bring the perpetrators to justice. Their meeting ended on a note of satisfaction over the successful reactivation of the Joint Working Group at the level of joint secretaries and designation of nodal points to deal with the issues of security and human trafficking. In the year 2008 India-Bangladesh maritime boundary talks held at Dhaka and leader of the Bangladesh team was M. A. K. Mahmood, Additional Foreign Secretary, while Indian side was led by Rear Admiral B.R. Rao. In the meeting both sides discussed all issues concerned with maritime boundary. Although talks held were fruitful but they agreed that further discussion on the issue was required. In nutshell they failed to agree on any of the differences continuing earlier and it ended inconclusively.

In a major breakthrough, the country had ever witnessed, Sheikh Hasina and her party Awami League alongwith its allies registered a historic win in the general elections held on December 29, 2008. It was held after two years of caretaker rule by an army- backed interim government installed on January 11, 2007. Of the 299 seats called the Awami League won 230 seats independently and with allies it became a grand alliance of 262 seats that would give the party the power to rewrite the constitution and bring about promised reforms. In contrast Hasina's arch-rival and leader of Bangladesh Nationalist Party (BNP) Begam Khaleda Zia was reduced to 27 only. It is said that while in power the BNP under Begam Zia with allies failed to address vital issues including soaring prices of essential commodities and power generation but focussed on consolidating all powers in its hands and misusing the same for personal and political gain. As the country has been plagued by political and economic crises for years, the election offered an opportunity to solve them in a planned way. All sections of the people have voted decisively for secular democracy and development and against religious fundamentalism and militancy. It is also a moment for Sheikh Hasina to mend fences with political rivals and together try to find solutions to the huge problems facing the country. If that does not happen, chances are that country will be back to zero sum politics which, in turn, could prompt the military to intervene again.[154] This is the only for Bangladesh to stop itself alarming slide towards the status of a failed state.

The people and the government in India have a tremendous goodwill for the Awami League and its leader Sheikh Hasina. On her success India's Prime Minister Dr. Manmohan Singh and his Minister for External Affairs Pranab Mukherjee recalling the close and friendly relations with Bangladesh, sent congratulating messages. The Indian Prime Minister noted that the successful conduct of free, fair and peaceful elections was a reflection of the desire of the people of that country for democracy, development and progress and hoped that under your leadership Bangladesh would attain even greater heights. He assured Sheikh Hasina of India's commitment to further strengthening and deepening of relations with Bangladesh.[155] He also invited her to visit India at her earliest. Likewise Pranab Mukherjee, India's Minister for External Affairs, described the victory of the Awami League and the grand alliance as landmark in democratic politics in South Asia. It is a resounding victory for democracy he added. Among others, Jyoti Basu, the former Chief Minister of West Bengal and Rajnath Singh, the Bharatiya Janata Party President congratulated Sheikh Hasina and her Party and hailed the win of democracy in Bangladesh. President of the BJP congratulating on her party's landslide victory hoped that the new regime in Bangladesh would strengthen the war on terror in South Asia. 'A stable and peaceful Bangladesh is not only in the interest of Bangladeshi people but it also builds a sense of coherence and consistency in the entire region.'

References

1. Janata Party's Election Manifesto, 1977 (New Delhi, 1977), pp. 23-24.
2. S. C. Gangal, Indian Foreign Policy-A Documentary Study of India's Foreign Policy Since the Installation of the Janata Government on 24 March 1977 (Young Asia Publications, New Delhi, 1980), pp. 158-59.
3. Ibid., pp. 45-46.
4. Shashi Tharoor, Reasons of State : Political Development and India's Foreign Policy Under Indira Gandhi 1966-1977 (Vikas Publishing House, New Delhi, 1982), pp. 382-83.
5. S. S. Bindra, Indo-Bangladesh Relations (Deep and Deep Publications, New Delhi, 1982), p. 53.
6. The proposal for the construction of a Barrage across the Ganga was recommended by Dr. Walter Hensen, a German engineer of International repute on tidal hydraulics, who came to this country on 22 February

1957, on the invitation of the Government of India and was asked to give a report in this connection. The project was taken up for implementation sometime in 1963. See Lok Sabha Debates, vol. IX, 15 December, 1977, colm. 236.

7. G. G. Mirchandari, ed., Reporting India 1977 (Abhinav Publications, New Delhi, 1978), p. 214.
8. The Hindu (Madras), April 16, 1977.
9. Ibid., May 8, 1977.
10. Ibid., April 19, 1977.
11. Ibid., May 12, 1977.
12. G. G. Mirchandari, op.cit., p. 213.
13. Robert Fraser, ed., Keesing's Contemporary Archives, vol. XXIII, no. 1616, 29 July 1977 (Longman Group, Scotland, 1977), pp. 28480-81.
14. The Hindu, June 11, 1977.
15. The Amrit Bazar Patrika, editorial (Calcutta), June 21, 1977.
16. G. G. Mirchandari, op.cit., p. 213.
17. Robert Fraser, vol. XVII, 6 January 1978, op.cit., p. 28763.
18. G. G Mirchandari, op.cit., p. 217.
19. See the text of a joint press released in New Delhi on 30 September 1977 in S. C. Gangal, op.cit., p. 258.
20. S. C. Gangal, "Trends in India's Foreign Policy", K. P. Mishra, ed., Janata's Foreign Policy (Vikas Publishing House, New Delhi, 1979), p. 45.
21. See the text of the agreement signed in Dacca on 5 November 1977 in S. C. Gangal, op.cit., pp. 267-71.
22. The Hindu, November 6, 1977.
23. See the Text of the official statement on the Agreement in S. C. Gangal, op.cit., pp. 259-67.
24. Lok Sabha Debates, vol. IX, 15 December 1977, colm. 218.
25. Ibid., colm. 232.
26. Ibid., colm. 236.
27. Ibid., colm. 268.
28. Inder Malhotra, "Beyond the Bangla Poll-New Delhi-Dacca Relations", The Times of India, June 8, 1978.
29. Robert Fraser, vol. XXIV, 24 February, 1978, op.cit., p. 28845.
30. The Times of India, December 21, 1977.

31. The Pioneer (editorial), "Indo-Bangladesh Report", 24 December 1977. See also, Indian Express (editorial), "A Useful Visit" December 22, 1977.
32. The Statesman (editorial), Investing in Goodwill", 24 December 1977.
33. Asian Recorder, Vol. XXIV, 26 March-1 April, 1978, p. 14229.
34. Foreign Affairs Record, August 1978, p. 278.
35. Ibid., April, 1979, p. 80.
36. Kuldip Singh, India and Bangladesh (Anmol Publications, Delhi, 1987), pp. 64-65.
37. See the joint communique in Foreign Affairs Record, April, 1979, p. 82.
38. The Hindu, April 18, 1979.
39. Kuldip Singh, op.cit., p. 65.
40. The Times of India (editorial), April 20, 1979.
41. Ibid.
42. Kuldip Singh, op.cit., pp. 66-67.
43. Ibid.
44. Virendra Narain, "India's Foreign Policy in the 1990s : Including some Reflections on Indo-Bangladesh Relations", M. Rasgotra, V. D. Chopra, K. P. Misra (eds), India's Foreign Policy in the 1990's (Patriot Publishers, New Delhi, 1990), p. 240.
45. Ibid., p. 243.
46. The Patriot (New Delhi), February 25, 1990.
47. The Times of India, January 6, 1990.
48. The Hindustan Times, December 4, 1989.
49. Ibid., January 23, 1990.
50. The Hindu, February 20, 1990.
51. The Times of India, February 17, 1990.
52. The Hindustan Times, February 19, 1990.
53. Bhabani Sen Gupta, "Regional Perspective : A Delhi-Dhaka Axis", The Indian Express, February 24, 1990.
54. The Times of India, June 10, 1990.
55. The Hindustan Times, February 19, 1990.
56. Foreign Affairs Record, Vol. XXXVI, no. 6, June 1990, p. 133.
57. The Hindu, June 20, 1990.
58. Bhabani Sen Gupta, op.cit.
59. Foreign Affairs Record, Vol. XXXVI, no. 1, January, 1990, p. 1.
60. Ibid., Vol. XXXVI, no. 5, May 1990, pp. 105-6.

61. Ibid., p. 105.
62. The Hindustan Times, March 13, 1990.
63. Ibid., February 2, 1990.
64. Babita Malhotra and S. Kumar, "Thaw in Indo-Bangla Relations", The National Herald, January 10, 1991.
65. Foreign Affairs Record, Vol. XXXVII, no. 1, January 1991, p. 1.
66. Ibid.
67. The National Herald, June 9, 1991.
68. Foreign Affairs Record, Vol. XXXVII, no. 3, March 1991, p. 36.
69. The Educational Consultant India is a public sector undertaking under the Ministry of Human Resource Development offering consultancy and technical services in different fields of education and human resource development both within the country and abroad. See, Foreign Affairs Record, Vol. XXXVII, no. 5, May 1991, p. 82.
70. Dr. Parmanand, "A Helping Hand of Friendship and Solidarity", The National Herald, June 9,1991.
71. Ibid.
72. Foreign Affairs Record, Vol. XLII, no. 5, May 1996, p. 89.
73. Ibid., no. 6, June 1996, p. 103.
74. Ibid., no. 7, July 1996, pp. 113-14.
75. Indian Recorder (a Weekly of Events and Happening), Vol. III, no. 41, 7-13 October, 1996, p. 2310.
76. Ibid., no. 43, October 21-27, 1996, p. 2338.
77. Ibid., no. 51, December 16-22, 1996, p. 2469.
78. Ibid., Vol. IV, no. 3, January 15 –21, 1997, p. 2543.
79. Ibid.
80. Ibid., no. 7, February 12-18, 1997, p. 2596.
81. Ibid., p. 2588.
82. Ibid., March 19-25, 1997, p. 2680.
83. SAARC SCAN, Vol. 1, no. 5, March 1997, p. 3.
84. The Hindustan Times, August 6, 1997.
85. Ibid.
86. Ibid., November 14, 1997.
87. Ibid., November 19, 1997.
88. Ibid., (editorial), November 24, 1997.
89. Ibid., January 20, 1998.

90. Ibid.
91. Ibid., January 15, 1996.
92. Ibid., January 17, 1998.
93. Ibid., January 16, 1996.
94. Ibid., August 15, 1997.
95. The Times of India (Patna), June 15, 1998.
96. Ibid., June 17, 1998.
97. Ibid., June 23 and 24 1998.
98. The Hindustan Times, June 23, 1998.
99. The Times of India, June 26, 1998.
100. The Hindustan Times, January 27, 1999.
101. Ibid., July 1, 1998.
102. Ibid., February 3, 1999.
103. Sugata Bose and Ayesha Jalal, Modern South Asia History, Culture, Political Economy, Second Edition (Oxford University Press, New Delhi, 2004), pp. 190-91.
104. Ibid.
105. Bruce Vaughn, "Bangladesh : Background and US Relations", Congressional Research Service Report for Congress, Updated August 2, 2007, p. 4.
106. The CIA World Factbook, also visit [http://www/cis.government/cia/publications/ factbook/goes/bg].
107. The Reuters News, October 2, 2001 and The Newyork Times, October 11, 2001.
108. Ibid.
109. Patricia Butenis, "Elections the Road Ahead", Dhaka University, 17 December 2006.
110. BBC News, July 3, 2003.
111. Xinhua News Agency, November 8, 2002 and International Herald Tribune, January 22, 2003.
112. Prem Shankar Jha, "Fear and Loathing", The Hindustan Times, September 27, 2004.
113. Kshitij Prabha, 'Terrorism Challenges Secular Fabric of South Asia', Mahavir Singh, editor, International Terrorism and Religious Extremism Challenges to Central and South Asia (Anamika Publishers, New Delhi, 2004), pp. 272-73.

114. Prem Shankar Jha, "That Other Neighbour", The Hindustan Times, August 13, 2002.
115. Ibid.
116. BBC News, February 25, 2005.
117. The Hindustan Times, August 3, 2006.
118. Ibid., Prem Shankar Jha, "That Other Neighbour".
119. Ibid., "Fear And Loathing".
120. The Indian Express, August 29, 2006.
121. The Hindustan Times, August 4, 2006.
122. Selig Harrison, "A New Hub for Terrorism ? In Bangladesh, An Islamic Movement with Al-Queda Ties is on the Rise', The Washington Post, August 2, 2006.
123. The Hindustan Times, July 19, 2006.
124. J. N. Dixit, "Calling on Neighbours", The Hindustan Times, 14 August 2002.
125. The Independent, December 23, 2002.
126. Ibid., J. N. Dixit, "Calling on Neighbours".
127. Heritage Foundation 2003 Index of Economic Freedom, November, 2002.
128. "Bangladesh", CIA World Factbook, August 2005.
129. Economic Statistics from Global Insight, "Bangladesh : Executive Summary", April 14, 2003.
130. Ibid., Prem Shankar Jha, "Fear and Loathing".
131. The Daily Star, January 5, 2008.
132. Siddharth Srivastava, "India Grapples with Energy Issues", Asia Times, March 24, 2007.
133. Deepender Kumar, "Global Climate Change : Bangladesh:, Babuddin Khan, ed., Third Concept, Vol. 16, no. 189, November 2002, New Delhi, 2002, pp. 56-57.
134. Ibid., p. 57.
135. Ibid., p. 55.
136. V. N. Khanna, Foreign Policy of India (Vikas Publishing House, New Delhi, 2001), p. 161.
137. S. Dutta, Student Movement in Arunachal Pradesh (Himalayan Publishers, Itanagar, 1998).
138. Robin Hissang, "Settling Chakma and Hajong Refugees in Arunachal Pradesh", Babuddin Khan, ed., Third Concept, vol. 20, no. 235, September

2006, New Delhi, 2006, p. 54.

139. Kavita Arora, "Trans-boundary Forest Management in South Asia-Geopolitical Concerns for India", Dr. Subhash Kashyap, ed., South Asia Politics, Vol. 5, no. 12, April 2007, New Delhi, 2007, pp. 31-32.
140. Ibid.
141. The Hindu, editorial, December 31, 2008.
142. BBC News, October 2, 2006.
143. Parveen Ahmed, "Bangladesh Political Alliance Threatens More Protests of Upcoming Election", Associated Press, December 18, 2006.
144. Report of the National Democratic Institute, Dhaka, September 11, 2006.
145. South Asia Analysis Group, Paper no. 8, February 26, 2007.
146. Joint Press Release, New Delhi, July 17, 2008.
147. Ibid.
148. Associated Press, August 1, 2006.
149. The Hindu, April 19, 2008.
150. Ibid., April 14, 2008.
151. Ibid., April 21, 2008.
152. Ibid., September 29, 2008.
153. Ibid., September 1, 2008.
154. The Hindustan Times, editorial, December 31, 2008.
155. The Hindu, December 31, 2008.

4

India-Sri Lanka Relations

REGIME OF JANATA PARTY

Premiership of Morarji Desai (24 March 1977—28 July 1979)

At the time when the Janata Government took over in India there were no outstanding problems between the two countries except that of the problem of absorption and repatriation of persons of Indian origin in Sri Lanka and, as such, at the initial phase an amicable relations existed between the two countries. At the July 1977 elections in Sri Lanka Jayawardene's United National party came out victorious which was a significant event and good for the relations between the two countries. It was to be noted that following the defeat of Mrs. Gandhi's Congress Party at the hustings, Jayawardene, leader of the UNP, the main opposition party then in Sri Lankan Parliament, stated promptly that the defeat of Mrs. Gandhi and her party was a lesson that "elected representatives were not to set undemocratically".[1] In course of the election campaign Jayawardene and his party had often pointed out to the overthrow of Mrs. Gandhi's Government in India as an example which could also be repeated in Sri Lanka. Obviously, Sri Lanka drew inspiration from India and when Jayawardene assumed the office of Prime Minister Desai sent an unusually warm message of felicitation congratulating the people of Sri Lanka for the "peaceful transition of power—yet another triumph of democracy in this part of the world".[2] He had also added that this victory in Sri Lanka afforded an interesting parallel with India which had encouraged the hope that the two governments should succeed in working together for the common good of the two countries.[3] Jayawardene, on his part, voiced his support for the new Indian regime and declared that it was also Sri Lanka's intent to follow the policy of "Genuine non-alignment in foreign policy.[4]

Ugly communal riots erupted in Sri Lanka between the Tamils and the Sinhalese in August 1977 which caused widespread anxiety and concern in India, particularly in the Southern State of Tamil Nadu. The Government of India was under considerable public pressure to take effective steps to ensure the protection of the lives and properties of Tamil settlers in Sri Lanka.[5] But the Government of India did not show any hasty reaction and was careful in dealing the situation. It expressed satisfaction over the steps taken by the Sri Lankan Government to deal with the situation. On 26 August 1977 Samarendra Kundu, India's Minister of State for External Affairs, expressed the confidence "that the steps taken by the Sri Lankan Government to protect the life and property of the minority and to restore confidence among them would succeed and the situation would return to normal speedily" [6] On the same day Desai sent a personal message through the Indian High Commission in Colombo to Jayawardene voicing his concern at the disturbances in the Island and expressing the hope that normalcy would return soon.[7] Such a modest and sober reaction of India was greatly appreciated by the Government of Sri Lanka and increased the level of understanding between the two countries.[8]

Early in 1978 Sri Lanka changed over from parliamentary system to the French type of presidential government. J. R. Jayawardene became the first president under the new constitution. Home Minister Charan Singh led the high level Indian delegation at the swearing-in-ceremony of Jayawardene He reiterated the close bonds between the countries. Relations between the two countries were very cordial at this time and there were no outstanding issues that called for settlement.[9]

A. C. S. Hameed, the Foreign Minister of Sri Lanka, paid an official visit to New Delhi 4-7 April 1978. Vajpayee hosted a dinner in honour of the visiting guest on 4 April 1978. His dinner speech was full of warmth and candour for Sri Lanka with which, as Vajpayee said, India shared "common commitments and aspirations and a common approach to world problem". He made a fervent appeal to redouble 'efforts to dissipate the suspicions of yesterday and to build for tomorrow new ties of confidence and trust." He was full of praise for Sri Lanka which, since the Non-aligned Summit in Colombo, had made an immensely valuable contribution in voicing the common urges and aspirations of the vast majority of human race" and hoped for continued co-operation between the two countries on this vital front.[10]

Vajpayee also re-emphasised his Government's approach to India's neighbours and to South Asia with a view to remove the suspicions, if there existed any, about India's real intentions in the region. He said that each state of the region would have to make a beginning to lay the foundation of peace in his own neighbourhood without loosing sight of world problems. He said that on the basis of shared sacrifices, India had taken" concrete steps and positive initiatives" to create a climate of peace in South Asia and added that India had succeeded in giving new momentum to the process of reconciliation, which should, in time, make South Asia truly a Zone of peace and friendship—a region free from conflict or confrontation and more than that an area of friendly and good neighbourly co-operation". He expressed the hope that" in not too distant a future the countries of South Asia could sit together and explore ideas of meaningful regional co-operation". As to India's relations with Sri Lanka he could "conceive of no possible relationship except one of friendship and good neighbourliness, based on mutual respect for each other's national identity and national interest."[11]

An atmosphere of trust and confidence had been created and in this atmosphere cordiality and shared perception existed between the two countries. It was not surprising, therefore, that at the very first round of talk the two Foreign Ministers agreed that the two neighbouring countries should work together to strengthen the non-aligned movement, transform the Indian Ocean into a Zone of Peace and strive for total and complete disarmament.[12] Hameed extended an invitation to Vajpayee to visit Sri Lanka which the latter accepted and the visit was scheduled for 29 June—1 July. However, the visit was postponed at the last minute due to the internal problems of the ruling party in India and it caused some disappointment in Colombo.[13]

The bilateral co-operation between the two countries expanded further when Sri Lankan President J. R. Jayawardene paid a state visit to New Delhi 27-30 October 1978. His visit highlighted the amity and cordiality existing between Colombo and New Delhi. He was accorded a warm welcome in New Delhi. Neelam Sanjiva Reddy, the President of India, welcomed him "as the leader of a friendly neighbouring country to which India was linked by close ties of history, culture and tradition and who was "considered close to us".[14] He said that India and Sri Lanka were in the happy situation of having a relationship that is entirely free from any bilateral problem. At a banquet given in the honour of the visiting President, Reddy emphasised the need of regional co-operation as the main answers to the problem of expanding the economic and commercial horizons of the non-aligned countries.[15]

Following his talks with Jayawardene Desai said that our dialogues were very friendly and that India and Sri Lanka had no bilateral problems. On 28th October Jayawardene addressed a press conference and replied to questions put to him on various issues. He did not give any hint that any problem existed between the two countries rather the conference created the impression that relations between the two countries were cordial and they shared a common perception on bilateral and regional co-operation and international relations.[16]

Jayawardene had very fruitful discussions covering a wide range of subjects of importance in bilateral co-operation and international relations with Reddy, Desai and other ministers concerned in a spirit of cordiality and friendship.[17] The president of Sri Lanka and the Prime Minister of India discussed various concrete possibilities for expanding the field of bilateral cooperation. It was felt that the climate was now more favourable for their development as considerable work had already been done for identifying suitable areas. It was, therefore, agreed that the India-Sri Lanka Sub-Committee on Economic Co-operation would meet more frequently, and that the working Groups would initiate action on their recommendations as early as possible. It was also agreed that the two governments would exchange delegations at the ministerial level at an early date to work out methods to increase the flow of trade and to stimulate Indian investment in joint ventures in Sri Lanka.[18]

Absence of any major bilateral problem between the two countries enabled their leaders to exchange views on bilateral co-operation in making Indian Ocean a Zone of Peace and exploring the possibility of expanding the area of economic co-operation amongst the Asian countries.[19] A daily newspaper of Ceylon very appropriately commented on 4 November 1978 that goodwill and friendship between the two countries had reached" a high point of cordiality and commonness of purpose"[20]

Morarji Desai, the Indian Prime Minister paid a return visit to Colombo 3-6 February 1979 for which invitation had already been extended during Jayawardene's visit to New Delhi. He was given a red carpet welcome in Colombo. In a spirit of warm cordiality and close friendship Desai had discussions with the President, the Prime Minister and other ministers of the Government of Sri Lanka which covered a wide range of subjects including bilateral matters and review of the regional and international situation. These talks revealed "a close identity of views" between the two countries.[21] On his return from Sri Lanka Desai informed the Lok Sabha on 2 March 1979 that the two sides agreed that there were no bilateral problems between the two countries.[22]

Desai had an opportunity to address a special session of parliament in Sri Lanka where he laid stress on the contributions made by Jayawardene to the promotion of good neighbourliness between India and Sri Lanka. He appreciated the role of Sri Lanka in world affairs, especially its contribution to world councils and in finding possible and concrete solutions to many world problems.[23] Desai in his address referred to the common democratic traditions of India and Sri Lanka and happily pointed out how attempts to mould governments into an authoritarian form was unsuccessful and short-lived and asserted that the two peoples would never "accept any but a truly democratic system". It is notable that Premdasa in his welcome address had expressed a similar sentiment when he referred to the "dark regime of mis- rule" that the people of both countries had rejected.[24] Desai repeated the theme when he told the Lok Sabha that India and Sri Lanka shared a common dedication to the democratic ways of life.[25] Desai participated in the inauguration ceremonies of the work on the Kotamale multipurpose reservoir project under the Mahaweli development scheme with which India was associated. Referring to this incident in the Lok Sabha Desai took the opportunity to reassert

India's firm intention to do whatever was possible within its resources to assist India's friends and neighbours in their growth.[26]

At the end of Desai's visit to Colombo a joint statement was issued which said that India and Sri Lanka had decided to pursue action to increase the trade between the two countries and the establishment of joint ventures in the industrial and export promotion zone in Sri Lanka. It said that during discussion on bilateral matters, there was an emphasis on economic and trade matters and closer co-operation between the two countries in cultural affairs, research and development.[27] The statement also mentioned that the two sides reviewed the implementation of Indo-Sri Lanka Agreements of 1964 on the status of persons of Indian origin in Sri Lanka. But it did not give further details on this subject. However, at a news conference, before his departure for New Delhi, Desai, in reply to question said that mutually satisfactory agreements had been reached between India and Sri Lanka on repatriation of persons of Indian origin residing in Sri Lanka.[28]

The visit of Desai to Sri Lanka perhaps represented the high watermark in the relations between the two countries. Very appropriately the visit was welcomed in both the countries as ushering in a new era in their relations.[29] The leaders had succeeded in establishing personal rapport. Mutual suspicions had melted. Trust and confidence had been created and a common approach and a shared perception in a common destiny had begun to emerge. In this atmosphere of mutual trust, confidence and goodwill the problems as they arose in the relations between the two countries were easily solved with understanding and without any bickering. But it was to be noted that the Janata Government had strove hard for creating such an atmosphere in its relations with its small neighbours.

Problem of Stateless persons

The problems of stateless persons of Indian origin in Sri Lanka had plagued Indo-Sri Lanka relations for long. A positive development took place in this connection in August 1978 which created further warmth in the relations between the two countries. The National State Assembly of Ceylon adopted a new constitution on 6 August 1978 which was to come into force on 7 September by a proclamation of the President of the

Republic. The new constitution guaranteed to the stateless persons of Indian origin numbering about half a million, fundamental rights, such as, those of freedom of speech and expression, of peaceful assembly, of association, and of freedom of religion for a period of ten years from the date of enforcement of the new constitution. It was to be noted here that these stateless persons had been discriminated against in respect of educational and employment opportunities and often denied free health facilities and subsidised food rations to which Sri Lankan nationals were entitled. New provision obviously reflected the government's hope of finding a solution to the problem of the stateless within that period. The Tamil leaders of Sri Lanka hailed the new provision not as an "ideal" or a "perfect" one, but, nevertheless, as a "great improvement" on all the contitutions that Sri Lanka so far had as it had given the "Tamils who had sweated and toiled to develop the country's economy a rightful place and a new status"[30] S, Thondaman, a member of parliament and President of Ceylon Worker's Congress said that the "10 year limitation" period was more than adequate as by then persons who were now stateless and who had been loyal and permanent residents of Sri Lanka would have required Indian or Sri Lankan nationality under the Sirimavo-Shastri Pact of 1964 and the subsequent Sirimavo-Mrs Gandhi pact of 1974. This step vastly improved the atmosphere for a cordial and warm relationship between the two countries.[31]

Trade Deficit and India's Acccommodation

In December 1978 India and Sri Lanka signed a trade agreement whereunder India agreed to provide tariff preference to Sri Lanka on such item as on cocaine, bear, gloves, torai rubber and graphite. Sri Lanka, on its part, agreed to give tariff preference to India on such items as automobiles, ancillaries, storage batteries and storage accumulations. India relaxed duties on certain items and lifted ban on some items, such as, crockery and fruit juice.[32]

Trade deficit with India had been a chronic problem of its small neighbours. Jayawardene had hinted at this problem at his press conference at New Delhi on the 28th October 1978 when he said that the Free Trade Zone 'scheme in Sri Lanka should attract Indian investors and that it would lead to a better balance of trade between the two countries.[33]

Following the signing of the agreement (December 1978), Sri Lanka's Minister for Foreign Trade Lalith Athoulath mudali was reported to have said that unless India gave the island "some special treatment in bilateral trade, it would be difficult to bridge Sri Lanka's yawning trade deficit with India.[34] He termed the agreement as an evidence of India's goodwill to improve trade relations with Sri Lanka. India's attitude of economic accommodation was described as a "magnanimous gesture".[35]

Apart from this, on 29 November 1977 an agreement signed in New Delhi between the two governments for the promotion and development of art, culture, education and sports which further strengthened relations between the two countries. The two countries agreed to undertake cultural and intellectual exchanges, reciprocal visits of representatives of educational literary and sport organisations and participation in symposia and seminars.[36] It also covered film festivals, exchange of educational, cultural and sports publications, the organisation of art exhibitions and display of archaeological findings. Scholarships were to be provided to students in one country seeking higher education in the other. The two sides agreed to examine the mutual recognition of university degrees and diplomas.[37] It was to be noted that it was for the first time that such an agreement had been signed between the two countries.

REGIME OF NATIONAL FRONT

Premiership of V. P. Singh (1 December 1989-7 November 1990)

The second non-Congress Government in India was formed under the premiership of Vishwanath Pratap Singh, with the support of Bharatiya Janata Party and took over the reigns of administration on 1 December 1989. The new government inherited a tense Indo-Sri Lankan relations. The inventionist approach adopted by the previous Government of Rajiv Gandhi resulted in the Indo-Sri Lanka Agreement of July 1987 that paved the way for interference of Indian Peace-keeping Force (IPKF) in the country and had created a very complicated situation, bristling with dangerous possibilities and unpredicatable consequences. With the change of government Sri Lankan Foreign Affairs and Defence Minister Ranjan Wijeratne hoped that the change in India would have no impact on either the Indo-Lanka Accord or the agreed time framework for IPKF withdrawal from the island country. He expressed the respect for the verdict of the people of India.[38]

The new dispensation was serious over the loss of confidence and mutual trust between Colombo and New Delhi. As such, it made initial attempts to redefine the parameters of Indian policy towards Sri Lanka. India had learned a lesson that while dealing with an independent sovereign country and that too during a destabilise situation there was a point beyond which India could not go. Yet India can not remain a silent spectator ignoring the ethnically based human rights violations quite often with support of the government. The National Front Government has viewed that the very presence of IPKF would pose a grave danger for mutual trust and confidence building from a small nation. In the circumstances there were three aspects which the National Front applied to the situation in Sri Lanka.

(i) That South Asia was a troubled region emphasising that in the context India's interest must be protected.

(ii) A Treaty of Peace and Friendship with Sri Lanka to bring the island back to India's sphere of influence and to put an end to the penetration of the international forces of subversion became an imperative need for India,

(iii) A good neighbourly relationship would make National Front comfortable at home and enable it to concentrate more on containing domestic subversive activities and justify its action in quelling it.[39]

The change of guard in New Delhi, as viewed by Colombo, was an opportune moment for seeking a turn around in New Delhi's Sri Lanka policy. A goodwill visit was paid to India by Ranjan Wijeratne, Sri Lanka's Foreign Minister and Minister of State for Defence as a head of the four member delegation who sought an immediate pull-out of the Indian troops from remaining six of the eight districts of the north-eastern Sri Lanka. The Minister was scheduled to meet V. P. Singh and was also carrying a personal message from President R. Premadasa for the new Prime Minister. The very composition of the delegation made it clear that the Sri Lankan Government attached considerable importance to the visit and would use the opportunity to put its case strongly for a quicker "de-induction of the Indian troops.[40] The delegation in course of its meeting with the new

Prime Minister hoped to have a firm commitment over the withdrawal of IPKF by 31 December 1989, as promised by the previous government but was disappointed when V. P. Singh assured the leader of the high powered delegation that the resolution of problems with Sri Lanka was the first priority of the new government and the withdrawal of the remaining Indian Peace-keeping Force personnel would be worked out between New Delhi and Colombo jointly.[41] The joint communique, issued on the occasion gave the hint that the new government would not reject Indo-Sri Lankan Agreement in the way it was expected to do and made specific mention of the mutual fulfilment of the obligations assumed by both governments. Mention is also made of the safety and security of all communities in the North-Eastern Provinces of Sri Lanka "a phrase which is one more link with the policy of the previous government.[42] However, the communique failed to satisfy the Sri Lankan side as commented by one of the members of the delegation after returning Colombo that the visit went off "very well" but had not produced the sort of unqualified commitment to the withdrawal of the IPKF that Sri Lanka would probably have wanted. Ranjan Wijeratne expressed his dissatisfaction over his talks with V. P. Singh and his Indian counterpart but pointed out the role of the Indian bureaucracy in guiding the foreign policy[43] and accused them of having stalled the withdrawal of the Indian peace-keeping forces from Sri Lanka and misleading the Indian Political leadership.[44] In fact, the visit of the delegation was not merely a gesture of prompt response to sentiments for improving ties with South Asian neighbours as expressed by the new government but for sounding out the new government on its Sri Lankan policy.[45] Within a week of the visit and after consultation with the then Tamil Nadu Chief Minister M. Karunanidhi the Prime Minister made it clear that the total withdrawal of the Indian peace-keeping force from Sri Lanka may not logistically be possible by 31 December 1989 as demanded by the island country. He also laid emphasis on the safety and security' of the Tamils in Sri Lanka.[46]

Initially, the National Front Government was charged with continuing the policy of the previous government but soon it was realised that it had different view of the problem. With all its concern for the security of the Tamils in Sri Lanka's Northern and Eastern provinces, the new government acknowledged the stern reality that the Indian peace keeping force can not do for the Sri Lankan Sinhalas but Tamils alone can do for themselves and therefore, must live in peace and social stability.[47] But the webs of confusion prevailed on the issue as Inder Kumar Gujral, the Minister for External Affairs, under new dispensation going by the reply to a parliament question stated that his government is committed to another deadline—31 March, 1990 for the withdrawal of the IPKF. New Delhi had assured President Premadasa that the Indian forces would leave Trincomalee and Jaffna districts much before the March deadline and possibly by January end.[48]

The declaration of the new deadline (March 31) for withdrawal of IPKF had surprised Colombo and in the background the second visit of Ranjan Wijeratne took place in the first week of January 1990. The frequency and speed of the visits suggested serious efforts for sorting out bilateral problems—the de-induction of the IPKF and related matters.[49] During his stay at New Delhi Wijeratne discussed with his Indian counterpart the schedule for the de-induction of the Indian peace-keeping force and related matters in the context of Sri Lanka's plea for speeding up the process. Gujral, while giving an assurance that he would personally look into the possibility of accelerating the withdrawal also expressed the desire that Sri Lanka should take care of logistical and other practical problems. However, his main concern was to impress upon the visiting minister about the new government's sincerity in sorting out its problems with Sri Lanka. In his opinion, this, and not the change in deadline by a few weeks here and there was material for a relationship of trust and confidence. At the same time Gujral clearly and emphatically expressed his concern over the ground realities in the North Eastern Province, the role of the LTTE, the likely increase in violence and its spill over to India. In course of the talk Wijeratne, on his part, was believed to have made a case for advancing the deadline to February 4, Sri Lanka's national day.[50]

The joint statement issued at the end of the visit, India and Sri Lanka agreed to make joint efforts to use their influence with the rival militant Tamil groups in the North Eastern Province and work towards a ceasefire. New Delhi had reaffirmed the commitment made in parliament to complete the withdrawal of the IPKF by 31 March 1990. Sri Lanka had pledged to ensure the safety and security of all communities in the north-eastern province. The two sides agreed to finalise a friendship treaty proposed by Sri Lanka that incorporated most of the elements of the 1987 Indo-Sri Lanka Accord and elements from the letters exchanged between New Delhi and Colombo.[51] Earlier, during the two rounds of talks between the two Foreign Ministers and in the discussions with V. P. Singh, the Indian Prime Minister, Wijeratne with his delegation was satisfied that India had no intention of creating problems for Sri Lanka.[52] The growing level of understanding between New Delhi and Colombo was welcomed by the United States of America who saw reason in India's inability to pull out the IPKF from Sri Lanka at a date earlier than March 31. A Bush Administration official had appreciated V. P. Singh's commitment to complete the withdrawal at the earliest and supported the recent concluded dialogue that brought the two neighbours back on 'conciliatory' terms.[53]

The statement as well as the visit itself found a general appreciation and both sides expressed happiness over the restoration of trust and confidence. A daily newspaper, *The patriot* commented "The Foreign Minister level talks had ended in a virtually unqualified success. The main outcome of the exercise, the one most highlighted, is an agreement on finalising the friendship treaty, proposed by Colombo in an updating or upgradation of the accord of July 1987.[54] Wijeratne, while addressing his press conference after his recent visit to New Delhi, sketched an optimistic scenario of the future of Indo-Sri Lanka relations stating that "We have to have a change of heart and bearing in mind the compulsions of both sides there must be a growing understanding of each other's problems.[55] He appeared to feel that the new government coming to power in New Delhi, a fresh chapter in Indo-Sri Lanka relations devoid of the irritants of the past few years could begin "I think the new Government is keen to establish good neighbourly relations... we in Sri Lanka must respond to this and take positive action to improve the conditions of our people", he added.[56]

However, the effects of much publicized successful visit was shortlived. In reply to the Sri Lankan treaty draft India transmitted its counter draft of the proposed friendship treaty to Colombo but the latter had opposed to sign the treaty with India before 31 March, the deadline for the withdrawal of IPKF stationed in the north and the east. A highly placed government source criticized Gujral's statement in Male that India would like the treaty signed before the end of next month (February) and opposed to linking issue of withdrawal and the signing of the friendship treaty.[57] The proposed draft treaty of friendship as put forward by New Delhi, included among other things, a suggestion that neither country should enter into or participate in the any military alliance directed against the other, that both countries should abstain from giving any assistance to a third party that engaged in an armed conflict with either of them. India had also proposed that the illegal movements of people, arms and contraband across the palk straits should be stopped. The Sri Lankan had let it be known that they are unhappy with the detailed security related clauses, and media commentators have portrayed the Indian draft as a "devious way" of reintroducing parts of the Indo-Sri Lanka Agreement which Sri-Lanka found unacceptable.[58] Although a comparison of the Indian and Sri Lankan draft showed that New Delhi's draft was a detailed document which seeks to put relations between the two countries on a firm footing and ensure that neither country would pose a threat to the other while the Sri Lankan draft was a shorter, more general document.[59]

Further, the two-day negotiations between Sri Lankan Foreign Secretary Bernard Tilakratne and his Indian counterpart S. K. Singh 'failed to make much headway and differences between the two persisted pertaining to the manner of the use of the Trincomalee Oil Farm, implementation of the Indo-Sri Lanka accord and India's proposal to have a joint consultative mechanism in the event of hostilities involving either country.[60] Colombo reacted sharply in the same month when New Delhi warned Sri Lanka that it would take a "very serious view" if the island government failed to safeguard the safety and security of the Tamils. Ranjan Wijeratne, Sri Lankan Foreign Minister, declared that his country would not sign a friendship treaty with India "under duress or coercion". He explained that Sri Lanka would refuse to do so until the complete pull-out, because they might evoke suspicion among the people that New Delhi had succeeded in arm twisting.[61] He said that there should be no room for suspicion on this count. The friendship treaty would be signed by two sovereign nations.[62]

A week ahead of the deadline (31 March), the last of Indian Peace-keeping Force left Sri Lanka ending a historic two and-a-half year long chapter in relations between the two countries. Soon after coming to power V. P. Singh on his part, fielded Karunanidhi to hold talks with the squabbling Sri Lankan Tamil militant groups. The Chief Minister, according to informed sources, "assured" the PM that he would try to bring all these groups together so that the IPKF could be withdrawn without the fear of a refugee backlash for. India.[63] No doubt, the present government can claim to have improved relation with Sri Lanka after they had suffered under the Rajiv Gandhi Government. The irony of that government's policy' was that India got deeply involved in the complex international contradictions of Sri Lankan politics. The fiasco of the policy of active intervention was writ large as our armed forces were virtually engaged in pulling president Jayawardene's chestnuts out of the fire.[64] Hardly ten hours after the IPKF left Sri Lanka, Premadasa, the President of Sri Lanka, thanked India profoundly for withdrawing its troops completely and said, "We were able to send home a mighty army not by war but by consultation."[65] He did not hesitate in praising New Delhi publicly and while addressing the Ceylon Workers' Congress referred to the Indian Prime Minister and said. "The premier has won our love and I am please to announce that his government has withdrawn its troops from the country without attaching any condition." "I thank the Government and people of India for respecting our sovereignty."[66] The Indian action was also hailed by the USA and state spokesman department Margaret Tutweiler, commenting on the withdrawal said that his country welcomed the departure of the Indian forces from Sri Lanka and that "it makes a step on that troubled country's road to normalcy".[67] With the peaceful withdrawal of IPKF from Sri Lanka the mission of Lakhan Lal Mehrotra, India's High Commissioner had been completed as the dispatch was made with single brief—to normalise relations with Sri Lanka. He reiterated the three pillars of India's policy' on Sri Lanka—commitment to the unity and territorial integrity of Sri Lanka, an equal commitment to the rights and the well being of Tamil community as ethnic harmony in this country depend on this factor and lastly the progress and stability of Sri Lanka and all its people. "It is in our interest to see Sri Lanka as a strong and stable society. .. since the lack of stability has a tendency to spill over and affect us and involve us in a way would rather not be involved."[68]

In the post-withdrawal period New Delhi maintained utmost precaution in its policy towards Sri Lanka. A tricky situation arose with the resumption of violence in the Tamil dominated regions of Sri Lanka in

June 1990. In the circumstances India could not afford to sit back and merely let that violence spread, on the other it would not afford to get involved in the same manner that the previous government did.[69] In response to Sri Lanka's request for moral support the Indian Prime Minister declared that Tamil rebels would be banished from Indian soil. At the sametime, perhaps with a view to pacify the Tamils, while talking to newsmen on his return from Maldives and earlier at Male before embarking he said with a perceptible hardening of attitude and it had been conveyed to the Sri Lankan Government that the human aspect of the ongoing conflict between the Liberation Tigers of Tamil Eelam and the security forces had to be taken note of.[70] Further in an interview in Madras he said, "while we stand for the sovereignty and integrity of all our neighbours, we rightfully do have concern for the lives of people of Indian origin, their safety, security and their democratic aspirations.[71]

It was in that kind of situation, two-day visit of Sri Lankan Foreign Secretary Bernard Tilakratne with a message from President R. Premadasa took place by the end of June 1990. The main purpose of Tilakratne's visit was to brief the Indian Government on the latest developments in Sri Lanka and the events leading to the flare-up. He also conveyed Colombo's desire to see that India's concern over the present situation did not affect its non-involvement policy. But Sri Lanka was worried about support to the militants from Tamil Nadu and wanted the present conflict to be seen as a war against terrorism and not Tamils. In fact this was essentially a probing mission. The Sri Lankan Government wanted to clear about India's stand on the current conflict in the North-East province.[72] No new policy pronouncement was made but I. K. Gujral, India's Minister for External Affairs repeated Indian policy while delivering a lecture on "Indian Foreign Policy-Reflections on Future", organised by the Institute of Asian Studies at the Administrative Staff College, Hyderabad and said, "Our options are to stay away from their internal affairs but tell them to settle the issue through a dialogue in the interests of the people of Sri Lanka".[73] In course of the visit he met his Indian counterpart Muchkund Dubey, Foreign Minister I. K. Gujral and both sides had reciprocated their sentiments of political goodwill while appreciating each other's concerns arising out of the latest flare up between Sri Lankan security forces and the Liberation Tigers of Tamil Eelam. The visiting Foreign Secretary' was satisfied with the outcome of the visit and disclosed that I. K. Gujral, "gave us a categorical assurance that India will not interfere in Sri Lanka's affairs".[74] Almost similar to the views of National Front's Government L. K. Advani, President of the BJP said in London that the diplomatic pressure should be exercised on Sri Lanka to end its war against the Tamils and India should also not allow any of its part to become a hinterland for terrorists.[75]

India's concern for the safety and security of Tamils residing in North- East Province of Sri Lanka continued and the matter was raised when a modest sized parliamentary delegation led by speaker M. H. Mohammed arrived New Delhi to brief the Indian political leaders and public opinion on the Sri Lankan Government's position in the current war with LTTE. Muchkund Dubey, India's Foreign Secretary reiterated his country's position and concern to Bradman Weerakoon, International Relations Adviser to Premadasa and the Sri Lankan High Commissioner Dr. S. Kalpage, when the two called on him.[76] The spokesman said that India was concerned over a "'possible involvement of outside powers in the current conflict in Sri Lanka" and over "large scale killings of innocent civilians" as well as the consequent increase in the number of refugees pouring into India.[77] At the juncture, New Delhi seemed impatient to help Sri Lankan victims on humanitarian ground and Gujral was bold enough to assure the Consultative Committee of Parliament on External Affairs that India "Will do everything possible and go out of the way to render humanitarian assistance to those suffering in the current warlike situation in Sri Lanka.[78] V. P. Singh, the Indian Prime Minister himself appealed to end the hostilities in Sri Lanka.[79]

Problem of Tamils

Still, peace remained a distant dream in Sri Lanka. The problem took a turn after 30 July 1987—the day, the then Indian Prime Minister Rajiv Gandhi and Sri Lankan President J. R. Jayawardene signed the historic Indo-Sri Lanka Accord which outlined solution to the vexed ethnic conflict within the framework of United Sri Lanka. The 1987 accord ran into trouble within months after the Liberation Tigers of Tamil Eelam (LTTE) took up arms against the Indian Peace-keeping Force (IPKF) which came to the island nation as part of the agreement. The treaty further witnessed a rough weather when the then Premadasa Government, after coming to an understanding with the LTTE, asked the IPKF to leave the country thereby virtually burying the agreement. However, the honeymoon between the LTTE and the Sri Lankan government did not last long as the Tamil Tigers guerillas renewed their armed struggle to achieve Eelam (separate country for Tamil).

Having an understanding with the LTTE on the withdrawal of IPKF, Colombo began to insist New Delhi for its implementation. Apart from huge wastage of resources, both material and human that the mishandling of the Sri Lanka's situation involved, it so brought no measure of goodwill between the two countries. It was, therefore, no mean accomplishment for the National Front Government to have pulled back Indian forces from the island in an effort to create the basis for restoring mutual confidence between Colombo and New Delhi.[80] Even before the coming of new dispensation India reached an understanding with Sri Lanka and 31 December 1989 was fixed as the deadline. In the meantime, the change of guard took place in India and in place of Rajiv Gandhi V. P. Singh leader of the National Front, with the support of BJP became the new Prime Minister of India on 1 December 1989. With the change of regime Colombo hoped that it would have no impact on the Indo-Sri Lanka accord and particularly on the agreed time framework for IPKF withdrawal from the island country.

Keeping in view mainly the withdrawal issue, within a week of the formation of new government in New Delhi, a high powered delegation under the leadership of Ranjan Wijeratne, Sri Lankan Foreign Minister and Minister of State for Defence, visited India and met with the new Prime Minister V. P. Singh who assured the delegation that the schedule for withdrawal of the remaining Indian Peace-keeping Force personnel worked out between the two governments jointly. He also assured the delegation that resolution of problem with Sri Lanka was the first priority of the new government. The visit of Sri Lankan delegation was termed as "good" but Colombo side was not satisfied with the development as he failed to have a commitment of the new regime on the withdrawal issue. Ranjan Wijeratne criticized the role played by the Indian bureaucrats for misleading the Indian Political leadership. As a result the Indian Peace-keeping Force and the Sri Lankan army had come dangerously close to an open confrontation for the first time as the relations between the two neighbours pass through another bad patch.[81]

In this background, the second visit of Ranjan Wijeratne took place in the first week of January 1990 and discussed the problem of de-induction of Indian Peace-keeping Forces with the Indian leaders including Prime Minister and the Minister for External Affairs. Earlier V. P. Singh had announced that the total withdrawal of IPKF was not possible by 31 December, and further it became crystal clear when Inder Kumar Gujral, India's Minister for External Affairs declared that his government was committed to another deadline—31 March 1990. During his second visit to New Delhi Wijeratne was assured that India would abide by the deadline although, Colombo on its part, wanted a firm date and probably February 4—Sri Lanka's national day. However the joint statement issued on the eve of the visit stated that Indian Foreign Minister had reaffirmed the commitment made in parliament to complete the withdrawal of the IPKF by 31 March. At the sametime Sri Lanka had pledged to ensure the safety and security of all communities in the north-eastern province.[82]

A happy moment came for Indo-Sri Lankan relations and the last IPKF left the island about a week ahead the deadline. Indian Prime Minister and Minister for External Affairs were thanked for this noble work. In a sense the removal of a major 'irritant' in Indo-Sri Lankan relations was the first real success that the Prime Minister could show in his relentless battle against a plethora of "inherited problems in the spheres of both foreign and domestic policies.[83] R. Premadasa, Sri Lanka's President also praised profoundly for withdrawing the Indian troops whereas the United States and its Congress had applauded the V. P. Singh Government's fufilment of commitment on the complete pull out of the IPKF from Sri Lanka. However, the things might take ugly turn as predicted by one analyst who cautioned Sri Lanka and suggested. "Premadasa should guard himself against any excessive euphoria on having succeeded in sending the IPKF packing. For him the troubles are just starting, particularly since the LTTE has given nothing away, not even the arms it has collected. It has filled the military vacuum that the IPKF has left and will soon fill the political vacuum left by the collapse of the EPRLF government and the demoralised Tamil groups. It is possible that it will abide by its time for the Eelam and in the meantime accept the limited political autonomy that has been granted to it " Tamil province.[84] The understanding between the LTTE and Sri Lankan government was short-lived and fresh violence erupted in the Tamil dominated regions of Sri Lanka. In the wake of this tricky situation, Sri Lanka's Foreign Secretary Bernard Tilakratne came to New Delhi mainly to brief the Indian government on the latest developments in Sri Lanka. In course of the visit and even later both Indian Prime Minister and the Minister for External Affairs made it clear that Tamil rebels would not be allowed to operate from Indian soil but at the sametime cautioned the visiting guest about the safety and security of Tamils in Sri Lanka. New Delhi's policy of non-involvement in the internal affairs was hailed by Colombo.[85]

Chandra Shekhar
(10 November 1990-21 June 1991)

In place of V. P. Singh, Chandra Shekhar became the new Prime Minister of India in November 1990. The change of regime in India did not make any change in New Delhi's policy towards Sri Lanka, but as its predecessor, the new dispensation continued to express its concern about the enormous civilian sufferings and casualties and the refugees influx, resulting from hostilities since June last year. The spokesman also hoped that all efforts would be exerted in this direction and lead to meaningful and sustained negotiations with the participation of all concerned parties. We believe that only a negotiated political settlement within the framework of the unity and territorial integrity of Sri Lanka which takes into account legitimate Tamil demands could lead to a durable and lasting solution.[86] However, the policy of non-interference would please the Sri Lankan Government but had disappointed many Tamils who feel that there could be no solution to the Tamil problem unless India takes an active role. As the prospect for peace has receded, even Tamils who were critical of India's role and of the IPKF had been suggesting that a fresh Indian initiative was necessary.[87]

Under the new dispensation the first visit undertaken by India was of V C. Shukla, the new Minister for External Affairs 28-31 January 1991. Speaking to journalists on his arrival the Indian Minister said that his visit would help further the existing friendly relations between the two countries. Even earlier the Indian side had made it clear that New Delhi was going to treat the war in the North and East as Sri Lanka's internal affair and the External Affairs Minister V. C. Shukla was not going to suggest any mediatory role for India or put pressure on the Sri Lankan Government to stop the fighting.[88] The first round of official talks between India and Sri Lanka went of extremely well in an atmosphere that was free from the suspicion and animosity that had characterised relations between the two countries. Shukla's meeting with his Sri Lankan counterpart, Harold Herat, lasted for three and half hours and talks were held from the Gulf crisis to the Indo-Sri Lankan agreement and the problems of Sri Lankan refugees in Tamil Nadu.[89] During the visit the Indian Foreign Minister suggested Sri Lanka's President R. Premadasa that the time was right for Sri Lanka to take a "bold initiative" to restart the peace process. Shukla also said that the success of peace process would depend on the extent to which the legitimate aspirations of the Tamils were satisfied. On the other, one of the main concerns of Sri Lanka had been to emphasise that the relations between the two countries should be based on equality and mutual respect for each others sovereignty.[90]

At the end of the visit, a joint press statement was issued by the Government of Sri Lanka and the Government of India on 31 January 1991, in which India appreciated the measures taken by the Sri Lankan Government to find a political solution to the problem. Shukla reiterated India's belief that the political framework created by Sri Lanka following the Indo-Sri Lanka agreement of 1987 provided a viable basis for a "reasonable and enduring settlement".[91] The two ministers expressed their concern that terrorist and separatist activities were serious threats to peace, security and development in their respective countries. They agreed to co-ordinate necessary measures in the context of the convention on suppression of terrorism.[92] Apart from political matters the two ministers discussed bilateral trade and economic relations. They agreed that efforts should be directed at stimulating a more balanced growth through the liberalisation of barriers affecting certain products. As stated in the statement the two ministers decided to take steps for the establishment of an Indo-Sri Lanka Joint Commission chaired by the respective Foreign Ministers on an alternative basis. The joint commission would initially incorporate two sub-committees at the level of secretaries devoted respectively to trade finance and investment and to social, cultural and educational matters.[93] Shukla's visit was a success to the extent that it had broken the ice, it was a welcome development. It should be followed up with more detailed discussions on how to put relations on an even keel permanently and specifically on how to bring the ethnic conflict to an early end.[94]

Despite New Delhi's repeated declaration that it would not interfere in the internal affairs of the island country recent visit of India's Foreign Minister V. C. Shukla was to assuage Tamil public opinion that India was not distancing itself from the Sri Lankan problem and that India was concerned about the impact of the war on the civilian population and the hardships caused to refugees and displaced persons. For instance, New Delhi expressed happiness on 14 March 1991 when asked to comment on the Sri Lankan Government's decision not to go ahead with the evacuation of the Madhu Church Area. The statement said, "If the reports that the Sri Lankan Government has decided to stop the evacuation operation are correct, we are happy because this would avoid unnecessary suffering and hardships to large segments of the population.[95]

REGIME OF UNITED FRONT

Premiership of H. D. Deve Gowda (1 June 1996—21 April 1997)

In line, the third non-Congress government was formed by the United Front (an alliance of thirteen Political parties) under the leadership of H. D. Deve Gowda who took the oath of office on 1 June 1996. Like his predecessors the new Prime Minister inherited a tense Indo-Sri Lanka relations mainly owing to the sufferings of the Tamils in North-East Province. Since I. K. Gujral became the Foreign Minister under H.D. Deve Gowda's dispensation, India had improved its relations with all the South Asian countries and was on the verge of taking a new turn in bilateral and multilateral ties in the region. The change of regime in New Delhi was hailed by Sri Lanka and its Foreign Minister Lakshman Kadirgamar came to India on 20 June 1996. During his two-day visit Kadirgamar met the External Affairs Minister on 20 June and hold discussions on issues of mutual interest. He would also call on the Prime Minister, Minister of Industry, Finance Minister and the Leader of Opposition.[96]

The visiting Foreign Minister described his trip to India as one of goodwill and conveyed Sri Lanka's interest in maintaining very close and cordial relations with India. He handed over a letter from the President of

Sri Lanka congratulating Gujral on his assumption of office and expressed the hope that there would be further enhancement of the close relations between the two countries. Lakshman's one hour meeting with External Affairs Minister I. K. Gujral aimed to convey the message of continued stability and understanding in the bilateral field. During discussion on specifics, Gujral responded favourably to Kadirgamar's plea for India's help in the reconstruction of the war ravaged areas in Sri Lanka. India, Gujral said, would contribute in its humble way. The Indian side accepted the Sri Lankan suggestion for convening the next meeting of the joint commission in Colombo.[97] While expressing satisfaction at the development of economic and commercial relations between the two countries, both Foreign Ministers agreed that ties could be strengthened and diversified. They also agreed on the need for taking steps to resolve problems faced by the fishermen of the two countries and discussed matters relating to SAARC and other matters of bilateral and regional interest.[98] India's Industry Minister Murasoli Maran held discussions with Kadirgamar who called on him at his office. During the 40-minute meeting, matters of mutual interests were discussed."[99]

The new National Front Government of H. D. Deve Gowda, in its first meeting held on 13 June 1996 decided to extend the ban on LTTE for two more years. The ban was first imposed in May 1992, a year after Rajiv Gandhi's assassination under the Unlawful Activities (prevention) Act, 1967, under which the period of ban lasts two years. The decision was significant in that DMK, being a member of the United Front ministry, was a party to the decision. Over the past few years, DMK was alleged to have links with the Liberation Tigers of Tamil Eelam, which was accused of having murdered former Prime Minister Rajiv Gandhi.[100] However, India's concern for the safety and security of Sri Lankan Tamils continued, as in the earlier regimes, and in October 1996, a total of 1750 tonnes of parboiled rice, valued Rs. 2 crore, was being dispatched by the government as food aid for relief operations in the Jaffna peninsula. India promised to help the Sri Lankan Government during a visit of Foreign Minister Lakshman Kadirgamar to New Delhi in June, and the first consignment of food aid arrived in Colombo port. The rice was to be sent in three instalments, to Colombo from the Madras port. Colombo would then decide how to use the rice, being sent as grant. Apart from the

Indian assistance, a $ 274-million rehabilitation plan for the Jaffna peninsula had been announced by Colombo for which it had been seeking the assistance of donor nations.[101]

In the field of bilateral trade, the Premiership of H. D. Deve Gowda registered a growth of 52 per cent during January 1996-97. This was clear from background paper prepared for the fifth meeting of the Indo-Sri Lankan Joint Business Council meeting held in Colombo. The meeting has been jointly organised by the Federation of Indian Chambers of Commerce and Industry (FICCI) and the Associated Chambers of Commerce and Industry of India. The paper added that India had become the largest exporter to the island nation for the first time in 1996, replacing Japan. It further pointed out that India's exports to Sri Lanka had declined from $ 43.5 million during 1995-96 to $ 41.2 million during January to December 1996-97. India's share in Sri Lanka's imports, which was no more than 4.5 per cent in 1989, increased to over 10 per cent during 1994-1995, ranking India in the second place to Japan.[102]

Inder Kumar Gujral
(21 April 1997-19 March 1998)

In place of H. D. Deve Gowda, I. K. Gujral became the new Prime Minister of India and took oath of the office on 21 April 1997. The change of guard in New Delhi did not witness any change in India's Sri Lanka policy. Like the predecessors, Gujral expressed his government's concern for the Tamils in Sri Lanka but ruled out any possibility or intention of getting involved in the internal affairs of the island country. In reply to a short notice question in the Rajya Sabha on the killings of Indian fisherman by Sri Lankan navy the Prime Minister said that India was working out a policy under which particular waters could be utilised by Indian fisherman for the purposes of fishing and trade. In a obvious reference to the IPKF operations in the island nation about a decade back he observed, "We have done it once and burnt our fingers, we do not want to get involved again"[103] Colombo appreciated the Indian points of view and perhaps, as a gesture of goodwill, Sri Lankan President. Chandrika Kumaratunga urged India to lead the "South's" efforts to "forge a just and equitable new order in the prevailing uni-polar world" while paying glowing tribute to India on its Golden Jubilee of Independence. On another occasion 'she spoke high about India's influence and recognised India as undisputed regional power in South Asia in an address to a special commemorative ceremony organised by the Indian High Commission in Colombo.

For the solution of ethnic problems in Sri Lanka, President Chandrika Kumaratunga offered a "peace package which provided for devolution of power to the units. It simply referred to the merger of the Tamil majority northern and eastern provinces. Despite the other nagging worries for the Sinhala parties, there was a general consensus in the country that devolution of power to the provinces was a must for a solution of the ethnic problem. On the other, the emotive issue of a separate homeland for Sri Lankan Tamils for which the Liberation Tigers of Tamil Eelam have wagged a bloody armed insurrection for the last 14 years, seemed a distant dream. Although LTTE is still fighting, but the rest of the militant Tamil groups have now laid down arms and joined the democratic mainstream. For the majority of Tamils now living in the island, an independent homeland is no longer the point. All that they want is a measure of self rule in the Tamil majority area within Sri Lanka.[104] However, the Indian origin Tamils in Sri Lanka feel that they are being sidelined and ignored by the people's Alliance (PA) Government of Chandrika Kumaratunga. S. Thondaman, Chief of the Ceylon Workers Congress (CWC), in a letter to the secretary of the ruling People's Alliance had bitterly complained that the Government's devolution proposals have no meaning for the community. CWC charged that neither the Government nor the devolution proposal have addressed the basic and pressing problems of the community. The letter dated 25 July also drew attention to the fact that the cabinet had gone back on its decision to increase the development cess on every kilo of tea by 50 cents. The money accruing from the increased cess was to go into the fund for plantation workers' welfare. In this context, the Government's devolution proposals had "absolutely no meaning" for the Indian Tamils, Thondaman declared.[105]

Sri Lanka's main political party in opposition, United National Party had, on several occasions, criticized President Kumaratunga's devolution of power to the units and suggested to talk with the LTTE before the finalisation of the scheme, Ranil Wickremesinghe in course of the talks with foreign correspondents favoured a new treaty with India to encompass a wide range of mutual interests specially the economic. "Sri

Lanka had been having a close and multifarious relationship with New Delhi for over 2,000 years", he said stressing the need for a comprehensive treaty.[106] Sensing the mood of opposition parties who were unwilling to support her radical constitutional proposals in Parliament, Kumaratunga declared that she would go in for a referendum on the question. In September 1997 the Sri Lankan cabinet decided to hold a referendum in the Trincomalee and Batticaloa districts of the Eastern Province on the question of the merger of the northern and eastern provinces to form a single North East Tamil Province. However the talks with the LTTE necessitated with the devastating bomb blast by the organisation on 15th October 1997. The Government in Colombo felt that the talks should be held with LTTE before finalising the devolution package. Despite the continued stalemate in regard to her devolution proposals, the Tamil minority in Sri Lanka, continued to pin its hopes for peace, security and an honourable settlement of its problem on Chandrika Kumaratunga because, "She is the first Chief Executive of this country to have said openly that injustice has been done to the Tamils in the last 50 years, and that devolution is the only answer to the problem.

The devastating bomb blasts, made by the LTTE in the middle of October 1997, was followed by the US ban on the organisation. Recently the United States has released a list of 30 organisations across the world, including the LTTE, which would from now be considered "terrorist" members of such organisations, would not be able to enter the US or collect funds there. Contributing to such organisations would also be a crime. Colombo had welcomed the US decision to ban LTTE and a foreign office spokesman said, "It is a victory for Sri Lanka's foreign policy and a testimony of the strong and healthy bilateral relationship that exists between Sri Lanka and the United States". Cornered by the US ban on it, the LTTE had assumed a defiant and belligerent posture. Its international spokesman, Anton Rajah, has told newspersons that the Tigers would continue to wage war against the Sri Lankan State. But the US too, by the time had started training Sri Lankan soldiers battling Tamil Tigers guerillas who have been declared "terrorists" by Washington.

As the solution of the Tamil problems in Sri Lanka was not in sight and the things were getting bad to worse India's Samata Party leader George Fernandes, while addressing a press conference, suggested that

India should use its clout with "major powers" to bring the Sinhalese government and Tamils into the negotiating table. This was stated in a convention organised by Samata Party in the International Convention for Solidarity with the Eelam Tamils of Sri Lanka that the Tamils in Sri Lanka have been suffering from the most inhuman violations of their human rights. In the circumstances, it was all the more necessary for India to extend their solidarity and support to the beleaguered Tamils who are in danger of being made the victims of India's internal politics.[107] The convention at its end adopted a resolution urging India to shed the "Gujral Doctrine" and come forward to play its "rightful" mediatory role in solving Sri Lanka's festering ethnic conflict.

Apart from this, the present dispensation in Sri Lanka seemed, sympathetic to the Tamils and its peace proposals, in order to bring the LTTE to the negotiating table were severally criticized. The National Joint Committee of Sinhala organisations—a body constituted to protect majority Sinhala interests against encroachments by the Tamils and other minorities had charged that the proposals were meant to "deceive the majority Sinhalas and sell the country to the Eelamists".[108] However, the moderate Tamil Party TULF, had expressed deep disappointment over the UNP's second list of constitutional proposals submitted to the chairman of the Parliamentary Select Committee M. Sivasithamparam. President of the Party complained that the central list had everything leaving only minor subjects to the provinces. "It has nothing in it for the Tamils". General elections to the Lok Sabha were held in March 1998 and a new regime took over the reign of administration in New Delhi on 19th of March 1998.

REGIME OF NATIONAL DEMOCRATIC ALLIANCE

Premiership of Atal Bihari Vajpayee
(19 March 1998-12 October 1999)

The change of guard in New Delhi did not witness any basic change in India's Sri Lanka policy. Except the problem of Tamils there was no contentious issue between the two countries. In a significant move, India, on account of developments in its relations with Pakistan and keeping in view the security considerations, exploded nuclear devices on 11 and 13 May, 1998. Countries of the world in general and world powers in particular condemned New Delhi's action that quickly followed the severe economic sanctions imposed on India. In this hour of dire need, even being a signatory of the Comprehensive Test Ban Treaty (CTBT), Sri Lanka backed India and denounced sanctions. Lakshman Kadirgamar, the Foreign Minister of Sri Lanka, said in a statement at Colombo, " We are not great believers in sanctions. Sanctions must be looked at in a broader context. Sanctions also imply judgement from a moral high ground. In the present world context, very few countries can take a moral high ground on such issues." He even did not question India's claim to be a member of the nuclear club." We cannot be against any country trying to become a member of the nuclear club. We want that there should be no nuclear club at all. We are for global disarmament."[109] However, a Sri Lanka paper, *The Sunday Leader*, termed New Delhi explosions as Russian bomb under an Indian mask and cautioned on Indian interference in Sri Lanka in future. The paper in its sharp editorial referred to the dropping of food parcels (1987) and described the week as the Black Week for Asia" and equated A. B. Vajpayee with Machiavelli. It also came down heavily on the Sri Lankan Foreign Minister for becoming New Delhi's" lap dog". But despite the expressions of deep understanding of India's security compulsions by the Sri Lankan Foreign Minister, the state-owned *The Sunday Observer* noted that the bombs were an attempt to inject "a massive dose of old style patriotism in the veins of the Indian polity" as a remedy for the ills of a "fragile BJP Government assailed by problems practically every day". After all, this healthy development in Indo-Sri Lankan relations did not suit the US interests in the region. The United States had asked the Sri Lankan Government to explain why it was not against any country trying to become a member of the nuclear club and that it was not questioning India's right to test nuclear bombs. Anne Barbaro, a spokesperson of the US embassy said, "We were very surprised by the statement and wanted to know the background to it"[110]

Sri Lanka's timely backing came as a great relief for New Delhi and in response, India made it clear that it would not support LTTE or terrorism of any kind. Sushma Swaraj, India's Minister for Communication had an opportunity'to attend the SAARC Communication Ministers meeting in May 1998 who declared, "Our government will never support the LTTE . I unequivocally state that we will not support any kind of terrorism under any circumstances. We are committed to a policy of not promoting terrorism, any where. She said that President Chandrika Kumaratunga was doing her best to solve the ethnic question. "We wish her well". But Sri Lanka's Foreign Minister, perhaps, as a part of country's strategy paid a visit to China and Beijing's Premier Zhu Rougji, during the visit said that it is a set policy of the Chinese government to develop bilateral friendship and cooperation on the basis of the five principles of peaceful co-existence. The two Foreign Ministers during their meeting discussed India's nuclear weapons programme and felt equally that more pressure should be brought to bear on India to get it to abandon its nuclear weapons development programme and join the Non-Proliferation Treaty and Comprehensive Test Ban Treaty. Beijing made acquainted the visiting Foreign Minister of China's strong views on India's nuclear tests on May 11 and 13 and told that India's actions would have grave consequences in the regional and international arena. The Chinese side sought Sri Lanka's help to smoothen the ruffled feathers in the larger interest of peace and stability in the Asian region. Sri Lanka, according to a Foreign Ministry Press release at Colombo, has accepted China's call to help settle the ongoing differences with India over the nuclear issue.

India and Sri Lanka witnessed the development of mutual understanding and it strengthened further when Colombo successfully organised SAARC Summit at the end of July 1998. As a gesture of goodwill and to resolve the ethnic issue Sri Lankan President Chandrika Kumaratunga, in an exclusive interview to PTI, expressed willingness to accept a third party facilitator to negotiate with the LTTE provided the rebel organisation agreed to give up the demand for a separate Eelam (State). She also referred to her constitutional reforms package containing devolution proposals for minority Tamils which, due to reluctance of the opposition UNP, got struck in the Parliament and failed to get two-thirds majority. But, at the same time the President reiterated her determination to find devious means of getting round strict constitutional provisions without being illegal or undemocratic. Above all, Chandrika Kumaratunga's willingness to allow a third party facilitator to start negotiations with the Tamil Tigers is a pointer to the flexibility, though it would not make the job any easier for whoever was persuaded to take up this onerous task. Any such initiative would have to be handled delicately. Getting the Tamil

Tigers to openly repudiate their demand for an independent Eelam is a major hurdle to cross. In case Colombo chooses not to insist on that as a pre-condition, as it had on earlier occasions, an initiative of that nature would have a better chance of getting off the ground. But until that happens, the Sri Lankan President should try harder to get the devolution package out of the dilatory procedural wrangles and put it on the firm ground for implementation.

At the end of December 1998, Chandrika Kumaratunga, the President of Sri Lanka came to New Delhi on a three-day state visit. The occasion was not only major turning point in bilateral relations but also, proved significant for South Asia as a whole on account of the free trade arrangement initiatives. The visiting President on 29th December reiterated her government's determination to carry the political reforms package for a political solution of the ethnic conflict. At New Delhi she met many leaders of the ruling political party and Sonia Gandhi, the Congress President. About the talk with her she disclosed that it was very good and said that they had discussed the problems the two countries faced. In course of the visit Kumaratunga blamed the main opposition party in the Sri Lankan Parliament, the United National Party, for it had refused to facilitate its package through a constitutional amendment requiring a two-thirds majority support. In fact, India had distanced itself from the Tamil cause, long ago, right from after Rajiv Gandhi's assassination in 1991. Since Rajiv Gandhi's death, there have been many Indian Prime Ministers from various parties, Chandra Shekhar, V. P. Singh, H.D. Deve Gowda, I.K. Gujral and now Atal Bihari Vajpayee, but India's policy of keeping off the Tamil question and cultivating the Sri Lankan government has continued. The Sri Lankan Tamils generally, and the pro-LTTE elements in particular, were sure that with the BJP assuming office in New Delhi in alliance with pro-LTTE parties, there would be a change. It was also said that the BJP and its allies did not have any attachment for Rajiv Gandhi and moreover it was a Hindu Party, which has supported the Tamil "Hindu" cause and had opposed the Sinhala-Buddhist cause of the Sri Lankan government in past. But all these theories proved to be groundless and none has been able to change or influence the Vajpayee government's policy on Sri Lanka. Again during the current visit when both the Prime Ministers held extensive discussions on the issues mounting international pressure on Colombo from some western nations and the rebel outfit to opt for third party mediation to sort out the differences, India had extended full support to Sri Lanka in rejecting LTTE supremo V. Prabhakaran's demand for third party mediation to resolve the country's decade-old ethnic problem. Vajpayee appreciated the Lankan government's approach that a third party "facilitator" not a "mediator" could arrange a platform for talks between the government and the LTTE.

However, the most important achievement of the visit was the signing of a trade pact between the two countries. As per the pact signed by India's Prime Minister Atal Bihari Vajpayee and the Sri Lankan President Chandrika Kumaratunga, India agreed to completely eliminate tariff on about 1,000 items in about three years. The list of such items would be finalised within sixty days. The agreement was hailed as a "path-breaking step" by Jaswant Singh, India's Minister for External Affairs, and as a landmark in the "already excellent relations" between the two countries by his Sri Lankan counterpart Lakshman Kadirgamar. The relations between the two had strengthened considerably was also evident from Indian President K. R. Narayanan's speech given in a banquet in honour of the visiting dignitary that Indians were very conscious of the challenges that Sri Lankans continued to face as they strove to live together in peace and harmony in a pluralistic society.

Regional Co-operation

By the time Atal Bihari Vajpayee became the Prime Minister of India, regional co-operation continued to be the crying need of the situation prevailing in and around India. The Congress Government that was in power for the larger part in past, was primarily concerned with economic liberalisation policies and impinged on the conduct of foreign policy in several ways. This regime's first three-year's preoccupation resulted in New Delhi being overly accommodative of Washington in the matter of a host of foreign policy issues. There were attempts to compromise India's position on strategic issues. All signs were that India was in the process of staging a historical retreat from the activist foreign policy that had own in the admiration of the developing world. The "Gujral doctrine" which encapsulated the United Front's neighbourhood policy, had already brought rich dividends to India as well as to countries in the neighbourhood. Its objective was to promote all-round economic and social development with justice and equity. The accelerated development of every country in the subcontinent was a key goal of the Gujral doctrine.[111] The first thing to note about it was that it had given a good deal of thought, rooted in concrete experience. This meant there is continuity in the sense of returning Indian foreign policy to an independent and upstanding orientation as well as a significant measure of new thinking. The exercise seemed reasonably well aligned with present political and coalition government realities in India and also with the emerging realities in the neighbourhood and the world at large.[112]

Vajpayee after becoming the Prime Minister of India followed his predecessor's foreign policy and reiterated Government's determination accordingly. Under the new dispensation the SAARC Communication Ministers meeting was organised in Colombo in May 1998 and was attended by Sushma Swaraj, India's Minister of Communications. The meeting, in principle, agreed to bring down the telecom tariffs between the SAARC countries. The host Minister Mangala Samaraweera said after the conclusion of the meeting that SAARC had also decided to relax exchange regulations to enable cellular roaming, relax rules for importing communications equipment, and to take a common stand in international telecom fora. At the meeting India's Minister impressed upon the other SAARC countries that it had technology appropriate to the conditions in the region. In her speech she referred to C-DOT that had developed telephone exchanges for rural areas which could do away with air-conditioning. The CORE DECT technology to improve route searching developed by the Indian Institute of Technology (IIT) was now being tested in several exchanges in Madras. India also took the opportunity to offer training facilities in telecom to the SAARC countries. During the stay Swaraj met President Kumaratunga, Leader of the Opposition Ranil Wickremesinghe and two leaders of the Sri Lanka Muslim Congress. M. H. M. Ashraff and Hisbullah.[113]

At the end of July 1998, the tenth summit of the South Asian Association for Regional Co-operation was held in Colombo. The meeting expected to be hot because it was being organised after the nuclear explosion by India and Pakistan and the two prime Ministers were to meet there. While, there had been some progress in recent years in stepping up trade between the SAARC countries, the investment potential remained virtually untapped. There had been no institutional framework by way of regional or bilateral investment agreements. Many of the SAARC countries are entering into collaboration the non-SAARC countries in areas where the member countries have sufficient expertise. Although the summit was to commence in a changed regional scenario, Naeem Hasan, Secretary General of the SAARC, who was to attend a meeting of the South Asian Growth Quadrangle (SAGQ) comprising Bhutan, Nepal, Bangladesh and the north-eastern states of India at Kathmandu said "Since our association is not concerned with bilateral issues and security matters, such developments are not supposed to create any problem in the functioning of SAARC". He laid emphasis to have some institutional reforms if it has to be effective in goal-oriented co-operation rather than general cooperation.

The beginning of the meeting was preceded by Foreign Ministers summit of the SAARC countries who discussed the Draft Declaration, prepared by host Sri Lanka. The discussions included both formal and informal, bilateral and multilateral issues among the SAARC countries. India was represented by Vasundhara Raje, Minister of State for External Affairs. According to spokesman of the Conference the Ministers agenda emphasised the consideration of the SAARC Food Security Reserve Board, review of the recommendation of the SAARC Commerce and Information Ministers, the report of the high-level committee on Telecommunications, the expert groups report on the Integrated Programme of Action, the visa exemption scheme etc. The two-day meeting had also taken up the report of the SAARC Chambers of Commerce and the agenda for the Heads of Government meeting. The Draft Declaration finalised the foreign secretaries of the seven SAARC countries said, "Heads of State and Government recognised that due to their particular vulnerability, small states require special measures of support from the international community for safeguarding their sovereign independence and territorial integrity." Sri Lanka's Foreign Minister Lakshman Kadirgamar was of the view that SAARC should focus its attention on the trade and economic co-operation. He, at the end of the meeting of Foreign Ministers said in a brief to the media at Colombo that the conflict between India and Pakistan over the nuclear and Kashmir issue has not cast a shadow on the proceedings of the SAARC summit and wished that the two would have fruitful discussions, as it was the desire of the region that there should be peace between the two countries.

Colombo, on its part, had emphasised that the summit was called to put through a comprehensive economic agenda with 104 listed items to discuss and decide on and there was no need at all to spend time on global, international or macro issues. Atal Bihari Vajpayee, in his inaugural address laid emphasis for strengthening regional co-operation in social, economic and other areas and it was an additional point of satisfaction for India that all the proposals contained in PM's speech found their due place in the draft declaration. India being the strongest economy among the SAARC members has rightly taken the initiative in lifting quantitative restrictions maintained for balance of payments on a preferential basis for SAARC countries with effect from 1 August, 1998. This announcement by Vajpayee meant the lifting restrictions on over 2000 products thereby substantially increasing the opportunities for the other SAARC members to access the Indian market and increase their exports. As a result of India's move, members could now earn dollars by trading with India instead of sending their goods to distant destinations. It would also persuade the smaller countries to open up their markets and overcome their fear of being swamped by Indian goods. Such apprehension was the reason why the road to SAFTA remained bumpy and unchartered even though the first round of selective tariff cuts became effective from 1 January 1996.[114]

The summit received a wide support, as also referred in Kumaratunga's remark that SAARC might end up considering political issues sooner rather than later. There was a general feeling that unless the political decks were cleared, there can be no real co-operation in any matter. Although the nuclearisation of India had also heightened fears of Indian domination, yet governments in the region, by and large, seemed to go along with the Indian view that co-operation in economic social and technical fields need not wait for the solution of political problems. New Delhi is in a position to facilitate the process of increased investments in joint ventures among the SAARC countries by focussing on joint ventures on bilateral issues. A framework of investment promotion in the three major countries of the region-India, Pakistan and Bangladesh can act as the bulwork for strengthening the process of increased investments in the region as a whole. However, it might be said about the regional co-operation in the SAARC region, no effective co-operation is possible without ensuring normal economic relations between the two major countries of the region, India and Pakistan.[115]

Economic Relations

By the time the Government of Bharatiya Janata Party under the Premiership of Atal Bihari Vajpayee assumed power in New Delhi, in March 1998, the global gloom had caught up the South Asia region. Sri Lankan economy was in fine fettle in 1997, touching up a growth rate of 6.4 per cent. Colombo did not catch the virulent East Asian contagion because it had taken the prudent decision not to go in for short-term borrowing. But as the 1998 came the growth rate was slashed down to 5.8 per cent in the first quarter and slumped to 4.1 per cent in the third quarter, forcing the country's Central Bank to revise its growth expectation for the entire year to 4.5 per cent. In 1998, the Sri Lankan rupee depreciated against all major currencies by 11 per cent, which is counted as bad for export industries. Internationally too, the big economies like US and the UK had failed and were not likely to make significant recovery soon. Indonesia is still not out of the woods and Russia continues to be mired. And all this is bad news for Sri Lanka, which survives on international trade. Even some had predicted a zero or negative growth that would inevitably touch Sri Lanka. The prevalent economic condition compelled Sri Lanka's opposition leader in Parliament and chief of the United National Party (UNP) Ranil Wickremesinghe to plea for a 10-year trade pact with India that would provide a market for farmers of Sri Lanka and held the view that there is no, alternative to this now.[116] Actually, the economic downslide and falling food production in the last four years, had contributed to keeping 18% of Sri Lanka's 18 million people below the poverty line as revealed according to the latest UNDP country report and economist Sandruwan Maduma Bandara.

As a major breakthrough in economic sphere the two countries signed a trade pact in December 1998 when Sri Lanka's President Chandrika Bandaranaike Kumaratunga came to New Delhi and held talks on mutual interest. Under the agreement, the contentious domestic value addition ratio was finally fixed at 35 per cent. India, according to the agreement, would complete the elimination of its tariffs within three years but Sri Lanka would do so in eight years. As for the negative list of items that remained to be resolved plus the preferential zero type items, the agreement would allow 60 days' time to finalise it. New Delhi would allow duty free import of around 1,000 items from Sri Lanka as per the free trade pact and Colombo would reciprocate by permitting duty free entry of around 900 items from India. Apart from the items in the negative list and those on which there would be a 50 per cent margin of preference as soon as the Act comes into force. Sri Lanka has said that there would be zero duty on about 300 items and on about 600 items there would be 50 per cent margin of preference. Although, by the pact Sri Lanka's immediate interests had been well protected yet the problem of finding markets in India for the island's products still remained as the economies of India and Sri Lanka were not complementary. India has done what it could for Sri Lanka and it is now up to the Sri Lankan entrepreneur and trader to find gaps in the Indian market and earmark goods that Indians might need. However, the yawning trade gap between India and Sri Lanka cannot be bridged overnight. India's exports to Sri Lanka is 13 times more than its imports from the island. After all, the pact is an affirmation of India's goodwill for Sri Lanka.

In Colombo, the Indo-Sri Lanka pact was criticized in many ways. The on-going has seriously affected the Sri Lankan economy by curbing developmental expenditure and being a deterrent to foreign investment. First of all the Tamil sources doubted that so long as the highly expensive and destructive war is on, the Sri Lankan economy would be weak and be unable to benefit from the free trade pact. India too would not be able to reap the full benefits if the island's economy is weak. An article in the top Tamil daily *Virakesari*, charged India that it had sacrificed the Tamil cause in the vain hope that the trade pact would help boost its economy. By dangling the economic carrot before the Indians, President Kumaratunga had made India ignore the Tamil question. The protests over the recently concluded Indo-Lanka Free Trade Agreement (FTA) continued. It was criticized by the Ceylon Chamber of Commerce and Industry (CCCI) that, in anguish, wrote a letter to president Kumaratunga pointing out that sectors of the small and medium industries in the island which were already closing down causing massive unemployment, would be further hit by the FTA. Columnist Bismarck, wrote in *The Sunday Leader* apart from opposing other aspects of FTA that the term insufficient working or processing" in annexure C of Rule 7 which interpreted that a product can be deemed not indigenous enough. He added further that most Sri Lankans are convinced that Colombo would never be able to ensure 35 per cent indigenization and that the trade gap with India would only widen as a result of the pact. Whereas Dayan Jayatilleke and Tissarani Gunasekara in their articles in *The Sunday Times* termed the Agreement as "a free fox among free chickens" and feared that the flooding of the Lankan market with cheap Indian goods would not only lead to the deindustrialization of Sri Lankan but also result in employers cutting wages and laying off workers in a vain bid to compete.

Problem of Tamils

When the BJP-led coalition assumed office Sri Lankans reacted in two different ways. The majority Sinhalese and the Government were apprehensive. The inclusion of avowedly pro-LTTE leaders and parties in the new Indian Government revived the nightmare of another Indian intervention in Sri Lanka in the Sinhalese of South. But the minority Tamils were elated and triggered hopes who wanted Indian backing for their cause. This Tamil perception sent Foreign Minister Lakshman Kadirgamar to New Delhi to seek clarifications. The new men at the helm assured the visiting minister that they stood for a united Sri Lanka and would have not truck with secessionism and terrorism. However, after the new regime took over, 35 Tamil organisations wrote a joint letter to Atal Bihari Vajpayee, the new Prime Minister of India, seeking his help to resolve the 15-year old ethnic conflict in the country. They blamed the two main political parties-the ruling people's Alliance and the opposition United National Party for the plight of the Tamil people. The organisations urged India to play an active and constructive role by persuading them to work out a just and reasonable political solution to satisfy the aspirations of the Tamils. This step of Tamils was strongly criticized by many but particularly by a major Sri Lankan-Buddhist federation who said that the ethnic problem was an internal affair of the country and urged Vajpayee to reject the Tamil demands. It noted in a statement that "while Tamil action groups have no national right to request the Indian Prime Minister to intervene in the internal affairs of this country the Prime Minister of India too has no international right to entertain any such request from any action group of another sovereign country.

Even as the Indian Prime Minister had told visiting Sri Lankan opposition leader Ranil Wickremesinghe that a solution to the ethnic conflict in the island must come from within Sri Lanka, the chairman of the Foreign Affairs Committee of the BJP, N. N. Jha, who had worked as India's High Commissioner five years ago, said in a statement, in Colombo that South Block was working on a "concrete, palatable; and immediately implementable" package for a solution. In his view India should take a friendly interest in Sri Lanka because we cannot be idle spectators when a house in the neighbourhood is on fire. New Delhi would also have to take the lead in South Asia, in view of the fact that it is the regional power. The statement of one time India's High Commissioner to Colombo created a storm in view of the fact that he was the convenor of the Foreign Affairs Committee of the ruling BJP and a member of its National Executive. It had triggered the majority Sinhalese and the Sri Lankan Government, fears of a second Indian intervention in Sri Lanka, but, at the sametime created hopes of deliverance among the minority Tamils. Both, Sri Lanka's Minister of Constitutional Affairs, Prof. G. L. Peiris and a foreign office spokesman had criticized Jha's views on merger of the Northern and Eastern provinces to form a single Tamil province if the ethnic issue was to be solved. The spokesman hinted that Sri Lanka would certainly object to India or for that matter any other country working out a "package" for the solution of the ethnic question, as this was essentially an internal matter to be solved by Sri Lankans themselves. He made it clear that such a "package would not be an expression of just' friendly concern" but amounted to interfering in the internal affairs of a sovereign country.

Sri Lanka did not react adversely when India exploded its nuclear devices in May 1998 which was quickly followed by Islamabad. The explosions were really an attempt to correct the current military and technological imbalance vis-a-vis China, which was already in the threshold of being a world super power. This sober statement by General A. S. Kalkat, former IPKF Chief and current Chairman of the International Committee for Conflict Resolution, had paved the way for strengthening of further relations between the two countries. The Government of India in response, had cornered the joint memorandum submitted by the AIADMK and three of its allies seeking a greater interventionist role in Sri Lanka to solve the ethnic tangle. The memorandum also spoke of a Tamil homeland and sending a parliamentary delegation to this homeland. The view, expressed in the memorandum, was a strident departure from the official policy of Delhi that any solution to the ethnic tangle had to be within the framework of the Sri Lankan constitution. Although barring the LTTE, none of the major Tamil parties in Sri Lanka were not talking in term of a Tamil homeland and even the issue of merging the north and eastern provinces had taken a back seat. Yet, the memorandum gave life to such contentious issues, which ideally should be sorted out between the Sri Lankan Tamil parties and the government. However, despite these all India's Minister of State for External Affairs Vasundhara Raje, in a written reply, in Rajya Sabha, reaffirmed New Delhi's continued support for a peaceful and negotiated settlement of the ethnic problem in Sri Lanka within the framework of the unity and territorial integrity of that country. She expressed India's firm belief that the ethnic issue is an internal matter for Sri Lanka to resolve and it is the policy of the 'Government not to interfere in the internal affairs of other countries.[117]

In the circumstances, even most of the Sri Lankans thought that war alone would not solve the ethnic problem. A recent survey conducted by Prof. S. T. Hettige, Head of the Department of Sociology of the Colombo University, revealed that 77.4 per cent of the respondents said "no" when asked if military action alone would solve the ethnic problem. Just 20.7 per cent said that war was the only way. To the question on how to solve the problem only 9.3 per cent said "by defeating the LTTE". Only 6.9 per cent said that peace would be ensured by defeating the LTTE, 77.8 per cent favoured a non-military way of bringing lasting peace. Most wanted some kind of a political solution by accommodation. When asked to specify what they wanted done in this respect, 22.2 per cent said the minority Tamils should be given equality with the majority, another 18.6 per cent suggested communal amity as a must for a lasting solution. Thus, the survey clearly indicated that the bulk of the Sinhalese at the grassroots level did not believe in a purely military solution and it gave a lie to the theory touted by a section of media that the Sinhalese favoured war.

Historically, the Tamil struggle in Sri Lanka dates back to the 1920s first in the form of a co-operative movement and later, under the Jaffna Youth Congress as a social movement against caste distinctions. In the 1960s, Marxist groups sprang up to fight the cause of economic freedom for the oppressed people. At another level, State oppression resulted in Tamil politics being taken over by the militant Tamil United Liberation Front. All the emerging militant movements represented shades of these two traditions, the former relying on democratic forces and the latter centralised an authoritarian and intolerant of dissent. When Prabhakaran formed the LTTE, in the early 1980s, it was a democratic group and decisions were taken collectively by a central committee. In 1984, Prabhakaran shocked his colleagues when he introduced the oath of personal loyalty to him. Rajni Thiranganama, who was earlier dedicated to Tamil Eelam in the eighties and later became a human right activist of Jaffna, predicted the inevitability of the break up of the LTTE and said, "The Tigers' history, their theoretical vacuum, lack of political creativity, intolerance and fanatical dedication will be the ultimate cause of their own breaking up. The legendary Tigers will go to their demise with their legends smeared with the blood and tears of victims of their misdoings. A new Tiger will not emerge from their ashes." But so far as the matter of Tamils were concerned, perhaps, they needed liberation from both sides. They have to politically defeat the LTTE if they want to regain the space to live in peace with dignity. Judging by the mood of the people of Jaffna and the 43 per cent vote in the council elections, they may be on the road to it. The second pointer is the resistence of parents to allow their children to join the LTTE. Third factor is the steady return of Tamils to the areas formerly held by the LTTE and recaptured by the army.

Despite the challenges faced by the LTTE and the Tamil, the community as a whole continued to be a vital force in Sri Lanka. In September 1998, leader of the opposition in Sri Lankan Parliament and Chief of the UNP, Ranil Wickremesinghe expressed his desire to talk to the LTTE to end the war. He also suggested that any talk with the LTTE should be preceded by an all-party conference to work out a genuinely unified stand on a political settlement. His call for a dialogue with the Tamil Tigers has raised the hope that nation's two political parties could, for once, be geared to evolve a consensus on the ethnic conflict. Although ever since independence whenever the Government has taken an initiative to offer some accommodation to the Tamils, the then opposition had sought to politicise the issue by shipping up chauvinistic sentiments among the majority Sinhalese population. The proposal of UNP was equally significant because it has suggested that the exercise be preceded by building a consensus among the southern political parties and an unconditional ceasefire. It had underlined the need for a mediatory role by a third country "not affected by the LTTE" in getting the dialogue underway. On the otherhand, Tamil Tigers too had recently indicated their preference for negotiations on the "principles enunciated at the Thimpu talks" held earlier. This, hopefully, should allow some space to the other Sri Lankan Tamil parties whose opinion and role are essential for arriving at a durable and democratic solution.[118]

In the circumstances, Raja Collure, General Secretary of the Communist Party of Sri Lanka, a partner of the coalition government, expressed Government's readiness for a third party mediation for negotiation with the LTTE and conceded to give regional autonomy to the Tamils in Jaffna and its neighbouring areas. Blaming the UNP for complicating the ethnic issue during the 1980s he said that the present government is against any military solution of the problem. It is said that with the coming of BJP the LTTE had started rebuilding its network in Tamil Nadu. Given the changed political scenario, in which it has lost international support, and with a long drawn out armed struggle ahead, the LTTE has had to turn to Tamil Nadu again for encouragement, support and sustenance. Garnering support is already underway and the pro-LTTE allies of the ruling BJP are said to be playing a key role in the re-establishment of the network. However, for any improvement in this regard getting Indian ban[119] lifted is crucial for LTTE. Further it would have some difficulties in playing its due role in view of the fact that the LTTE stood indicted by the Jain Commission for heinous crimes in India. But after all, the LTTE needed Tamil Nadu because of its increasing isolation in the world. The US banned it last year and the UK is in the process of bringing in tough legislation to curb foreign terrorist groups. France, Canada and Germany are keeping a close watch on the extortion and other activities of the LTTE among Tamil refugees. Norway and Denmark are contemplating repatriation of Sri Lankan Tamil refugees.

This uncertain situation is bad for its morale in the long run and could affect fund raising and motivational campaigns. In the meantime President Chandrika Kumaratunga, in an exclusive interview to the state-owned ITN TV, blamed UNP for making the Tamil question a "complete mess" that gave India an opportunity to interfere but said that New Delhi did not want to interfere now because it was satisfied with the way Sri Lanka was tackling the issue. In January 1999 Lt. General Srilal Weerasooriya, the new Army Chief, rejected LTTE's key pre-condition for talks and declared that the Army would not be withdrawn from areas which it had liberated from the LTTE. He said, "As a soldier, I am 100 per cent for peace. If there is a definite chance for peace, we are all for it. But it has to be peace with meaning. I think there needs to be a political ' solution. But let us talk from where we are". After all, the Indo-Sri Lankan relations had strengthened since president Kumaratunga has taken over, the solution is not a distant possibility. Recently on 4 February, 1999, speaking on the occasion of country's 51st Independence Day she said, "It is time for all of us to find a just and satisfactory solution taking into serious consideration the great loss of life and property caused by unpatriotic elements. Without naming LTTE she added further that let us dedicate ourselves to achieving peace, prosperity and unity, preserving the rich diversity of all, thus ensuring economic and social stability". The present dispensation of Sri Lanka seemed more willing 'to solve the ethnic issue because, for the first time it was felt in the island that justice had not been done with the Tamils.

Foreign Involvement

Since long collection of funds from abroad had been an important source of income for Tamils. The Sri Lankan Government was happy with the news that the LTTE is getting unpopularity in foreign countries, among them, some have banned its (LTTE's) activity on their soil. In September 1998, President Chandrika Kumaratunga, in a impassioned speech at the UN General Assembly, appealed to member nations to prevent the LTTE from collecting funds in the guise of humanitarian work, as these funds were being used for "murdering and brutalising" her countrymen. She said, "Only through such action would be able to ensure that terrorist are compelled to renounce violence and enter the democratic process".

Kumaratunga also took the opportunity to reiterate her government's firm commitment for a peaceful solution of the Tamil question and added that the doors for a dialogue were always open to the LTTE, if it eschews terrorism and its bloody call for a separate state.

The island country was hit badly by the ethnic conflict since 1980s and occasional offer of mediation was made by the world powers including United Kingdom (UK) and the United States of America (USA). In October 1998 it was announced that Derek Flatchett, the British Minister of State for Foreign Affairs would be at Colombo, in November this year to inaugurate the British Trade Fair. The occasion reminded the speculation for renewing UK mediation offer. It was based on the fact that there is a standing British mediation offer since the time Dr. Liam Fox, Flatchett's predecessor in the Foreign and Commonwealth office, made it. Dr. Fox had even, at the time got the Sri Lankan President and the leader of the opposition to sign what came to be known as the Fox Pact on 1 April, 1997. The proposal envisaged mutual consultation and agreement on what should be discussed with and offers to the LTTE if there were talks to it. Unfortunately, both the ruling People's Alliance and the opposition UNP wanted to deny each other the credit for solving the ethnic problem, no joint effort was possible. While the UNP was keen on accepting the British offer, the government plainly rejected any third party mediation. All it would consider was facilitation under certain conditions.

The US government had designated the LTTE as a terrorist organisation and banned it in September 1997. Although the LTTE had challenged it in the US appeal court, there are indications that the US government and the Congress continue to view the LTTE as terrorist and are keen on keeping it on the list of banned organisations. Karl Inderfurth, US Assistant Secretary of State, in course of his visit to Colombo in February 1999, reiterated his country's stand that the LTTE was terrorist and untrust worthly but had added that the US would be quite happy to be a facilitator or be part of a group of facilitators,if it was called upon to assume that role by the two parties to the conflict. The visiting US Assistant Secretary discussed with his Sri Lankan conterpart, the question of having an extradition treaty between the US and Sri Lanka. This is crucial for Sri Lanka, because, Colombo might in future want LTTE fugitives and fund raisers to be extradited. He also denied that the US was giving "military assistance" to Sri Lanka but said that Lankan army personnel were being trained in the US as part of routine international programme.

In recent past LTTE's campaign in major countries had disappointed it and now Sri Lanka had confirmed reports that the LTTE is trying to establish a base in South Africa. To quote Foreign Minister Kadirgamar, "we are not confronting the South African government on the LTTE issue. We are just saying to them this is a serious problem. We have information that the LTTE trying to make a base in South Africa. Please do not allow that to happen". He pointed out that if the LTTE really made a base in South Africa it would try to do so within the South Africa Indian community. On the occasion he reminded South Africa the assassination of Rajiv Gandhi on Indian soil and banning of it by several countries of the world including India itself. In other words, he appeared to have conveyed to the South African government the necessity of not repeating the mistake that the Indian authorities did by indulging the LTTE.

Keeping in view the problem of the base of LTTE, Lakshman Kadirgamar, the Sri Lankan Foreign Minister visited South Africa in November 1998. The Sri Lankan government has been bringing the LTTE factor to the notice of the Mandela government since 1996. That year a White National Intelligence Agency official had told the visiting Sri Lankan Foreign Minister that the LTTE had four front organisations to do propaganda and collect funds. An Indian journalist in Johannesburg also revealed that the LTTE was culturally and politically "Tamilising", the Tamils of South Africa in the Sri Lankan Tamil way. "Many of the new Tamil Hindu priests have a Sri Lankan Tamil rather than an Indian Tamil background. President Chandrika Kumaratunga took up the matter with President Mandela in Edinburg, in October 1997. The meeting followed a raid order by the President on LTTE camps in Laudium near Pretoria, Lenasia near Johannesburg, and New Castle in KwaZulu-Natal. But these proved to be a fiasco and gradually it acquired serious proportions. The precious little had been done to allay Colombo's fears that necessitated the current visit of Lakshman Kadirgamar, Sri Lanka's Foreign Minister to South Africa.

Thus, aimed the report that the Tamils are setting up bases in South Africa and taking advantage of the pressure of the large Indian

Tamil community there, resulting in opening of a number of military camps, this important visit took place. As a gesture of goodwill towards the Tamils President Chandrika Kumaratunga expressed her readiness for talks with the LTTE without a prior agreement on ceasefire if the rebels settled for a stipulated timeframe for negotiations. The visit was undertaken to hold discussions with leaders of the African National Congress (ANC) which was alleged to have been maintaining close relations with the LTTE. Although the LTTE, on its part, has denied that it is trying to build a base in South Africa, for collecting funds and getting training, what Colombo wanted from South Africa, was an assurance that Pretoria would not allow the extremist Tamil Tigers to establish a base there. Denying any chance of South African President Nelson Mandela's facilitating talks between the government and the rebel LTTE, disclosed on 18 January 1999 in Colombo, the South Africans had told the visiting President in no uncertain terms that they would not tolerate any LTTE activity on their soil.

Second Term of Atal Bihari Vajpayee (13 October 1999-22 May 2004)

India experienced the third front's managed governments between 1996-98 and the government formed on 19th March, 1998 headed by Atal Bihari Vajpayee was defeated by one vote in the Lok Sabha in the third week of April 1999. Viewing no possibility of the alternative government, to be put in place, on 26 April 1999, President K. R. Narayanan dissolved the 12th Lok Sabha and as a result having consulted nation's political parties M. S. Gill, the then Chief Election Commissioner of India, announced that the poll dates for the 13th Lok Sabha would be in September-October and new House would be constituted before 21 October 1999. Meanwhile Vajpayee's government remained in office in what is called, caretaker capacity. However, the National Democratic Alliance (NDA) led by the Bharatiya Janata Party got clear majority in the general election and Vajpayee for the third time on 13 October, 1999 took over as the Prime Minister of India.

In Sri Lanka Presidential election was held in December 1999 and Chandrika Kumaratunga was re-elected as the President. Further in the general election held in October 2000 no party got a clear majority to form the government and ultimately the People's Alliance formed the government with the help of the EPDP and the Muslim NUA, an offshoot of the SLMP. On account of narrow margin of majority the Kumaratunga government remained insecure and after a year it was forced to call for another in December, 2001 in which 26 political parties and 120 independent groups contested. The verdict went in favour of the United National Party (UNP) but as it could not get enough number of seats to form the government of its own, the UNP-led government was formed with the support of Sri Lanka Muslim Party (SLMP) and Ranil Wickremesinghe became the Prime Minister of the country.

Bilateral relations between the Democratic Socialist Republic of Sri Lanka and the Republic of India have been generally friendly but were controversially affected by several factors. While discussing the prospects of India-Sri Lanka relations, it is necessary to keep in mind two historical realities. First, India's abiding and seminal influences on all aspects of Sri Lankan life; second; despite the shared cultural heritage, the asymmetrical power equation has made the Sinhalese deeply suspicious of India's foreign policy objectives.[120] In recent years India-Sri Lanka relations have undergone a qualitative and quantitative transformation. Political relations are close, trade and investments have increased dramatically, infrastructural linkages are constantly being augmented, defence collaboration has increased and there is a general broad-based improvement across all sectors of bilateral cooperation.[121] There exists a broad consensus within the Sri Lankan polity on the primacy of India in Sri Lanka's external relations matrix. Both the major political parties in Sri Lanka – the Sri Lanka Freedom Party and the United Nationalist Party have contributed to the rapid development of bilateral relations with India.

Exchange of Visits

Relations between India and Sri Lanka strengthened in the period as a result of the important visits undertaken by both sides. Chandrika Kumaratunga visited India from February 22-25, 2001 accompanied by Lakshman Kadirgamar, Sri Lanka's Minister of Foreign Affairs and held talks with the Prime Minister Atal Bihari Vajpayee and Jaswant Singh, India's Minister for External Affairs. The talks between the two sides were held in an atmosphere of cordiality and understanding and covered bilateral, regional and international matters of mutual interest. Both sides expressed great satisfaction at the excellent state of bilateral relations and the warmth and understanding that existed between the two countries.[122] In course of the talks the two sides noted with satisfaction the progress in the implementation of the India-Sri Lanka Free Trade Agreement, which took effect on March 1, 2000 and reiterated their commitment to the realization of the full potential of the Agreement. They agreed that the two sides would attend to any problem in the implementation of the FTA and resolve them. New Delhi, as earlier, reiterated its consistent support for the unity, sovereignty and territorial integrity of Sri Lanka and for a negotiated political settlement of the conflict, as the only way to restore lasting peace which would meet the aspirations of all elements of Sri Lankan society.[123] Thus, the discussions held during the visit reflected the high priority attached by both countries to the maintenance of close and friendly relations based on mutual trust and understanding.

At the close of the year 2001 (December 22-24) Ranil Wickremesinghe, the Prime Minister of Sri Lanka visited the country at the invitation of the Government of India. After assuming power it was his first official visit abroad and it underlies the significance he attached to bilateral relations. He was accompanied by Tyronne Fernando, Minister of Foreign Affairs, Milinda Maragoda, Minister of Economic Reforms, Science and Technology and other high officials. Their visit proved most productive and wide-ranging discussions were held in the most cordial atmosphere reflecting the close relations between the two countries. They met the Indian leaders across the political spectrum. Substantive discussions were held with the Indian Prime Minister and Minister for External Affairs. In the talks India reiterated its commitment to the sovereignty and territorial integrity of Sri Lanka. During the visit they agreed to cooperate in a number of other areas with immediate priority on agriculture, power and the Information Technology Industry.[124] Keeping in view the spirit of the closest of historical, cultural and social ties that has bound the two countries over the millennia, both sides agreed to work on commissioning a feasibility study on a land bridge between the two countries.[125]

Again at the invitation of the Government of India Wickremesinghe, the Prime Minister of Sri Lanka, visited India June 8-12, 2002 along with

Milinda Moragoda, Minister of Economic Reform, Science and Technology and other high officials. The visit marked the wide-ranging discussions held in a cordial atmosphere reflecting the close relations between the two countries. The Sri Lankan Prime Minister met Indian leaders across the political spectrum and substantive discussions were held with the Indian Prime Minister and Minister for External Affairs in which he appraised the current status of the process to initiate talks to end the ethnic conflict in Sri Lanka. In response the Government of India reiterated its commitment to the unity, sovereignty and territorial integrity of Sri Lanka and to restoration of a lasting peace through a peaceful, negotiated settlement. It was made clear during the visit that the Government of India remained fully supportive of the measures taken by the Sri Lankan Government to take the peace process forward. Apart from expressing satisfaction over the economic progress made so far both sides agreed to initiate a multi-disciplinary feasibility study envisaging private sector expertise and investment under the guidance of the Planning Commission of India and the Policy Development Ministry of Sri Lanka.[126] They also agreed that global terrorism is a threat to international peace and security. They agreed that terrorist acts cannot be justified on political, ethnic, religious, social, economic or other grounds. Terrorism is an absolute evil; it is a global scourage to be collectively countered.

In response to Sri Lankan visits Yashwant Sinha, India's Minister for External Affairs, paid a visit to Sri Lanka in the second week of July 2002 and held wide-ranging discussions with Ranil Wickremesinghe, the Prime Minister of Sri Lanka and Tyronne Fernando, Foreign Minister on July 11 and talks were held in the cordial and friendly spirit that characterized the close relations between the two countries. In the meeting the two sides reiterated that global terrorism is a threat to international peace and security, and can not be justified on any grounds. They stressed that this evil phenomenon must be combated unequivocally, and expressed their commitment to support all global initiatives to eradicate this menace. On the same day India's Foreign Minister met the President of Sri Lanka, senior minister and other dignitaries. The interactions reflected the high priority attached by both countries to the maintenance of close and friendly ties based on mutual trust and understanding.[127]

At the invitation of the Government of India Ranil Wickremesinghe, the Prime Minister of Sri Lanka, visited India 19-21 October 2003, accompanied by Tyronne Fernando, Minister of Foreign, Milinda Moragoda, Minister of Economic Reforms, Science and Technology and other senior officials. The visit gave Sri Lankan side an opportunity to held wide-ranging discussions with Prime Minister Atal Bihari Vajpayee, Ministers of External Affairs, Commerce and Industry, Civil Aviation and Petroleum and Natural Gas and which were held in a cordial atmosphere, reflective of close relations between the two countries. The two Prime Ministers noted with satisfaction the significant contribution made by the India-Sri Lanka Foundation towards fostering exchanges in cultural, educational, scientific and technological areas and announced a further contribution of Rs. 1 crore each to enable the Foundation to sustain its diverse activities.[128] The India-Sri Lanka Foundation was established on December 28, 1998 by a Memorandum of Understanding signed between the Government of India and Sri Lanka, with the objective of fostering Indo-Sri Lanka relations in diverse fields and the promotion of greater understanding between the peoples of the two countries. The thrust areas of the Foundation were identified as education and culture, archaeological studies, agricultural research, science and technology, health, technical training, development studies and women's studies. It is financed, as per provisions of the signed MoU, through revenues from a Trust Fund set up with grants made available by the two Governments. Each country has contributed an equal share of the corpus of the Foundation in their respective currencies.

In course of the visit other issues such as the problem of fishermen, civil aviation links and continuing acts of terrorism found prominence and several decisions were taken related to these burning irritants between the two countries. The two Prime Ministers expressed satisfaction that existing understandings on dealing sympathetically and humanely with fishermen who stray into each other's maritime zone were working well. In the meeting it was agreed that while it was important that the fishermen should be released early, the boats may be held till the judicial processes in the two countries are completed. They agreed on the need to undertake enhanced survellance to minimize incursions, institutionalize assistance for salvage operations of released vessels, pay attention to ecological and conservation aspects and consider licensed fishing within a bilateral Memorandum of Understanding on fisheries. The two Prime Ministers expressed satisfaction at increased civil aviation links between India and Sri Lanka. It was agreed to do away with the existing requirements of Commercial Agreements between designated airlines of the two countries for asymmetrical operations. With a view to increasing tourist flow and connectivity, it was also decided to encourage private scheduled airlines of India, who operate only in the domestic sector at present, to extend their operations to airports in Sri Lanka.[129] The Sri Lankan Prime Minister agreed to reciprocate in terms of the access that airlines from India could have to Sri Lankan airspace.

Like earlier taking note of the continuing acts of terrorism world wide and in our region, the two Prime Ministers emphasised the need for concerted opposition to terrorism in all its forms and manifestations. They agreed that there can be no justification for terrorism, be it political, religious or ideological. At the occasion they recalled the Kathmandu Declaration adopted at the 11th SAARC Summit held in Kathmandu on 6 January 2002 on criminalisation of financing for terrorist purposes and the need to prevent the abuse of financial systems of States. They reaffirmed the need to finalise and adopt, at the earliest, the proposed Comprehensive Convention on Terrorism, which would send a strong signal that the international community was united and determined in its efforts to eliminate the scourage of terrorism. Their meeting also discussed the ongoing cooperation in training and the supply of equipment to the Sri Lankan defence forces and agreed that the two sides would commence discussions with a view to concluding a defence cooperation agreement at the earliest. India again reiterated its support for the process of seeking a negotiated settlement acceptable to all sections of Sri Lankan society within the framework of a united Sri Lanka and consistent with democracy pluralism and respect for individual rights.[130] It remained committed to Sri Lankan sovereignty and territorial integrity. Further Sri Lankan President visited India in November 2004.

Economic Relations

India's economic and commercial relations with Sri Lanka had undergone a significant change since the signing of Free Trade Agreement which became operational in March 2000. The FTA between India and Sri Lanka has radically transformed their relationship, replacing mutual debilitating confrontation by peaceful co-existence, trade, investment and tourism. India is no longer a significant player in the bitter ethnic conflict, which is the main political issue in Sri Lanka. India's energies are now directed towards building economic bridges with its southern neighbour for mutual advantage. Apart from the FTA juridical framework for the relationship has been provided by a Double Taxation Avoidance Agreement (DTAA), a Bilateral Investment Protection and Promotion Agreement (BIPPA) and agreements/MoUs on Air Services, Small Development Projects, Cooperation in Small Scale Industries, Tourism, Information Technology, Space, Agriculture and Education. India is active in a number of areas of development activity in Sri Lanka. About one-sixth of the total development credit granted by Government of India is made available to Sri Lanka. There are three lines of credit extended to Sri Lanka – US$ 100 million for capital goods, consumer durables, consultancy services and food items, US$ 31 million for supply of 300,000 MT of wheat and US$ 150 million for purchase of petroleum products. All of these lines of credit have been fully utilized. A number of development projects are also implemented under 'Aid to Sri Lanka' funds.

For a long sugar was the main item of export to Sri Lanka but over the years and especially from the 1990s the pattern of India's exports to Sri Lanka has diversified into industrial goods such as petroleum products, pharmaceuticals, iron and steel products, auto rickshaws, buses, lorries, chemical products and vegetables etc. The post – FTA periods witnessed a new momentum in India-Sri Lanka bilateral trade and since 2000 Indo-Sri Lankan trade rose 128 per cent by 2004 and quadrupled by 2006 reaching USD 2.6 billion. India-Sri Lanka bilateral trade for 2002 touched USD 1 billion for the first time ever. In 2003, bilateral trade touched USD 1338 million with exports from India to Sri Lanka amounting to USD 1093 million; while exports from Sri Lanka to India in the same period amounted to USD 245 million. In 2004, bilateral trade touched USD 1732 million with Indian exports amounting to USD 1350 million and Sri Lankan exports amounting to USD 382 million. The trade balance in favour of India has declined from 15.7:1 in 1998 to 3.5:1 in 2004, demonstrating a faster rate of growth of Sri Lankan exports as compared to India's. India accounts for almost 15% of total Sri Lankan imports and is the third largest export destination for Sri Lanka. In comparison to India, Sri Lanka is a relatively small market and it accounts for around 2% of total Indian exports and less than 1% of its imports. With USD 450 million in FDI approvals India is the fourth largest overall investor in Sri Lanka.

Thus in post-FTA phase India's exports to Sri Lanka had gone up three-fold and Sri Lanka's exports to India nine-fold since 2000, the trade gap is still a yawning one. It rose from $542 million to $48 billion in seven years in absolute terms, becoming an eyesore for Sinhalese nationalists. In Indian view the Sri Lanka should also realise that many of the things Colombo would like to sell are grown or made in India. Tea, rubber and garments are Sri Lanka's major exports, but India has its own thriving tea, rubber and garment industries to safeguard. The position of India-Sri Lanka trade during Vajpayee's premiership is given below.

India-Sri Lanka Bilateral Trade in USD million

Year	*Imports from India*	*Exports to India*	*Trade Deficit*	*Total Trade*
1999	512	49	463	561
2000	600	58	542	658
2001	602	72	530	674
2002	835	171	664	1006
2003	1093	245	848	1338
2004 (August)	1350	382	656.45	1732

In addition exchange of visits, as earlier, remained a significant factor in promoting economic relations between the two countries. In February 2001 when Chandrika Bandaranaike Kumaratunga, the President of Sri Lanka, visited India the two sides reiterated their commitment to the realization of the full potential of the agreement and agreed to attend any problems in the implementation of the FTA and resolve them. India agreed to provide 2500 tonnes of wheat per month for the next twelve months from December 2001 when Sri Lankan Prime Minister came to New Delhi and made request in this regard. Further in June 2002 Ravi Karunanayake, the Sri Lankan Minister of Trade was accompanied with country's Prime

Minister's visit to India and decided following the meeting with Murasoli Maran, India's Minister of Commerce, that an Indian delegation will visit Colombo in the first week of July to resolve outstanding procedural issues. Taking into account Sri Lanka's Prime Minister's intention to widen the ambit of the FTA to include the services sector and impart renewed impetus and synergy to the process it was decided to set up a Task Force for 'FTA II and beyond'. During the visit the two Prime Ministers noted with satisfaction the progress made in operationalisation of the bilateral agreement for the supply of wheat to Sri Lanka. India also offered to share its experience and technical expertise in agriculture and to work together with Sri Lanka for farm and food security in the region.

Yashwant Singh, India's Minister for External Affairs visited Sri Lanka in July 2002 and the two foreign ministers in their meeting expressed satisfaction with the momentum in the economic relationship between the two countries. They acknowledged the progress made in the expeditious resolution of outstanding issues relating to tea, garments and cement under the Free Trade Agreement at the meeting of senior officials held in Colombo 4-5 July 2002. Both sides noted with satisfaction the recent signing of Agreements providing for concessional terms for the USD 31 million supply of wheat by India to Sri Lanka and a programme loan of USD 20 million provided by India for facilitating the economic stabilization of Sri Lanka, as part of the programme negotiated under the Standby Agreement with the International Monetary Fund in April 2001. The Sri Lankan side expressed appreciation to the Government of India for its contribution of USD 7.5 million to the Government of Sri Lanka for setting up an Indian Cancer Centre in Colombo. Both sides also expressed satisfaction over the imminent commencement of flights to Bangalore by Sri Lankan Airlines, and stressed the need for further enhancing air links in the context of growing economic ties. The decision to set up a India-Sri Lanka Joint Study Group which would made recommendations for the establishment of a Comprehensive Economic Partnership Agreement, was taken in October 2003 when Ranil Wickremesinghe, the Prime Minister of Sri Lanka visited India and the two Prime Ministers also noted the successful holding of the 5th session of the Joint Commission Meeting, co-chaired by the Foreign Ministers, in Colombo on 15th October 2003.

Problem of Tamils

The present ethnic conflict in Sri Lanka is not amongst the common Tamil and Sinhalese people as in the previous days, but it is between the LTTE and the government as well as between stubborn Sinhalese and Tamils. This is not the problem particularly of Sinhalese or Tamils or Muslims, but it has encircled the entire population in Sri Lanka which is tired of violence and is dreaming of peaceful habitation.[131] When Chandrika Kumaratunga was elected President of the country she was very keen on bringing about ethnic reconciliation and expressed her readiness to imitate discussions without preconditions.[132] In fact she realised the earlier mistakes and blunders made by the early governments after independence in 1948 and began pondering on the new pattern of political system which would be based on the federal style without using the term 'Federation'. Gradually the Government of Sri Lanka began to feel comfort on Tamil problems and were confident that New Delhi would never support separatism in the region because in the event Colombo would make good relations with China. From the beginning India's consistent position has been in favour of a politically negotiated settlement acceptable to all sections of Sri Lankan society within the framework of an undivided Sri Lanka and consistent with democracy, pluralism and respect for human rights.

Although devolution of political powers in Sri Lanka among the communities was not an issue in the election campaign, it posed a real challenge for the government that took over in December 2001. The new dispensation was also in favour of military action, it however, taking a positive view, initiated peace talks with the LTTE and announced a month's ceasefire. It was reciprocated by the LTTE the very next day and at the end of the period on 24 January 2002, the government extends the cease-fire by another month. The Government of India welcomed the cessation of hostilities announced by the LTTE and the positive response of the Government of Sri Lanka and hoped that this would begin a process to restore lasting peace. It was stated in India- Sri Lanka joint statement issued at the end of Ranil Wickremensinghe's visit to India in December 2001. Earlier too India reiterated its consistent support for the unity, sovereignty and territorial integrity of Sri Lanka and for a negotiated political settlement of the conflict, as the only way to restore lasting peace which would meet the aspirations of all elements of Sri Lankan society.

For the time being the confidence building measures between the LTTE and the Sri Lankan government worked and on 22 February 2002 a long-term cease-fire agreement was signed. In early September the government lifted the ban on the tigers and within a few days peace negotiations started in Thailand with Norwegian facilitation. Perhaps due to the very weakness of the political situation in New Delhi both Sri Lanka and the LTTE were able to get the help of the perennial peace keeping nation of Norway's good help in facilitating and even mediating a peace making process. Sri Lanka was able to achieve this inspite of a vociferous negative reaction in India in certain quarters to the involvement of western peacemaker within South Asia. These forces were fearful that the peace made in Sri Lanka with the help of the West would end up leading to a just and potentially fissiparous solution in Kashmir. However, the Sri Lankan side informed Yashwant Sinha, India's Minister for External Affairs, the current status of the process to initiate talks to end the ethnic conflict when he had paid a visit to the country in July 2002. The Indian minister reaffirmed India's full support to the measures taken by the Sri Lankan government to take peace process forward.

Further too the Government of Sri Lanka kept the Indian government aware of the developments in this regard. In October 2003 Ranil Wickremesinghe, the Prime Minister of Sri Lanka, paid an official visit to India and he apprised the Indian leadership of recent developments in the peace process and proposals made by his government for the establishment of an Interim Administration. India expected that the response to the proposals made by the Sri Lankan government in July 2003 would be reasonable and comprehensive. In course of the talks India supported the process of seeking a negotiated settlement acceptable to all sections of Sri Lankan society within the framework of a united Sri Lanka and consistent with democracy pluralism and respect for individual rights. It was made clear on India's part that it would welcome a resolution of the current impass in the peace process and an early resumption of negotiation. Any interim arrangement should be an integral part of the final settlement and should be in the framework of the unity and traditional integrity of Sri Lanka. New Delhi also reiterated the same sentiment and view when Chandrika Kumaratunga, president of Sri Lanka visited India in November 2004 and the visiting president apprised the Indian leadership about the current status of peace process in Sri Lanka and the steps she had taken to advance it further. However, the security situation in Sri Lanka remained delicately poised and an agreement on resumption of peace talks is yet to emerge.

REGIME OF UNITED PROGRESSIVE ALLIANCE

Premiership of Manmohan Singh (22 May 2004-22 May 2009)

Indo-Sri Lanka relations have seen the best of times as well as the worst times. In between these a change of guard took place in India in which Dr. Manmohan Singh of Congress Party formed the government with the support of the Communistsand succeeded Atal Bihari Vajpayee as the new Prime Minister of India on 22 May 2004. The change of government at New Delhi witnessed no any policy shift in regard to Sri Lanka and as earlier regular contacts at different levels continued. In December 2004 India was the first country to respond to Sri Lanka's request for assistance after the tsunami tragedy. The Government of India, taking a generous view sent immediate assistance to Sri Lanka and reiterated that India remained committed to assist Colombo's remarkable efforts to recover from the tragedy of the tsunami of December 2004. New Delhi's grant consisted Rs. 100 crores for relief and reconstruction projects, a moratorium on debt repayments for three years as well as the factoring of post-tsunami reconstruction priorities into existing and proposed lines of credit.[133] India also announced further that it would provide equipment to set up a fully-equipped obstetrics and Gynaecology unit in the existing hospital at Dickoya. The President of Sri Lanka had thanked the Prime Minister and the Government and people of India for the generous assistance.

November 2005 witnessed the change of guard in Sri Lanka and Mahinda Rajapaksa replaced Chandrika Kumaratunga as the President of the country. Earlier in November 2004 and June 2005 President Chandrika Kumaratunga paid an official visit to New Delhi and exchanged views with Indian leaders on various issues of bilateral interest. On 10 June 2005 India and Sri Lanka conducted the sixth meeting of the Joint

Commission, co-chaired by External Affairs Ministers in Colombo. Mahinda Rajapaksa, the President of Sri Lanka, made his first visit abroad after his victory to India in December 2005. On the sidelines of NAM Summit in Havana on 16 September 2006, the new President of Sri Lanka met Indian Prime Minister and reached bilateral understanding on a number of issues. Rajapaksa's second visit to India took place in 2006 and it was followed by Sri Lankan Prime Minister's visit of India in January 2007. In the year 2008 Mahinda Rajapaksa came to India on a two-day pilgrimage tour and Rohitha Bogollagama, the Foreign Minister of Sri Lanka, visited India in September 2008. From Indian side too K. Natwar Singh, the External Affairs Minister of India, paid an official visit to Sri Lanka in June 2005 and India's Foreign Minister went to Colombo in January 2007 to hand over the SAARC Summit invitation to the Sri Lankan President. The visits undertaken so far have paved the way for furthering India's understanding with Sri Lanka in ways more than one.

Among the important visits paid to strengthen India's relations with Sri Lanka in diverse fields was the visit of the President of Sri Lanka Chandrika Bandaranaike Kumaratunga from November 3-7, 2004. She came at the invitation of the President of India Dr. A. P. J. Abdul Kalam and was accompanied by Lakshman Kadirgamar, Minister of Foreign Affairs and Susil Premajayantha, Minister of Power and Energy; and senior officials. In the discussions both sides reaffirmed the traditional convergence of views between them on a wide range of international issues. They remained deeply committed to opposing terrorism in all its forms and manifestations. Both sides agreed that there could be no justification for terrorism, be it political, religious or ideological. They also touched international issues and a meeting of minds on the need for urgent reform of the UN system to meet global challenges, including the expansion of the permanent membership of the Security Council was held. On the occasion India and Sri Lanka expressed their identity of views and agreed to cooperate in other forums, including the WTO.[134] Sri Lanka endorsed India's candidature for the permanent membership of the UN Security Council for which the latter had expressed sincere appreciation.

In their discussions both sides expressed happiness and deep satisfaction at the dynamism and energy in bilateral economic ties since the entry into force of the India-Sri Lanka Free Trade Agreement in March

2000. The President of Sri Lanka apprised the Indian leadership of the current status of peace process in Sri Lanka and New Delhi, on its part, reiterated its support for the process of seeking a comprehensive, negotiated settlement acceptable to all communities of Sri Lanka. The two sides agreed to explore the possibilities of intensification of cooperation in power sector. In fisheries while agreeing to continue with the existing understandings on the human treatment and early release of apprehended fishermen, it was decided to constitute a Joint Working Group which could meet frequently to deal with issues relating to fishermen between the two countries.[135] In cultural side they admitted that cultural exchanges is an area which has great scope in bringing the two peoples together. Both sides also agreed that the Cultural Exchange Programme, which was signed in October 2003, needs to be actively implemented. In addition both sides also discussed the activities relating to Buddhism, health, defence and canal project.

In succession Chandrika Bandaranaike Kumaratunga paid a working visit to India 2-4 June 2005 and held cordial, wide-ranging discussions with the Prime Minister of India. The discussions with Dr. Manmohan Singh were substantive and covered the gamut of bilateral relations between the two countries, post-tsunami reconstruction efforts in Sri Lanka, and regional and international issues. In the discussions both sides expressed their satisfaction with the excellent state of bilateral cooperation in diverse areas particularly in economic sphere. They also made known each other on the status of Tamil problems in which India emphasised the need for a negotiated settlement acceptable to all communities of the country. The discussions between the two leaders reflected a large measure of convergence of views between the two countries on a number of international issues including reform of the United Nations, the elimination of terrorism, SAARC, and regional cooperation. In course of the visit the President of Sri Lanka also met with Sonia Gandhi, Chairperson of the UPA, P. Chidambaram, Minister of Finance, and Mani Shankar Aiyar, Minister of Petroleum and Natural Gas and Minister of Panchayati Raj and discussed with them several issues of mutual interest.

At the invitation of Lakshman Kadirgamar, Minister of Foreign Affairs of Sri Lanka, K. Natwar Singh, Minister of External Affairs of

India, paid an official visit to Sri Lanka 9-11 June 2005 consisting of senior officials. On 10 June the Foreign Ministers of India and Sri Lanka Co-chaired the 6th Session of the Sri Lanka-India Joint Commission and reviewed the full range of bilateral relations in the context of growing cooperation between the two countries. They reaffirmed the importance of the Joint Commission and agreed on the need for it to meet regularly to address bilateral issues and to discuss ways and means to further intensify bilateral ties. In their discussions both sides welcomed the establishment of a Joint Working Group on fisheries, which held its first meeting in April 2005. It was agreed that the Joint Working Group should continue to meet to examine and made recommendations to further the cooperation in fisheries sector. Other issues discussed in the meeting were related to economy, health, education, research and defence. They welcomed the on-going close cooperation between the two countries in the areas of defence and security and felt the need for the regular exchange of visits by senior defence and security officials to enhance cooperation between India and Sri Lanka.

In September 2006 the Prime Minister of India and the President of Sri Lanka met at Havana on the sidelines of NAM Summit and reached bilateral understanding on a number of issues. As earlier both sides remained resolutely committed to opposing terrorism in all forms and manifestations. They agreed that the current global challenges require the reinvigoration of multilateralism including through strengthening of the UN system. Their thrust area included the commitment of India and Sri Lanka to work for the full realisation of the objectives identified by the 13th SAARC Summit in Dhaka last November and expressed the view that the South Asia Free Trade Agreement (SAFTA) once operationalised should pave the way for the SAARC nations to move towards even closer economic cooperations. They, in their meeting discussed several aspects of economic relations with emphasis on credit line, power project, renewable energy and collaboration in Information and Communication Technology (ICT). The President of Sri Lanka apprised the Prime Minister of India of recent attacks on Sri Lankan security forces and other ceasefire violations, and the two leaders deplored violations of the ceasefire which could undermine the prospects for peace in Sri Lanka. The Government of India welcomed the Sri Lankan Government's offer for early resumption of peace talks in the interest of country's sovereignty. In particular, their meeting desired to accelerate the cooperation in the field of Human Resource Development and fashioning of educational policies to meet the challenges of 21st century.

Union Finance Minister P. Chidambaram went to Sri Lanka in the second week of November 2007 to deliver the second Lakshman Kadirgamar Memorial Lecture on 'Growth Prospects in South Asia Challenges and Opportunities'. His lecture and a talk to the journalists in Colombo covered a wide range of subjects-bilateral as well as regional. He took the opportunity to caution the island that continuation of the armed conflict in Sri Lanka would deepen the divisions in society and make a negotiated settlement more difficult. When asked how the dialogue was possible with the LTTE seeking a separate state Chidambaram said that as both sides had taken an 'irreconcilable' stand there was need for a negotiated settlement. He, however, conceded that it was not an easy situation and India was conscious of the hurdles.[136] About the perception of India that had frozen its Sri Lanka policy after the assassination of Rajiv Gandhi he clarified that just because New Delhi was no longer the mediator it was not correct to say that Indian policy was stagnant. 'India is concerned and continuing encouragement of a political settlement acceptable to all'.[137]

In his lecture the Indian Finance Minister referred to the potential of South Asia as a potent economic bloc in the context of the island nation in order to make full use of the opportunities and laid emphasis on the atmosphere of peace, stability and security. Lamenting that South Asia is the least economically integrated region in the world, he underlined the urgent need for the leaders of the region to address non-controversial issues such as travel and communication. 'It is now generally acknowledged that South Asia in view of its recent economic performance, can match East Asia's growth rates. Sound macro-economic policies can attract huge investments to the region. Capital joining hands with the abundant and talented human resources of the region can turn it into a veritable economic power house.[138] He also spoke on multi-culturalism and added that plural societies such as Sri Lanka, there was no model of governance better suited to reflect and respond to the needs and aspirations of people than democracy. As part of a courtesy call he also met Mahinda Rajapaksa, the President of the island nation.

Regular exchange of visits and discussions on various issues concerning mutual benefits of India and Sri Lanka continued as earlier despite heavy fighting between the LTTE and the Sri Lankan security forces. In July 2008 Mahinda Rajapaksa, the President of Sri Lanka, paid a two-day pilgrimage journey to India and reiterated his government's readiness to resume talks with the Liberation Tigers of Tamil Eelam (LTTE) provided it laid down arms. In his talks to journalists at Tirumala he defended even earlier governments by saying that it was the government which had been negotiating with the LTTE for the past 20 years expecting some positive outcome every time. Rajapaksa expressed deep concern on the killing of innocent people and said that they become a casualty even when the ceasefire was declared. He, however, appreciated India's cooperation on the issue and said that New Delhi had always remained helpful to his country. 'The relations between the two countries, I can say, are at best.[139] In course of the talks he denied the charge that Indian fishermen were being harassed by the Sri Lankan defence forces. Emphasising the efforts to strengthen ties with all member countries of SAARC he said that Sri Lanka would provide necessary security to all leaders attending the SAARC meeting scheduled in the first week of August 2008.

India's Prime Minister Dr. Manmohan Singh when visited Sri Lanka to attend a SAARC Summit at Colombo, exchanged views on a wide range of issues of concern with Mahinda Rajapaksa, his Sri Lankan counterpart. The plight of fisher folk straying into each other's waters figured prominently in course of the talks and the two Prime Ministers agreed on the need to deal with fishermen apprehended in Sri Lankan waters in a humanitarian manner. The Indian authorities were also urged to discourage Indian fishermen from crossing the International Line of Demarcation, as their presence is used by the LTTE as cover for its activities. In the talks Dr. Singh laid emphasis on strong links between the two and Rajapaksa reiterated his government's commitment to implement comprehensively the provisions of the 13th Amendment to the Constitution on power devolution. He also told the Indian Prime Minister that Sri Lanka valued the economic benefits derived from the investments of Indian entrepreneurs and thanked the Indian government for the development and cooperation to Sri Lanka.[140] Further Rohitha

Bogollagama, the Foreign Minister of Sri Lanka, emphasised in a 90-minute interview to *The Hindu* at his office in Colombo on 6 September 2008 that democracy is the only answer we have for sustainable peace and terrorism in the hands of the LTTE has to be eliminated in order to sustain that progress for the people of the island as a whole.

Sri Lankan Tamils and LTTE

With the advancement of struggle between Sri Lankan security forces and the LTTE and weakening of the latter in the battlefield, Rajapaksa, the president of Sri Lanka, now concentrated on safety of Tamil brethren and providing them humanitarian help. He addressed the All Party Representative Conference at presidential palace and said, 'I wish to once again very clearly call on the LTTE to lay down arms and surrender. They should act in this manner and enter the democratic political process. Our aim should be to ensure the democratic political rights of our Tamil brethren. He remained firmly committed to a just and enduring political solution to the Tamil question in Sri Lanka and was clear that there were no military solutions to political questions. As to the humanitarian situation of displaced people and civilians affected by the military conflict he noted that his government was doing its utmost to meet their essential needs. Rajapaksa also made the point that the solution had to be given to the Tamil people and not to the LTTE, 'what is the use of giving a solution to terrorists? They are not giving up terrorism.' However the political parties of Tamil Nadu expressed its concern over the ongoing fighting in Sri Lanka and criticized the apathy of the Government of India in this regard. In six resolutions adopted at a recent all party meeting chaired by Tamil Nadu Chief Minister M. Karunanidhi the event was considered a 'ethnic genocide' and issued an ultimatum to the Central Government to provide humanitarian assistance to Tamils, cease all military assistance to the Sri Lankan Government and bring about a ceasefire. The passed resolution also threatened that failing these all Tamil Nadu MPs would resign from the regime of United Progressive Alliance.

Not only the government and people of Tamil Nadu but the Government of India too responded favourably to the humanitarian crisis of Sri Lanka. The Indian Government had communicated to Colombo the need for a peacefully negotiated political settlement to the Tamil issue in Sri Lanka. The very next day President Mahinda Rajapaksa telephoned Indian Prime Minister to give an assurance that all necessary measures were being taken to ensure the safety and welfare of Tamils in the island nation. In conversation Manmohan Singh stressed the need to ensure that rights and welfare of the Tamil community were not enmeshed in the ongoing hostilities and the LTTE and reiterated India's stance that there could be no military solution to the conflict. He also urged Rajapaksa to initiate the process for a political settlement within the framework of a united Sri Lanka. Assurance on Tamil's safety as given by Sri Lankan government, was informed by Pranab Mukherjee, India's Minister for External Affairs, in a statement in the Lok Sabha and Rajya Sabha respectively after the several members expressed their views on the situation in Sri Lanka.

In this hour of crisis India and Sri Lanka in the last week of October 2008 reached an agreement on ensuring the protection of Indian fishermen entering Sri Lankan waters and in addition Sri Lanka promised to guard against civilian casualties in the war against the LTTE. The positive developments in relations between the two countries and M. Karunanidhi's meeting with Pranab Mukherjee provided them a practical way out of the political crisis and they agreed to shift the focus from the issue of forcing a ceasefire in the war between the Sri Lankan armed forces and the LTTE to extending humanitarian aid to the Tamil civilian population affected by the conflict. The Sri Lankan President in an interview to the English daily '*The Hindu*' reiterated his commitment to avoiding harm to civilians and to ending their suffering in a short time. He also welcomed the offer of relief material from India and particularly from Tamil Nadu and added that his government would facilitate delivery and cooperate with the Government of India in addressing the humanitarian issue.[141]

In response to an appeal issued by M. Karunanidhi, the Chief Minister of Tamil Nadu, the Dravida Munnetra Kazhagam's (DMK) Central and State Ministers, Members of Parliament and State Assembly contributed liberally towards providing relief materials to Sri Lankan Tamils. From the funds collected for the humanitarian help of Sri Lankan Tamils as disclosed by Karunanidhi, would be sent to the island nation in the form of different relief materials and would be routed through the

Centre. Earlier to this decision under the United Nation's programme its agencies had delivered 750 metric tonnes of food to an estimated 2,30,000 civilians in country's north where the military and the LTTE were engaged in battles. The UN agencies would also monitor the distribution at three locations where there is a heavy concentration of affected civilians. The world body's humanitarian help to affected civilians of Sri Lanka continued on regular basis even thereafter.

By the time Basil Rajapaksa, a member of Parliament and Senior Advisor to the President of Sri Lanka visited India as the special envoy of the president and the issue was raised in Sri Lankan parliament by the United National Party members. There was also an speculation in Sri Lankan media about a secret deal with the New Delhi on the current political crisis. In reply to member's question and media's apprehension it was asserted that there was a clear understanding between New Delhi and Colombo on its efforts to defeat terrorism and restore democracy in the north. Sri Lanka's Foreign Minister Rohitha Bogollagama refuting the charges by members and media characterised the strong bonds of friendship and trust that the present government of Sri Lanka had forged with the political leadership of India as a manifestation of the long standing historical ties between the two countries. He also tabled two official communiqués issued jointly by India-Sri Lanka Joint Press Release and the India-Sri Lanka Joint Statement on fishing arrangements.[142] Regarding India's humanitarian assistance to affected civilians the minister stressed that India had come forward with the help as a gesture of goodwill which reflected the friendship and spirit of the good neighbourliness between the two countries.

As a follow up of October 26, 2008, India-Sri Lanka joint statement in which both sides decided that India would provide humanitarian relief assistance in Sri Lanka the former had formally handed over, 1680 tonnes of relief material to the International Red Cross Committee for distribution to civilians in north Sri Lanka. It would be involved in a supervisory capacity and the actual distribution would be done by the government agents. The consignment of relief materials was handed over by Alok Prasad, India's High Commissioner to Sri Lanka and consisted of food, clothing and personal hygiene items in 80,000 family packs. Despite extending humanitarian relief New Delhi did not forget to remind Sri

Lanka that India would do everything possible to find a political solution to the Sri Lankan Tamil's issue. Indian Prime Minister Manmohan Singh assured this to a delegation of altogether 35 members of Parliament from Tamil Nadu and Puducherry who wanted Centre's more serious intervention to bring about a ceasefire in the island nation.[143] On the other in view of Mumbai terror attacks, conveying Sri Lankan condolences to the people of India, Nirmal Siripala De Silva, its Minister for Healthcare and Nutrition called on the South Asian countries to come together and chalk out a strong plan to stamp out terrorism.

Economic Relations

In economic sphere the change of guards in India in May 2004 followed by Sri Lanka in November 2005 cast no negative shadow on India-Sri Lanka economic relations. In post-FTA phase both are thinking of expanding it to include more items and to remove some non-tariff barriers, liberalise the Rules of Origin and undertake trade facilitation. Like earlier the growth in trade continued and bilateral trade rose to US $ 2.025 billion in 2005. Exports from India to Sri Lanka in 2005 amounted to US $ 1.437 billion, while exports from Sri Lanka to India in the same year amounted to US $ 588 million. At 15% of the total, India is the biggest source of Sri Lankan imports. It is also the 3rd largest destination for Sri Lankan exports. In September 2006 Indo-Sri Lanka Chamber of Commerce and Industry was inaugurated by Finance Minister Chidambaram. In comparison to earlier the ratio of trade has come down from 10.3:1 in 2000 to 3.7:1 in 2006.[144] Recently, as a gesture of friendship, India overlooked the fact that it was also a producer of tea and garments and agreed to take a limited quantity of these items from Sri Lanka. India has given Sri Lanka an annual quota of 15 million kg. of tea besides eight million pieces of garments. In October 2007, India undertook to lift the restriction on the port of entry for garments. Of the quota of eight million pieces, three million would be exempt from the requirement to source the basic fabric from India. Experts even say that there is still a lot that Sri Lankans can do under the existing FTA as most of the tariff lines provided in the said agreement remain unutilised. Much can be done to fully exploit the mammoth Indian market of over one billion people.

After the change of government in India in May 2004 in which Dr. Manmohan Singh became the new Prime Minister of the country, the Sri

Lankan President Chandrika Kumaratunga, at the invitation of the President of India came to New Delhi 3-7 November, 2004. In the talks both sides expressed happiness that bilateral trade has exceeded US $ 1.5 billion in 2003-04. In course of the visit the leaders of India and Sri Lanka resolved to inject impetus to the process of further economic integration of the two economies by expediting negotiations on the Comprehensive Economic Partnership Agreement (CEPA) between the two countries. Further the visit of Sri Lankan President took place in June 2005 and wide ranging discussions were held between Chandrika Kumaratunga and Indian Prime Minister Manmohan Singh. They expressed satisfaction with the excellent state of bilateral cooperation in diverse fields. The two leaders noted that bilateral trade recorded a volume of US $ 1.8 billion in 2004 with the trade imbalance between them having narrowed significantly. Taking stock of the encouraging progress on negotiations on a Comprehensive Economic Partnership Agreement the two leaders directed that the negotiations on the CEPA be concluded by the end of 2005 so as to give a new thrust to overall bilateral business activity as well as to encourage investments in several areas of mutual interest and thereby strengthen the partnership in economic development between the two countries.

In line the visit of K. Natwar Singh, India's Minister for External Affairs, to Sri Lanka in June 2005, provided the two countries an opportunity to discuss their problems and prospects of economic relations. Although in course of the visit Indian minister exchanged views on several bilateral, regional and international issue, his journey to the island nation was concentrated around the 6th session of the Sri Lanka-India Joint Commission scheduled on 10th June. Reviewing the full range of bilateral relations the joint commission noted the contribution of Free Trade Agreement between the two countries which had enhanced bilateral economic activity and now represented by a two-way trade volume of US $ 1.8 billion. In the meeting both sides decided to provide avenues for widening economic cooperation and agreed that closer people-to-people contact would contribute positively to strengthening the friendship between the two countries.

The Joint Commission unanimously emphasised the need for greater cooperation in joint promotional activities in order to attract tourists to the region. It stressed the fact that frequency of air travel between the two countries could be further increased by additional liberalization of the aviation sector, particularly with regard to flights to major Indian cities. During the meeting the Indian side announced that it would give a grant of Sri Lankan Rupees ten million to finance a pilot project of establishing 20 e-libraries. Both sides urged the need for close cooperation in the field of science and technologies between the two countries and Sri Lanka thanked India for the offer made to Sri Lankan scientists to join Indian scientists in carrying out research in the Antarctic under the Indian Antarctic Research Programme. Apart from this project investments in the power, energy and transport sectors were discussed and they agreed to explore the further development of the oil storage complex in Trincomalee into an expanded facility catering to the region. Successful conclusion of the joint commission's session witnessed furthering of India-Sri Lanka relations in diverse fields with particular emphasis on economic issue.

In the change of guard in Sri Lanka Mahinda Rajapaksa was elected the President of the island nation in November 2005 replacing Chandrika Kumaratunga. Under the new dispensation the re-engineering of an alternative policy strategy was articulated in the document entitled 10-Year Horizon : A Development Framework for 2006-16 based on his manifesto for the 2005 presidential election. The new policy recognised market-oriented strategies and endorsed the need to balance the roles of private and public sectors. The strategy has a four-pronged approach. (i) The expansion of government revenue efforts through institutional capacity development and the introduction of technology to administer move effectively Value Added Tax (VAT) and Income Tax, in Sri Lanka's service sector-led economy (ii) The elimination of unsustainable and economically costly fiscal losses, such as the dramatic reduction of the fuel subsidy which was Sri Lanka's Rs. 26.4 billion in 2004 to Rs. 0.6 billion in 2007; (iii) Mobilisation of long term funding in support of large infrastructure projects, including hydro and coal power plants, highway networks, irrigation and water supply projects and the expansion of part facilities; and (iv) Restructuring of national debt to reduce associated fiscal costs, including through the recent entry of the Government into international capital market and the opening of treasury bonds for foreign investors.[145]

The strategy was launched in a difficult environment marked by the post-tsunami recovery, the effort to counter terrorism, the rise in international oil prices and the lapse of the Multi-Fibre Agreement that had provided assured access for apparel exports to Western markets. However, the outcome of the fiscal policy reforms was encouraging. The reform process has raised revenue to 16 per cent of GDP and reduced recurrent expenditure to 17.4 per cent of GDP. Public investment has increased to 6.7 per cent of GDP and the overall deficit has declined to 7.7 per cent of GDP. The progress in reducing the public debt level is satisfactory and the 2007 level of public debt to GDP, is the lowest since 1997. With this fiscal transformation the economy of Sri Lanka saw an average growth of 6.7 per cent during 2005-2006. Per capita income, which was $1.030 in 2004, reached $ 1.630 in 2007. Unemployment has declined to 6 per cent. Despite these positive responses of the new strategy inflation remained high with core inflation itself reaching 9 per cent, demanding greater fiscal consolidation.[146] The policy makers of Sri Lanka, in the context of global uncertainties and fears of an economic slow down, feel that sustaining the growth process would require the continued attention.

Wide ranging discussions were held in September 2006 when Mahinda Rajapaksa, the President of Sri Lanka met with Indian Prime Minister Manmohan Singh on the sidelines of NAM Summit at Havana. On the occasion the two leaders exchanged their view on contemporary issues of the world and matters of mutual benefit. In economic sphere they welcomed the bilateral understandings being reached on identifying joint ventures for the development of the eastern Sri Lankan Port City of Trincomalee and its surrounding regions. In this context it was agreed to set up a coal based power project of 2×250 MW capacity in the Trincomalee region of Sri Lanka as a joint venture between the National Thermal Power Company of India and the Ceylon Electricity Board, a Government of Sri Lankan entity. As the Rajapaksa's government had aimed to revitalise the agriculture and infrastructure, they agreed that there was great potential for cooperation in the areas of agriculture and renewable energy. Both sides discussed collaboration in the Information and Communication Technology (ICT) area and as a step further India and Sri Lanka decided to set up an ICT Park in Sri Lanka.

In addition to the earlier treaties and agreements including the benefits of FTA for Sri Lanka the Tea Research Association of India and

Tea Research Institute of Sri Lanka entered into a research collaboration in the first week of September 2008 and signed a Memorandum of Understanding (MoU). The signed MoU would include plant breeding, studies on maximum residue level, biological control of pests, mechanisation of field and factory operations, development of chemical index for quality tea, development of water harvesting techniques and development of soil health.[147] It was signed by C. S. Bedi, Chairman, Tea Research Association of India and G. Jayawardene, Chairman, Tea Research Board of Sri Lanka at Jorhat (Guwahati) in the presence of D. M. Jayaratne, Sri Lankan Minister of Plantation. Jayawardene, the Sri Lankan Chairman after signing the Memorandum said that it would be beneficial for both the countries in the international scenario as India, being the largest black tea producer, and Sri Lanka, being the largest exporter of tea could work and represent to international organisations.

Defence

Defence cooperation between India and Sri Lanka formed an integral part of overall relations between the two countries. In June 2005 when K. Natwar Singh, India's Minister for External Affairs, visited Sri Lanka the two sides welcomed the on going close cooperation in the areas of defence and security. In this connection Sri Lanka thanked India for the offer of training for police personnel in India and other facilities extended. About 53% of the training of Sri Lankan Armed Forces are carried out in India and there has been a significant increase in the number of training slots offered to Sri Lankan armed forces personnel in recent years. For 2006-07, the allotted slots had been 870 with 545 for the Army, 216 for Navy and 109 for Air Force. In 2005-06, 977 courses were offered; and for 2007-08, courses have been near 2579 with 1208 for Army, 518 for Navy and 853 for Air Force. Besides this, there is continued cooperation in terms of exchange of visits and cooperation between Navies. It is hoped that the regular exchange of visits by senior defence and security officials would contribute to enhance cooperation in this field between the two countries.

References

1. Institute of Defence Studies and Analysis, News Review of South Asia (New Delhi) March 1977, p. 65.

2. India and Foreign Review, August 1, 1977., p. 20.
3. Ibid.
4. Arthur A. Banks, ed., Political Handbook of the World (New York, 1978), pp. 30-33.
5. The Hindu (Madras), August 25, 1977.
6. India and Foreign Review, September 1, 1977, pp. 8-9.
7. See; Lok Sabha Debates, 8 December 1977, colm. 98.
8. S. C. Gangal, Trends in India's Foreign Policy", K. P. Mishra, ed., Janata's Foreign Policy (Vikas Publishing House, New Delhi, 1979), p. 45.
9. The Financial Express (Bombay), February 1, 1978.
10. S. C. Gangal, India's Foreign Policy-A Documentary Study of India's Foreign Policy since the Installation of the Janata Government on 24 March, 1977 (Young Asia Publications, New Delhi, 1980), p. 307.
11. Ibid.
12. The Hindu, April 5, 1978.
13. The Hindustan Times, June 30, 1978.
14. The Hindu, October 28, 1978.
15. Ibid.
16. Asian Recorder, 3-9 December 1978, p. 14627.
17. Foreign Affairs Record, October 1978, p. 319.
18. Ibid.
19. The Patriot (New Delhi), October 30, 1978.
20. The Ceylon Daily News (Colombo), November 4, 1978.
21. Asian Recorder, 19-25 March 1979, pp. 14800-14801.
22. Lok Sabha Debates, Vol. XXII, 2 March 1979, colms. 277-79.
23. Asian Recorder, op.cit., pp. 146-271.
24. Ibid.
25. Lok Sabha Debates, op.cit., colms. 277-79.
26. Asian Recorder, op.cit.
27. Ibid.
28. Ibid.
29. The Hindu, February 3, 1979.
30. See the brief summary of S. Thondaman, M. P. and President of Ceylon Worker's Congress in Asian Recorder, 1-7 October 1978, pp. 14533-34.
31. Ibid.
32. "New Avenues of Firmer Economic Ties", Commerce (Bombay), 10 February 1978, Vol. 138, p. 154.

33. Asian Recorder, 3-9 December 1978, p. 14627.
34. New Review on South Asia, December 1978, p. 717.
35. Ibid., January 1979, p. 798.
36. Foreign Affairs Record, November 1977, p. 239.
37. Ibid.
38. The Indian Express, December 1, 1989.
39. V. N. Viswanathan, "Indo-Sri Lanka Relations", India Quarterly, A Journal of International Affairs, Vol. XLVI. no. 1, January-March 1990 (Indian Council of World Affairs, New Delhi, 1990), pp. 90-95.
40. The Hindustan Times, December 7, 1989.
41. Ibid.
42. The Hindu, December 10, 1989.
43. The Indian Express, December 11, 1989.
44. The Hindu, December 22, 1989.
45. The National Herald, December 11, 1989.
46. The Patriot, December 16, 1989.
47. Bhabani Sen Gupta, "After IPKF is Out", The Hindustan Times, December 23, 1989.
48. The Times of India, January 1, 1990.
49. The Hindu, January 1, 1990.
50. Ibid., January 6, 1990.
51. The Hindustan Times, January 7, 1990.
52. Ibid.
53. Ibid, January 9, 1990.
54. The Patriot, January 9, 1990.
55. The Hindu, January 13, 1990.
56. Ibid.
57. The Tribune, January 21, 1990.
58. The Hindu, February 5, 1990.
59. Ibid.
60. The Times of India, February 11, 1990.
61. Ibid., February 16, 1990.
62. Ibid.
63. The Indian Express, March 26, 1990.
64. Nikhil Chakravartty, "Foreign Ties : Why so Formal ?" The Times of India, June 10, 1990.

65. The Hindustan Times, March 26, 1990.
66. The Indian Express, March 27, 1990.
67. The Hindustan Times, March 29, 1990.
68. The Hindu, June 5, 1990.
69. The Statesman, June 22, 1990.
70. The Hindu, June 29, 1990.
71. Ibid.
72. Ibid., July 3, 1990.
73. The Indian Express, July 1, 1990.
74. Ibid., July 4, 1990.
75. The Times of India, July 8, 1990.
76. The Statesman, July 18, 1990.
77. The Indian Express, July 18, 1990.
78. Ibid., July 31, 1990.
79. The Hindu, August 28, 1990.
80. The Times of India, June 10, 1990.
81. The Hindustan Times, December 26, 1989.
82. Ibid., January 7, 1990.
83. The Indian Express, March 26, 1990.
84. N. S. Jagunnathan, "The End of a Misadventure", Ibid., April 2, 1990.
85. Ibid., July 18, 1990.
86. Foreign Affairs Record, Vol. XXXVII, no. 1, January 1991, pp. 7-8.
87. The Hindu, January 26, 1991.
88. Ibid.
89. Ibid, January 30, 1991.
90. Ibid., January 31, 1991.
91. The Statesman, February 1, 1991.
92. Foreign Affairs Record, Vol. XXXVII, no. 2, February 1991, p. 17.
93. Ibid.
94. The Times of India, February 2, 1991.
95. Foreign Affairs Record, Vol. XXXVII, no. 3, March 1991, pp. 38-39.
96. Ibid., Vol. XLII, no. 6, June 1996, p. 109.
97. Indian Recorder, 22-28 July 1996, p. 2135.
98. Foreign Affairs Record, op.cit.
99. Indian Recorder, op.cit., p. 2135.
100. Ibid.

101. Ibid., Vol. III, no. 50, 9-15 December 1996, p. 2457.
102. SAARC, SCAN, Vol. 1, issue 8, June 1997, (New Delhi), p. 5.
103. The Hindustan Times, August 15, 1997.
104. Seema Guha, "The Lankan Tug-of-War", The Times of India, July 28, 1997.
105. The Hindustan Times, August 21, 1997.
106. Ibid., August 30, 1997.
107. Ibid., December 12, 1997.
108. Ibid., March 3, 1998.
109. Ibid., March 15, 1998.
110. Ibid., May 15, 1998.
111. Ibid., May 19, 1998.
112. John Cherian, "Clear and Coherent-Indian Foreign Policy Under I. K. Gujral", Frontline Vol. 14, no. 6, March 22-4 April, 1997 (S. Rangarajan, Chennai, 1997), pp. 4-5.
113. Ibid., p. 8.
114. The Hindustan Times, May 25. 1998.
115. Ibid., editorial, August 1, 1998.
116. Nitya Chakraborty, "SAARC : Bumpy Road Ahead", Ibid, August 3, 1998.
117. Ibid., November 6, 1998.
118. Ibid., editorial, September 5, 1998.
119. India's ban on the LTTE was imposed in May 1992, a year after the assassination of Rajiv Gandhi. It has to be reviewed every two years. Ibid., November 5, 1998.
120. The Hindu, December 21, 2001.
121. Brief on India-Sri Lanka Relations, Ministry of External Affairs BMS Division, February 26, 2007.
122. See, the Press Release, New Delhi, February 23, 2001.
123. Ibid.
124. India-Sri Lanka Joint Statement, New Delhi, December 24, 2001.
125. Ibid.
126. India-Sri Lanka Joint Statement, New Delhi, June 11, 2002.
127. Ibid., Colombo, July 12, 2002.
128. Joint Press Release, New Delhi, October 21, 2003.
129. Ibid.

130. Ibid.
131. Vinod F. Khobragade, 'Re-Thinking Power Devolution in Sri Lanka', Dr. Subhash Kashyap, ed. South Asia Politics, Vol.6, no.1, May 2007, New Delhi, pp. 23-26.
132. V. Suryanarayan, 'Explaining Prabakaran's Persistent Defiance', The Hindu, December 21, 2007.
133. Joint Press Statement, New Delhi, June 3, 2005.
134. Joint Press Release, New Delhi, November 7, 2004.
135. Ibid.
136. The Hindu, November 12, 2007.
137. Ibid.
138. Ibid.
139. Ibid., July 13, 2008.
140. Ibid., August 2, and September 11, 2008.
141. Ibid., editorial, October 29, 2008.
142. For detail see the Joint Press Release and the Joint Statement issued at New Delhi on 26 October 2008.
143. The Hindu, December 3, 2008.
144. Brief on India-Sri Lanka Relations, Ministry of External Affairs, BSM Division, February 26, 2007.
145. P. B. Jayasundera, 'Moving to Create More Fiscal Space', The Hindu, June 5, 2008.
146. Ibid.
147. Ibid., September 5, 2008.

Bibliography

A. Books

Abbas, B.M.A.T., Ganges Water Dispute (Dhaka University Press Dhaka, 1982).

Agrawal, Govind R and Jai P. Rana, Nepal and Non-Alignment (Centre for Economic Development and Administration, Tribhuvan University, Kathmandu, 1982).

Aggarwala Adish C., Rajiv Gandhi : An Assessment (Amish Publication, New Delhi, 1993).

Ahluwalia B.K. and Shashi Ahluwalia, Rajiv Gandhi- A Profile in Courage (Intellectual Publishing House, New Delhi, 1985)

Ahmed, Kamruddin (ed.), Bangladesh Politics, Centre for Social Studies, Dhaka, 1980).

Appadorai, A., The Domestic Roots of India's Foregin Policy (Oxford University Press, Delhi, 1981).

____________ (ed), Selected Documents on India's Foreign Policy and Relation 1947-1972 (Oxford University Press, Newyork, 1982).

Arthur, S. Banks, (ed.) Political Handbook of the World (Newyork, 1978).

Ayoob, Mohammed, India, Pakistan and Bangladesh, Search for a New Relationship (Indian Council of World Affairs, New Delhi, 1975).

____________(ed.) The Politics of Islamic Assertion, (New Delhi, Vikas, 1982).

Bhargava, G.S. (ed.), Perestroika in India : V.P. Singh's Prime Ministership (New Delhi, 1990).

Bhatia, Shyam, India's Nuclear Bomb (Vikas Publishing House, UP, India, 1979).

Bhuiyan, Abdul Wadud, Emergence of Bangladesh and Role of Awami League (Vikas, New Delhi, 1982).

Bhasin, A. S. (ed) Nepal's Relations with India and China, Documents 1947-1992, Vol. 1 (Siba Exim, Delhi, 1994).

Bose, Sugata and Jalal, Ayesha, Modern South Asia-History, Culture Political Economy (Oxford University Press, New Delhi, 2004).

Bose, Sumantra, Kashmir-Roots of Conflict and Paths to Peace (Vistaar Publications, New Delhi, 2003).

Chavan, Yashwant Rao B., India's Foreign Policy (Somaiya Publishers, Bombay, 1979).

Chakravarty, S. K., The Evolution of Politics in Bangladesh 1947-1978 (Associate Publishing House, New Delhi, 1978).

Chaudhuri, Sailen, Maoist Betrayal: India a Case Study (Sterling Publishers NewDelhi, 1980).

Chatterjee, R. K., India's Land Border—Problems and Challenges (Sterling publishers, New Delhi, 1978).

Chopra, Surendra, ed., Studies in India's Foreign Policy (Amritsar, 1980).

Cohen, Stephen P. and Park, Richard L., India: Emergent Power (Crane, Russak & Company, Newyork, 1978).

Christopher, Clapham, Foreign Policy Making in Developing States : A Comparative Approach (Praeger Publishers, Newyork, 1977).

Cope, David R., Hills Peter and James peter, eds., Energy Policy and Land Use Planning : An International Perspective (pergamon press, Oxford, London, 1984).

Doctor, Adi H., Essays on India's Foreign Policy (National Publishing House, New Delhi, 1977).

Dutta, S., Students Movement in Arunachal Pradesh (Himalayan Publishers, Itanagar, 1998).

Dutt, Subimal, With Nehru in the Foreign Office (minerva Associates, Calcutta, 1977).

Dutt, V. P., India's Foreign Policy (Vikas Publishing House, New Delhi, 1984).

Evans, Nigel and Hope Chris, Nuclear Power–Future Costs and Benefits (Cambridge University Press, London, 1984).

Foreign Affairs Record (Ministry of External Affairs, External Publicity Division, Government of India, New Delhi, 1977-1980,1989-1991 and 1996-1997).

Gaige, Frederick H., Regionalism and National Unity in Nepal (Vikas Publishing House, New Delhi, 1975).

Gangal, S. C., India's Foreign Policy—A Documentary Study of India's Foreign Policy since the Installation of the Janata Government on 24 March 1977 (Young Asia publishers, New Delhi, 1980).

Haksar, P.N., Premonitions (Inter press, Bombay, 1979).

Imam, Zafar, ed., Soviet View of India 1957-1975 (Kalyani Publishers, Delhi, 1977).

India 1983, Compiled by Research and Reference Division (Publication Division, Ministry of Information and Broadcasting, Government of India, New Delhi, 1983).

Islam, Nurul, Development Planning in Bangladesh : A Study in Political Economy (London, C. Hurst and Co., 1977).

J. Bandyopadhyaya, The Making of India's Foreign Policy (Bombay, 1980).

Jackson, Robert, South Asian Crisis: India, Pakistan, Bangladesh,-(Chatto and Windus, London, 1975).

Jain, R. K., China-South Asian Relations 1947-1980 (Radiant Publishers, New Delhi, 1981).

Jha, S. K., Uneasy Partners: India and Nepal in the Post-Colonial Era (Manas, New Delhi, 1975).

Kaul, T. N., India, China and Indo-China (Allied Publishers, New Delhi, 1980).

______ Diplomacy in Peace and War : Recollections and Reflections (Vikas Publishing House, New Delhi, 1979).

Khanna, V. N., Foreign Policy of India (Vikas Publishing House, New Delhi, 2004),

Kodikara, Shelton, U., ed., External Compulsions of South Asian Politics (Sage Publications, New Delhi, 1993).

Koithara, Verghese, Society, State and Security-The Indian Experience (Sage Publications, New Delhi, 1992).

Kukreja, Veena, Contemporary Pakistan-Political Process, Conflicts and Crisis (Sage Publications, New Delhi, 2003).

Kumaraswamy, P.R., ed., Security Beyond Survival (Sage Publications, New Delhi, 2004).

Kumar, D. P., Nepal: Year of Decision (Vikas Publishing House, New Delhi, 1980).

Madan Gopal, India as a World Power : Aspects of Foreign Policy (Sagar Publications, New Delhi, 1974).

Madhu Limaya, India and the World (New Delhi, 1979).

______ Problems of India's Foreign Policy, N. C. Mehrotra, ed. (Atma Ram and Sons, New Delhi, 1984).

Majumdar, Asis Kumar, South East Asia in Indian Foreign Policy (B. Mitra, NayaPrakash, Calcutta, 1982).

Mallik, Deva Narayan, Post-war International Politics-A Quadripartite Survey (Veena Mandir Publishers, Muzaffarpur, 1973).

Maniruzzaman, Talukdar, Radical Politics and the Emergence of Bangladesh (Dhaka, Bangladesh Book International, 1975).

___________ Bangladesh Revolution and Its Aftermath (Dhaka, Bangladesh Book International, 1980).

Mirchandari, G. G., ed, Reporting India 1977 (Abhinav Publications, New Delhi, 1978).

Mishra, Pramod K., South Asia in International politics (Udh Publishers, Delhi, 1984).

Muhith, A. M. A., Bangladesh: Emergence of a Nation (Dhaka, Bangladesh Book International, 1980).

Naik. J. A., ed., India in Asia and Africa—Documents: 1976-1978 (Avinash Reference Publication, Maharashtra).

______ The Great Janata Revolution (S. Chand and Company, New Delhi, 1977).

______ The Pak Bomb and Rajiv's India (National Publishing House, New Delhi, 1986).

Narayan, Shriman, India and Nepal : An Exercise in Open Diplomacy (New Delhi, 1971).

Nath, Tribhuvan, The Nepalese Dilemma 1960-74 (New Delhi, 1975).

Panda, Kamalakanta and Mishra, Pramod, The New Perspectives in India's Foreign Policy, The Janata Phase (Sandeep Prakashan, Delhi, 1980).

Ramakant, Nepal, China and India (Abhinav Publications, New Delhi, 1976).

Rasgotra, M., Chopra, V D. and Mishra K. P. eds., India's Foreign Policy in the 1990s (Patriot Publishers, New Delhi, 1990).

Razzaq, Abdur, Bangladesh: State of the Nation (Dhaka University, 1981).

Saini, M. K., ed, Aspects on Non-Alignment (Kalamkar Prakashan, New Delhi, 1980).

Shaha, Rishikesh, Nepali Politics: Retrospect and Prospect (Delhi, 1975).

__________Politics in Nepal 1980-1991 (Manohar Publishers, New Delhi, 1992).

Shelly, Mizanur Rahman, Emergence of a New Nation in a Multipolar World: Bangladesh. (Dhaka, University Press, 1979).

Singh, Kuldip, India and Bangladesh (Anmol Publications, Delhi, 1987).

Singh, Mahavir, ed., International Terrorism and Religious Extremism (Anamica Publishers, New Delhi, 2004).

Singh, Rajkumar, Less Tasty Indo-Nepal Political Relations 1947-1997 (Novelty & Co., Patna, 1998).

__________, Indo-Pak Nuclear Tension 1974-1998 (Samiksha Prakashan, New Delhi, 2001).

__________, India's Foreign Policy : The First Study in Continuity and Change (Samiksha Prakashan, New Delhi, 2001).

__________, Past, Present and Future of Kashmir (Gyan Publishing House, New Delhi, 2008).

__________, India and Pakistan-Social, Political and Military Perspectives (Regal Publications, New Delhi, 2009).

__________, Global Dimensions of Indo-Nepal Political Relations: Post Independence (Gyan Publishing House, New Delhi, 2010).

Sobhan, Rahman, The Crisis of External Dependence: The Political Economy of Foreign Aid to Bangladesh (Dhaka University Press, 1982).

Tharoor, Shashi, Reasons of State: Political Development and India's Foreign Policy Under Indira Gandhi 1966-1977 (Vikas Publishing House, New Delhi, 1982).

Ulyanovsky, Rostislav, National Liberation (Progress Publishers, Moscow, 1978).

Vajpayee, Atal Bihari, New Dimensions of India's Foreign Policy (Vision Book New Delhi, 1979).

Vohra, Dewan C., India's Aid Diplomacy in the Third World (Vikas Publishing House, New Delhi, 1980).

Wesson, Robert G., Foreign Policy for a New Age (Houghton Miffliu Company Boston, London, 1977).

Zaidi, A. M. and Zaidi, S. G., eds., The Encyclopaedia of Indian National Congress (S. Chand & Company, New Delhi, 1981).

B. Articles in Periodicals and Newspapers

Ahmad, Emajuddin, "Current Trends in Islam in Bangladesh" , Economic and Political Weekly, Vol. XVIII, no. 25,18 June, 1983.

Ahmed, Parveen, "Bangladesh Political Alliance Threatens More Protests of Upcoming Election", Associated Press, December 18, 2006.

Ahmar, Moonis, "The Role of CBM's in the Post Cold War Era", ACDIS, Occasional Paper (Department of International Relations University of Karachi, Pakistan, October, 1993) pp. 9-12.

Ahmed, Naveed, "The Non-aligned Movement and Pakistan", Pakistan Horizon (Karachi), Vol. 32, no.4, Fourth Quarter, 1979, pp. 79-91.

Anand, R. P., "Role of New Afro-Asian Countries in the Present Legal Order" , American Journal of International Law, Vol. 56.

Anita, S. N., "Islamic Bomb and India: An Appraisal", Mainstream (New Delhi) Vol. 17, no.45, 7 July 1979, pp. 11-12 and 34.

Ayoob, Mohammed, "Two Faces of Islam", Asian Survey, Vol. 19, no. 6, June, 1979.

Bagchi Ajoy, "The General Just Cannot Deliver", The Pioneer, January 26, 2002.

Bahadur Kalim, "India and Pakistan", Bimal Prasad, ed, International Studies, Vol. 17 (Vikas Publishing House, New Delhi, 1978), p. 517.

Bajpai, K.Shankar, "Three in This Marriage", The Hindustan Times, March 15, 2005.

Baral, J. K., "From Simla to Delhi : A Case Study of a Sub-system Diplomacy", Indian Journal of Political Science (Bombay), Vol. 38, no. 2, April-June 1977, pp. 918-37.

Baral, L.S., "India and Nepal", Bimal Prasad, ed., India's Foreign Policy-Studies in Continuity and Change (Vikas Publishing House, New Delhi, 1979), pp. 170-71

Barnds, William J., "United States Policy towards South Asia : Shifting Perceptions and Policy Choices" , Pacific Community, Vol. 8, no. 4, July 1977).

Beri, H. N., "Pakistan and CENTO", Strategic Analysis (New Delhi), Vol. 1, no.3, January 1977, pp. 9-14.

Bista, K. N., "Nepal and India Stand for Cooperation with All Nations", The Rising Nepal, April 20, 1972.

Bull, Hedley, "The Conduct of American Foreign Policy: A View from Abroad Consisting Under Pressure", Foreign Affairs, Vol. 57, 1978, p. 459.

Chakravartty Nikhil, "Foreign Ties: Why So Formal", The Times of India, June 10, 1990.

Chari, P. R., "India's Nuclear Policy", K. P. Misra, ed., Janata's Foreign Policy (Vikas Publishing House, New Delhi, 1979), p. 57

Chaturvedi, S. K., "Indo-Nepal Relations: Tension Area", Vol. XXXIII no.5, May 1989 (Indian Council of World Affairs, New Delhi, 1989) p. 77.

Chellaney, Brahma, "Hard Words Soft Actions", The Hindustan Times, February 29, 2000.

______, "A Perilous Course", Ibid., January 11, 2001.

______, "Flailing in the Shadows", Ibid., October 3, 2001.

______, "Pakistan's Janus Face", Ibid., February 20, 2002.

______, "Closet Nehruvian", Ibid., August, 7, 2003.

______, "LoC, Stock and Barrel", Ibid., August 31, 2004.

Chowdhury, G. W., "Bangladesh : Coup and Counter Coup: International Implications", ORBIS, Vol. XIX, no. 4, Winter, 1976.

Dar, A. N., "Mr. Bhattarai Plays Right", The National Herald, June 16, 1990.

___________"Need for a Cautious Approach in Kashmir", The Hindustan Times (New Delhi), August 27, 1997.

Desai, Morarji, "Farakka Agreement: An Acid Test of India's Foreign Policy", India and Foreign Review (New Delhi), Vol. 15, no. 4, 1 December 1977, pp. 10-12

Dev. S. Kumar, "Towards Mature Indo-Nepal Ties", Commerce, Vol. 135, no. 447, December 1977, p. 1152.

Dieter, Bram, "Changes in South Asia Intra-regional and External Relationship", The World Today, vol. 34 (London, October 1978), p. 393.

Dixit, J. N., "In the General's Own Words", The Hindustan Times, February 2, 2000.

______, "Slowly But Surely", Ibid., May 10, 2001.

______, "Calling on Neighbours", Ibid., August 14, 2002.

Dixit, Kanak Mani, "Enter Nepal's Maoist Establishment", The Hindu, April 14, 2008.

Dutt, Vijay and Ninan Servanti, "The Route of Discontent", India Today, Aroon Purie,ed. (Living Media, New Delhi, 16-31 July 1978), p. 16.

Gangal, S. C., "Trends in India's Foreign Policy", K. P. Misra, ed., Janata's. Foreign Policy (Vikas Publishing House, New Delhi, 1979), p. 35.

_________,"A Successful Visit", The Indian Express, February 14, 1978

Guha, Seema, "The Lankan Tug of War", The Times of India, July 28, 1997.

Hossain, Mosharaf, "Nature of State Power in Bangladesh", Journal of Social Studies, no.5, (Dhaka University, Dhaka, 1979).

Huq, Abdul Fazal, "The Problem of National Identity in Bangladesh", The Journal of Social Studies, no.24, April 1984, Dhaka.

Jagunnathan, "The End of a Misadventure", The Indian Express, March 26, 1990.

Jain, Girilal, "Foreign Policy Consensus—Some New Factors at Work", The Times of India, April 6, 1977.

Jha Prem Shankar, "Where Next With Pakistan", The Hindustan Times, February 12, 2000.

_______, "That Other Neighbour", Ibid., August 13, 2002.

_______, "Fear and Loathing", Ibid., September 27, 2004.

_______, "A Question of Trust", Ibid., April 22, 2005.

Joshi Manoj, "A Tale of Two Countries", The Times of India,February 5, 2005.

Jayasundera, P. B., "Moving to Create More Fiscal Space", The Hindu, June 5, 2008.

Kamal, A. Nazir, "Karakoram Highway-A Nation Building Effort", Strategic Studies, Vol. II, no. 3 (Islambad, Spring 1979), P.16.

Kapur, Ashok, "EmergingProblem in India's Foreign Relations in the Seventies", Foreign Affairs Report (New Delhi), Vol. 20, no.7, July 1971, pp. 148-56

Kohli Manorama, "Foreign Policy" Initiatives of the National Front Government in India", Ramakant (ed), South Asian Studies), Vol. 25, no. 1 & 2 January-December 1990 (University of Rajasthan, Jaipur, 1990), p. 141.

Kumar, Vinod, "Great Powers and Nepal", S. D. Muni, ed., Nepal: An Assertive Monarchy (Chetana Publishers, New Delhi, 1977), pp. 143-59.

Kurve, Mavin, "Nepal's Peace Zone Move: Attempt to Change 1950 Treaty", The Times of India (New Delhi), January 14, 1981.

Lone, Sajad, "Exile on Main Street", The Hindustan Times, November 1, 2004.

Madhu Limaye, "India's China Policy", The Illustrated Weekly of India, vol. XIIX, (The Times of India Press, Bombay, November 12-18, 1978), p. 6.

Malhotra, Babita and Kumar, S., "Thaw in Indo-Bangla Relations", The National Herald, January 10, 1991.

Malhotra Inder, "Beyond the Bangla Poll-New Delhi-Dhaka Relations", The Times of India, June 8, 1978.

___________,"China's Stance on Kashmir", The Times of India, 22 February, 1990.

Manchanda, Rita, "The Ugly-Indian Image Remains", The Hindustan Times (New Delhi), 28 July 1997.

Mehta, Ashok, K., "A Borderline Case", The Hindustan Times, August 6, 2003.

Mehta Jagat, "Blazing a New Trial", The Indian Express (Chandigarh), 31 August 1990.

Menon, N. C., "An Unequal Bargain", The Hindustan Times, 3 November 1997.

Mohanty, Manoranjan, "China Commentary-Course of Sino-Indian Normalisation", The Amrit Bazar Patrika (Calcutta), 19 May 1978.

Mukarji, Apratim," Friendliness is not Weakness", The Hindustan Times, 6 October 1997.

Muni, S. D., "Chinese Arms Pour into Nepal", The Times of India, 1 September 1988.

______, "A Common Destiny", The Times of India (Patna), 23 April 1989.

______, "On a Hot Tin Roof", The Hindustan Times, August 30,2003.

______, "Thy Hand, Great Monarch", Ibid., February 9, 2005.

______, "Dealing with a New Nepal", The Hindu, September 15, 2008.

Narain, Virendra, "Bangladesh and Changing International Context : An Analysis of Perceptions", in S. P. Verma and Virendra Narain, eds., Pakistan Political System in Crisis : Emergence of Bangladesh, Jaipur, South Asia Studies Centre, 1972.

Nayar, Kuldip, "Estranged Neighbour: The Arrogant India", The Indian Express, 12 December 1994.

Noorani, A. G., "India-Nepal Relations: The Heart of the Matter", The Indian Express, April 11, 1989.

Padgaonkar Dileep, "Pak Crisis and India's Choices" The Times of India, August 19, 1990.

Pant, Pushpesh, "Major Developments in India's Foreign policy and Relations" , International Studies, January- June 1979, Vol. 90, p. 52.

Poulose, T. T, "The Politics of Nuclear Free Zone in South Asia", Pacific Community (Tokyo), Vol. 6, no. 6, April 1977, pp. 541-60.

Puri, Rakshat, "Delhi's Kowtowing to Beijing", The Hindustan Times, November 12, 1997.

Rajan, M. S., "Bangladesh and After," Pacific Affairs, Summer, Vol. 45, no. 2.

Ramachandran, Rajesh, "War as Politics", The Hindustan Times, June 7, 1999.

Ramakant, "Nepal's Foreign Policy and China", India Quarterly, Vol. XXVI, no. 3, July-September 1971.

Raman, B., "Attack of the Clones", The Hindustan Times,January 5, 2004.

Raman, A. S.," India: Democracy in Danger", Contemporary Review, Vol. 233, no. 1355, December 1978, p. 305.

Rao, Chandrasekhar," Janata Government and the Soviet Connexion", World Today, vol. 34, no. 2, (London, February, 1978), pp. 70-76.

Roa, P. V Narasimha, "Nepal-India Relations", Nepal Council of World Affairs, Journal, Souvenir Issue, December 1981.

Rehman, Shahidur, "In a Hole and Digging", The Hindustan Times, June 24, 2001.

Roy, Jayant Kumar, "A View From Outside", Bimal Prasad, ed.. International Studies, Vol. 17 (Vikas Publishing House, New Delhi, July-December 1978), p. 393.

Sahay, S., "A Close Look Indo-Nepal Relations", The Statesman, December 10, 1981.

Sahay, Anand. K., "Kashmir As General Fodder", The Hindustan Times, January 29,2002.

Sandhu Kanwar, "Why Are We Tongue-tied?", The Hindustan Times, August 1, 2001.

Sareen, Rajendra, "Dimensions of Turmoil", The Tribune, February 5, 1990.

Sengupta Bhabani, "Towards Good Neighbourliness", Bimal Prasad, ed., India's Foreign Policy-Studies in Continuity and Change (Vikas Publishing House, New Delhi, 1979).

_______________, "A Deeply Divided Nation", Prem Chopra, ed., Contemporary Pakistan-New Aims and Images (Vikas Publishing House, UP, India, 1983), p. 83.

______________, "Waiting for India: India's Role as a Regional Power", Journal of International Affairs (Newyork), vol. 29, no. 2, Fall 1975, pp. 171-84.

_________, "After IPKF is Out", The Hindustan Times, December 23, 1989.

__________, "How to Avoid War with Pakistan", The National Herald, February 13, 1990.

___________, "Global Change Cripples Pakistan", The National Herald, February 22, 1990.

___________, "Regional Perspective: A Delhi-Dhaka Axis" The Indian Express, February 24, 1990.

Shaha, Rishikesh, "The Nepal-India Imbroglio", The Indian Express, June 24, 1989.

Sharma, R. C, "Geography as a Base for India's Foreign Policy", Indian Geographical Journal, Madras, vol.6, March 1976, pp. 1-6.

Sharma, R. S., "Process for Formulation and Execution of National Security and Defence Policies in the 1990s", Kouser J. Azam, ed., India's Defence Policy for the 1990s (New Delhi, 1992), p. 27.

Singh, S. Nihal, "India-China : Time of Move Forward", The Statesman, May 22, 1979.

____________, "Edging Back from the Brink", The Tribune, April 17, 1990

Shreedhar, "Indo-Pakistan Relations in Post-Benazir Period", Strategic Analysis, vol. XIX, no. 12, March 1997 (Institute for Defence Studies and Analysis, New Delhi, 1997) pp. 1695.

Sinha, S. K., "Value of National Front's Policy", The Statesman, February 11, 1991.

Sobhan, Rahman, "Politics of Food and Famine in Bangladesh", in Emajuddin Ahmed, ed., Bangladesh Politics, Dhaka, Centre for Social Studies, 1980.

Srivastava, Siddharth, "India Grapples With Energy Issues", Asia Time, March 24, 2007.

Suryanarayan, V., "Explaining Prabhakaran's Persistent Defiance", The Hindu, December 21, 2007.

Thapa, Bhekh Bahadur, "Foreign Aid and Economic Development in Nepal", Souvenir Issue, The Nepal Council of World Affairs Journal, Kathmandu, June 1971.

Thapliyal, Sangeeta, "Nepal in India's Security Parameters", Strategic Analysis, Vol. XVIII, no.9, December 1995 (Institute for Defence Studies and Analysis, New Delhi, 1995), p. 1201.

Varadarajan, Siddharth, "In Nepal Time to Check Dangerous Drift", The Hindu, September 20, 2006.

Varshney, R. L. and Raj Kumar, Foreign Affairs Report, Vol. XXXIX, nos. 1 & II January-February 1990 (Indian Council of World Affairs, New Delhi, 1990), p. 17

Victor, Cecil, "Busting Terrorist Bases no Solution", The Patriot, May 18, 1990

Vishwanathan, "Indo-Sri Lanka Relations", India Quarterly, A Journal of International Affairs, Vol. XLVI, no. 1, January-March 1990 (Indian Council of World Affairs, New Delhi, 1990), pp. 90-95.

Vohra, Pankaj, "Strike at Parliament is Attack on India's Sovereignty," The Hindustan Times, December 17,2001.

Wriggins, W. Howard, "Pakistan's Search for a Foreign Policy After the Invasion of Afghanistan", Pacific Affairs, Vol. 57, no.2 (The University of British Columbia, 1984), p. 285.

C. Newspapers

The Hindu (Madras).

The Times of India (New Delhi).

The Statesman (Delhi).

The Hindustan Times (New Delhi).

The Indian Express (Delhi).

The Pioneer (Lucknow).

The Patriot (New Delhi).
The Tribune (Chandigarh).
The Motherland (New Delhi).
The Indian Nation (Patna).
Amrit Bazar Patrika (Calcutta).
The Sunday Standard (New Delhi).
The National Herald (New Delhi).
Nagpur Times (Nagpur).
The Newyork Times (Newyork).
The Pravada (Moscow).
The Times (London).
The Financial Times (London).
The Ceylon Daily News (Ceylon).
The Pakistan Times (Lahore).
The Dawn (Karachi).
The Bangladesh Observer (Dacca).
Naya Samaj (Kathmandu).
Gorkhapatra (Kathmandu).
The Commoner (Kathmandu).

D. Periodicals

American Political Science Review (Newyork).
Eastern Economists (Bombay).
Economic and Political Weekly (Bombay).
Foreign Affairs (Newyork).
Foreign Policy Report (New Delhi).
Illustrated Weekly of India (Bombay).
India Today (New Delhi).
Indian Journal of Political Science (Hyderabad).
International Affairs (Moscow).
International Studies (New Delhi).
Link (New Delhi).
Modern Review (Calcutta).
Pacific Affairs (Newyork).
Political Science Quarterly (Newyork).
Time (New York), The Weekly News Magazine.

The News Week (Newyork).
SAARC News (Calcutta).
SAARC, SCAN (New Delhi).
Survey of China Mainland Press (Peking).
World Politics (Princeton).
World Today (London).

E. Digests
Asian Recorder (New Delhi).
Indian Recorder (New Delhi).
Keesings Contemporary Archives (London).
Nepal Trade Directory (Nepal Trading Corporation, New Delhi).

Index

C

J

L

Q

V